Bicycling
America's National Parks

Bicycling
America's National Parks

UTAH AND COLORADO

The Best Road and Trail Rides from
Canyonlands to Rocky Mountain National Park

SARAH BENNETT ALLEY
Foreword by Dennis Coello

BACK COUNTRY WOODSTOCK, VERMONT

With time, road numbers, signs, park regulations, and amenities referred to in this book may be altered. If you find that such changes have occurred along the routes described in this book, please let the author and publisher know, so that corrections may be made in future editions. Other comments and suggestions are also welcome. Address all correspondence to:

Backcountry Guides
P.O. Box 748
Woodstock, VT 05091

Copyright © 2000 by Sarah Bennett Alley

Foreword copyright © 2000 by Dennis Coello

Library of Congress Cataloging-in-Publication Data
Alley, Sarah Bennett.
    Bicycling America's national parks. Utah and Colorado : the best road and trail rides from Canyonlands to Rocky Mountain National Park / Sarah Bennett Alley ; foreword by Dennis Coello.
    p. cm.
    ISBN 0-88150-426-2 (alk. paper)
    1. All terrain cycling—Utah—Guidebooks. 2. All terrain cycling—Colorado—Guidebooks. 3. National parks and reserves—Utah—Guidebooks. 4. National parks and reserves—Colorado—Guidebooks. 5. Utah—Guidebooks. 6. Colorado—Guidebooks. I. Title: Utah and Colorado. II. Title.
    GV1045.5.U8 B46 2000
    917.9204'33—dc21   99–058158

Maps by Bryan Steven Jones, © 2000 by The Countryman Press
Interior photographs by Dennis Coello, Sarah Bennett Alley, and Lee Cohen
Cover photographs by Dennis Coello
Cover and interior design by Joanna Bodenweber
Series editor, Dennis Coello

Published by Backcountry Guides
A division of The Countryman Press
P.O. Box 748
Woodstock, VT 05091

Distributed by W. W. Norton & Company, Inc.
500 Fifth Avenue
New York, NY 10110

Printed in the United States of America
10 9 8 7 6 5 4 3 2 1

For Tim. And for Ruby.

ACKNOWLEDGMENTS

Many thanks are due to the numerous people who assisted me over the many weeks I was on the road gathering information for this project. The enthusiasm and encouragement I received from family, friends, and strangers who all share a love of adventuring on two wheels kept me rolling when I was far from home and more than a little road weary. Whether it was shower and a bed, directions, or simply a smile and a few comforting words, their generosity and kindness helped make this book possible.

My respect and gratitude go out to the men and women of the National Park Service, who are committed to preserving and sharing some of this country's most fantastic natural and historic treasures. They are under a great deal of pressure to accommodate the needs of a growing number of visitors to our parks each year. Cyclists who care about riding safely in their parks and would like their presence considered in future park transportation funding need to seek out park service employees and make themselves heard. Let's give them our input and help them do the best job they can.

I also tip my helmet to the dedicated folks who work for the National Forest Service and the Bureau of Land Management, the agencies that manage the road and trail systems in the country surrounding the parks that make for such great cycling. They are responsible for building and maintaining many of the trails and routes in this book and deserve our cooperation and respect.

The riders who appear in the pages of this book, many of them complete strangers who were more than willing to pull over, smile for my camera, and share their tales of the road or trail, are greatly appreciated for their spirit of adventure and love of cycling. And to my family and friends who took time to travel, camp, explore the trails, and pose for my pictures; thank you!

Last, but not least, I would like to thank my editor and friend, Dennis Coello, for offering me the chance to do this project and the opportunity to, once again, wander and revel in the spectacular country of the American Southwest.

Bicycling America's National Parks: Utah

1. Arches National Park
2. Bryce Canyon National Park
3. Canyonlands National Park
4. Capitol Reef National Park
5. Cedar Breaks National Monument
6. Golden Spike National Historic Site
7. Grand Staircase–Escalante National Monument
8. Natural Bridges National Monument
9. Timpanogos Cave National Monument
10. Zion National Park

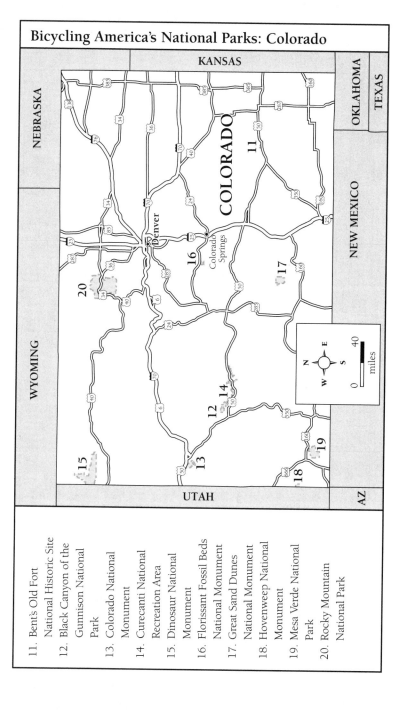

Bicycling America's National Parks: Colorado

11. Bent's Old Fort National Historic Site
12. Black Canyon of the Gunnison National Park
13. Colorado National Monument
14. Curecanti National Recreation Area
15. Dinosaur National Monument
16. Florissant Fossil Beds National Monument
17. Great Sand Dunes National Monument
18. Hovenweep National Monument
19. Mesa Verde National Park
20. Rocky Mountain National Park

Bicycling America's National Parks: Utah & Colorado
Map Legend

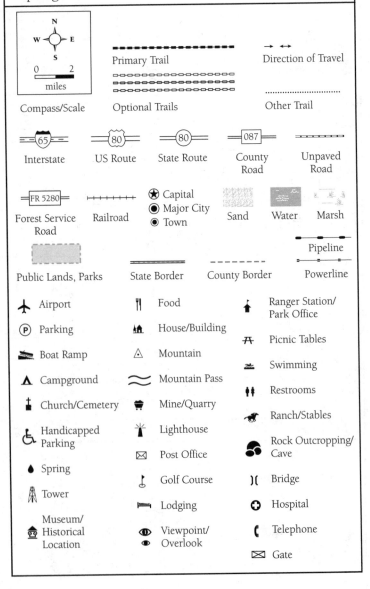

Compass/Scale

Primary Trail

Optional Trails

Direction of Travel

Other Trail

Interstate

US Route

State Route

County Road

Unpaved Road

Forest Service Road

Railroad

⊛ Capital
◉ Major City
◉ Town

Sand

Water

Marsh

Public Lands, Parks

State Border

County Border

Pipeline

Powerline

Airport

Food

Ranger Station/ Park Office

Ⓟ Parking

House/Building

Picnic Tables

Boat Ramp

△ Mountain

Swimming

▲ Campground

Mountain Pass

Restrooms

Church/Cemetery

Mine/Quarry

Ranch/Stables

Handicapped Parking

Lighthouse

Rock Outcropping/ Cave

Spring

⊠ Post Office

)(Bridge

Tower

Golf Course

✪ Hospital

Museum/ Historical Location

Lodging

(Telephone

Viewpoint/ Overlook

⊠ Gate

CONTENTS

20 ROCKY MOUNTAIN NATIONAL PARK   **445**

"The problem isn't too many people, it's too many cars." So says Interior Secretary Bruce Babbitt when discussing how we Americans are loving our national parks to death. You're skeptical? Then take a look at the statistics: Each year more than 285 million "recreation visitors" (non-service or -ranger personnel) visit the parks. That's right—more than the entire population of the United States. Great Smoky Mountains National Park leads the list with almost 10 million visitors annually. Grand Canyon is next with 4 million-plus. Yosemite, Yellowstone, Rocky Mountain, and Olympic National Parks all host more than 3 million visitors every 12 months. Wyoming's Grand Teton, Maine's Acadia, Utah's Zion, and Kentucky's Mammoth Cave National Parks each see more than 2 million people every year, most of them motoring in from May through September. Drive to the Grand Canyon on any summer weekend, and you and six thousand other drivers will spend much of your time competing for the two thousand parking spaces. You have better odds at the local mall.

And with all those cars come noise, air pollution, and the clogged roads you thought you left at the mall back home. It's gotten so bad in Yosemite, Zion, and the Grand Canyon that most cars will soon be banned from certain areas or left outside the park entirely, with propane-powered buses and, in time, light-rail systems shuttling people to "central dispersal sites." How you explore the park from there—whether by boot or bike or on an "alternatively powered bus" to some distant location and then a hike or bike ride from there—will be up to you. It will be different. For some this change in the way we experience our parks may be disturbing. And that's where *Bicycling America's National Parks* steps in to help.

Most national park bookstores are filled with hiking guides, and handouts are available for the shorter walks to the most popular attractions. But not until this series have in-depth guides existed for those wishing to see our country's grandest scenery and most important historic sites from the saddle. Whether you're peering through a windshield in those parks that still allow personal cars, or through the window of a bus you are sharing with 30 others, it doesn't begin to compare with the wide-screen, wind-in-the-face feeling of a park viewed over the handlebars. It is an intimate experience, a chance to sense exactly the conditions that helped shape what you are there to see. Zion's towering white and red walls are even more imposing, Organ Pipe's weirdly shaped cacti even odder, Hovenweep National Monument's ancient Indian towers and dwellings more dramatic when you bicycle up to them to say hello. Pedal Gettysburg's hills and you'll gain a soldier's appreciation of topography. Be forced to stop to let the buffalo pass in Yellowstone, and you will see how much more magnificent these beasts are when viewed from beyond the confines of a car. And—for some this is the best reason of all to pedal a bike—you can pull over and park almost anywhere.

Sarah Bennett Alley, the author of this guide, tells road cyclists and fat-tire bikers alike where to ride to see the sights, when to go for the least traffic and best weather, how to select a route to suit your mood and energy that day, and even whether there's good outside-the-park cycling. There's information on camping, on lodging in the parks and in nearby towns, on flora and fauna, and on where to refuel (as in food, not gas)—even the location of the nearest Laundromat. Sarah has logged all the miles, interviewed the rangers, and kept both seasoned cyclists and beginning bikers in mind during her research. She's done her part.

Now is the time for all of us to do our part in saving these places of stunning beauty and important history. Our national parks—hundreds of them across America—are our natural, secular cathedrals. It's time to get the cars out of church.

Dennis Coello
Series Editor

Visiting our national parks is something we Americans love to do; it's almost a rite of passage for us as kids, and it's a family ritual, designed to strengthen our bonds to one another and reacquaint us with the magnificent wilderness landscapes that distinguish our nation. More than two centuries of American literature, art, public policy, and popular myths regarding the West and this country's wild frontier reflect how important the idea of wilderness is to our national identity. These wild and beautiful places, in addition to having historical and archaeological significance, all have a story and a message about what we value and how we see ourselves. We come away from them feeling refreshed, and maybe even inspired.

The only glitch in this otherwise happy relationship that we Americans share with our national parks is our insatiable love for the automobile. It's not that we are loving our parks to death, as recent newspaper headlines would have us believe, but that there's just not room for the number of private vehicles we bring to them. This is not entirely the park-goers' fault; our national transportation systems are designed for cars. The National Park Service, which has happily accommodated us and our cars over the decades, must also share some of the blame. Recent traffic problems and the negative impact they have had on the national park experience for thousands of visitors are forcing the park service to rethink its mission and change the way it manages cars in the parks.

During the month that I mulled over this project, I visited a few national parks, including Capitol Reef and Zion in my home state of Utah. I wanted to see how much of a presence vehicles in the parks actually were, and how they might impact a cycling experience. As I pulled into Springdale, Utah, just outside of Zion National Park, I immediately took notice of the number of bikes on car racks, and the number of happy cyclists pedaling around town. Sure, people had driven their vehicles here, but it looked as though they were ready and willing to get out of their cars, see the park up close, and contribute to solving the problem.

As I was getting ready for what I anticipated to be a spectacular ride up Zion Canyon, I was immediately immersed in my surroundings. Any worry I had about traffic and crowds seemed to melt away. I pedaled out of town, made the requisite stop at the entrance station tollbooth, and after a few minutes and some friendly words with the ranger, I was on my way. As I pedaled through the lower canyon I noticed that the West Temple and the Towers of the Virgin were bathed in the deep, golden glow of afternoon sun. The cottonwoods along the Virgin River were just leafing out; tiny heart-shaped leaves that looked as though they had been fashioned out of shiny, lime-green vinyl fluttered in the breeze. The dry air felt delicious.

The shadows of the canyon were chilly, holding firm to the frost of winter. I push hard on the pedals to ward off the goose bumps that jumped to attention on the exposed skin of my arms and legs. Suddenly I caught a movement out of the corner of my eye. A beautiful, muscular six-point mule deer buck bounded through the trees, splashed across the river, turned to look at me, and froze. I squeezed my brakes momentarily, just in time to catch a glimpse of his glistening nose and a pair of dark brown eyes. Several cars whizzed by, unaware of the presence of this magnificent "other" with which we share our parks.

Farther into the canyon I hit my brakes again as I entered a shaft of sunlight coming over the canyon wall. I rolled slowly through the warm light and let my eyes travel upward, over pink canyon walls streaked with desert varnish to the shining white crowns of Zion's impressive sandstone formations. Ahead I again noticed some movement near the road, this time a flock of wild turkeys. Probably a dozen of the enormous birds pecked and scratched at the ground. I stopped to watch them, and soon traffic had stopped in both directions. We all watched in amusement as a nervous tom ran circles around the flock, anxiously herding his seemingly unconcerned harem to the far side of the road.

Back at the car I felt flushed, slightly giddy from the ride. Sure, there were cars and people, but I was so absorbed in my surroundings I hardly noticed them—and even when I did, they seemed to be having a great time. Besides, I'd learned that in another year there was going to be a major reduction of traffic on the Zion Canyon Scenic Drive. Many of the biggest and most popular parks are now involved with extensive transportation studies aimed at reducing vehicle congestion and improving visitors' park experience. The results of those studies, combined with an

injection of federal dollars, are putting several new transportation strategies into action; in Zion's case this means that as of 2000, sight-seers will be required to ride a bus through the canyon. And bicycles are finally getting some consideration as a transportation alternative.

In the days that followed I traversed the Kolob Terrace north of Zion Canyon in almost complete solitude; rode the fun, fast-paced singletrack of the JEM Loop; and got seriously humbled on the ultratechnical slickrock trails atop Gooseberry Mesa. By the time I was ready to leave I had seen the park from several different angles—from inside and outside park boundaries, from canyon floors and the tops of high mesas. The variety of cycling experiences in and around Zion, and the insights those different routes and trails gave me on the park and its celebrated resources, convinced me there was a great cycling guidebook waiting to be written. Of course the main scenic drive in each of the national parks in Utah and Colorado would be included, along with everything they revealed about each park's outstanding feature. But other trails and routes around the park, I knew, could add to the park experience and appeal to cyclists of different abilities and persuasions.

I took on this project because, first and foremost, I felt there was an audience that needed and could enjoy this guide. I am convinced that a bicycle is one of the best ways to really see and experience the country you've made an effort to get to. I also saw this book as the chance to be an advocate both for the parks themselves and for cyclists during a time of change. The parks are grappling with a variety of issues now and they are open to hearing from us, the public, about how we want to experience them in the future. Changes are needed, and if we don't make ourselves heard now, we may not get the opportunity later.

In putting together this book I've tried to present riding options for both road and mountain bikers, while maintaining a focus on the kinds of natural resources and natural settings that make each park special. This means you'll find everything from a 2-mile ride on a paved trail suitable for trailers and bikes with training wheels inside a park, to a strenuous and technical ride to a peak or overlook that encompasses an entire geographic region outside the park. In some cases—such as Arches National Park outside Moab, Utah, and Colorado National Monument outside Grand Junction, Colorado—I have included trails that not only highlight the particular resource of the park but that also speak to the overall popularity of the area as a biking destination.

I have tried to include both road and mountain-biking routes in each chapter, although you will generally find more options for mountain bikers than road riders. There are a number of reasons for this, including the fact that many more people own mountain bikes these days than road bikes. Also, the undeveloped character of the country that surrounds many of the national parks in Utah and Colorado simply means there are more dirt roads and trails than paved routes for biking. The main routes and scenic drives through parks are almost always paved and usually make for great road rides, but park back roads and roads accessing country surrounding the parks are usually better suited to mountain biking.

Now to the nuts and bolts (or should I say cogs and sprockets?) of how this book works. Each chapter is devoted to a single park, to what makes it so fascinating and special, and to the road- and mountain-bike rides you can find there. The chapters are grouped by state and arranged in alphabetical order. The rides within each chapter are grouped depending on their proximity to one another. Each grouping of rides is listed from easiest to most difficult. At the beginning of each chapter is an introduction to the park and a discussion of its historical, geologic, ecological, or archaeological significance. Please note that the term *park* is often used generically to refer to all parks, monuments, historic sites, or national recreation areas managed under the national park system. The one exception to this is Grand Staircase– Escalante National Monument, which is managed by the Bureau of Land Management and referred to throughout that chapter as a monument.

After the park introduction you'll find a section titled "Cycling in the Park," in which I discuss the particular geography, climate, and other characteristics of the area and how they impact the riding experience in and around that park. I also reference each ride in this section, identifying its general location and difficulty and remarking on its particular attributes: "fun family ride," "great hike along the way," "fantastic overlook at the end," "takes you to a spectacular ruin," and so on. Next come the rides themselves. In the sidebars and in the Trip Planning Appendix for each chapter you will find all the information you need to make your visit to the park as enjoyable and hassle-free as possible.

Let's cruise through a typical ride outline:

Sample Ride

Immediately after the trail name and an indication of what kind of bike you'll need comes a very brief introduction to the ride. The length of the ride is listed here and the type or configuration of the trail is identified (an out-and-back, for instance, or a loop, or a point-to-point ride). In some parks where routes are very long, you may find that a vehicle-supported overnight trip is recommended. The type of trail and the riding surface it presents (singletrack, dirt road, doubletrack, smooth, rocky, or washboarded) are also briefly described here. Level of difficulty is identified both in terms of the physical demands and technical riding skills required. Suggestions for trail options, which may include shortening the ride, making it longer, riding an additional spur, or changing the configuration of the route—may also appear here.

Starting point: The exact place the ride begins is listed here along with instructions on how to get there if it's somewhere other than the main visitors center of the park. Parking areas are also identified.

Length: The ride's total distance in miles is listed here, sometimes along with mileages for portions of the ride or optional spurs. Mileages listed here are approximate—they're close to exact, but differences in the calibration of your cyclometer may result in slightly different readings. A rough estimate of the amount of time in hours that it will take to ride the route is also listed here.

Riding surface: Under this heading is listed the trail type (singletrack, dirt road, doubletrack) and the kind of surface on the trail (rocky, smooth, rutted).

Difficulty: Terms for difficulty include *easy, moderate, difficult* and *strenuous.* Again, both the physical demands and technical riding ability or bike-handling skills required to ride the route are factored into this rating and are explained. Any other significant aspect of the ride—a long climb or a rocky surface, for example—that was factored into the difficulty rating is also referred to here.

Scenery/highlights: Whatever is significant about this ride in terms of the park's geology, history, or other natural resources is described here. Scenery, points of interest, or any other relevant information is also listed. Sometimes I remark on the riding and the physical qualities of the trail here as well, and I note hikes along the route.

Best time to ride: Here I make suggestions about the best time of year and time of day in an area or on a particular ride. One ride in a chapter might be at a higher elevation than the others, for instance, and so I recommend riding it later in the spring or summer. Spring and fall are often recommended for riding in southern Utah because of the area's hot summers. Riding in the morning or evening is a good idea in these areas for the same reason, but also because these are the times of day when wildlife is most active and the light is best for viewing scenery. Certain kinds of weather that may affect your ride are referred to here, such as wind in the spring or thunderstorms on summer afternoons.

Special considerations: In this section you'll find information designed to make your ride as safe and enjoyable as it can be. The water and rest rooms nearest to the trailhead or along the trail are always listed here. If there are safety issues relating to traffic, weather, trail surface, or anything else, they are discussed here. I also remark upon the remoteness of the country, the difficulty of route finding, or any other consideration that you should keep in mind when preparing for your ride. If there are some good hiking opportunities or particular points of interest along the route that are away from the road or trail, I usually recommend that you consider bringing a lock to secure your bike.

After these summaries, you will find a general description of the route, its heading and changes in direction, major geographic features that the route traverses or that can be seen from the route, changes in trail surface, and mileages at points along the way. At the end of the ride description you will find options for spurs and amendments to the route.

Sidebars

Cycling options: A very brief rundown of all the rides listed in the park is given here.

Flora: Here you will find a classification of the life zone and habitat type (transition life zone and piñon-juniper woodland, for example) found in and around the park. Dominant tree and shrub species are listed for each habitat type and life zone type. The most common and showy wildflower species are noted, grouped according to the season in which they bloom. These lists will give you a basic idea of what you'll see in the park.

Fauna: I have listed a number of the different kinds of animals you might see, including birds, mammals, reptiles, and amphibians, giving special attention to species that are either endangered, endemic, or unique to the ecosystem of the region. Raptors, songbirds, hummingbirds, and any avian creatures adapted to aspects of the park's environment are listed. These lists are, once again, designed to give you a good idea of the fauna that resides in the park, either seasonally, occasionally, or year-round.

It's interesting to know . . . : Here you will find an interesting tidbit of information—historical background on the park, basic information on the native peoples who formerly lived in the area, or a piece of folklore that relates to the park or the history of the surrounding area.

Don't miss . . . : A particularly spectacular hike, a beautifully constructed ruin, or a unique geologic feature not accessible by bike may be listed here. You might also find a museum, state park, or some other entity outside the park that can provide insight into the park and general region.

Trip Planning Appendix

Camping: Here you will find information on campgrounds within the park, the facilities they offer, and the procedure for obtaining a campsite. Availability of sites and any other pertinent information on staying in the park is listed here.

Private campgrounds make a good stopover for tent campers who have been in the backcountry, because they often have showers and laundry. I include private campgrounds with those types of facilities.

State parks often are located next to national parks and can be a great alternative to camping in the park. They usually have more facilities and a greater number of sites. Where state parks are found next to parks, I've provided information on their amenities and how to contact them.

I also make suggestions for wilderness camping on adjacent public lands. The agencies that manage those lands and have more information on campsites and procedures are listed at the end of each chapter under "For further information."

Please note: Because prices for campsites both inside and outside the national parks tend to fluctuate over time, I haven't given exact rates.

Lodging: Here you will find only very basic information about the kinds and locations of lodging options in the area surrounding the park. Chain hotels, motels, B&Bs, and a few out-of-the-way lodges are listed. For a more thorough description of your choices, please visit the local chamber of commerce or visitors center.

Food: The dining options listed here are similarly basic. I make suggestions for where to find a good cup of coffee and a good breakfast, and different kinds of food, be it Mexican, Chinese, continental, steaks, and so on. Again, a more complete list is available at the local chamber of commerce or visitors center.

Laundry: The closest place to do a load of laundry is listed here. Private campgrounds often have laundry facilities, but they're usually reserved for their paying guests.

Bike shop/rental: Here you will find a listing of the nearest bike shops, an indication of which ones rent, and what specialties they might have. Business hours for shops are not listed due to their tendency to change seasonally.

For further information: Here you will learn how to contact the park and obtain park-related information, as well as the address and phone numbers of nearby chambers of commerce and visitors centers. You will also find contact information for the public land management agencies that oversee surrounding land.

Remember, it is always best to supplement this, or any guidebook, with topographical maps and to use a compass when you are adventuring outside the parks. Riding a bike is an activity that has inherent risks; use your best judgment, always wear a helmet, and don't overdo it your first day out. Don't forget to play by the rules: Stay on designated roads and trails, do not climb on or disturb archaeological sites, and never remove any naturally occurring or archaeological object from federal lands. Federal fines and penalties are routinely given for these types of violations, which often occur unwittingly. We're not just visitors, but also part owners of America's parks and monuments, and the many dedicated folks who manage them need us to help them do the best job they can. Give them your input and let them know you're here as a cyclist and as a caring member of the populace that the parks are designed to benefit.

Visiting and riding around our national parks is an incredible opportunity for a rewarding learning experience. Take pictures, or maybe just mental snapshots, and leave only tire tracks. You'll be sure to take away a wealth of memories that you'll treasure for a lifetime. Happy trails!

Part One   UTAH

1

Concentrated inside the 73,379 acres of Arches National Park is the greatest density of naturally occurring stone arches in the world. More than 900 named arches are sprinkled along two major anticlines, or upfolds, running northwest to southeast through the park. Created by a combination of geologic happenstance, water, wind, and time, these arches, along with the many other fins, spires, hoodoos (fantastic or even grotesquely shaped columns and pinnacles of stone), and balanced rocks that accompany them, make for a thrilling natural spectacle. The ingredients that went into the creation of these arches, ranging in size from 3 feet across to the awe-inspiring 306-foot span of Landscape Arch, coalesced here some 300 million years ago when an inland sea evaporated. Left behind was a 3,000-foot layer of salt, gypsum, and fine sediment across a broad area referred to as the Paradox Basin.

The entire region was then covered by sand dunes, river deltas, and shallow seas that periodically encroached and receded over the eons. With each of these geologic events, layers of sandstone, siltstone, mudstone, and limestone were deposited on top of the salt bed. Several faults running through the park were overlaid with thinner, weaker rock layers. The plastic salt and gypsum material then flowed into these fault zones, creating intense pressure on the rock layers above. Eventually this pressure on the rock layers overlying the faults forced them skyward into domes. Many of these domes were fractured by the faults trending in a northwest-southeast direction. The cracks and fissures in the rock allowed water to seep in and dissolve the salt, causing portions of the rock domes to collapse, leaving hundreds of freestanding rock fins.

Exfoliation of the rock along weak zones due to freezing and thawing gradually worked to create alcoves and arched caves in the fins. Sometimes they formed from both sides and joined to create a window high above the ground. These openings were slowly widened by continued weathering and fracturing of unsupported rock layers, creating arches. Often the damaged fins and partial arches simply crumbled, but those that shed layers of stone evenly and maintained a certain degree of hardness, survived to become the famous arches.

Exfoliation due to weathering is an ongoing process that will eventually cause all the arches in the park to collapse, but even as they do, others are being formed out of the many fins and domes that remain. Almost all of the arches in the park are formed out of the Jurassic dune-deposited Entrada sandstone. The light, buff-colored Navajo sandstone is also prevalent throughout the park.

Cycling in the Park

In Arches National Park bikes are restricted to established roads and must abide by vehicle regulations. There are, however, 48 miles of paved road and almost 28 miles of dirt road that are open to cyclists. There are two important issues to keep in mind when planning a biking trip to Arches: The first is the large amount of vehicle traffic these roads experience during peak tourist season, running from May through September, and the second is the blistering temperatures during the summer months. Temperatures remain comfortable throughout the rest of the year here when the crowds have abated, making for some truly enjoyable bike adventures along the paved main road, or on one of the backcountry roads through Salt Valley or across Willow Flats. The BLM land surrounding the park and the greater Moab area feature some of the most popular trails in the country and have become a bike mecca for the thousands of mostly off-road cyclists who flock here every spring and fall.

The fascination with riding in Utah's gorgeous redrock country all began in the early 1970s with the Slickrock Trail just outside of Moab. The trail was originally designed and built for motorcycles but was taken

CYCLING OPTIONS

There are six rides listed in this section, one on roads, and the other five for mountain bikes. Intermediate-level road riders will enjoy riding the park's main road from the picnic area near Balanced Rock to the end, 20 miles total. Superfit and experienced road riders may want to ride this route from the visitors center, which makes this ride almost a half century. The ride out to Tower Arch in the northwest corner of the park is a long but fairly easy 24-mile pedal on dirt roads. Courthouse Wash is a 26-mile loop route that traverses redrock country both inside and outside the park on doubletrack jeep trails, dirt road, and pavement. This ride is moderately difficult and best suited for fit and experienced riders.

The Gemini Bridges ride is a classic Moab singletrack mountain-bike ride that is 13.5 miles in length, moderately difficult, and best done with a vehicle shuttle. The loop route that takes you to Monitor and Merrimac Buttes is just over 13 miles and is also moderately difficult. The Slickrock Trail, arguably the most famous mountain-biking trail in the world, offers some route options but is difficult to strenuous for even the experienced mountain biker. This route is extremely challenging; please use caution.

over in the 1980s by mountain bikers, who continue to swarm the area by the thousands during spring break in March and then again in October for the annual Canyonlands Fat Tire Festival. Stop in at the Moab Information and Visitors Center on the corner of Center and Main Streets to get whatever brochures or information you need. The boom-and-bust economy of the former uranium mining town of Moab has stabilized and is thriving due to the seemingly endless stream of fat-tire enthusiasts who come from all over the world to pedal these trails every year. There are probably more bike shops, bike-touring companies, and cyclists in Moab than in any other town its size in the country, possibly the world.

During June, July, and August temperatures frequently blaze beyond 100 degrees, and it is not uncommon to have days close to that in May and September. If you have to ride in the park during these months, an early-morning or evening ride is best.

The dry air, elevation, and strong sun common to desert environments will quickly deplete your body of the precious fluids it needs to keep running smoothly. When you are exerting yourself in the desert during the warmer months you should plan on drinking at least a gallon of fluid a day, and about half that in the winter months. A long-sleeved shirt is your best bet for preventing sunburn; the next best is a sunblock with an SPF of at least 15. A baseball cap under your helmet will provide extra shade for your face if you don't have a visor on your helmet.

Unless you're a native of the Sahara you'll find the temperatures out here during the summer months intolerable.

Early spring in the desert is one of the best times of year here—as is late fall, when the crowds have thinned out. Temperatures throughout the winter months can be quite comfortable, getting into the 50s during the day and sinking into the 20s at night.

1. ARCHES TOUR–MAIN PARK ROAD (See map on page 34)

For road bikes. The tour of Arches National Park from the main road provides not only a wonderful view of the park's magnificent rock formations, but also spectacular panoramas of surrounding redrock landscapes and desert mountain ranges. The route described here traverses the northern half of the park's scenic drive and includes the two main spur roads out to the Windows Section and Delicate Arch Viewpoint. Possibilities exist for riding this entire route, a 45.5-mile day that serious road riders will relish, or simply riding out the Windows Section road (5.4 miles total) which is suitable for families. Be forewarned: The main park road through Arches National Park experiences heavy traffic from May through September. Riding in the early morning, in the evening, or during the off-peak months is strongly recommended.

Starting point: Picnic Area 4 across from Balanced Rock. If you are up for the whole trip out-and-back, begin at the park visitors center. Parking is extremely tight at the visitors center, picnic area, and all the trailheads. Make sure you are parked legally or the park service will ticket you.

Length: 26.2 miles. This mileage includes the section of road beginning at Picnic Area 4 across from Balanced Rock extending north to the end

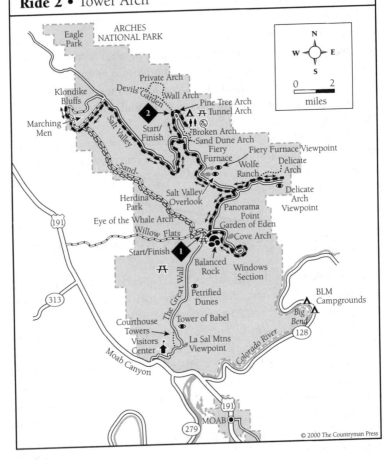

of the road at Devils Garden trailhead, with spur roads to the Windows Section and Delicate Arch Viewpoint.

Riding surface: Pavement; narrow with almost no shoulders.

Difficulty: Moderate to easy. The length and rolling terrain add some difficulty. Elevations vary between 4,400 and 5,200 feet above sea level.

Scenery/highlights: The 2.5-mile Windows Section Road and the short trail at the end of this spur lead to some massive arches. North Window,

South Window, Turret Arch, and Double Arch vary between 51 and 105 feet high and 39 and 163 feet wide. Garden of Eden Viewpoint provides a great view of the Salt Valley, where the body of salt responsible for the arches lies just beneath the surface. The old Wolfe Ranch buildings on the way out to Delicate Arch reflect the pioneering efforts of John Wesley Wolfe, who homesteaded here in 1888. A trail leads to some petroglyphs above the ranch.

Delicate Arch is perhaps the most famous arch in the park, and the one that was selected to grace the sesquicentennial license plates for the state of Utah. The view through Delicate Arch to the La Sal Mountains beyond is truly spectacular and should not be missed. A 1.5-mile trail beginning at the Wolfe Ranch takes you out to Delicate Arch. The Fiery Furnace is a tightly packed group of fins with arches and at least one natural bridge hidden among them. A free permit is needed to explore among this brilliantly colored maze of slots and fins. The Devils Garden Trail takes you to as many as 10 arches, including Landscape Arch, spanning 306 feet—6 feet longer than a football field.

Best time to ride: Despite the hot temperatures, the summer months see a steady stream of tourists, many of them international. Riding in the park between the months of November and March is your best bet for a safe experience that avoids the numerous campers and cars that can cause traffic on some of the spur roads to come to a standstill.

Special considerations: A pit toilet is available at Picnic Area 4, but not drinking water. Water and bathrooms are available at the Devils Garden trailhead and Campground. It is a good idea to bring plenty of water with you when you start out and refill when you get there.

Car and camper traffic is a hazard on this road. Please ride in single file on the right-hand side of the road, always wear a helmet, and stay alert. People driving this road are looking at the scenery and may not be looking at you. Be especially wary around turnouts and in parking areas. Also, a white or bright-colored shirt will help make you more visible.

It is a good idea to carry a lock with you on this ride so that you can secure your bike while you hike out to the arches.

From Picnic Area 4 (elevation 5,040 feet), directly across from Balanced Rock, pedal out onto the main park road and head northeast for approximately 0.2 mile to the road leading out to the Windows Section. Go right onto this road and pedal 2.5 miles to the end, where you can take one of several short trails out to the windows and arches. You will climb less than 100 feet on your way out here.

When you are ready, pedal back out to the main park road, go right, and continue heading northeast for just over 1 mile over level terrain to Panorama Point. After taking in the view here pedal onward, descending 1.3 miles to the road that takes you to Wolfe Ranch, the Delicate Arch Trail, and Delicate Arch Viewpoint. Turn right onto this road and descend a few hundred more feet to Salt Wash, where you will find the old Wolfe Ranch. It is 1.2 miles from the main road to Wolfe Ranch, where you can pick up the 1.5-mile hiking trail out to Delicate Arch. If this hike isn't something you want to do, continue for another mile up to Delicate Arch Viewpoint. After marveling at this fantastic view, ride the 2.2-mile spur road back out to the main road and continue pedaling northward.

In just over 2 miles (and a 400-foot elevation gain) the short spur out to Salt Valley Overlook is on your right, and just after that is the Fiery Furnace Viewpoint (a pit toilet is available here). The road continues to climb for another 2 miles past these lookouts to Sand Dune Arch, which can be accessed by a short trail. Another 0.5 mile beyond this, the dirt Salt Valley Road takes off to the left. From this intersection it is approximately 1 mile to the end of the road at Devils Garden trailhead.

Out the Devils Garden Trail you will find six more named arches, including Landscape Arch. There are also bizarre hoodoos (fantastic or even grotesquely shaped columns and pinnacles of stone), sandstone fins, and a maze of passageways winding around through this redrock wonderland. When you're ready to go, ride back to the picnic area at Balanced Rock. The first few miles you will be coasting downhill toward the Salt Valley Wash, but once you cross the wash you will have to climb back up to the picnic area where you left your car.

---

2. TOWER ARCH (See map on page 34)

For mountain bikes. This ride is a fairly easy 24-mile (total distance) out-and-back adventure into the northwest corner of the park to see the impressive span of Tower Arch and the sentinel spire that stands guard over it. The way follows a well-used dirt road and a section of jeep road. Beginning and intermediate riders in reasonably good condition will have little problem tackling this route. One steep section of jeep road that ascends the ridge leading up to Tower Arch will be a challenge for even the seasoned rider and may have to be negotiated on foot.

Starting point: Devils Garden trailhead or one of the pullouts nearby.

Length: 23.6 miles.

Riding surface: Dirt road, four-wheel-drive jeep roads. The Salt Valley Road can become badly washboarded.

Difficulty: Moderate. The distance and climb up a section of jeep road make this ride a bit more difficult.

Scenery/highlights: The Klondike Bluffs, Tower Arch, Marching Men, and surrounding scenery are spectacularly strange and beautiful. The Marching Men pinnacles are a legion of red fingers that seem to be traipsing up a slope. The clusters of salmon-pink fins and spires that surround these formations are also notable.

Best time to ride: Spring and fall; early morning start will give you a couple of hours of cooler temperatures but it will still be warm and dry, so be sure to drink plenty of water.

Stay away if it is raining or the ground is supersaturated! The sticky mud will ruin your day. You may not have much choice in this, because the park closes the gate to the Salt Valley Road if conditions warrant. However, if the gate is open and it has rained recently, or you can wait a day or two, you may want to consider riding this as a loop, heading south on the jeep road to the main park road. Rain actually improves this road tremendously by firming up the sand, but if the road is traveled by too many vehicles it will turn into a sand bog once again.

Special considerations: Water and toilets are available at the Devils Garden trailhead and Campground. There are no facilities out at Tower Arch so bring plenty of water, snacks, and sunscreen with you.

The Salt Valley Road can become very washboarded and dangerous; the best remedy is to shift to a lower gear and ride at a slower speed on the uphill sections. If you encounter sections of washboard on a downhill, be sure to check your speed.

From the Devils Garden Trailhead, pedal south on the main park road for just over a mile to the start of the Salt Valley Road. Go right and begin your descent into Salt Valley. The road winds downhill in a southerly direction, following the northern fork of the wash for approximately 2.5 miles. For the next 1.5 miles the road winds between low red hills, slowly gaining in elevation before entering a narrow part of the wash—a place you don't want to be if a thunderstorm is imminent.

Just beyond, the road rises over a hill and then descends into the broad plain of Salt Valley. You'll traverse the 2-mile-wide valley floor for the next 3 miles before encountering the intersection with the jeep road that takes you to the Tower Arch Trail from the southwest. (A few hundred yards beyond this left-hand turn is another road that takes you to a hiking trail, accessing the Marching Men formation and Tower Arch from the northeast.) Go right onto the jeep road and ride 1 mile across the sagebrush-dotted desert to the western margin of the valley. At this point you come to a steep grade covered with broken sandstone; this is the hard part, but the views are worth the effort. From here you can see the jagged fins of Devils Garden and beyond to the peaks of the La Sal Mountains. You descend slightly and then climb to another ridge where views of the Klondike Bluffs and surrounding formations are superb.

Approximately 1.7 miles from your last turn onto the jeep road, you will encounter the sandy jeep road that heads southeast and intersects the Willow Flats Road near the Balanced Rock Picnic Area. The pinnacles of the Marching Men come into view to the north from here. The trail descends into a sandy wash and follows a jeep trail as it passes through piñons and junipers while skirting the west side of Klondike Bluffs. The road zigs and zags through this section before ending 3.3 miles from the junction with the Salt Valley Road, at a sign and trailhead for Tower Arch. It is a short, 0.5-mile hike to the arch. When you are done, retrace your route back to Salt Valley, and ride the road back out to where you left your car.

---

3. COURTHOUSE WASH (See map on page 41)

For mountain bikes. This 26-mile loop takes you on a five-star tour of this area's magical redrock terrain. Along the way you pass by deep red cliffs of Entrada sandstone topped by swirls of buff-colored Navajo sand-

FLORA

The plant community that dominates in Arches National Park is piñon-juniper woodland. Here the trees, faced with harsh living conditions, constitute a pygmy forest of twisted, gnarled individuals often far older than they appear. Cliffrose, four-wing saltbush, rabbitbrush, horsebrush, blackbrush, shadscale, and Mormon tea (in the Ephedra genus) are some of the shrubs you will find scattered across the arid valleys and canyons of the park, but in the moister areas near the base of cliffs with seeps or springs you might find Gambel oak, single-leaf ash, Utah serviceberry, or Fremont barberry. Yucca and big sagebrush are very common, as are prickly pear and fishhook cacti.

The wispy branches and foliage of the invasive tamarisk, or salt cedar, are covered with either white or pink blooms in spring and are quite lovely despite the damage they do to desert environments. Tamarisks are giant sponges, perspiring as much as 40 gallons of water into the air on a hot day. In this way they dry up springs that are critically important to desert life. Many parks in southern Utah have embarked on tamarisk-eradication campaigns that have proved as futile as they are costly. Cliffrose is covered with fragrant creamy white blossoms in spring and summer, and is joined by the brilliant red of claret cup cactus, the tall spears of yucca blooms, and the yellow and peach of prickly pear blossoms. During spring and early summer you are also likely to see the reds of paintbrush; the yellow of goldenweed, wallflower, and puccoon; the white of evening primrose and twin-pod; and the pink of milk vetch and rock cress. Rabbitbrush, which is quite common in the park, blooms into great mounds of golden yellow in fall.

stone. Slickrock meets the trail in several places and will tempt you off course. This ride is best suited for intermediate and advanced riders with a good amount of stamina, though for an excellent easy, family-type or beginner-level ride, ride a portion of the Willow Flats Road west from the picnic area at Balanced Rock to the park boundary, giving you an out-and-back distance of 8 miles total.

Starting point: Arches National Park Visitors Center. If the parking lot here is full or you do not want to pay the fee to enter, park at a pullout approximately 0.5 mile beyond the turnoff for the park on the right-hand side of US 191. For the easier option, go into the park and drive 10 miles to Picnic Area 4 across from Balanced Rock and begin there.

Length: 26 miles. Allow at least 5 hours to complete this loop. The easier 8-mile option takes 2 to 3 hours, tops.

Riding surface: Pavement, dirt road, doubletrack, singletrack.

Difficulty: Moderate to difficult. There are just a few spots that require some technical riding skills. The overall distance and the sometimes difficult route finding add difficulty. Almost 1,000 feet of elevation change occurs along this ride.

Scenery/highlights: Incredible scenery, including beautiful redrock formations, views to the La Sal Mountains, and a possible side trip out the Windows Section Road to see the park's famous arches, makes for a stellar two-wheeled adventure.

Best time to ride: Early spring; avoid the crowds that throng the park midspring through midfall. Get an early start to avoid the scorching temperatures of midday on the uphill section of this ride, and to avoid the mass of tourists seeing the park from behind the wheel of a car or camper.

Special considerations: There is water available at the visitors center but none along the way, so bring plenty of your own. Bathrooms are available at both the visitors center and at the picnic area across from Balanced Rock.

Vehicle and camper traffic on the main park road can be very heavy during peak tourist season. Be safe! Ride in single file to the right and always wear a helmet.

From the visitors center ride out onto US 191 and head north for approximately 0.5 mile to a large pullout. From here you pick up the old highway road, or what's left of it, and pedal uphill on a fairly moderate grade. Continue following the old highway for 3 miles to an intersection. The old highway continues north; a right-hand turn heads east and eventually takes you to the same place, but it traverses some really interesting terrain in between. Go right and be prepared to be a little confused

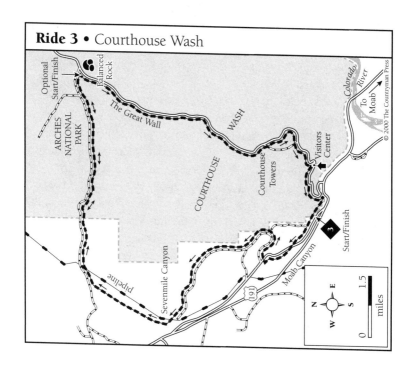

Ride 3 • Courthouse Wash

by the multitude of faint jeep roads leading in all directions. You are in between the park boundary to the east and the old and new highways to the west, so it is difficult to get too lost out here.

Follow this doubletrack east for about 0.5 mile before it swings around and heads north. As you pedal northward, you are tracing the boundary between rolling, sage-covered red hills to your left and slickrock on your right. Keep following the doubletrack that skirts this boundary for the next 2 miles. You will be tempted by several different routes taking off to your right over the slickrock; feel free to play around and explore, but know that they end at the park boundary. Please do not ride across the lumpy, black-coated soils known as cryptobiotic crust. They are very fragile, complex communities of lichens and bacteria that form the building blocks of life in the desert.

You pass by a large anvil-shaped rock just before this doubletrack disappears over sections of slickrock. Keep heading in the same northerly direction and pick up the trail again as it passes the head of Sevenmile

Canyon. The trail again becomes a doubletrack with numerous spurs heading off in all directions. Follow the best-worn track for another 3.5 miles as it rolls along before hitting the pipeline corridor. Go right onto the pipeline road that is marked with orange signs. The road crosses several washes in the next 2 miles. Be careful—some of the descents into these washes are steep and dangerous. Expect stretches of sand in the washes.

Just over 10 miles from the start of this ride you come to the intersection with the Willow Flats Road, where an old gas company structure stands. Go right onto the Willow Flats Road, and follow it east. This road has sandy stretches and some challenging hills. Pedal eastward for the next 2 miles over a rough four-wheel-drive road, at which point you reach the park boundary. Half a mile past the park boundary is Willow Springs.

The next 4 miles of Willow Flats Road inside the park are much smoother, bringing you to Picnic Area 4 directly across from Balanced Rock. Take a break and consider whether you want to ride the 5-mile (total distance out and back) spur road out to the Windows Section. It's a small price to pay for the fantastic scenery that awaits you. If you decide to head back, simply go right onto the main park road and ride 10 miles downhill to the visitors center. Be careful of car and camper traffic on this road; stay to the right and ride in single file.

Option: For an easy 8-mile (total distance) adventure the whole family can do, park at Picnic Area 4 across from Balanced Rock and ride west on the Willow Flats Road for 4 miles to the park boundary. This section of road traverses beautiful piñon- and juniper-covered flats, rolling through some mellow hills and around sandstone humps and mounds. Traveling the road west, you will lose close to 500 feet of elevation that have to be regained on the return trip. (If the gang is up for it, you can ride out of the park toward US 191 for another 4 miles.) When you've had enough, retrace your route back to your starting point.

---

4. GEMINI BRIDGES (See map on page 44)

For mountain bikes. This route is an easy-to-moderate 13.5-mile (one-way) point-to-point ride that is best done with a shuttle. The highlight is the twin bridges that run parallel to each other, but the scenery, stunning views, and multitude of geologic wonders make this a superlative biking adventure. Beginning and intermediate riders will encounter only a few moderately technical sections along this route, which follows relatively smooth four-wheel-drive roads most of the way. Expect to find a few sandy sections near the bridges.

Starting point: A dirt road (signed for Gemini Bridges) off UT 313, 13.2 miles southwest of US 191. Leave a shuttle vehicle or plan to get picked up 1.5 miles south of the turnoff for UT 313 on US 191. To do this drive north on US 191 10 miles from Moab, or 5 miles from the park entrance, to a dirt pullout on the west side of US 191 next to the railroad tracks. There is a BLM sign here with information about the roads and trails in the area. Leave a vehicle here. Continue driving north for 1.5 miles to UT 313, which is the access for Canyonlands National Park and Dead Horse Point State Park. Go left onto UT 313 and drive 13.2 miles to the dirt road signed for Gemini Bridges on the left-hand side of the road. Park or get dropped off here.

Length: 13.5 miles point to point. If you do not do this as a shuttle, you can ride out and back to the bridges from the pullout on US 191, a total distance of 15.5 miles. Allow at least 3 hours to do this ride.

Riding surface: Slightly rocky dirt road, doubletrack with some sections of sand.

Difficulty: Easy to moderate. One short, technical descent over loose rock and one short climb require some technical riding ability; otherwise this tour is all downhill over good riding surfaces.

Scenery/highlights: Views into Arches National Park and Gold Bar Rim to the east, into the Behind the Rocks area to the southeast with the peaks of the La Sal Mountains beyond, and to Monitor and Merrimac Buttes to the north are awe inspiring. Instead of viewing Gemini Bridges from below as you do most arches and bridges, you approach them from above. You can even walk out across these flat bridges and peer down into the chasm below. Use caution!

Best time to ride: Anytime spring or fall. You may run into more bikers at this time of year, but it is better than frying in the summer heat.

Special considerations: There is no water available at either trailhead, so bring plenty of your own. If you only have one vehicle and would like to

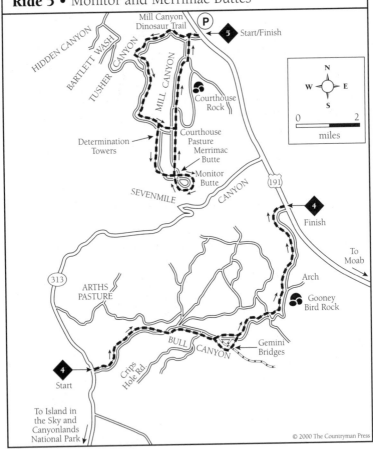

Ride 4 • Gemini Bridges
Ride 5 • Monitor and Merrimac Buttes

Mill Canyon
Dinosaur Trail

HIDDEN CANYON

BARTLETT WASH

TUSHER CANYON

MILL CANYON

P

5 ◆ Start/Finish

Courthouse Rock

Determination Towers

Courthouse Pasture
Merrimac Butte

Monitor Butte

SEVENMILE CANYON

191

4 ◆ Finish

To Moab

313

ARTHS PASTURE

Arch

Gooney Bird Rock

BULL CANYON

Gemini Bridges

Gnps Hole Rd.

4 ◆
Start

To Island in the Sky and Canyonlands National Park

N
W E
S

0   2
miles

© 2000 The Countryman Press

do this as a shuttle, consider contacting one of the bike shops or touring companies in Moab; many are happy to run shuttles for day riders.

Begin pedaling east through rolling piñon and juniper woodlands. Soon this first section of graded road begins to drop, descending rapidly for 3.5 miles before emerging onto a wide open flat. Just after reaching the flat a road on the left heads towards Arths Pasture, stay right following

The snowcapped peaks of the La Sal Mountains offer a breathtaking backdrop to Arches National Park.

DENNIS COELLO

trail markers for Gemini Bridges. Another spur at 4.2 miles takes you to the Four Arches Trail and Crips Hole. Pass this spur and continue for 1 more mile toward Bull Canyon and the road that accesses Gemini Bridges.

As you get closer watch for painted stripes on the rock leading to the spans; follow them, ignoring the multitude of old trails scaring the landscape. Ride with caution here; canyon walls and rock ledges drop away without warning. A fall here would be lethal. Follow the painted stripes until you arrive at the bridges (6 miles from the start). If you choose to explore the bridges, leave your bike behind and be careful—it is 200 feet to the canyon floor below. After you've had a chance to marvel at these spans, remount, ride back out the spur you came in on, and turn right onto the main road.

Continue heading east as the trail descends through more piñon and juniper, crossing sections of slickrock. In 2 miles you arrive at a major intersection; the road to the right takes you out and around into Bull Canyon where you can view the bridges from below. Stay left to continue on the main route. At 0.5 mile past this intersection, 8.5 miles from the start, is the steep, technical descent into Little Canyon that many will choose to walk. At the bottom of the canyon is an intersection; stay left and follow a double track up Little Canyon 1.5 miles to the pillar called the Gooney Bird.

Beyond Gooney Bird the trail continues its ascent of Little Canyon. The trail crosses back and forth over the wash through some sandy sections for 1 mile before making a steep climb out of Little Canyon. For the last mile of this ride you will have to negotiate the rough and sometimes dangerous descent into Moab Canyon. Don't forget to enjoy the view across to Arches on the way down. At the bottom of this descent follow the powerlines back to where you left your car.

Option: If you do not have two vehicles for a shuttle you can simply ride 15.5 miles out-and-back to the bridges from the pullout on US 191. This means negotiating the two rough, steep hills on this ride going and coming back. Another option, one that avoids riding up those two hills on the way to the bridges, is to ride around on the pavement on US 191 and UT 313 to the upper trailhead and riding this route as described above.

---

5. MONITOR AND MERRIMAC BUTTES (See map on page 44)

For mountain bikes. This moderate 14-mile loop with several side-spur options takes you through open desert, up Tusher Canyon, and then plays around in slickrock among these wondrous geologic formations before dropping down Mill Canyon. Those well versed in American history will recognize the two buttes as named for the ironclad warships that did battle in 1862 during the Civil War. The Monitor is on the left and the Merrimac on the right as you head out. The slickrock that swirls around the base of the buttes provides a great opportunity to test your technical riding skills, while the great equalizer—sand—will require almost everyone to get off and push a little here and there. At the end of this ride you can tour some dinosaur tracks at the mouth of Mill Canyon.

Starting point: A BLM trailhead with a registration box and a sign. To get there travel north on US 191 approximately 16 miles north of Moab, or 11 miles north of the Arches National Park entrance, to the dirt Mill Canyon Road just past mile marker 141. Go over the railroad tracks and follow the dirt road for a short distance to the trailhead.

Length: 14 miles. Allow 3 to 4 hours to complete this loop.

Riding surface: Gravel road, four-wheel-drive jeep road, some sandy wash bottom, slickrock.

Difficulty: Moderate. Some of the slickrock sections are technical but there are usually easier ways around. Sections of sand are a nuisance.

Scenery/highlights: This is a great opportunity to get comfortable riding on slickrock and to work on your bike-handling skills. The battleship buttes are a scenic destination, with plenty of rolling slickrock around them. Determination Towers, along with the many other weather-sculpted features of this landscape, are endlessly fascinating. Great views to Arches National Park and beyond abound.

Best time to ride: Spring and fall are delightful; summers are sizzling hot. Get an early start. This ride is especially good after rain, which helps firm up the sandy spots.

Special considerations: There is no water out here, so make sure your water bottles or hydration packs are topped off.

If it hasn't rained in a while you can bet it will be sandy in the wash bottoms, but too soon after a rain you'll find it gets pretty muddy. There are a lot of jeep roads taking off in all directions out here, but the distinctive geologic features looming ahead make for good geographic markers. Still, it's pretty easy to get sidetracked.

I've described the route in a counterclockwise direction, but it is frequently ridden the other way as well. Use caution on the slickrock.

Please do not ride across the lumpy, black-coated soils known as cryptobiotic crust. They are fragile, complex communities of lichens and bacteria that form the building blocks of life in the desert.

From the parking area ride a short distance before taking a right-hand fork leading up Tusher Canyon. This route begins with a pedal across open desert dotted with sagebrush and bunchgrass. A major power line passes overhead before crossing a large wash; stay left instead of following a fork that goes under the line. In just over 2 miles, after crossing the wash, the trail bends around to the left and heads up into Tusher Canyon. Stay in the wash while the main road heads right into Hidden

Canyon and Bartlett Wash. There is often water in this wash, which helps keep the sand firm.

Another 0.7 mile down the wash the road climbs up and to the right, and then continues through the wash again for another 1.3 miles. At this point the wash can get pretty sandy. In another 0.5 mile the trail branches left, up a fork of the wash, through a gap in a large wall. Determination Towers come into view through this gap. At this gap is a gate; go through it and leave it as you found it. Continue following this jeep road as it climbs up out of this wash toward the towers. Don't take the short, steep spurs right, at 0.2 mile, or left, at 0.5 mile past the gate, but continue climbing up and out of the wash on the main route.

On top, several spur roads take you over to Mill Canyon as you approach the towers. Stay on course as you make your way around the east side of the towers, reaching them 2.3 miles from the gate. Just past Determination Towers you ride up onto slickrock, where it is sometimes difficult to discern your route. Cross over this slickrock area and pick up another four-wheel-drive road that takes you to the base of Merrimac Butte. There are several sections of sand along the 1.3-mile stretch between Determination Towers and Merrimac.

After you've played around the base of Merrimac Butte, go left (east) for 0.7 mile to a crossroads of at least five different jeep trails. Take a fork to the right that heads toward Monitor Butte over slickrock. As you cross the slickrock platform between the two buttes there are fabulous views into Sevenmile Canyon, and south and east to Arches and the La Sals beyond. After you've spent some time in the shadow of the mighty Monitor, the Union ship that became the protector of the North's wooden fleet but could not sink the Merrimac, retrace your tracks to the five-way intersection and go right, dropping down into Mill Canyon.

Stay right as you descend into Mill Canyon, ignoring spurs to the left leading back to Determination Towers. In a short distance you encounter a sandy section that turns to a semitechnical rocky stretch in 0.5 mile. Stay on this main road as it heads down the canyon, crossing several more sandy sections. Approximately 3 miles from the five-way intersection you come to the Mill Canyon Dinosaur Trail on the right. Leave your bike on the road and enjoy this short walk to footprints and other interesting sites. When you're ready to go, ride the 1.6 miles back to your car.

6 . SLICKROCK TRAIL (See map on page 51)

For mountain bikes. The smooth, undulating, and unbelievably scenic Slickrock Trail undoubtedly ranks as one the most famous fat-tire routes in the world, and played a large role in making Moab the epicenter of the mountain-biking craze. An incredible number of bikers make the pilgrimage here to ride the Slickrock Trail. Marked by painted lines, the Slickrock Trail loops around a totally barren, stair-stepped sandstone mesa that overlooks the Colorado River and the Moab Valley. Stunning views to the rock spans of Arches National Park across the river, and to the towering 12,000-foot-plus peaks of the La Sal Mountains to the south, add to the mystique of this area. Riders of all abilities will find ample opportunities for exploring, testing their skills, and taking in the scene that put both mountain biking and Moab on the map. There are several loops out here but no requirement for the route, distance, or time you must ride. The route is considered technical and demands a good level of overall body strength.

Starting point: Fee station and parking lot at the trailhead 3.6 miles from Moab off Sand Flats Road. To get there drive south through Moab on Main Street (US 191) to Center Street. Drive east on Center Street for four blocks to 400 East. Go right on 400 East and head south for about half a mile to Mill Creek Drive. Turn left onto Mill Creek Drive at Dave's Corner Market (a good place to pick up refreshments after your ride), and then bear left onto Sand Flats Road in another half a mile. It is 1.8 miles to the Sand Flats Recreation Area, where you must pay a fee. The pass you receive is good for 3 days.

Length: The practice loop is just over 1 mile long round-trip from the start, and the main loop is about 11.

Riding surface: 100 percent slickrock. The Navajo sandstone that comprises this riding surface is not "slick" as the name implies, but has a smooth, grainy surface that provides maximum traction.

Difficulty: Difficult. If you're unfamiliar with slickrock riding, start out slow on the practice loop; it is easier technically but is still demanding physically. If you're confident of your ability to negotiate some of the hair-raising dips, cross-slope angles, and ledges out here, go for it. There's plenty of technical challenge on this ride, probably some that you've never even considered before. The most difficult sections are marked with white-and-yellow "fried egg" markers, and with black diamonds. Spending a good part of the day out here provides a full-body workout, the upper half often working just as hard as the lower.

Scenery/highlights: The lithified sand dunes of the Navajo sandstone are frozen here as beautiful, buff-colored swirls that change to reflect the pink of morning, lavender and golds of sunset, or bright white of midday. A good pair of sunglasses is a must for riding out here. Out on this mesa you will find only a few pockets of sand supporting cryptobiotic communities, perhaps a shrub or two, and maybe some prickly pear cacti. Potholes that fill with rainwater are also communities of bacterias that support bugs, amphibians, and other wildlife and are an important resource for life in the desert.

The views in all directions are some of the most fantastic in the Moab area. The throngs of bikers who come in all different sizes, shapes, and attitudes are a fascinating sideshow in their own right. It is always fun to watch the really accomplished technical riders show off for the crowds.

Best time to ride: Spring and fall, though expect huge crowds around spring break in March and again in the third week in October during the Canyonlands Fat Tire Festival. During the hot months, get out early or in the evening to beat the heat on this reflective rock. You will also have to contend with fewer bikers on the trail at these times of day.

Special considerations: There is a fee to get into the Slickrock Trail parking lot and ride the trail. There are bathrooms available at the trailhead but no water. Carry plenty of fluids and some high-energy snacks.

Although the Navajo sandstone is amazingly "grippy," be wary of the tumbles that are all too common out here. The surface of these ancient dunes is rock hard and abrasive, and can leave you with painful "raspberries" should you slide in a fall. Always wear a helmet that fits properly, is not tipped too far back, and doesn't jostle around loosely. Be sure that your front wheel is set properly in the front forks of your bike, and that the front skewer is snug. Also, check your brakes and make sure they are adjusted. If there are any sections of the trail you are unsure of, dismount and walk your bike.

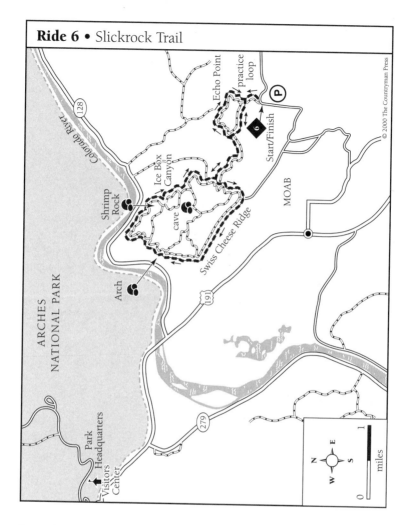

© 2000 The Countryman Press

From the parking lot, ride to the well-marked trailhead. Odometer readings, which start at the gate, read 12.5 miles by BLM figuring, but your actual mileage will likely be different. After you pass the gate you immediately climb what is called Hurry Up and Wait Hill, where riders sometimes form a traffic jam hundreds deep. In 0.2 mile you come to the intersection where the routes divide; to the right is the practice loop, to the left is the main loop. If you choose to go right to warm up on the practice loop you'll head east, where stellar views of the La Sals unfold. As the route

FAUNA

White-throated swifts and violet-green swallows love to play in the updrafts and winds that circulate around the arches. The song of the canyon wren, which starts high and then cascades in lovely clear notes, is synonymous with canyon country. Other songbirds such as the blue grosbeak, song sparrow, red-shafted flicker, warbling vireo, house wren, and Bullock's oriole find an ample supply of insects to feed on near the park's water sources. A variety of sparrows and finches, pinyon and scrub-jays, and ravens are the most commonly seen avian residents of the park, but you might also see a western meadowlark, a horned lark, or one of a variety of woodpeckers. Red-tailed hawks, sparrow hawks, and prairie falcons prefer the wide-open grasslands to do their hunting. If you're out at dusk, you may see nighthawks diving and maneuvering in short, sharp circles in pursuit of insects.

Mule deer are the largest of the park's mammals, but they stay away from human traffic and tend to be near water sources. Populations of desert bighorn sheep were bolstered by a transplant of 30 animals from nearby Canyonlands National Park in 1985. They favor the southwest side of the park, west of the Windows and the Great Wall. Black-tailed jackrabbits, rock squirrels, white-tailed antelope squirrels, and a variety of kangaroo rats and pocket mice live in the park, but are not as commonly seen as the northern plateau lizard, western whiptail lizard, short-horned lizard, and collared lizard. Only one poisonous snake is found in the park —the midget faded rattlesnake, about 18 inches long and a light pink to straw color. These are uncommon but are most likely to be seen near water.

swings around and heads northwest you'll find yourself peering into Echo Canyon. Obey all warnings indicating where to dismount at viewpoints; these overlooks come up quickly and you don't want to tumble over the edge here. Pedaling onward toward Abyss Canyon, you encounter a couple of sand traps before rejoining the main trail 0.8 mile from the intersection. If you choose to bypass the practice loop it is a quick 0.3 mile of rolling slickrock that descends to the beginning of the main route.

Back at the junction with the practice and main loops you are faced with a steep, luge-like descent that terminates in the kind of half pipe you might find at a skateboard park. The trail routes you around the half pipe to the Abyss Viewpoint, past which you descend a bumpy, dangerous, staircase section into a gully. The bottom of this gully, called Woolly Gully by locals, is sandy and a technical move is required to escape it. After you emerge from the gully, 1.3 miles from where the practice loop rejoined the main trail, you'll find "easier" and "harder" routes indicated by painted markers. The easier route takes the clockwise direction around the loop, although both routes pass over the same terrain. This clockwise loop is described here.

Now almost 3 miles into your slickrock odyssey go left, riding another half mile to Mountain View Cave on your right. A spur trail takes off on the right near the cave, and another trail 0.2 mile further comes in on the left. After a short sandy section you'll be faced with the intimidating wall of rock known as Cogs Too Spare. Gear low, spin your brains out, and hope for the best. The next challenge, 4.2 miles along the trail, is the climb up Swiss Cheese Hill. Most climb this one on foot. Once atop Swiss Cheese Hill take in the view; Moab Valley lies below, and beyond it are the Moab Rim, Poison Spider Mesa, Gold Bar Rim, and Portal, where the Colorado River crosses the Moab fault and flows southwest. Portal Viewpoint lies just ahead. A quick descent takes you to a spur leading to Panorama Viewpoint, where you can peer over into the murky Colorado River. The vertical relief here is dizzying; please be careful near this drop-off.

After a stretch of sand and some more rolling slickrock, the spur to Updraft Arch (4.8 miles from the start) takes you to an overlook of the river below. Continue almost another 2 miles as the route winds around to Natural Selection Viewpoint; use caution near the edge. In another 0.5 mile is Shrimp Rock, which doubles as a shrine where legions of fat-tire faithful bikers come to worship the slickrock gods. Just beyond is another challenging stair-stepped hill that will require all of your technical know-how and strength. Now 7.5 miles into the ride the trail mellows a bit, delivering you back to the "harder-easier" junction in another mile. Stay left here to go to the trailhead. There is some fun slickrock formations to play on as you continue toward the last big challenge—Fried Egg Hill leftovers. At almost 11 miles from the start you come to the junction with the practice loop. There is only one more steep descent to test your stamina and control—and it's a doozy. Now to the car and the cooler.

CAMPING

The **Devils Garden Campground** is located at the end of the park's scenic road, 18 miles from the visitors center at the park entrance. There are 52 tent and trailer sites, plus two walk-in group sites limited to tenting for 10 or more people. Facilities include flush toilets and water until frost. Chemical toilets are available after frost. Fire grates are provided but wood gathering is prohibited. You must preregister for individual campsites at the visitors center between 7:30 and 8 a.m., or at the entrance station after 8. Group campsite reservations are made by calling (435) 259-4351. The group campground fills every day from mid-March through October, often by early morning. A fee is required.

Dead Horse Point State Park is located between Arches and Canyonlands National Parks in a spectacular location overlooking the Colorado River. It's also at the slightly cooler elevation of almost 6,000 feet. This park has 32 tent sites and 22 RV sites. A per-night fee is required. It's open from the beginning of March through the middle of October. Facilities include modern rest rooms, drinking water, and waste disposal. You can make reservations from 3 to 16 days in advance by calling (800) 322-3770.

There are many possibilities for camping on surrounding **BLM land.** Contact the agency at (435-259-6111) to get a complete list of campgrounds or suggestions for wilderness camping.

You can also try these private campgrounds: **Canyonlands Campground** at 555 S. Main in Moab, the **KOA Campground** at 3225 S. US 191, or the **Up the Creek Campground** at 210 E. 300 S., also in Moab. Showers are available at all of these places for a fee.

LODGING

You can find almost any kind of accommodations you want in Moab these days, from hostels and fairly cheap motels to fancy lodges and exclusive spa resorts. Most of the big chain hotels are represented here now, including **Days Inn, Super 8, Best Western,** and **Ramada Inn.** You can rent a condo at **Cedar Breaks Condos** (435-259-7830), or cottages at **Desert Gardens** (800-505-5343). There are a handful of good B&Bs in town as well, including the **Blue Heron** (435-258-4921), **Sunflower Hill** (435-259-2974), **Canyon Country Bed & Breakfast** (435-259-5262), and the beautiful and secluded **Castle Valley Inn** (435-259-6012).

FOOD

For a good cup of coffee in Moab try **Mondo Coffee** (57 S. Main), or **Kayenta Coffee House** (92 E. Center Street), a popular spot that offers baked goods and has a deli, too. **The Jailhouse Café** (101 N. Main Street) and the **Moab Diner and Ice Cream Shoppe** (189 S. Main Street) have traditional fare for breakfast. **The Slick Rock Café** (5 N. Main Street) is a good place to go for breakfast, lunch, or dinner. If it's Mexican you want try the **Rio Colorado Restaurant** (100 W. Center Street) or **Dos Amigos** (56 E. 300 South). **Poplar Place Pub & Eatery** is a longtime

IT'S INTERESTING TO KNOW . . .
Evidence suggests that people lived and hunted in the area that is now Arches National Park as long as 10,000 years ago. Folsom projectile points, stone tools such as scrapers, and small split-twig figurines fashioned into the shapes of animals from willow branches found in and around the park constitute some of the scant evidence of a Paleo-Indian culture that is thought to have hunted large mammals long since vanished from this landscape. Many archaeologists believe that this archaic culture evolved into the Fremont culture, which flourished in this general region some 2,500 years ago. The Fremont culture was followed by the Ancestral Puebloans, or "Anasazi," who were responsible for the stone ruins found throughout the Four Corners region.

favorite in town (Main and 100 N.), as is **Eddie McStiff's** brewery (57 S. and Main Street). **The Moab Brewery** (686 S. Main Street) is another excellent choice for grog and food and is usually less crowded than McStiff's. **Catarina's** (51 N. Main) serves excellent Italian food, and **Thai House** (84 W. 200 N.) is a real treat if you like spicy food. **Center Café** (92 E. Center St.) is a wonderful choice for a nice meal, and you can always get a good steak at **Buck's Grill House** (1393 N.US 191).

LAUNDRY

Moab Speedqueen Laundromat, 702 S. Main St.; (435) 259-7456

BIKE SHOP/BIKE RENTAL

Chile Pepper, 702 S. Main St.; (435) 259-4688

Kaibab Mountain Bike Tours, 391 S. Main St.; (435) 259-7423

Poison Spider Bicycles, 497 N. Main St.; (435) 259-7882

Rim Cyclery, 94 W. 100 N.; (435) 259-5333

Western Spirit Cycling, 478 Millcreek Dr.; (435) 259-8732

FOR FURTHER INFORMATION

Arches National Park— Superintendent, P.O. Box 907, Moab, UT 84532; (435) 259-9161; http://www.nps.gov/arch/

Moab Visitors Center, 805 N. Main St. (corner of Main and Center), Moab, UT 84532; (435) 259-8825 or (800) 635-MOAB

Grand County Travel Council, P.O. Box 550, Moab, UT 84532; (435) 259-8825 or (800) 635-6622

Bureau of Land Management (BLM), Moab District Office, 82 E. Dogwood, P.O. Box 970, Moab, UT 84532; (435) 259-6111

Manti–La Sal National Forest, P.O. Box 386, Moab, UT 84532; (435) 259-7155

Community Sand Flats Team (Slickrock Trail camping and biking); (435) 259-2444

2

Bryce Canyon National Park is a continuation of the redrock theme found throughout southern Utah's national parks, but instead of massive sandstone formations rising out of the desert, the intricate canyons and delicate hoodoos found at Bryce Canyon drop away from a forested, green plateau. The series of headwater drainages that are the focus of the park do not constitute a true canyon, but are instead a row of huge natural amphitheaters carved into the soft sedimentary rocks of the 9,000-foot-high Paunsaugunt Plateau. The downsloping eastern edge of this plateau has been beautifully chiseled away by wind, water, and time, leaving behind delicate towers, turrets, crenellated ridges, and windows in fantastic shades of bright orange, white, and pink.

The siltstone and sandstone layers responsible for the stunning shapes and variety of the formations at Bryce Canyon are part of the Claron formation, deposited close to 65 million years ago in a Paleocene lake about the size of Lake Erie. Chalky limestone sediment from an earlier period, when shallow seas encroached into and then receded from the area, washed into the lake with other silt and sediments to be deposited there in layer upon layer. Volcanic activity then covered much of this region with a protective layer of lava. Later, the country throughout southern and central Utah faulted and uplifted in enormous blocks that remain as plateaus. These uplifted fault blocks, capped with lava that prevented them from being eroded down, have nonetheless experienced extensive erosion along their unprotected flanks. The soft rock layers of Bryce exposed along the eastern edge of the Paunsaugunt Plateau are subject to erosion from water running off the plateau as well as rain, snowmelt, hail, and wind. They are also sensitive to the extended periods of freeze-thaw cycles that take place at these elevations. Tree-ring studies done on some of the larger trees along the rim of the plateau reveal that the canyon rims are receding at the rate of 10 to 40 inches each century—quite rapid by geologic standards. The dazzling legions of brilliantly colored spires, hoodoos, fins, and pillars of Bryce Canyon, surrounded by the lush aspen and pine forests of the plateau and the spectacular 100-mile views to as far away as the Kaibab Plateau of Arizona, make this park one of the crowning jewels of our national park system.

Cycling in the Park

Pedaling across the rooftop of the Paunsaugunt Plateau, catching the scent of evergreens wafting on a cool breeze while the desert sizzles below, stopping along the way to peer down into a geologic wonderland or gaze out at the stunning vistas is a two-wheeled adventure that ranks with the best of them. The shorter ride to Bryce Point and the longer 18-mile ride out to the tip of the plateau at Rainbow Point on the main park road both offer fantastic opportunities to get out and experience the wonders of Bryce Canyon National Park up close.

Every year over 1.5 million people visit Bryce Canyon from all over the world. The summer months are the busiest. Parking spots are very limited in summer inside the park. Drink plenty of water to help your body combat the dehydrating effects of exertion, sun exposure, high altitude, and an arid climate. Bring something to eat as well. Snacking is the best strategy for keeping your energy up during a long day in the saddle. Temperatures in the summer are delightful, with highs in the 70s and 80s and lows dipping down into the 40s. Fall and spring offer more solitude and fewer cars along the park road, but the temperatures are cooler. Riding up here in the fall when the aspens are ablaze in hues of gold and red is spectacular, but make sure you check with forest service rangers and avoid riding in the woods when the deer and elk hunt is on. If you have to ride, wear something bright to help alert hunters to your presence.

CYCLING OPTIONS

There are seven rides in this chapter, three for road bikes and four for mountain bikes. In the park the ride out to Bryce Point is an easy-to-moderate ride of 10 miles. The ride out to Rainbow Point is a 32-mile round trip out to the southern end of the park best suited for intermediate to advanced road riders who don't mind a long day in the saddle.

The off-road ride into Daves Hollow is an easy route the whole family can enjoy just outside the park's northern boundary. The Sunset Cliffs Loop is a longer easy-to-moderate 17.5-mile ride on dirt roads that accesses a stunning display of orange pinnacles similar to those found in the park. The singletrack trail up Casto Canyon is one of this area's most popular rides. It is 11 miles out and back and is rated moderately difficult. The road ride up Red Canyon is a skinny-tire version of Casto Canyon but gains 1,100 feet in elevation and has a total of 24 miles. The ride up to Powell Point gives options for a longer (21-mile) or shorter (9-mile) ride out to one of the most spectacular overlooks in southwestern Utah. Although neither option requires advanced bike-handling skills, the longer route gains 2,000 feet of elevation and requires a good-to-excellent level of physical fitness.

Although you can't ride your mountain bike on any of the trails inside the park, nearby Casto Canyon features the same delicate spires and hoodoos in shades of flaming peach and salmon in a backcountry setting. Red Canyon offers road riders a skinny-tire version of Casto Canyon and traverses part of the scenic open ranching country atop the Paunsaugunt Plateau. Riding out to the Sunset Cliffs that rim the plateau's western edge is a gorgeous pedal through the Dixie National Forest that provides more of a peaceful backcountry experience than in the park and a similar, but far less visited, fairyland of pink and orange towers.

Nearby Brian Head—a small, quiet ski town turned summer biking destination—is the main resource for the region. The rural, wild nature of this part of the country and few paved roads mean there are many more off-road riding opportunities than exist for road riders. Still, if you spend a few days or weeks poking around in the fabulous country surrounding Bryce, you're sure to find plenty of riding to keep you happy.

7. BRYCE POINT (See map on page 61)

For road and mountain bikes. This ride is a good choice for your first day at Bryce Canyon, allowing you to get out, find your way around the park's facilities, and do some sight-seeing while adjusting to the higher elevations and thin, dry air atop the plateau. From the visitors center you can pedal south via back roads through the campground and park facilities to Sunrise Point and the main lodge, and then ride the spurs taking you out to Sunset Point and Inspiration Point before heading out to Bryce Point. Taking the back roads south as far as you can, riding all the spurs out to the overlooks, and riding back on the main park road gives you an out-and-back distance of 10 miles. An alternate starting point at the Ruby's Inn resort complex adds 5 miles.

Starting point: Park visitors center, about 1.5 miles inside the park boundary and 2.5 miles from Ruby's Inn. If you are here when it is busiest, consider parking at Ruby's Inn and riding from there. Just 2.5 miles outside the park entrance is Ruby's Inn, a complex of hotel buildings, cabins, and a campground.

Length: 10 miles. Bypassing the back roads shaves about a mile off the total distance. Starting from Ruby's Inn gives you a total distance of approximately 15 miles. Depending on how long you linger at the lookouts, 3 to 4 hours should suffice for most.

Riding surface: Pavement; narrow and rough in spots.

Difficulty: Easy to moderate. Elevations on this ride range between almost 7,900 feet at the visitors center and 8,200 feet just before Bryce Point. If you have come from a lower altitude, the elevations atop the plateau will have more of an impact on your wind and overall energy.

Scenery/highlights: From Sunrise Point you can look north across Campbell Canyon to Boat Mesa and the wealth of fanciful formations just beyond known as Fairyland. In the distance to the north are the Table Cliff Plateau and the Escalante Mountains. Sunset, Inspiration, and Bryce Points all exist at varying points above Bryce Canyon amphitheater, giving different views into the spectacular array of pinnacles, turrets, towers, and knobs. Distant views into the Tropic Valley and beyond to the Paria

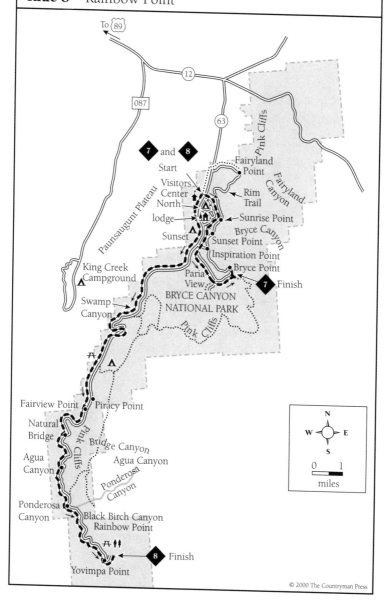

Ride 7 • Bryce Point
Ride 8 • Rainbow Point

To 89

12

087

63

Pink Cliffs

7 and 8

Start

Fairland Point

Visitors Center

North

Rim Trail

Fairland Canyon

lodge

Sunrise Point

Sunset

Bryce Canyon

Sunset Point

Inspiration Point

Bryce Point

Paria View

7 Finish

King Creek Campground

BRYCE CANYON NATIONAL PARK

Swamp Canyon

Pink Cliffs

Fairview Point

Piracy Point

Natural Bridge

Pink Cliffs

Bridge Canyon

Agua Canyon

Agua Canyon

Ponderosa Canyon

Ponderosa Canyon

Black Birch Canyon

Rainbow Point

8 Finish

Yovimpa Point

N
W — E
S

0   1
miles

© 2000 The Countryman Press

River drainage and Navajo Mountain in the south are astounding. The alpine environment atop the rim of the plateau provides cooler temperatures and greenery that's a beautiful contrast to the brilliant reds and oranges of the desert below.

Best time to ride: Anytime spring through fall, provided summer thunderstorms aren't in the forecast. During the busy summer months get an early start or take an evening ride to avoid the traffic. Mornings are superb for looking into the amphitheaters when they are flooded with sunlight from the east.

Special considerations: Water and bathrooms are available at the visitors center but not at Bryce Point. Bathrooms and water are also available along the back roads at the lodge, near the general store and nature center, and in the campground. Snacks, drinks, and fast-food items are available at the general store.

Be careful around pullouts, riding through the campground, and anywhere vehicle traffic becomes congested. Tourists are anxious to get in and out of scenic overlook areas and may not pay attention to you. Also, be careful around the canyon rims; the drops are precipitous and the soft soils underfoot can easily give way.

At the visitors center, hop on your bike and head out to the main road. Go left and ride about 100 yards, turning left on the road signed for North Campground. (If you would rather ride the back roads on your return trip or bypass them altogether, simply keep riding straight here.) Ride through this spacious campground and continue past a picnic area to the junction with the one-way road taking you to the general store and nature center. Follow this road around to make a stop at Sunrise Point, the store, or the nature center (otherwise continue on toward the Bryce Canyon Lodge). Eventually the road swings around to the southwest, taking you by the lodge, and intersecting the main park road approximately 2 miles from the visitors center.

At the main park road go left, coming to a spur road in 0.25 mile. It is half a mile out and back to Sunset Point. Back on the main road, ride 0.5 mile through a pine forest to a three way junction; bear left, then left again to catch the next spur out to Inspiration Point.

After taking in the view at Inspiration Point, ride back to the three-way junction (0.5 mile out and back), bearing left again onto the road out to Bryce Point and Paria View Overlook. The road now climbs along some weathered slopes of bright soils and rock, reaching an intersection where routes to the two overlooks divide in 1.5 miles. Take the left fork to Bryce Point (0.6 mile) where some of the best views of Bryce Canyon await. If you've got the time and energy on your return trip, go left back at the last intersection you passed, and ride another 0.5 mile out to Paria View Overlook. When you are ready to return, simply reverse your route, riding the Bryce Point spur road (2 miles) to the intersection with the main park road, and another 2 miles to the visitors center, ignoring the three spur roads you rode earlier on your right.

Option: A much shorter trip (4 miles total) leaves from the visitors center, heads out to the main road, and goes left. It's 1 mile to the turnoff for Fairyland Point, then 1 more mile out to the end of the road overlooking Fairyland. Because this overlook is a mile before the visitors center it receives far fewer visitors and less car traffic than the other overlooks.

---

8. RAINBOW POINT (See map on page 61)

For road bikes. Riding to the end of the main park road at Rainbow Park is a world-class tour of the many beautiful hoodoo-filled amphitheaters and sweeping vistas that make Bryce National Park so spectacular. Elevations along this route range from almost 7,900 feet at the visitors center to 9,100 feet at the overlook at Rainbow Point. This 16-mile one-way tour is well suited for experienced road bikers or recreational riders in good-to-excellent physical condition who have had a day or two to acclimate to the high elevations atop the plateau.

Starting point: Park visitors center. During the busy summer months consider starting from Ruby's Inn, 2.5 miles north of the visitors center, where you will find many more parking spaces.

Length: 32 miles out-and-back. From Ruby's Inn, total distance is 37 miles. Riding out to Bryce and Paria Viewpoints adds another 4 miles. Plan on spending the better part of a day out here.

Riding surface: Pavement; little or no shoulder, rough in spots.

Difficulty: Moderate to strenuous. The distance and elevation gain of 1,200 feet make this a more difficult ride.

Scenery/highlights: The views, the views, the wonderful alpine scenery, and the views. Sunrise, Sunset, Inspiration, and Bryce Points encircle the top of Bryce Canyon, the largest and by many estimates the most fantastic of the natural amphitheaters in the park. If you ride out to Paria View you gaze into a bowl full of hoodoos carved by Yellow Creek. The Paria River is fed by all the drainages coming off the eastern edge of the plateau. It flows into the Colorado River near Lees Ferry, where it often turns the water a milky pink after a thunderstorm. From here the White Cliffs, eroded out of Navajo sandstone, can be seen to the south.

Farview Point provides vistas reaching all the way to the Kaibab Plateau, which forms the North Rim of the Grand Canyon. The bridge at Natural Bridge is not really a natural bridge, it's an arch weathered out of the rock. At Agua Canyon you look down over almost vertical cliffs into the Willis Creek drainage and beyond to the Cockscomb and Kodachrome Basins. At Ponderosa Canyon the brilliantly colored turrets and pinnacles in the canyon are set off against pine-cloaked foothills. At Rainbow and Yovimpa Points enjoy views that take in much of southern Utah. On most days you can see Navajo Mountain and the Kaibab Plateau 90 miles away. On the very clearest days you may be able to see Shiprock in northwestern New Mexico.

Best time to ride: Spring and fall, to avoid the crush of traffic; get an early start if you are here in the summer to avoid the daily crunch and view the pinnacles and hoodoos of this wonderland is at their best.

Special considerations: Water is available at the visitors center but at no other point along the way; bring your own.

Bring a cable lock to secure your bike if you are interested in any of the short hikes from the overlooks to the spires and hoodoos of the canyons. Be careful when venturing among these rock formations and near the edge of the canyon rim; soils are soft and give way easily.

Be especially wary around pullouts and overlooks. Drivers often have their eyes on the scenery and are anxious to get into and out of these congested areas. Chances are they won't be looking at you.

From the visitors center head south on the main park road. In just 100

A heavily-laden touring bike and rider beginning the climb up scenic Red Canyon on the way to Bryce Canyon.

yards is a road on your left signed for North Campground. If you want to ride some of the paved back roads leading to the park's general store, nature center, and main lodge, go left here and wind your way around passing Sunrise Point overlook and rejoin the main park road in approximately 1.5 miles. You can also save these roads for the return trip.

If you choose to bypass these back roads altogether you will reach the spur road for Sunset Point approximately 1.3 miles from the visitors center. Go left here and ride 0.25 mile to take in the massive hoodoo-filled basin of Bryce Canyon. Back on the main road you pass a road on your right leading out to Sunset Campground, and come to a junction 0.5 mile from Sunset Point. Stay left here to ride the 0.25-mile spur road out to Inspiration Point, one of the most fantastic views of Bryce Canyon. When you get back from Inspiration Point to this junction, go left if you are interested in riding out to Bryce Point and Paria View. To continue south, bear right and then left through this junction, again on the main park road.

Beyond this intersection the road skirts a large alpine meadow and then climbs through a mostly ponderosa pine forest. The road emerges at the edge of the meadow, reaching the Swamp Canyon pullout approximately 3 miles from the junction at Inspiration Point. From this junction the road climbs steadily, gaining through switchbacks above Shaker and Trough Springs, reaching Whiteman Bench and a shady picnic area on the west side of the road approximately 3 miles from the pullout at Swamp Canyon. The Whiteman Bench narrows as the road continues to climb 1.2 miles beyond the picnic area to the Farview Point pullout. A short trail takes you out to Piracy Point, offering more stunning panoramas of the Tropic Valley and southeastern Utah. The 85-foot span of Natural Bridge is another 2 miles south on the east side of the road.

For the next 3 miles the road alternately climbs through pine forests and regains the rim, passing Agua Canyon, Ponderosa Canyon, and Black Birch Canyon lookouts. Now cruising through mixed conifers and aspens, you make your final push toward Rainbow Point, reaching it 1.7 miles past the last viewpoint at Black Birch Canyon. Spend some time breathing in the clean air and tremendous views from here, have a snack and plenty to drink, and decide whether or not you want to hike the Bristlecone Loop Trail (1 mile round-trip) from Rainbow Point, or make the short walk out to Yovimpa Point. When you're ready to go, saddle up and enjoy the rolling 16-mile descent back to the visitors center.

9. DAVES HOLLOW (See map on page 67)

For mountain bikes. This easy 8-mile loop route traverses the lovely meadows and pine forests typical of Utah's high plateaus, gaining and losing very little elevation. The whole family will enjoy traveling part of the Great Western Trail on their way through peaceful, wooded Daves Hollow just west of the park entrance. Several options allow stronger riders to explore farther south, toward Tropic Reservoir.

Starting point: The trailhead that leaves from the Bryce Canyon National Park boundary 1 mile south of Ruby's Inn and about 1.5 miles north of the visitors center. Park on the west side of the road.

Length: 8 miles round-trip. Allow at least 2 hours to complete this ride.

Riding surface: Dirt roads, mellow doubletrack.

Difficulty: Easy. There is no real technical riding along this route and not much climbing, although elevations are relatively high, ranging between 7,700 and almost 8,000 feet.

Ride 9 • Daves Hollow
Ride 10 • Sunset Cliffs Loop

Scenery/highlights: This is simply a nice cruise through the woods, serving as a good introduction to the backcountry that exists across the Paunsaugunt Plateau. The stands of ponderosa pine and open meadows here constitute a unique habitat for birds, deer, and other creatures.

Best time to ride: Anytime spring through fall. Be aware of fall hunt schedules; try to avoid riding in forests where hunters are out.

Special considerations: Water and bathrooms are available at the Pink Cliffs Village tourist complex at the intersection of UT 12 and 63 and at the park visitors center just a few miles to the south of this junction. Be aware of forecasted summer thunderstorms and all-terrain vehicle traffic.

From the trailhead at the park boundary, ride west about half a mile to a junction. Go left and pedal southward on FR 090, part of the Great Western Trail. In approximately 0.75 mile turn right, following a doubletrack down Daves Hollow. This doubletrack eventually picks up FR 088 and ends at the gravel road that takes you to Tropic Reservoir (FR 087). Dave's Hollow Forest Service Station is just up this well-traveled road a few hundred yards on the right. When you are ready to return you can follow the same route back, or approximately 1 mile east of the gravel road to Tropic Reservoir bear left onto FR 1173. Follow this road east until it comes to an intersection just before the trailhead where you began.

Option: For a slightly longer route, at the junction at 0.75 mile stay straight instead of right to Daves Hollow. Ride FR 088, and then a short section of FR 096, another 3 miles into Johnson Hollow. This road also ends where it hits the road to Tropic Reservoir (FR 087). You can ride FR 087 to the reservoir, or continue heading south on FR 185 as it climbs up onto Whiteman Bench. Whichever way you choose to go adventuring out here, retrace your route to get to your starting point.

---

10. SUNSET CLIFFS LOOP (See map on page 67)

For mountain bikes. This 17.5-mile loop up Badger Creek and down Skunk Creek on the way out to Sunset Cliffs is a refreshing crowd-free trip out to some of the same spectacular bright pink and orange formations found inside the park. Beginning and intermediate riders in good condition who are able to tackle rides at elevations between 7,800 and 9,250 feet will be richly rewarded for their efforts on this route.

Starting point: Boat ramp day-use parking lot at Tropic Reservoir 15 miles west of Bryce Canyon National Park. To get there drive west approximately 3 miles from the intersection of UT 12 and UT 63 (the road leading into the park), and go south onto FR 087 (signed for Kings Creek Campground and Tropic Reservoir). Drive south 7 miles on this gravel road to Tropic Reservoir, cross over the dam at the north end of the reservoir, and park at the boat ramp.

Length: 17.5 miles. Allow 4 hours to complete this loop.

Riding surface: Dirt road, doubletrack; a few loose, rocky sections.

Difficulty: Easy to moderate. Although this route does not require much in the way of technical riding ability, the distance and elevation gain make it more difficult.

Scenery/highlights: This is a great tour of the alpine country of Utah's high plateaus, with open, grassy meadows; fragrant stands of mixed conifers, and great views at Sunset Cliffs. To the west you look across the Sevier River Valley to the Markagunt Plateau, crowned by the distinctive shape of Brian Head Peak (11,307 feet).

Best time to ride: Spring and summer; these dirt roads are ridable as soon as the ground is dry and free of snow, usually by late April. In the fall the area is popular with hunters during the deer and elk season.

Special considerations: Water and pit toilets are available at Kings Creek Campground and at the Tropic Water Stop, a spring-fed fountain just south of Tropic Reservoir near the end of the ride.

Be aware of hunt schedules in the area and predicted afternoon thunderstorms. Be careful around the cliffs themselves; stay back from the edge, as the ground is soft and can give way beneath you.

From the day-use parking area at the boat ramp, ride south past the entrance to Kings Creek Campground, and traverse the west side of the reservoir for approximately 1 mile before turning right onto FR 109, signed for Badger Creek and Proctor Canyon. Head west up a meadow-filled valley flanked by tall stands of ponderosa pine and rock formations reminiscent of those inside the park. After 2 miles you come to an intersection; bear left onto the fork signed for Skunk Creek and Proctor Canyon. (The right fork leads up the Left Fork of Blue Fly Creek.)

The road begins to climb through stretches of meadow and forest. Ponderosa pines give way to stands of mixed spruce, fir, and aspen as you reach elevations of 8,500 feet. Follow the road as it climbs up two switchbacks and arrives at an intersection 6.5 miles from the start. Bear left heading south on FR 233 toward Skunk Creek. Follow this road as it

FLORA

The 2,500 feet of vertical relief found inside Bryce Canyon National Park provides for a number of different habitat types, supporting entirely different plant communities. At the lowest elevations of the park, ranging between 6,500 and 7,000 feet, piñon-juniper woodlands dominate, with Gambel oak in slightly moister areas. Here temperatures can dip below zero in the winter and frequently soar past 100 degrees in the summer. As you move up to elevations between 7,000 and 8,500 feet, the tall, straight, ruddy-colored ponderosa pine with its long needles becomes the dominant tree. These elevations receive more precipitation than the desert below, enabling the meadow grasses in pockets around the plateau to thrive. Ponderosa pines like the sun-drenched southwest-facing slopes and will persist on these exposures as high as 9,000 feet. Beginning around 8,500 feet Douglas fir, white fir, blue spruce, and aspen—trees that like the cooler temperatures and moister soils of the Canadian life zone—become dominant. Growing on the most barren, inhospitable spots along the plateau rim are bristlecone and limber pine. These trees manage to thrive in the nutrient-poor limestone soils other plants cannot tolerate. Bristlecone pines can grow to be hundreds, and sometimes thousands, of years old; they shed their needles only once every 25 to 30 years.

Utah serviceberry and cliffrose are shrubs commonly found in piñon-juniper woodlands, but here they occur at higher elevations as well. Big sagebrush and green-leaf manzanita are also found throughout the park at varying elevations. Manzanita thickets are present among stands of ponderosa pine, where you will also find mountain mahogany, Oregon grape, and blue elderberry. At the highest elevations snowberry, wax currant, and a ground-spreading juniper are the most common shrubs.

In the lower, more arid parts of the park you may find several varieties of milk vetches, purple tansy asters, white evening primroses, goldenrod, Indian paintbrush, red and purple penstemons, and succulents such as prickly pear, claret cup, and fishhook cactus. The delicate white sego lily (Utah's state flower), white yarrow, purple bellflower, and the distinctive green gentian can also be found here. Wildflowers native to a mountainous Canadian life zone are also present in the cooler, moister reaches of the plateau, including lupine, columbine, and wild geranium.

Hikers descending into one of the brilliantly colored "amphitheaters" inside Bryce Canyon National Park.

wiggles its way along the cliffs, just out of sight to the west. After 1 mile the road meets the rim.

Stop here and make the short hike out to the knob where you can get a better perspective on the span of Sunset Cliffs. That's the Sevier Valley below you, and Markagunt Plateau, home of Brian Head Ski Area and Cedar Breaks National Monument, beyond to the west. When you're ready to go, mount up, check your brakes, make sure your helmet is on snugly, and get ready for the thrilling descent down Skunk Creek. The way down is hard-packed and fast, but some of the turns may be washboarded. Check your speed and watch out for those tight turns with loose gravel. Stay to the right and be prepared for upcanyon traffic.

After approximately 5 miles you intersect FR 087. Turn left and ride north 1.5 miles to FR 109. Just before this junction is the Tropic Water Stop, where you'll probably want to glug down some refreshing springwater. Go left onto FR 109 and ride 1 mile along the west side of the reservoir back to the boat ramp and your car.

---

11. CASTO CANYON (See map on page 73)

For mountain bikes. The ride up Casto Canyon is a five-star tour through a wonderland of the same fiery orange-pink spires, pinnacles, and hoodoos found in Bryce Canyon—only here you're in the backcountry surrounded by towering pines and chirping birds instead of Winnebagos and tourists. The fanciful shapes of the formations in this canyon require frequent stops to avoid dumping over your handlebars, not because the trail is so technical but because of the eye-popping scenery. The 11-mile out-and-back excursion up this canyon is moderately difficult for intermediate riders with some technical skills. A good level of physical fitness is recommended for this ride.

Starting point: The trailhead parking lot at the mouth of Casto Canyon. To get there from the intersection of UT 12 and UT 63, drive west on UT 12 toward Panguitch. Drive down Red Canyon toward US 89 for about 12 miles, going right (north) approximately 2 miles before you reach the junction with US 89. Drive north on this gravel road, passing the turnoff for Losee Canyon in 2 miles, and at 3 miles reach the parking lot at the mouth of Casto Canyon.

Length: 11 miles out-and-back. Stop at the Red Canyon Visitors Center for information about trails around Bryce and Red Canyons.

Riding surface: ATV doubletrack, singletrack; stretches of hard-packed dirt, loose rock in stream channels.

Difficulty: Moderate. Intermediate levels of both technical riding ability and physical fitness are recommended for this ride.

Scenery/highlights: The incredibly vibrant orange, peach, pink, and red of this landscape are almost surreal, and in some places the turreted canyon walls seem literally to glow. The drainage itself is quite lovely, coursed by an intermittent stream that remains dry most of the summer.

Butch Cassidy and his gang supposedly used this and nearby canyons to evade capture on at least one occasion. A trail intersecting this route bears the bandit's name.

Best time to ride: Anytime April through October provided the ground is dry and free of snow. Don't ride up here if it has been raining or is just free of snowmelt; the pernicious mud will do nasty things to your bike.

Special considerations: No water or bathrooms are available at this trailhead, but you will find both at the Red Canyon Visitors Center.

From the parking area ride east on the ATV trail, which takes you immediately into the fiery gullet of Casto Canyon. The trail winds its way up

Ride 11 • Casto Canyon
Ride 12 • Red Canyon

this strikingly beautiful canyon, frequently crossing back and forth over loose stream-deposited gravels and rocks. Recent rain may erase the trail, but it is difficult to get lost in this orange-walled gauntlet.

Approximately 3.5 miles from the start of this trail you come to an intersection. (The doubletrack ATV trail heads left up the side of the canyon; it makes a loop and rejoins the canyon farther up.) Stay right and continue on what becomes a singletrack taking you up the upper part of Casto Canyon. At this point the orange pinnacles and high canyon walls begin to melt into pine-covered slopes. The canyon becomes a bit wider as the main route passes the Cassidy Trail on the right. Almost 2 miles from where the trail turned to singletrack you arrive at FR 121 (Sanford Road). This is the end of the trail. Turn around here and head back the way you came.

Options: Strong riders with an adventurous bent might want to consider traversing the Cassidy Trail south to where it dumps into Losee Canyon. This is an extremely technical but gorgeous 4-mile stretch that takes you over to the neighboring canyon. It is 3 miles out Losee Canyon to the gravel road you drove north on to access Casto Canyon. Go right when you reach this road and ride 1 mile back to the Casto Canyon trailhead. Another option is to ride the Sanford Road all the way out to UT 12, where you ride out Red Canyon and ride back to the Casto Canyon trailhead via the gravel road you came in on.

12. RED CANYON (See map on page 73)

For road bikes. The ride up Red Canyon is a five-star tour of 12 miles from the mouth of Red Canyon to the turnoff for Bryce Canyon at the intersection with UT 63, a total distance up and down the canyon of 24 miles. This is a great beginning-to-intermediate road ride that climbs approximately 1,100 feet on the way up. Elevations are relatively high—between 6,700 and 7,800 feet—so a good level of physical fitness is recommended.

Starting point: The pullout and parking area on the right side of the road at the mouth of Red Canyon, just over 2 miles east of the intersection of US 89 and UT 12.

Length: 24 miles. Allow 3 to 4 hours to complete this ride.

Riding surface: Pavement; shoulders narrow in places.

Difficulty: Moderate. Length and elevation gain may be difficult for some.

Scenery/highlights: Red Canyon is very pretty; fantastic orange-to-pink spires and columns, a beautiful forested canyon, and some graceful plateau country, all unique to this area. Stop in at the Red Canyon Visitors Center just 1.5 miles from the start to see its books and maps on the area.

Best time to ride: Anytime spring through fall when weather and temperatures permit. Car and camper traffic are heaviest during summer.

Special considerations: Water and rest rooms are available at the Red Canyon Visitors Center and at the nearby campground.

Head out onto UT 12, a designated Utah Scenic Byway, and pedal east up Red Canyon. The entrance of the canyon is well defined by brilliant orange pinnacles that accompany you through most of this tour. In 1.5

FAUNA

Most common among the park's avian residents are pinyon jays, gray jays, gray vireos, blue grosbeaks, house finches, chickadees, mountain bluebirds, Say's phoebes, and rufous-sided towhees. Among the meadows and forests of the plateaus you may see sage grouse, blue grouse, horned larks, western meadowlarks, Williamson's sapsuckers, Steller's jays, Clark's nutcrackers, and brown creepers. Ravens often caw and croak at you as you walk along the trails of the park. The violet-green swallow and the white-throated swift delight in playing in warming updrafts near the rim of the plateaus.

Alpine-loving yellow-bellied marmots, skunks, porcupines, spruce squirrels, northern flying squirrels, and threatened white-tailed prairie dogs all live atop the plateau, along with several species of chipmunks and pocket mice. Gray foxes and long-tailed weasels, which both feed on the abundance of rodents on the plateau, are occasionally seen but are quite shy. Cougars sometimes follow mule deer, their primary quarry, onto the plateau, but not often. Mule deer are the most common large mammal in the park and can be spotted near dusk around the fringes of the plateau's meadows. Short-horned lizards are also quite common among the lower elevations of the park, as are Great Basin rattlesnakes. These can grow to be up to 5½ feet long and generally will not strike unless surprised or provoked. They sometimes find that park hiking trails make handy places to stretch out and get warm in the morning. If you happen upon one of these beautiful creatures, back away to a safe distance and make noise; the snake will leave once its solitude has been disturbed.

miles is the Red Canyon Visitors Center, where you can pick up information on the area or use the facilities. Beyond the center the road makes several gentle curves as it climbs through the canyon. You emerge from the canyon onto the Paunsaugunt Plateau, elevation 7,775 feet, approximately 5 miles from your start.

The road climbs just slightly over the next 2 miles before dropping toward the Pine Hills and crossing into the Emery Valley—beautiful open ranch country intermingled with ponderosa pine forests. You pass the graded dirt road that heads south toward Tropic Reservoir 9 miles from the start, 3 miles before the turnaround point at the turnoff for Bryce Canyon National Park (approximate elevation 7,600 feet). There are several places to get a drink and a snack at Bryce Junction before heading back to your vehicle at the mouth of Red Canyon.

---

13. POWELL POINT (See map on page 77)

For mountain bikes. The 21-mile up-and-back ride to Powell Point atop the Table Cliff Plateau delivers you to one of the most breathtaking viewpoints in southern Utah: an awe-inspiring aerie where you can take in almost the whole of the sprawling Grand Staircase–Escalante National Monument. You'll need a strong pair of legs and a good set of lungs to negotiate the long climb that winds its way up through forests of ponderosa pine and mixed stands of spruce, fir, and aspen to a lofty perch 2,000 feet above the Paria River Valley. An intermediate level of technical riding skills is recommended for the steep sections of loose rock and the long climbs. An alternate starting point farther along the route makes this a 9-mile out-and-back adventure with very little climbing.

Starting point: Pine Lake in the Dixie National Forest, approximately 16 miles northeast of Bryce Junction (the intersection of UT 12 and UT 22 just north of the entrance to Bryce National Park). To get there drive north on UT 22 for 11 miles toward Pine Lake and Antimony. Go right onto the gravel FR 132 and drive just under 6 miles to Pine Lake. Park here.

If you are interested in the shorter version of this ride, continue driving (a four-wheel-drive, high-clearance vehicle is recommended) past Pine Lake on FR 132 for another 6 miles to where the road gains the top of the plateau and a doubletrack to Powell Point takes off on the right for driving to this starting point.

Length: 21 miles. The shorter ride is approximately 9 miles.

Riding surface: Rough dirt road (loose in spots), doubletrack, short section of singletrack.

Difficulty: Moderate to strenuous. Although this ride does not require expert bike handling skills, some of the rough spots along the route and the long climb make it more difficult. The 2,000 feet of elevation gain to

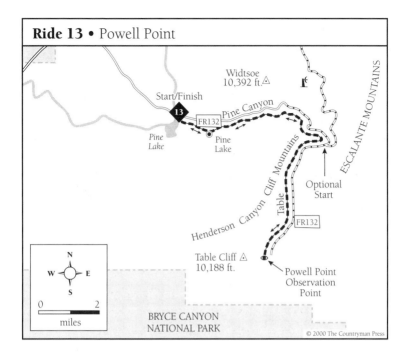

Widtsoe
10,392 ft. △

Start/Finish

13

FR132   Pine Canyon

Pine
Lake

Pine
Lake

ESCALANTE MOUNTAINS

Table Cliff Mountains

Optional
Start

Henderson Canyon Cliff Mountains

FR132

Table Cliff △
10,188 ft.

Powell Point
Observation
Point

N
W   E
S

0   2
miles

BRYCE CANYON
NATIONAL PARK

© 2000 The Countryman Press

the high point of this ride (at 10,300 feet) require a good-to-excellent level of physical fitness.

Scenery/highlights: From atop Table Cliff Plateau, to the north and east you can see the Aquarius Plateau; to the east are the Straight Cliffs and Kaiparowits Plateau; and southward is the vast expanse of desert wilderness now included in the Grand Staircase–Escalante National Monument. The Henry Mountains, created by a volcanic intrusion, are the isolated peaks amid the jumble of mesas, canyons, and plateaus receding into the distance. To the west are the glowing pink ramparts that fringe the Paunsaugunt Plateau inside Bryce Canyon National Park. The land beyond the Paunsaugunt drops away in great steps to the Skutumpah Terrace, the White Cliffs, the Vermilion Cliffs, and, finally, the Grand Canyon.

Best time to ride: Anytime spring through fall, provided the ground is dry and free of snow. Be aware of local forecasts predicting afternoon thunderstorms, and of hunt schedules in the area.

These fantastic formations, in bright hues of pink and orange, have been chiseled out of ancient lake bed sediments in Bryce Canyon.

Special considerations: Bathrooms are available at Pine Lake but not water. Be sure to bring plenty with you.

Be careful near the edge when you're out at Powell Point or anywhere along these high plateaus. Also, check your speed and be wary of the loose and rutted sections of road on your way down.

From the parking area at Pine Lake head back onto FR 132 and go right, following this road as it climbs 6 miles up, up, up Pine Creek Canyon to the edge of the plateau. The higher you go, the steeper and rougher the road gets. In places the road is rutted from runoff, and in others it's covered with coarse gravel-like deposits of rocks that make it challenging to maintain traction. After several switchbacks you gain the top of the plateau. The main road turns abruptly north (left) here, with a lesser-used doubletrack forking to the south (right). Go right onto this doubletrack (start here for the shorter ride) and follow it as it rolls along through the alpine environment atop Table Cliff Plateau. Gaps in the trees reveal mind-bending views to the east as you make your way south toward Powell Point.

Approximately 4 miles from the last intersection with the main road, the doubletrack ends and a singletrack begins. It is 0.5 mile to Powell Point. When it's time to go, head back the way you came. Check your speed on your descent of FR 132 and beware of sections of loose rock.

CAMPING

There are two campgrounds in Bryce Canyon National Park, offering 216 sites with space for tenters and RVs (no hook-ups). Both **North Campground** and **Sunset Campground** have picnic tables, drinking water, and toilets, and are managed on a first-come, first-served basis. There is a 14-day stay limit at both campgrounds. North Campground also has showers and is open year-round. Sunset Campground is open from mid-May to the first of October and has a group site available (reservations required). A fee is assessed for each night's stay. Backcountry camping permits are available at the visitors center for a per-night fee. Arrive early in the day to secure a campsite, as these campgrounds tend to fill up quickly in the summer.

There are at least three campgrounds in the Dixie National Forest that are close to the park; often they have room when the park is full. Try **Pine Lake Campground**, located 11 miles north and 6 miles east of Bryce Junc-tion; **Kings Creek Campground**, located 3 miles west and 7 miles south near Tropic Reservoir; or **Red Canyon Campground,** located in Red Canyon 10 miles west of Bryce Junction. Contact the Dixie National Forest's Escalante Ranger District for more information.

Ruby's Inn, just a mile outside the park entrance, has tent sites and RV sites with hook-ups, as well as showers, a store, a restaurant, and laundry facilities. **Bryce Canyon Pines Store & Campground,** about 6 miles west of the park turnoff right next to the Bryce Canyon Pines Motel, has tent sites and RV sites with hook-ups, as well as showers, laundry, a swimming pool, and a store.

LODGING

Nestled among ponderosa pines a short walk from the canyon rim is the **Bryce Canyon Lodge,** built in 1923 by the Union Pacific Railway that brought tourists practically to the front door via a spur line for almost 30 years. Now on the National Register of Historic

Places, the lodge has standard motel rooms, western-style cabins, and lodge suites. It is open from April 1 to November 1. You can also arrange through the lodge to go on horseback rides, park tours, and ranger-led talks. There is often live entertainment in the evenings. Make lodge reservations at least 8 months to a year before your visit. Contact AMFAC Parks and Resorts, 14001 E. Illif Ave., Suite 600, Aurora, CO 80014; (303) 292-2757; http://www.amfac.com/. Or you can contact the lodge directly in season: Call (435) 834-5361.

There are several other good lodging options close to the entrance of the park, the most notable being **Best Western Ruby's Inn.** This year-round resort complex has hundreds of hotel rooms, rooms with kitchenettes, tent sites, and RV sites with hook-ups and is very conveniently located 2.5 miles outside the park entrance. A general store, post office, laundry facilities, and two swimming pools are also available for guests. Rooms are more expensive at peak season and fill up fast. Make your reservations well in advance if you plan to visit during the summer months. Call (800) 528-1234 or (435) 834-5341.

Near the turnoff to the park is the **Pink Cliffs Bryce Village Inn,** offering motel rooms, cabins, and hostel rooms. Call to get more information or make reservations: (435) 834-5303 or (800) 834-0043. An on-site restaurant offers three meals a day. Farther west on UT 12 toward Panguitch are other lodging options, including **Foster's, the Bryce Canyon Pines Motel,** and **the Bryce Junction Inn.**

The town of Panguitch, 20 miles northwest of the turnoff to the park, has at least 20 hotels, motels, lodges, and B&Bs. **Bear Paw Lakeview Resort,** rents mountain bikes and boats, and has a store, restaurant, and RV park.

FOOD

The restaurant at **Bryce Canyon Lodge** has a good menu of mostly American fare three meals a day. With a 12-hour advance notice it will pack a box lunch for you. The **General Store** located near Sunrise Point parking area has groceries, fast-food items, and camping supplies. **The Canyon Diner** at Ruby's Inn is a good choice for breakfast, lunch, or dinner. It also has a snack bar that serves more casual lunch and dinner items, and a general store well stocked with groceries and camping supplies. Farther west on UT 12 your options include **Foster's Family Steak House,** serving three meals a day and offering a supermarket, bakery, and a gas station. A restaurant at the **Bryce Canyon Pines Motel** also serves meals anytime, as does **Harold's Place Café** near the Red Canyon Indian Store and RV Park.

In Panguitch try **Buffalo Java**

DON'T MISS

Several short (1.5 to 5 miles) trails take you down through a maze of brilliantly colored pinnacles and turreted ridges that can sometimes boggle the senses. The Rim Trail between Fairyland Overlook and Bryce Point is a longer 5.5-mile trail that can be hiked with a vehicle shuttle or done halfway as an out and back. The Queens Garden Trail is one of the most popular trails accessing the fantastic Bryce Canyon amphitheater. The Navajo Loop provides a great walk among formations such as Wall Street, Two Bridges, and Thors Hammer and is one of your shorter hike options. The Peekaboo Loop Trail, a superb 5-mile hike that traverses the southern half of the Bryce Canyon Amphitheater, is another great day-hike option.

(47 N. Main St.) for coffee, pastries, and bagels. You can get a meal at the **Cowboy's Smokehouse Bar-B-Q** (95 N. Main St.) or, if you prefer something different, **Grandma Tina's Spaghetti House** (523 N. Main St.),which has Italian favorites as well as a few vegetarian choices.

LAUNDRY

Coin-operated showers and laundry facilities are at the general store inside the park near the Sunrise Point parking area. Laundry and shower facilities are also available at the campground at **Ruby's Inn** just outside the park, and at the **Bryce Canyon Pines Store & Campground** 6 miles west of the park turnoff on UT 12.

BIKE SHOP/BIKE RENTAL

Ruby's Inn has it all, including mountain-bike rentals. Call ahead to reserve bikes: (435) 834-5341 or (800) 528-1234. Your other options include one shop in Panguitch and three in Brian Head (about an hour's drive from the park). The **Bear Paw Lakeview Resort** in Panguitch also rents serviceable mountain bikes: (435) 676-2650 or (888) LKE-VIEW.

Brian Head Cross Country Ski & Mountain Bike Center, 223 Hunter Ridge Dr., Brian Head; (435) 677-2012

Brian Head Resort Rentals, 223 W. Hunter Ridge Dr., Brian Head; (435) 677-2035

Brian Head Sports Inc., 269 S. Brianhead Blvd., Brian Head; (435) 677-2035

Mountain Bike Heaven, 25 E. Center S., Panguitch; (435) 676-2880

FOR FURTHER INFORMATION

Bryce Canyon National Park-Superintendent, P.O. Box 170001, Bryce Canyon, UT 84717; (435) 834-5322; brca_reception_area@nps.gov; http://www.bryce.canyon.national-park.com/info.htm

Bryce Canyon Information Line—Reservations; (800) 444-6689

Garfield County Travel Council, Box 200, Panguitch, UT 84759; (435) 676-8421

Dixie National Forest, Supervisor's Office, 82 N. 100 E., Cedar City, UT 84720; (435) 865-3700

Dixie National Forest, Powell Ranger District, Box 80, Panguitch, UT 84759; (435) 673-3431

3

The layer-cake geology distinctive of the Colorado Plateau is elegantly revealed by the work of two rivers in Canyonlands National Park: the Colorado and the Green. Here the plateau's many layers of sedimentary rock, laid down eons ago by successive sand dunes, shallow seas, and river deltas, have been cleaved by these two mighty rivers, exposing more than 150 million years of the earth's history. The beautiful pink, salmon, rust, peach, cream, and crimson hues of the different layers are the result of the amount of iron oxide minerals present, while the shapes of the buttes, canyon walls, and pinnacles, as well as the general lay of the land, have been determined by the varying hardness of those layers.

Rivers that flowed during the Triassic era deposited thick layers of mud and sand across broad deltas that became the poorly consolidated Moenkopi and Chinle formations. These soft layers eroded away from the distinctive bench-forming layers of the Cedar Mesa and White Rim sandstones prevalent in the park. The Wingate sandstone is another erosion-resistant layer that stands in pink skyscraperlike walls, helping define the park's canyons, while the buff-colored swirls of Navajo sandstone cap the mesas like frothy meringue. Both of these layers tell stories of vast deserts and shifting dunes, of a time when the western half of North America must have looked much like Africa's Sahara Desert does today. The Kayenta formation that separates these two wind-deposited layers is comprised of mudstones and shales, indicating that a river once cut through the dunes, only to be overtaken by blowing sand again.

The park is split by the Green and Colorado Rivers into three major sections that all meet in the center. The northern section, a pie-shaped wedge that pinches off at the confluence of the rivers, is called the Island in the Sky District. The eastern section, distinguished by fantastic pinnacles and rock formations, is referred to as the Needles District, and the western section, defined by an incredible network of canyons and drainages, is known as the Maze District. A fourth section, detached from the rest of Canyonlands, is referred to as the Horseshoe Canyon Unit. Here you can visit the Great Gallery, one of the most intriguing pictograph panels in the Southwest.

Cycling in the Park

The mesas, deep canyons, and remote areas of fantastic rock formations found inside the 527 square miles of Canyonlands National Park are decidedly primitive in character, although hundreds of miles of jeep roads and foot trails access much of the area. As in all other national parks, bikes are permitted on roads accessible to licensed vehicles but are prohibited from using any hiking trails. Each section offers excellent opportunities to take in the beauty of this quiet, removed national park.

Biking in Canyonlands requires the consideration of three main factors, the first being the distances between the different sections or districts of the park. The park is carved up into these sections by big rivers and even bigger canyons, across which there are no bridges. Getting from one section to another by car requires 2 to 6 hours of driving. Once you get to where you are going, you will be faced with the second important issue: the remote nature of this park. At the Needles or Maze District you will find very little in the way of lodging, food, and other conveniences. It is a good idea to plan on camping when visiting these areas, and riding from a base camp. Finally, consider the extremely hot weather this region experiences during the summer months. June through August temperatures frequently soar past the century mark, making spring and fall your best choice for adventuring on two wheels here. Even during the spring and fall temperatures can get quite warm, and when combined with the dry air and strong sun, you'll find your body takes a beating. When exerting yourself in the desert, plan on consuming at least a gallon of water a day. This will ensure that all your body's systems keep running smoothly, allowing you to concentrate on the riding and beautiful sur-

CYCLING OPTIONS

There are seven rides in this chapter. One is a road-bike ride, six are mountain-bike tours, and one is short enough to be ridden as either—the ride out to Upheaval Dome from the Willow Flat Campground (11 miles total). The ride out to Grand View Point on the park's main road, however, is long enough (26 miles total, with the option of an additional 10-mile spur) that riding it on a road bike is best. The Colorado River Overlook is reached by an easy-to-moderate 14.5-mile (total distance) pedal well suited for intermediate-level riders in good shape. The ride out to the Confluence Overlook is another scenic fat-tire adventure that is slightly longer (15 miles) and more difficult. The mountain-bike ride out to Panorama Point is longer still (17 miles) but not as difficult, as it traverses mostly well-traveled dirt roads. The 9-mile trip out to Horseshoe Canyon is not long or difficult but, combined with the hike that takes you down to the petroglyph panel,s it makes for a long day. The 100-mile-long White Rim Trail is enjoyed by most as a multiday vehicle-supported trip, but can be ridden in a single day by ultrafit and experienced riders, or in several by bikers who don't mind carrying the necessary along with them in panniers.

roundings, not how on lousy you feel. It's a good idea to stay covered up with a long-sleeved shirt; if you've got to feel that friendly desert breeze on your skin, use liberal amounts of sunscreen frequently. A bad sunburn will exacerbate the effects of dehydration and can ruin your trip.

Taking several days to do a vehicle-supported trip on the almost 100-mile White Rim Trail is considered the ultimate canyon-country riding experience, perhaps the ride of a lifetime. Heading out to the massive formation of Cleopatra's Chair and then taking in views of the Maze District from Panorama Point will give you a perspective on the size of this landscape that is sure to make your head spin. Indeed, biking any of the primitive jeep roads that wind their way across the wild and colorful country of Canyonlands offers you not legions of Lycra-clad bike fiends on singletracks over miles of slickrock but, rather, the space, serenity, and wildness that we celebrate in our national parks.

14. UPHEAVAL DOME (See map on page 87)

For road and mountain bikes. This ride is an easy 12-mile (total) out-and-back adventure from the Willow Flat Campground to Upheaval Dome Overlook and Picnic Area. Riders of all abilities enjoy this delightful cruise across the gently undulating terrain of the Island in the Sky Plateau with its beautiful high-desert scenery, incredible views, and the geologic mystery of Upheaval Dome. Elevations are between 5,700 and 6,100 feet, so the air might be a little thinner than you're used to.

Starting point: Willow Flat Campground. Do not park in one of the campsites unless you are camping there; park alongside the road near the entrance instead. An alternate parking area is another 0.3 mile past the turnoff for the campground at the Green River Overlook.

Length: 6 miles. Allow at least 2 to 3 hours to ride out to the overlook and back.

Riding surface: Pavement, short stretch of gravel; roads are narrow with little or no shoulder.

Difficulty: Easy. There are a few gentle hills.

Scenery/highlights: Upheaval Dome is a curious mound of Triassic and Jurassic sandstone and mudstone surrounded by rings of much younger sedimentary rock. Many of the rock rings around the dome are vertically tilted layers of sandstone that have weathered into fins and other interesting formations. It was long thought that salt deposits buried deep beneath the sedimentary rock layers of this area caused this formation, forcing the rock layers above to arch skyward. The exterior layers were thought to have fractured and weathered away, leaving the vertical layers of stone surrounding the remaining inner dome.

But scientists now believe that Upheaval Dome is the result of a large meteorite that struck the earth during the late Cretaceous or early Tertiary era. The impact and resulting shock wave is believed to have created an underground cavity that the shattered rock surrounding the impact site slid into, converging and surging upward in the middle. At the time this event occurred the formation you see today was buried some 2 miles below ground, giving you some idea of the size of the

Ride 14 • Upheaval Dome
Ride 15 • Grand View Point
Ride 16 • White Rim Trail

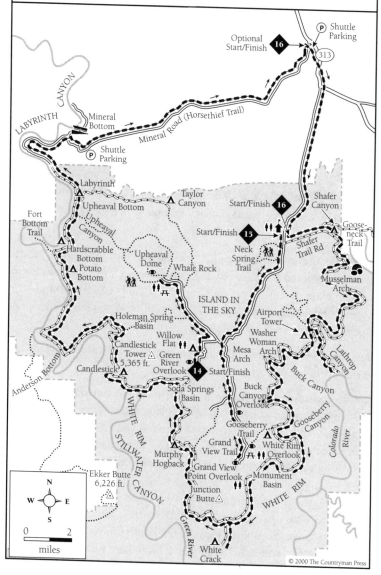

Taking time out to enjoy one of many expansive views in Canyonlands.

SARAH BENNETT ALLEY

meteorite and intensity of its impact. Surface rock layers have eroded away to reveal the evidence of what must have been a cataclysmic event. You can make the hike down the Crater View Trail (1.8 miles round-trip) to get a better look at this curious formation or, if you have time, circle Upheaval Dome via the 8-mile-long Syncline Loop Trail.

Best time to ride: Spring and fall; the summer months are simply too hot to exert yourself out here.

Special considerations: There are bathrooms but not water at Willow Flat Campground and Upheaval Dome Picnic Area. Bring plenty of your own water, and make sure you have some in your car for your return. Even in the spring and fall you can count on warm temperatures, dry air, and strong sun, all of which work to dehydrate your body.

From the campground ride out to the spur road you came in on and go left, out to Green River Overlook. A short trail takes you to the rim, where you can enjoy sublime views of Labyrinth Canyon, the White Rim Bench, the Maze, and the Orange Cliffs. From here you can also see the distinctive shape of Cleopatra's Chair as well as Ekker and Elaterite

Buttes. To continue, ride the gravel spur road approximately 1 mile out to the main road heading out to Upheaval Dome. Go left when you reach this paved road and ride in a northwesterly direction across the grassy Willow Flat area for 0.3 mile to the Aztec Butte Trailhead. This is a short (under 1 mile) trip out to the base of the butte, where you can also see some Ancestral Puebloan cliff dwellings. Another 1.5 miles up the road the Wilhite Trail takes off on your left, descending into Holeman Spring Basin. Eventually this foot trail meets the White Rim Trail.

The road to Upheaval Dome continues heading northwest, passing very close to the canyon rim above Holeman Spring Basin. Another 1.5 miles beyond the Wilhite Trailhead is the Alcove Spring Trail, leading to a beautiful alcove. This hiking trail continues into Trail Canyon and to Taylor Camp, one of the camps used by bikers riding the White Rim Trail. The trail out to Whale Rock leaves the main road about 0.75 mile beyond the Alcove Spring Trail, and a mile beyond that you reach the Upheaval Dome Overlook and Picnic Area. Take a break, drink your fluids, and have a snack. If you feel like it, make the short hike out the Crater View Trail. When you're ready to go, simply ride back the way you came.

---

15. GRAND VIEW POINT (See map on page 87)

For road bikes. This is a fabulous 24-mile tour of the Island in the Sky District from the visitors center to the end of the park's main road at Grand View Point. A 5-mile spur out to Upheaval Dome Overlook lets riders with stamina make a complete circuit of this park's rooftop plateau with gently rolling terrain, gorgeous high-desert scenery, and fantastic viewpoints along the way.

Starting point: Island in the Sky Visitors Center.

Length: 24 miles (total) out-and-back. The 5-mile spur out to Upheaval Dome Overlook adds 10 miles, for a total of 34 miles. Allow 3 to 4 hours to complete this ride.

Riding surface: Pavement; narrow with little or no shoulder.

Difficulty: Moderate, but only because of the distance. The terrain is very friendly with no major gains or losses in elevation.

Scenery/highlights: There is a lot to see along this route, making it hard to complete in less than half a day. Grand View Point is a 6-mile arm of the Island in the Sky Plateau that juts southward, toward the confluence of the Green and Colorado Rivers. As its name suggests, it offers one of the most comprehensive views of Canyonlands. From the overlook the cliffs drop away 400 feet to the bench below. Just beyond lies the isolated Junction Butte, cut off from the main plateau by erosion. At 6,400 feet, this butte forms the apex of the of Island in the Sky Plateau and is one of the most prominent features of the Canyonlands Basin. The erosion-resistant White Rim sandstone highlights the edge of the next bench below, where the 100-mile-long jeep road winds its way along above the two rivers. Looking southeast you can see the La Sal and Abajo ranges; more directly to the south are the Henry Mountains, all formed by intrusions of igneous rock. Sweeping vistas abound.

Best time to ride: Spring and fall, but these are also when the Island in the Sky District sees most of its tourist traffic. An early morning or evening ride avoids the heaviest traffic during midday and are also the times the lighting on this vertical world of many colors most spectacular.

Special considerations: There are bathrooms available at Grand View Point but not drinking water. Be sure to bring plenty of fluids to replace those being soaked out of your system by the dry air and strong sun.

From the visitors center (elevation 5,945 feet) ride south on the main park road, crossing the neck of the plateau at the top of Shafer Canyon about 0.5 mile from the visitors center. To the east of the overlook the Shafer Canyon Trail makes the plunge down the South Fork of Shafer Canyon, where it picks up the White Rim Trail. To the west you look into Taylor Canyon and beyond to Upheaval Dome. You can pick up the Neck Spring Trail from the Shafer Canyon Overlook if you are interested in doing this hike. About 1.5 miles past the overlook you pass the Lathrop Trail on your left; this hiking trail makes a hair-raising descent off the plateau to the White Rim.

The next 4 miles roll along across the sparsely vegetated plain of Grays Pasture, with expansive views in almost every direction. Just before you reach the junction of the road that takes you out to Upheaval Dome, you come to a short trail leading out to Mesa Arch. A short distance past

Mesa Arch is the junction where the southernmost 6-mile leg of the journey to Grand View Point begins. From here the route climbs steadily for approximately 2.6 miles to the highest point on the route (about 6,200 feet) just before the intersection with the gravel road leading out to Murphys Point. Another 0.6 mile past this intersection is the Buck Canyon Overlook where you can take a moment to try to comprehend the vastness of the landscape before you.

Another 1.2 miles beyond is the turnoff for the Gooseberry and White Rim Canyon Overlook Trails, and 1 mile beyond that you come to the end of the road at Grand View Point Overlook. A trail from the overlook that's just under a mile long takes you out to the farthest point of the plateau; it's well worth the extra time and effort. When it is time to go, head back the way you came 6 miles to the junction with the road out to Upheaval Dome. If you still have the energy and the desire, bear left here and ride the 5 miles out to the Upheaval Dome Overlook. Otherwise, bear right and continue back to the visitors center and your car.

16. WHITE RIM TRAIL (See map on page 87)

For mountain bikes. The 103-mile circuit of the pie-wedge piece of redrock desert between the Colorado and Green Rivers on the terrace-forming White Rim sandstone is the West's premier multiday mountain-bike adventure. It's best done with a vehicle for support. If you are a superfit long-distance maniac you can probably knock this off in a single day. If you don't mind pulling panniers full of camping equipment along with you, you can do the White Rim as a multiday self-supported ride. Doing this trip with a sturdy, spacious four-wheel-drive vehicle allows riders who might not be up to the rigors of a 25- to 30-mile day to pack it in and ride along to camp when they get tired. To do a White Rim trip, apply for a permit well in advance.

Starting point: Island in the Sky Visitors Center. An overnight parking area is located 0.5 mile south of the center, but you need to check in with the rangers at the center before you begin your ride. This route can be ridden in either direction, but is described here in a clockwise direction.

If you want to eliminate the 13 miles of gravel road and 10 miles of pavement that it takes to get back to your vehicle from where the

Thousands of ancient Indian petroglyphs (chipped into stone) and pictographs (painted on stone) can be found throughout southeastern Utah.

Horsethief Trail emerges from the canyon, consider leaving a second vehicle at the Horsethief Trailhead or arranging for a shuttle service through one of the bike-touring companies in Moab.

Another option is to split the difference and leave your car at the parking area at the junction of UT 313 and the road out to the Horsethief Trail. This way you ride the 10 miles of pavement at the start of your ride and the 13 gravel miles at the end.

Length: 103 miles. Most groups choose to do this loop over 3 or 4 days, spending 2 or 3 nights in designated campgrounds along the way.

Riding surface: Four-wheel-drive jeep roads, pavement, gravel; rough in places, sandy stretches.

Difficulty: Moderate to strenuous. While the majority of this route requires only intermediate bike-handling skills, several steep hills, rough sections, and sandy areas demand experience. Long days in the saddle combined with hills make this ride more strenuous.

Scenery/highlights: The astounding scenic beauty of this landscape was created over 150 million years of the earth's history; the magnificent natural beauty of this place and the awesome sense of time it can't help but impress upon you are the biggest highlight of this adventure. The lacy fringe of White Rim sandstone has created a well-defined, erosion-resistant bench that floats about midway between the 2,000 vertical feet of strata stretching from the river bottom to the top of Island in the Sky. Whitecapped pinnacles march outward away from the bench in many places, while 400-foot ramparts of rich, red Wingate sandstone form the bulwark that supports the mesa above. The sweeping panoramas constantly change as you work your way south above the Colorado, bending around the apex of the wedge above the confluence, and then north along the Green River. Other points of interest along the way—such as Musselman Arch, Washer Woman Arch, and the hike out to White Crack or Upheaval Dome—offer daily opportunities to explore and marvel at the wonders of this desert wilderness.

Best time to ride: From the middle of March to the middle of May in the spring, and mid-September through October in the fall, but these are also the most popular times to visit Canyonlands and the most difficult times to get a permit. Riding the White Rim during the summer is not recommended because it's simply too hard to stay properly hydrated and feeling good in the 100-plus temperatures that are common in summer.

Special considerations: Permits are required for all bicycle and vehicle camping in the backcountry of Canyonlands National Park. To get one, see the Camping section in the Trip Planning Appendix following this chapter.

All campsites are equipped with pit toilets but no drinking water is provided; you are responsible for carrying in all that you need. Plan on at least a gallon of water per person per day plus extra for cooking and cleanup. Wood collecting is prohibited, so you will need to bring a gas stove or charcoal for cooking. All trash must be packed out.

As in all national parks, bikes are restricted to roadways and are pro-

FLORA

One of the most unique plant communities found in and around Canyonlands is what is referred to as cryptobiotic crust. This knobby, black crust is made up of fungi, lichen, algae, moss, and bacteria living together in a symbiotic relationship. Cryptobiotic crusts are the foundation of life in the desert due to their ability to prevent erosion, stabilize soils, retain moisture, and provide nutrients such as nitrogen to plants struggling to survive in this hostile environment. This living crust is extremely fragile; once it has been crushed by a footstep or bike tire, it turns to dust. Recovery and regrowth of cryptobiotic crusts takes decades.

Although piñon-juniper woodlands are usually restricted to elevations found atop the highest mesas, they survive much lower in the park, their roots seeking moisture where it collects in the cracks of slickrock. Single-leaf ash, ephedra (Mormon tea), mountain mahogany, buffalo berry, Utah serviceberry, Fremont barberry, cliffrose, and squawbush are some of the other trees and shrubs that coexist with piñon and juniper. Blackbrush grows everywhere except along the river. Sagebrush thrives in the sandy areas of the park, as do Harriman, narrowleaf, and Datil yucca. Rabbitbrush, also found throughout the park, is most noticeable in autumn when it is covered with showy clumps of golden flowers. In the wet spots and along the rivers you will find large, beautiful Fremont cottonwoods, narrower-leaved lanceleaf cottonwood, coyote willows, and the ever-present tamarisk.

Tamarisk, also called salt cedar, was introduced into the Southwest from the Middle East over 100 years ago to control erosion along streambanks. The plant species favored by birds and animals have been forced out, and many of the water sources on which desert life depends have been dried up by the water-sucking ability of these trees. A concerted effort by the park service to eradicate tamarisk from along the river and near springs continues, although they have proven tough to kill.

Common wildflowers include several varieties of milk vetches, purple tansy asters, white evening primroses, goldenrod, Indian paintbrush, red and purple penstemons, and the large white-flowered jimsonweed, also called locoweed, moonflower, thorn apple, and, sacred datura. Succulents such as prickly pear, claret cup, and fishhook cacti are all magnificent spring bloomers that can be found throughout the park, producing brilliant blossoms in yellow, red, and pink, respectively.

hibited from using any footpath. The desert ecosystem is fragile, and what life there is depends on the tiny lichen and bacterial communities that comprise the black, knobby cryptobiotic crust you find everywhere. Do not step on or ride over these crusty soils. If you are hiking, stay to the footpaths, slickrock, or washes to avoid disturbing them.

Make sure you have a four-wheel-drive, high-clearance vehicle that can handle your gear load if you are doing this as a vehicle-supported trip.

Ride north from the visitors center 1 mile and go right onto the Shafer Trail. Approximately 1.8 miles from the start of the dirt, pause as this jeep road plunges over the edge and gaze out over the many switchbacks leading down to the White Rim almost 1,000 feet below. Make sure your front wheel is snug in your forks, that your brakes are working properly, and that your helmet fits securely.

When you're ready to go, push off, preparing yourself for a long, sometimes bone-jarring descent. Be sure to check your speed going around some of these hairpin turns; you don't want to end up like the piles of broken automobiles scattered below. After 5 miles you come to a fork; stay right to begin your White Rim odyssey.

Your first chance to get off your bike and have a look around comes 1.3 miles past this intersection at the Gooseneck Trail. This short, 0.3-mile walk takes you to an overlook of a graceful, 180-degree bend in the river of the same name. Just 2 miles farther is Musselman Arch, a flat-topped natural bridge that spans a dizzying chasm below. Leave your bike at the pullout and walk to the arch.

After cruising along a mostly level stretch for 5 miles you climb up the ridge separating Little Bridge and Lathrop Canyons, reaching the top of the ridge 1 mile beyond. The day-use road approximately 18 miles from the start of your ride down Lathrop Canyon takes you to the river. Airport Tower juts skyward just past the head of Lathrop Canyon, and keeps guard over the campsite of the same name just below. The stern face of Washer Woman Arch and watchful Monster Tower mark the north fork of Buck Canyon at mile 20. For the next 7 miles the road skirts around each of the three forks of this drainage.

Two miles farther, the Gooseberry Trail heads up to Island in the Sky, just before the road winds around the top of Gooseberry Canyon. Views into Monument Basin just beyond are awe inspiring. Here the White

The Colorado River twists through canyons below as bikers begin their descent down to the White Rim via the Shafer Trail.

Rim sandstone has capped many eroded pillars, including the Totem Pole standing out in front of you. Approximately 37.5 miles from the start is the left turn taking you out to White Crack Campground (1.5 miles from the main road) and the fantastic rock formations that exist at the very tip of the White Rim.

After another 6 miles of delightful desert cruising you begin the short but brutal climb up Murphys Hogback, reaching the top 45 miles from the start. The views from up here are vast. If you're not lucky enough to have one of the three campsites on Murphys Hogback, continue onward, reaching Candlestick Campsite another 10 miles down the road. The few miles beyond Candlestick are some of the most technical, but don't get so wrapped up in what your front wheel is doing that you miss the Holeman Slot, 2 miles from Candlestick. This is a fun descent into a shady crevice in the rock that is a good place to take a break.

From here the road begins its descent to the bottomlands along the Green River. In 8 miles you reach the first of the Potato Bottom Campsites (there are three). Another mile past Potato Bottom you will begin the merciless climb up Hardscrabble Hill, featuring lots of broken sandstone and steep grades. On the other side of this hill, 0.5 mile past where a road takes you down to Fort Bottom, a trail leads 1.2 miles to an ancient ruin and an old cabin. The ruin may have been a defensive structure. The cabin was supposed to be a rest stop for tuberculosis patients on their way to a lodge at the confluence of the Green and Colorado Rivers that was never built.

Back on the road you pass the Syncline Trail, leading to Upheaval Dome, in 3 miles. Another 0.7 mile beyond is the road leading up to Taylor Camp and the impressive towers known as Zeus and Moses, which are a magnet for rock climbers. The next couple of miles are sandy; you pass Labyrinth Campsite along the way.

Just under 78 miles from your start, make a right-hand turn onto the Horsethief Trail and begin the gut-busting climb up, up, up to the rim above. After 1.7 miles you reach the rim, but if you didn't leave a shuttle vehicle here, the climbing isn't over. Granted, from here back to UT 313 it is a steady, mellow grade, but it *is* uphill and there's 13 miles of it! You can do it. After you reach UT 313, turn right and ride the 9 miles of pavement back to the visitors center. Congratulations, you made it!

---

17. COLORADO RIVER OVERLOOK (See map on page 98)

For mountain bikes. Located in the Needles District of Canyonlands National Park, this route is an easy-to-moderate 14-mile (total distance) out-and-back trip to an overlook perched almost 1,000 feet above the Colorado River. The route follows doubletrack jeep roads through some sandy spots and over some rough, potholed sandstone surfaces toward the end, but does not require a lot of experience or technical skill.

Starting point: Needles Entrance Station and Visitors Center. To get there drive south of Moab on US 191 for approximately 42 miles to the

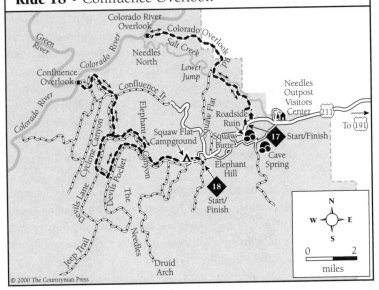

Ride 17 • Colorado River Overlook
Ride 18 • Confluence Overlook

well-signed turnoff for UT 211. Go right onto UT 211 and drive 35 miles west to the visitors center. You will have to pay a fee if you do not have a pass from entering the park at one of the other entrance stations.

Note: You may want to plan time on either your way out or your way back for stopping at Newspaper Rock State Park, which features one of the largest panels of petroglyphs in the Southwest. Used by successive cultures of native peoples, this sandstone billboard undoubtedly tells thousands of stories and is well worth a look. It is located 13 miles west of the intersection of US 191 and UT 211.

Length: 14 miles. Allow at least 3 hours to complete this ride, not including time spent at the overlook.

Riding surface: Doubletrack jeep roads; sections of sand and potholed sandstone.

Difficulty: Moderate. Total elevation gain of about 650 feet.

Scenery/highlights: The Colorado is a river at work, carrying an estimated 500,000 tons of silt and sediment downstream through the can-

Getting off the beaten path and finding your own route can pose unexpected challenges.

yons every day to where it now deposits behind the Glen Canyon Dam. It is this fine, red-colored desert sediment that clouds the river's waters and earned the river its name. *Colorado,* a Spanish term meaning "reddish," was given to the river by early Spanish explorers. The river's headwaters are high in the Colorado Rockies north of Denver, where it begins an almost 1,500-mile journey to the Gulf of California. The river actually no longer reaches the sea because its precious water is all consumed along the way by the thirsty states of Utah, Arizona, Nevada, and California. Farmers in the central valleys of California, where most of this country's year-round vegetable crop is grown, are the biggest consumers of Colorado River water. From the overlook the river winds its way through the Loop, an enormous meander that almost completely doubles back on itself. Although some of the river's fury is siphoned off by farmers between the mountains of Colorado and the Utah border, the river runs wild through these canyons, much as it has for eons.

Best time to ride: Early to midspring or fall. It is simply too hot to ride in this country during the summer months. Piñon gnats and biting flies can also be a problem out here late May through August.

Special considerations: You must pay a fee to enter the park. Bathrooms and water are available at the Needles Visitors Center.

From the parking lot at the visitors center, look for a trail leaving to the left (north). The road forks almost immediately; follow the sign pointing left. As you begin pedaling, the road gradually descends through open grass and shrublands with only a few rock outcroppings. In 2.5 miles you arrive at the head of Salt Creek Wash where a trail on the left leads a few hundred feet down the wash to Lower Jump, a 100-foot pour-over when the creek is running. Climb to the right out of the wash and head west, toward the river. The doubletrack across the next open stretch of desert is often sandy, but delivers you to the edge of barren sandstone about 5 miles from the start.

The next 1.3 miles of slickrock are anything but slick. Deposits of harder material among weaker pockets makes this stretch rough, but before you know it you'll be gazing into a 1,000-foot abyss created by the Colorado River. Scrambling over the rocks provides different perspectives of the canyons below, but be careful near the edge. When you've spent some time out here, head back the way you came.

---

18. CONFLUENCE OVERLOOK (See map on page 98)

For mountain bikes. Rock formations that may cause you to drop on bended knee and pray—Elephant Hill, Devils Pocket, Devils Kitchen, Devils Lane, and Cyclone Canyon—are just a few of the geologic wonders you'll marvel at. Although it sounds like hell it's much closer to heaven, especially for intermediate and advanced riders who aren't afraid of a little sand. This 15-mile (total) out-and-back trip, with a one-way loop in the middle, is a fairly strenuous ride to the heart of the park. A short hike takes you to a breathtaking view of where two of the West's mightiest rivers meet.

Starting point: Elephant Hill trailhead in the Needles District. To get there drive south of Moab on US 191 for approximately 42 miles to the well-signed turnoff for UT 211. Go right onto UT 211 and drive 35 miles west to the Needles Entrance Station and Visitors Center. You will have to pay a fee if you do not have a pass from entering the park at one of the other entrance stations. Stop in at the visitors center and spend a few minutes gathering information that will help make your ride more enjoyable. Then continue west on UT 211 for approximately 3 miles, following signs for Squaw Flat Campground and Elephant Hill. Past Campground B, pick up the gravel road that takes you to the Elephant Hill trailhead in 3 more miles. Park here. An alternate starting point at the campground allows a few miles to warm up before you hit the trail.

Note: You may want to plan time on either your way out or your way back for stopping at Newspaper Rock State Park, which features one of the largest panels of petroglyphs in the Southwest. Used by successive cultures of native peoples, this sandstone billboard undoubtedly tells thousands of stories and is well worth a look. It is located 13 miles west of the intersection of US 191 and UT 211.

Length: 15 miles. Beginning at the campground adds a total of 6 miles to your distance. Allow at least 4 hours to complete this ride.

Riding surface: Doubletrack jeep roads; sections of sand and rock.

Difficulty: Moderate to strenuous. The two biggest challenges on this ride are negotiating the ledges and steep pitch of the sandstone mound known as Elephant Hill right at the start, and the few stretches of sand found intermittently along the way.

Scenery/highlights: The brilliantly colored sandstone pinnacles, spires, fins, and arches found in the Needles District are endlessly fascinating. At the end of the trail you come to the very heart of Canyonlands National Park, the place where its four regions—the Island in the Sky, the Maze, the Needles District, and the two rivers—converge. The Maze District is to the west and the Island in the Sky and the White Rim are to the north. It is a powerful place of almost incomprehensible vastness in both time and space.

Best time to ride: Spring and fall; the summers are too darned hot. Even during these shoulder seasons you'll find the sand and rock can heat up during the day, even if nighttime temperatures still hover around freezing. If you have to ride during the warmer months, get an early start and plan on a siesta during the hot afternoon hours. Bugs, especially the piñon gnats, can be bad during the warmer months.

Special considerations: You will have to pay a fee at the Needles Entrance

Station. There are bathrooms available at both Squaw Flat Campground and the Elephant Hill trailhead, but not drinking water. Water is available at the Needles Visitors Center. Be sure to bring plenty with you for your ride and for when you get back to your car.

You may want to carry a cable lock with you for locking up your bike at the beginning of the short trail out to the overlook. No bikes are allowed on any of the hiking trails in the park.

You'll be jumping right in on this ride—tackling the biggest, hardest hill right off the bat with no warm-up. This hill is infamous among the four-wheelers who flock here every Easter for the annual Jeep Jamboree, and a trip over the top will tell you why. The trail is steep and technical going up, and a nerve-racking trip across barren rock on the way down. You'll start out descending Elephant Hill, but don't worry, it will be here waiting for you on your way back.

Shortly after Elephant Hill, approximately 1.5 miles from the start, there is a junction; go left to begin the one-way section. After a wash you pass through Devils Pocket and negotiate the winding path between sandstone walls on either side. The trail then turns west at the next junction, Devils Kitchen. You may want to go left at this intersection and make the sandy 2-mile slog out to Cave of 100 Hands. The numerous handprints left here by the ancients are startling for their small size, an indication of the toll that surviving hand-to-mouth in this country took on these people. Once you're out here you can enjoy superb views into Chesler Park and the many pinnacles and spires that undoubtedly help to earn this region its name. If you choose to bypass this side trip, though, turn right, away from Devils Kitchen.

Half a mile later turn right onto Devils Lane and be prepared to encounter the sand monster from hell. You descend for a time, following the north-south-trending grabens (faulted and sunken valleys) this part of the Needles is known for. Approximately 1.5 miles down the trail from the last intersection you pass the one-way return road on your right; stay left and continue on toward Cyclone Canyon and the Confluence Overlook. After this you make a U-turn consisting of two almost right angles to the head of Cyclone Canyon, another graben valley. Bear right past the road up Cyclone Canyon and pedal another 0.5 mile to the parking area and trail taking you out to the Confluence Overlook.

FAUNA

Anyone visiting Canyonlands during spring through fall can't help but notice the lovely descending song of the canyon wren. Not often seen but frequently heard, this little brown bird provides a memorable serenade for your canyon-country experience. Atop the mesas ravens, pinyon jays, gray jays, mountain bluebirds, blue-gray gnatcatchers, Audubon's warblers, mourning doves, horned larks, and western meadowlarks are all quite common. Turkey vultures, kestrels, golden eagles, and several hawk species soar on the thermal updrafts that waft off canyon walls in the park, while acrobatic fliers such as white-throated swifts and violet-green swallows delight in playing in these updrafts right along the canyon rims.

Lizards are among the most often seen of the park's wildlife. Gray- and red-colored leopard lizards, collared lizards, whiptail lizards, the side-blotched tree lizard, and the western fence swift are found at most elevations in the park. Two kinds of snakes are here: the gopher snake and the midget faded rattlesnake. Gopher snakes are not poisonous but can grow to be almost 6 feet in length. The light straw-colored to pinkish midget faded rattlesnake does not grow beyond 2 feet and is quite shy, but it's poisonous.

A variety of jackrabbits, pocket mice, and kangaroo rats are the prey of gopher snakes and raptors, as well as the bobcats, mountain lions, and coyotes that live in the park. Mule deer live in the bottoms near the river, where you might see desert bighorns coming to drink. Bighorn sheep can also be spotted high on broken slopes, their powerful bodies and sticky hooves allowing them to move freely among the steep slopes and rock ledges of the canyons. If you are lucky enough to catch a glimpse of these regal creatures, please report the sighting to a park ranger. These animals are sensitive to human intrusion and researchers are working to better understand their behavior. Amazingly, a population of black bears, known to exist in the Abajo Mountains, sometimes makes its way into the Salt Creek drainage. Report any bear sighting to a park ranger as well.

The hike to the overlook is a short 0.5-mile jaunt out to an 800-foot-high perch on the canyon rim almost directly above the confluence. Take some time here, breathe in the mingled energies of the two rivers below, and consider the vast emptiness of the landscape before you. When you are ready to begin the ride back, return to the intersection at the north end of Devils Lane and go left. Follow the sign for Elephant Hill, and ride for 2 miles to the start of the one-way loop. Continue left on this one-way stretch (it's approximately 3 miles from the Confluence Trail parking lot), ride another 2 miles, and turn left again for Elephant Hill. Once you have made it up and over Elephant Hill, you're home free.

---

19. PANORAMA POINT (See map on page 107)

For mountain bikes. The 17-mile (total) out-and-back ride out North Point Mesa to Panorama Point offers an entirely different perspective on Canyonlands, this time from the west. Located just outside Canyonlands National Park but inside Glen Canyon National Recreation Area, this lookout's perspective is not dissimilar to the one a hawk soaring above the canyons might enjoy. Beginning and intermediate riders who aren't put off by sand and a few rocky spots are richly rewarded for the moderate-to-strenuous effort it takes to get out here. The 600 feet of elevation gain along this route has to be negotiated on the return trip.

Starting point: The turnoff to North Point Mesa just south of the Hans Flat Ranger Station. To get there from Green River, Utah, travel 12 miles west on I-70 to UT 24. This is exit 147, signed for Hanksville and Capitol Reef. Head south for 25 miles on UT 24. Just past the turnoff for Goblin Valley State Park, turn left onto a gravel two-wheel-drive road, and drive east for 46 miles to the Hans Flat Ranger Station. Be aware that this road can become impassable due to weather. From the Hans Flat Ranger Station go southeast, following signs for the Flint Trail. After 2 miles you pass a fork for French Spring, and immediately beyond that is the start of the North Point Road accessing Panorama Point and Cleopatra's Chair. Park your car at this intersection near the camping area.

Length: 17 miles. An optional 2.5-mile spur out to Cleopatra's Chair is well worth the effort. Allow 3 to 4 hours to complete this ride.

Riding surface: Jeep roads; packed sand, broken rock, bedrock, sand bogs.

Difficulty: Moderate. Negotiating the sand and a few of the rocky sections takes some technical skill. A solid base of physical fitness is recommended for this ride.

Scenery/highlights: Panorama Point is at the very end of North Point Mesa, which juts out from the phalanx of rock referred to as the Orange Cliffs. At the point you are almost 2,500 feet above the Green River. The tangled maze of canyons that give this area of Canyonlands its name lie to the southeast, directly south is the distinctive shape of Elaterite Butte, and to the east is Ekker Butte. Farther east is the glowing outline of the White Rim. Junction Butte and Grand View Point, part of the mesa known as Island in the Sky, are also to the east, a mere 40 miles as the crow flies but several hours away by car. Words can't quite describe the sensory experience that awaits you at Panorama Point.

The massive sandstone butte known as Cleopatra's Chair is a beautiful salmon-colored, sheer-walled monolith that is breathtaking in its enormity. This distinctive butte can be seen for hundreds of miles around on a clear day, and is one of the most easily recognized landmarks in Canyonlands.

Best time to ride: Spring and fall; summer is ridiculously hot out here. The elevations make riding tolerable into late May, but by the time mid-June rolls around you don't want to be anywhere near here. If you are visiting during the hotter months, get an early start and stay hydrated.

Special considerations: This is a remote area where few conveniences exist. Make sure that you have a full tank of gas, a cooler full of drinks, some food, and at least a gallon of water a day for every person. You may want to consider camping out here so you do not have to drive in and out in the same day. Check in with the ranger at Hans Flat if you are interested in camping. Permits are required to camp in the Orange Cliffs area. (Permits are issued by Canyonlands National Park; call 435-259-7164 for more information.) You'll find no water and no bathrooms at any of the primitive campgrounds out here. Bury all human waste and carry out all your garbage.

LEE COHEN

A campsite in an area of Canyonlands National Park called the Doll House.

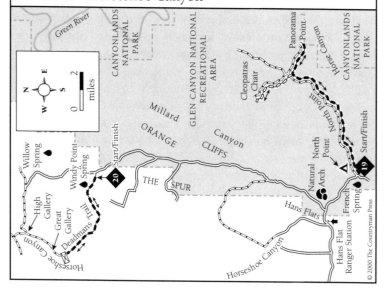

From the parking area ride north on the North Point Road across the delicate desert landscape, dotted with sage and pygmy forests of piñon and juniper. As you pedal along, descending gently, you cross over a land bridge to another sky island supported by ramparts of Wingate sandstone, referred to here as the Orange Cliffs. Just under 7 miles from the start of this ride you come to a fork in the road. Turn right to Panorama Point, left if you first want to visit Cleopatra's Chair. You may want to save that excursion for the way back.

Another 2 miles past that fork you come to Panorama Point. Breathe deep and try to take it all in. It's easy to imagine being on the wing up here, a lone hawk with only the wind in your ears. When you decide it's time to go, saddle up and ride back to the junction with the spur road taking you out to Cleopatra's Chair. If you haven't had enough, take an hour or so to make the 5-mile (total) out-and-back trip up close to this enormous rock formation. When you're done exploring, ride the North Point Road back to where you left your car.

20. HORSESHOE CANYON (See map on page 107)

For mountain bikes. The trip out to Horseshoe Canyon on the Deadmans Trail Road is a moderately difficult excursion taking you to one of the most exquisite rock art panels in North America. The Great Gallery, a panel featuring a handful of ghostly, human-sized figures—some adorned with breastplates, masks, and headdresses—floating on a wall of pale Navajo sandstone, is a haunting yet beautiful expression of the life and imagination of an ancient people thought to have inhabited this region as long as 8,000 years ago. The Fremont, and the Anasazi or Ancestral Puebloans who came after them, also left their mark at several other sites in the canyon. You'll need some technical riding ability to negotiate the alternating stretches of rock and sand out here, and a good amount of stamina to make the 3-mile (one-way) trek through the canyon. This is a superb, all-day desert adventure through empty country requiring shoes suitable for hiking as well as biking.

Starting point: The start of the Deadmans Trail Road, 16.5 miles north of the Hans Flat Ranger Station. To get there from Green River, Utah, travel 12 miles west on I-70 to UT 24. This is exit 147, signed for Hanksville and Capitol Reef. Head south for 25 miles on UT 24. Just past the turnoff for Goblin Valley State Park, turn left onto a gravel, two-wheel-drive road, and drive east for 46 miles to the Hans Flat Ranger Station. Be aware that this road can become impassable due to weather.

From the Hans Flat Ranger Station, go north for 16.5 miles on a doubletrack signed for Horseshoe Canyon. This stretch of road is rougher and is not recommended for two-wheel-drive vehicles. Park at the at the start of the Deadmans Trail.

Length: 9 miles of biking and at least 4 miles of hiking round-trip to get to the Great Gallery. Plan on spending at least half a day out here riding and exploring the major rock art panels in the canyon.

Riding surface: Doubletrack jeep road; sand and rock.

Difficulty: Moderate. The ride is not long or very difficult, but the hike into Horseshoe Canyon makes this a long day requiring some stamina. Like many of the rides in Canyonlands, you lose elevation on your way

Cyclists traverse an open stretch of country on the White Rim Trail.

out to the canyon that has to be regained on your way back to your starting point. The elevation change between the start of the trail and the canyon rim is about 400 feet.

Scenery/highlights: Crossing the vast, empty plateau that slopes gently away to the west from the Orange Cliffs toward the San Rafael Desert on your way out to the rim of the canyon provides soul-nourishing desert solitude. The canyon itself, a hidden gash in the layers of Navajo sandstone that cover this plateau, is also stunningly beautiful. A small, intermittent stream burbles over slickrock and whispers across the sand. The canyon has been used for thousands of years by prehistoric Indians, ranchers, and even outlaws as a haven from the world beyond.

There are four major rock art panels in the canyon that have been identified as unique to an archaic Indian culture. This canyon (formerly called Barrier Canyon, because Barrier Creek runs through it) contains the greatest concentration of these type of petroglyphs in the Southwest. The style of these major rock art panels is therefore referred to as Barrier Canyon style. The archaic culture that left these drawings is believed to have thrived in this arid region beginning some 8,000 years ago, dying out by A.D. 450. Archaeologists believe that these drawings were most likely painted here between 2,000 and 3,000 years ago. Other petroglyphs, artifacts, and stone granaries in the canyon indicate that the Fremont and Ancestral Puebloan peoples also used the canyon.

Please do not touch any of the rock art drawings or remove any artifacts you might find. Oil from your hands stains the rock and works to destroy the thousand-year-old pigment used to create these images. Disturbing archaeological sites also carries stiff penalties under federal laws. Take only pictures, leave only footprints.

Best time to ride: March through early April and September through November; the summer months are simply too hot. Anytime of day is good, but if you are interested in taking pictures of the Great Gallery figures, get an early start—they are shaded by afternoon.

Special considerations: This is very remote country with little in the way of conveniences. Come prepared! Make sure you have a full tank of gas, plenty of water (a gallon per person per day), and some food. There is a cell phone and a ranger on duty most days at Hans Flat Ranger Station. Pit toilets are available here but not water. Camping requires a permit issued through Canyonlands National Park. Call (435) 259-7164 for information about camping, or check in with the ranger at Hans Flat.

Bikes are not allowed on any of the hiking trails in the park. Bring a lock for your bike if you plan to leave it unattended at the trailhead.

Ride the Deadmans Trail Road northwest, as it strikes a course across the empty plateau for the hidden gouge of a canyon beyond. The route rises and falls across sections of sand and broken, barren rock, passing by curiously striped mounds of earth and buttes capped with sandstone swirls in the distance. In 4.5 miles you reach the end of the road and the trailhead for the Deadmans Trail, taking you into the bottom of the canyon. You must leave your bike here. Pamphlets in a dispenser box at the head of the trail offer insights to the archaeological wonders in the canyon below. You descend via several switchbacks to the sandy canyon floor and reach the first rock panel, the High Gallery, via a short spur in about 2 miles. The height of the drawings and their unique style both attest to the antiquity of this site. Continue onward to the Great Gallery a short distance beyond, and farther to the other panels. When you're done, retrace your steps to your bike and ride back out the way you came.

CAMPING

There are two developed camp-grounds in Canyonlands National Park that offer some amenities. Both are open year-round and are operated on a first-come, first-served basis. There are, however, at least 20 vehicle backcountry camps. A permit, and in some instances a reservation, is needed for all backcountry camping in the park.

Willow Flat Campground is located in the Island in the Sky District and has 12 sites, vault toilets, picnic tables, and grills, but no water; it takes no reservations. A per-night fee is required.

Squaw Flat Campground is located in the Needles District and has 26 sites, water, vault toilets, fire rings, and picnic tables; it takes no reservations. A per-night fee is required.

GROUP CAMPSITES

There are three group campsites, all in the Needles District: **Split Top** (15 people), **Squaw Flat** (50 people), and **Wooden Shoe** (25 people). A minimum of 11 people is required for each. Reservations are recommended for all group campsites. A per-night fee is required.

BACKCOUNTRY CAMPING AND PERMITS

A permit and a fee are required for all backcountry vehicle and backpack camping. Permits are issued to walk-ins on a space-available basis, and to confirmed reservation holders. All members of your camping party must be present for a regulation talk when the permit is issued. Rangers will not issue permits during the last hour of visitors center operations.

Permits must be obtained at the district visitors center nearest to where you plan to camp. If you are riding in the Needles and plan to camp in that area, you must pick up your permit at the Needles Visitors Center. Permits for camping along the White Rim Trail may be mailed in advance. The reservation office at park headquarters in Moab issues all mail permits.

In order to receive permits by mail, you must contact the reservation office at least 2 weeks prior to your visit. Groups must provide information for all vehicles that will be in the park overnight (license plate number, make, model, and color) and coordinate parking arrangements for any vehicles left at trailheads before a permit can be mailed.

Reservations are highly recommended for all backcountry campsites. Competition for White Rim trips is greatest during spring and fall, so start planning early. Group campsites are also hard to get.

Reservations may be made by mail or fax only. Contact the reservation office in Moab for more information: Canyonlands National Park, Reservation Office,

IT'S INTERESTING TO KNOW . . .

The first people of European descent to visit the area that is now Canyonlands were the Fathers Escalante and Dominguez, who passed near here in 1776 during their expedition to find a route between Santa Fe, New Mexico, and the missions of California. Then a French trapper named Denis Julien took beaver out of the Southwest's desert rivers and left inscriptions throughout both the Colorado and Green River Canyons with dates ranging between 1836 and 1838. But the rivers and the canyons of Canyonlands National Park weren't thoroughly explored until the 1869 and 1871 expeditions led by John Wesley Powell.

Powell's first expedition, sponsored by the U.S. Geological Survey, began at the headwaters of the Green River near present-day Green River, Wyoming, and took him and a handful of men 900 miles down through the confluence of the Green and Colorado Rivers and into the Grand Canyon on an epic journey that nearly cost them their lives. Powell's efforts put much of this area on the map, and his insight as to the arid nature of this country and the difficulties it would create for human settlement, while disregarded at the time, have now come back to haunt us. Stop in at the Powell Museum in Green River, Utah, to learn more about this brilliant and determined man who foretold many of the problems water managers are confronting today. Wallace Stegner's examination of Powell's journey, *Beyond the Hundredth Meridian*, is an excellent read about the history of this area and the West.

There are at least half a dozen rafting outfits based in Moab and Green River offering trips down through Labyrinth and Stillwater Canyons on the Green River, and through the goosenecks and loops on the Colorado. Although a float down through the park in either of these canyons generally takes several days, sections of the two rivers farther upstream can be floated in a single day. Seeing Canyonlands as you float along on churning currents provides an entirely different perspective on the forces that created this vertical landscape. It also gives you an introduction to the riparian habitat that is a precious ribbon of life for so many wild creatures in the desert. Sitting comfortably on a raft, enjoying the cool air that hovers around the water and the refreshing splash of water that has trickled down from the Colorado Rockies or the high peaks of Wyoming's Wind River range, is a delightful respite from the hot, dusty trail and makes a trip to Utah's canyon country complete.

2282 S. W. Resource Blvd., Moab, UT 84532-8000; (435) 259-7164; fax (435) 259-4285; http://www. canyonlands. national-park. com/camping.htm.

Other options for camping include **Dead Horse Point State Park,** conveniently located just outside Canyonlands National Park's Island in the Sky entrance in a spectacular location overlooking the goosenecks of the Colorado River. There are 32 tent sites and 22 RV sites. A per-night fee is required; the park is open from the beginning of March through the middle of October. Facilities include modern rest rooms, drinking water, and waste disposal. You can make reservations from 3 to 16 days in advance by calling (800) 322-3770.

There are many possibilities for camping on surrounding **BLM land.** Contact the agency to get a complete list of campgrounds or suggestions for wilderness camping.

You can also try these private campgrounds in Green River: the **Green River KOA** (550 S. Green River Blvd.), with a pool, laundry facilities, and showers, or **United Campground,** where they have a pool, store, and showers (910 E. Main St.). Both have tent sites and sites with hook-ups.

In Moab try **Canyonlands**

Campground (555 S. Main St.), the **KOA Campground** (3225 S. US 191), or the **Up the Creek Camp Park** (210 E. 300 S.). Showers are available at all of these places for a fee.

There is a variety of chain hotels and a few motels to choose from in Green River. **Comfort Inn, Motel 6, Rodeway Inn, Budget Inn,** and **Super 8** are here, but if you want something a little different try the **Budget Host Bookcliff Lodge** or the **Tamarisk,** both with dining rooms that offer three meals a day. **The Best Western River Terrace Hotel,** like the Tamarisk, is right on the river and has the nicest rooms in town. Less pricey rooms can be found at the **Robber's Roost Motel,** the **Oasis Motel,** or the **Sleepy Hollow Motel.**

If you are basing yourself out of Moab, see the Trip Planning Appendix on pages 62–63 for lodging suggestions, or visit the Moab Information Center on the corner of Main and Center Streets. There are also several sites on the Internet that provide information about lodging in Moab (try http://moab-utah.com/ or http://www.moab.net/).

FOOD

Your choices are pretty limited in Green River. Other than motel food and fast food, your best bet is **Ray's Tavern** (25 S. Broadway). Ray's has long been a favorite of river runners and thirsty desert adventurers. You can get chops, burgers, a steak, and most other standard café fare here, along with a variety of cold microbrews.

There are many more choices for dining out in Moab; see chapter 1 for suggestions there.

LAUNDRY

Your only real choice for doing laundry in this neck of the woods is in Moab. Several of the private campgrounds have laundry facilities but they are not usually available to nonguests. **Moab Speedqueen Laundromat,** 702 S Main St, (435) 259-7456.

BIKE SHOP/BIKE RENTAL

The knowledgeable folks in Moab are your best, and only, resource in the vicinity of the park. Here are just a few shops:

Chile Pepper, 702 S. Main St.; (435) 259-4688

Kaibab Mountain Bike Tours, 391 S. Main St.; (435) 259-7423

Poison Spider Bicycles, 497 N. Main St.; (435) 259-7882

Rim Cyclery, 94 W. 100 N.; (435) 259-5333

Western Spirit Cycling, 478 Millcreek Dr.; (435) 259-8732

FOR FURTHER INFORMATION

Canyonlands National Park—Superintendent, 2282 S. W. Resource Blvd., Moab, UT 84532-8000; (435) 259-7164; fax: (435) 259-4285; http://www.nps.gov/cany/

Grand County Travel Office—Green River (at the Powell Museum), Box 335, 885 E. Main St., Green River, UT 84525

Moab Visitors Center, 805 N. Main St. (corner of Main and Center), Moab, UT 84532; (435) 259-8825 or (800) 635-MOAB

Grand County Travel Council—Moab, P.O. Box 550, Moab, UT 84532; (435) 259-8825 or (800) 635-6622

Bureau of Land Management (BLM), Moab District Office, 82 E. Dogwwod, P.O. Box 970, Moab, UT 84532; (435) 259-6111

4

The Waterpocket Fold is a giant 100-mile-long upwarp in the earth's crust, and the magnificent centerpiece of Capitol Reef National Park. Called Land of the Sleeping Rainbow by the Navajo, the beautifully hued rock layers found here have been revealed by a process that began during the late Cretaceous period between 50 and 70 million years ago. During that tumultuous era of mountain building, a fault deep within the earth's crust shifted, forcing overlying rock layers upward, creating a long, sinuous hump with one very steep side and one gently sloped side. Rock layers on the west side of the park are tilted at nearly 60 degrees and are more than 7,000 feet higher than those on the east side.

Nearly 10,000 feet of sedimentary strata are found in the Capitol Reef area, representing more than 200 million years of geologic history. Among these layers is evidence that rivers and swamps once covered this region, followed by Sahara-like deserts and warm, shallow seas. The varying thickness and hardness of the different rock layers and the forces of erosion have determined the shape of the many glorious castles, sheer cliffs, domed buttes, and deep, shadowy gorges in the park. The swirls of white Navajo sandstone that cap the layers on the sloped side of the monocline are dotted with numerous potholes or natural tanks that help support the park's wildlife and contribute to the name *Waterpocket Fold.* This same sandstone layer is responsible for the white domes that top many of the buttes and cliffs in the park, and reminded early settlers of the domes atop American capitol buildings; hence the name *Capitol*. Early travelers, many of whom came to America aboard sailing ships or were sailors themselves, likened the stone barrier that stretches across this land to a reef, resulting in the second half of the park's moniker.

Besides the almost 380 square miles of impressive geologic features inside the park, there are also many fascinating archaeological sites, including several petroglyph panels that you can visit. Also preserved are the historic buildings erected by Mormon pioneers along the Fremont River, and the prolific fruit orchards they tended that earned the settlement the name *Fruita*. Cherries, apples, apricots, peaches, and pears are still grown in the park, and picking orchards are open to the public. You can eat as much as you want in the orchards for free, but if you want to pick to take away with you, a fee is requested at a self-pay station.

The many scenic roads through the park's backcountry, the hiking trails among twisted canyons and around these fascinating rock formations, as well as the archaeological and historical resources of the park, make for a rewarding visit to Capitol Reef no matter what your interests.

Cycling in the Park

The 140 miles of paved and dirt roads through Capitol Reef, the close proximity of such features as the Aquarius Plateau and Thousand Lakes Mountain—both within the Dixie National Forest—along with the wonderful climate of this area, offer fantastic opportunities for exploring on two wheels. The remote nature and wilderness character of much of this country mean that there are many more possibilities for getting out on a mountain bike than there are for riding a road bike, though several road-riding possibilities should keep the skinny-tire folks happy.

The long distances and fabulous scenery traversed by some of the park's backcountry roads make them prime candidates for vehicle-supported overnight trips. Closer in, there are a handful of biking adventures sure to please almost everyone. Capitol Reef now receives close to 800,000 visitors annually, the majority of them visiting in late spring, summer, and early fall. While this park does not get as crowded as Arches or Bryce, the roads can still get pretty busy during these times. Late spring and early fall are probably the busiest at Capitol Reef—the times

CYCLING OPTIONS

There are five rides in this chapter; two are recommended for road bikes but are not so long that a mountain bike won't suffice, while the other three are mountain bike rides. The mostly level cruise through the Fremont River Canyon that runs through the park is 17 miles (total) out and back and is well suited for novice and intermediate riders. The paved Capitol Reef Scenic Drive is 8 miles one-way (16 miles total), but is more difficult due to the rolling nature of the terrain and absence of shoulders on the road. The ride up South Draw Wash is an off-road adventure on one of the park's dirt roads that has options for riders of varying fitness levels and abilities. Families can ride for just 3 miles to Pleasant Creek and back (6 miles total), or the superfit and adventurous mountain bikers can ride all the way up to UT 12 and back (42 miles total). The Pleasant Creek–South Draw Wash ride is a one-way 24-mile downhill that requires a shuttle. This is a spectacular descent from UT 12 on Boulder Mountain that ends inside the park at the end of the scenic drive. The 60-mile adventure through Cathedral Valley in the northern section of the park is described here as a multiday vehicle-supported trip. A solid four-wheel-drive, high-clearance vehicle is recommended for negotiating the water crossings and rough terrain along this backcountry road.

of year when the temperatures aren't so hot and the kids are out of school. If you are riding in the park during these times, it's best to ride in the morning before the roads get busy. Early spring and late fall are some of the most spectacular times here, and there are far fewer people. In mid- to late autumn you can pick apples and delight in the flaming gold and yellow of the park's cottonwoods as they flutter in against a deep blue sky. Springtime you can enjoy the blossoms of the park's fruit trees and many desert wildflowers. Spring and fall are the most desirable times to visit the park, but the weather can be cool at the extreme ends of those seasons due to the high elevations here. Summers are hot, frequently climbing up toward the century mark.

Capitol Dome and other distinctive formations have been weathered out of light, buff colored Navajo sandstone, and helped to earn Capitol Reef its name.

SARAH BENNETT ALLEY

---

21. FREMONT RIVER CANYON–HIGHWAY 24 (See map on page 121)

For road and mountain bikes. This ride is a scenic, sight-filled tour of the gorge cut through Capitol Reef by the Fremont River. Both the ancient Fremont Indians and the Mormon settlers took advantage of the beautiful, year-round stream that flows through this canyon, growing their crops in the fertile soils that have collected between the canyon's vertical sandstone walls. Along this mostly level route you can see Fremont petroglyphs, a pioneer schoolhouse, and the fruit orchards that made this Mormon settlement famous. There is no set distance that must be completed; simply ride east on UT 24 as far as you like, and turn around when you've had enough. Riding from the visitors center to the eastern boundary of the park is just over 8.5 miles one-way. A good turn around point is the picnic area on the north side of the road 4 miles east of the center.

Starting point: Capitol Reef Visitors Center on UT 24, 9 miles west of the east entrance or 8.5 miles east of Torrey, Utah.

Length: 17 miles round-trip; 8 miles round-trip for shorter option. Plan at least 2 to 3 hours cruising this canyon.

Ride 21 • Fremont River Canyon–Highway 24
Ride 22 • Capitol Reef Scenic Drive
Ride 23 • South Draw Wash
Ride 24 • Pleasant Creek–South Draw Wash
Ride 25 • Cathedral Valley Loop

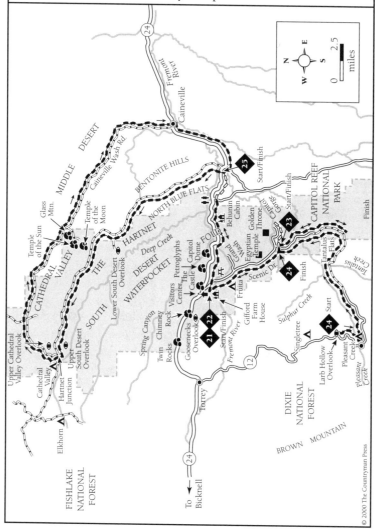

© 2000 The Countryman Press

Riding surface: Pavement. Narrow, winding road with some shoulders.

Difficulty: Easy to moderate. Higher elevations, car traffic.

Scenery/highlights: The Fruita Schoolhouse was built in 1896 by Leo Holt, Amasa Pierce, and E. C. Behunin. Behunin's daughter, Nettie, had been teaching school in their home since she was 12, but was able to move her classes to this building after it was completed.

A petroglyph panel featuring several humanoid shapes and a parade of sheep across the bottom of a towering wall is located in the shade of large trees. The short hike up to Hickman Bridge is also well worth your time and effort. If you want to do this hike, consider bringing a cable lock to secure your bike.

Best time to ride: Spring and fall; if you are here during summer, get an early start to avoid the heat and traffic that gets worse at midday.

Special considerations: Water and rest rooms are available at the visitors center. Vault toilets are available at the picnic area 4 miles east of the center.

Be aware of traffic on this road. Although speed limits are low, it is still a highway. Stay to the right-hand side of the road and ride in single file. When you want to cross to the opposite side of the road stop, dismount, look both ways, and walk your bike across the road. A white or light-colored shirt will also help alert motorists to your presence. Always wear a helmet; if you wear glasses make sure they are shatter-resistant.

From the visitors center ride out onto UT 24 and go right. Just a mile from your start you encounter the old Fruita Schoolhouse. The structure also served as a community center where town meetings, dances, elections, and church services were held. The school was closed in 1941 due to a lack of students and restored in 1964 by the park service in an effort to preserve the cultural heritage of the area. Immediately beyond is a short trail that leads through the orchards and shady riparian foliage to the Fremont River. Continuing eastward on UT 24, you come to the petroglyph panel 0.3 mile beyond the schoolhouse. This panel is on the north side of the road so you will need to dismount and cross the road to see it, or save it for the way back.

Just beyond the petroglyphs the canyon narrows. Towering sandstone walls of light pink and beige, many striped with desert varnish, rise on

Canyon walls and cliff faces, stained with desert varnish and common throughout Southern Utah, provided an ideal canvas for ancient people to express their ideas and beliefs.

either side of the river. Cottonwoods, box elders, and other streamside vegetation create a stunning contrast to the crimson hues of the rock. The trailhead for Hickman Bridge is on the north side of the road 2 miles from the visitors center. For the next 2 miles the road winds along through the river-carved ramparts of stone. Several canyons begin to come in on either side of the road. At mile 4 you reach the picnic ground and parking area for people hiking up Spring, or Chimney Rock, Canyon, which joins the main canyon from the northwest.

The highway then bends south, reaching the Grand Wash trailhead in 0.5 mile. In another 0.5 mile you come to the Behunin Cabin, beyond which the canyon begins to widen. The sloping eastern edge of the Capitol Reef monocline gently gives way to the South Desert and the grays, greens, and purples of the Morrison formation. In 8.5 miles you reach the east entrance to the park, where you will find a pullout, picnic tables, rest rooms, and an information board. The Notom-Bullfrog Road heads south another 0.5 mile from here, and the River Ford (Hartnet) Road leading to Cathedral Valley leaves the highway and heads north another 2.7 miles beyond that. Turn around when you are ready, and be prepared for some of the best views of the ride. Heading this direction you have a good perspective on Capitol Dome, a giant dollop of sandstone that helped give the park its name, and the east-facing slope of the fold covered by buff-colored Navajo sandstone.

22. CAPITOL REEF SCENIC DRIVE (See map on page 121)

For road and mountain bikes. A ride out this park's 8-mile (one-way) scenic drive takes you south over rolling terrain along the dramatic sheer sandstone cliffs of Capitol Reef. The road climbs and descends over successive hills of eroded debris that have crumbled away from the towering cliffs of the reef, providing many small summits where you can catch your breath and gape at the fantastic scenery. Several dirt spurs explore canyons that intersect this route, providing for shorter or longer rides if you are on a mountain bike. The short dirt spur roads up Grand Wash and Capitol Gorge are ideal for family outings. This scenic drive can become busy with car and camper traffic, so you should feel comfortable sharing the road with vehicles. An intermediate level of physical fitness is recommended if you plan to go the entire distance.

Starting point: Visitors center at the intersection of UT 24 and the scenic drive.

Length: 16 miles round-trip; if all the spurs are ridden, total distance is 22 miles.

Riding surface: Pavement; Sections of cement cross the washes.

Difficulty: Easy to moderate. Although there are no technical riding sections to speak of along this route, the many hills make it more difficult.

Scenery/highlights: The dizzying wall of sandstone that stretches along the entire length of the scenic drive, colored in delicate hues of gold, peach, pink, cream, and red artistically streaked with desert varnish, is the showstopper on this ride.

Best time to ride: Spring and fall; if you have to ride during summer, be sure to get an early start to give yourself a couple of cooler hours to pedal.

Special considerations: If you do not stop in at the visitors center before you begin your ride and pay your park fee there, you will need to stop at the pay station 1.5 miles past the center on the scenic drive.

FLORA

While the extreme northwest corner of the park includes a small portion of Thousand Lakes Mountain and the Canadian life zone found there, the majority of the park falls within the upper Sonoran life zone, where piñon-juniper woodlands dominate. Buffalo berry, single-leaf ash, green ephedra, gray Torrey ephedra, Utah serviceberry, Fremont barberry, and the little-leaved mountain mahogany are other trees and shrubs commonly found. Cliffrose, big sagebrush, yucca, and rabbitbrush, which blooms brilliant yellow in fall, are some of the most recognizable of the shrubs that grow in Capitol Reef. Blackbrush is also quite common.

The riparian habitat created by several streams that run throughout the park hosts a variety of trees, including box elders; Fremont, narrowleaf, and lanceleaf cottonwoods; and a variety of willows. A little farther back from the water you might see Gambel oak and hackberry. The invasive exotic from Eurasia known as tamarisk is also found near water.

Several species of native grasses used to cover some of the valleys along the eastern margin of the Waterpocket Fold, but they have been overgrazed and now shrubs, such as sage, have taken over. Common flowering plants include the daisylike yellow mule's ears, lupine, groundsel, badlands Bahia grass, and prickly pear. The large, tissuelike petals of evening primrose are always easy to spot, as are the delicate spikes of orange globe mallow. Pink desert four-o'clock, white sand verbena, yellow blanketflower, and showy milkweed also bloom in the park.

As in all national parks, there is no shoulder on the scenic drive. Ride in single file, stay to the right-hand side of the road, and always wear a helmet plus a light-colored or white shirt to help make you visible.

Another safety issue here is the danger of flash floods. A cloudburst or sudden downpour can cause these normally dry washes to suddenly fill with an angry torrent of water. The scenic drive dips across many of these dry washes, which should be avoided if heavy rains are in the area. The washes in Grand Wash and Capitol Gorge can also fill with rushing water and should not be entered if heavy rains are forecast.

Water and bathrooms are available at the visitors center. Vault toilets are located at the end of the road at Capitol Gorge.

The impressive buttes and sandstone cliffs of Capitol Reef National Park are part of an enormous monocline called the Waterpocket Fold.

From the visitors center go left and ride out onto the scenic drive. Just beyond the center the road passes by fruit orchards and the pioneer-era buildings of Fruita. These buildings now house park employees. The road heads south past a picnic area and a group campsite before crossing over the Fremont River. Just beyond, in the middle of the fertile Fruita Valley, is the Gifford Homestead, consisting of rock walls, a home, a barn, and a smokehouse. This farm was built in 1908. Continue past several spur roads to campgrounds, the amphitheater, and the pay station. Beyond the pay station the road climbs up a long, steady grade known as Danish Hill, no doubt named for the Danes who settled in the area.

Approximately 3.5 miles from the start of your ride you come to the spur road for Grand Wash. Do not enter Grand Wash if thunderstorms are threatening. This 1-mile dirt spur twists and turns as it plunges into the sculpted orange walls of Wingate sandstone that rise on either side. At the end of the road a hiking trail leads farther into the canyon.

Back on the main scenic drive, the route rolls up and over numerous red hills and dives through several washes as the beautiful cliffs of Capitol Reef continue to unfold before you. This section of road continues for 4 miles and should be avoided during heavy rains. Approximately

4.5 miles from Grand Wash the pavement ends at the spur road leading into Capitol Gorge. If you are on a road bike, this is the end of the trail for you. If you are on a mountain bike, you can keep going.

The Capitol Gorge Road turns east and follows a road that wiggles its way into a cleft in the sandstone reef. This dirt road served as UT 24 to Hanksville until 1962 but is now closed by the park service 2 miles from where it leaves the scenic drive. There is a parking area at the end of the pavement.

Option: If you've got the kids along and you're interested in a short, off-road ride, this could be the one for you. The road descends just slightly over 2 miles on a dirt surface that becomes a little washboarded in spots and a little sandy in others, but otherwise presents no real technical challenges. It ends at a trailhead and parking area where you'll find a picnic area and rest rooms. A hiking trail takes you farther into this cool, shadowy gorge. When you're done, simply ride 2 miles back out the way you came in.

---

23. SOUTH DRAW WASH (See map on page 121)

For mountain bikes. Here's an opportunity for beginning and intermediate riders to get off the beaten path and do some exploring beyond the end of the park's well-traveled scenic drive. Beginning at the end of this drive, the dirt road up South Draw winds its way up a hill, crosses Pleasant Creek, and then follows the course of the wash itself. You climb very gradually for just over 6 miles before beginning a steep, unending climb up the flank of Boulder Mountain to where it ends at UT 12 some 15 miles beyond. You may want to ride just the 3 miles to Pleasant Creek and back, or ford the creek (where you will get your feet wet) and ride to where the road begins to climb. Ride for as long and as far as you like.

Starting point: The parking lot at the end of the scenic drive, 8 miles from the visitors center.

Length: 6 miles out-and-back to Pleasant Creek; 12 miles round-trip to where the road begins to climb skyward.

Riding surface: Dirt road, wash bottom with sections of loose gravel and sand.

FAUNA

The ever-present raven is found throughout this park, as it is throughout the other parks of southern Utah. Among the piñon-juniper woodlands you might hear the squawk of scrub- and pinyon jays, or see a common flicker or yellow-bellied sapsucker darting through the bush. Mourning doves, sage thrashers, meadowlarks, mockingbirds, and beautiful chukar partridges also live among the trees of the high desert. A variety of songbirds, including yellow and Wilson's warblers and black-headed grosbeaks, prefer the streamside setting found along the Fremont and the other streams of the park. Sharp-shinned hawks, American kestrels, and nighthawks are here, as are white-throated swifts and violet-green swallows, which like the vertical environment found in the deep canyons.

Cottontails and desert black-tailed jackrabbits share their desert home with the white-tailed antelope squirrel, wood rats, and pack rats. Ringtails, mistakenly referred to as cats, are nocturnal raccoonlike animals that feed on fruit, insects, birds, and lizards. Badgers are also nocturnal and live in the park. Skunks, muskrats, and minks like the riparian zones, while yellow-bellied marmots like the high mountainous country of Thousand Lakes Mountain. Mule deer are here, as is that ever-present but secretive stalker, the mountain lion. Lizards are abundant in the park, but snakes are rare. Only one poisonous snake is found in the park—the midget faded rattlesnake, which never grows longer than 2 feet. There are several species of frogs and toads that live near the river and in the water pockets among the Navajo sandstone, including the Great Basin spadefoot toad, the Rocky Mountain toad, and the leopard frog.

Difficulty: Easy to moderate. If you want to tackle the steep, rough road up the side of Boulder Mountain, you can make this ride very strenuous.

Scenery/highlights: The Wingate sandstone cliffs are dazzling for their exquisite hues of peach, salmon, buff, and red. Capitol Gorge recedes into the cliff wall, a narrow, shrouded cleft in the stone. The dark, forested brow of the Aquarius Plateau looms above you on the other side, promising cool, pine-scented breezes.

Best time to ride: Spring and fall; if you have to ride when the weather is hot, get an early start.

Special considerations: Rest rooms are available in the parking lot at the end of the scenic drive and the start of the South Wash Road, but there is no drinking water. Be sure to bring along plenty of water and have some waiting for you when you get back to the car.

Capitol Creek and Pleasant Creek both have to be negotiated along this route. Just stepping in, getting your feet wet, and walking your bike across is the safest, albeit wettest, option. There are places where you can jump across on rocks—but the rocks are often wet and slippery, making it dangerous to try to cross while pushing your bike.

From the parking lot at the end of the scenic drive go south, immediately crossing through Capitol Creek. Then you simply follow the dirt South Draw Road as it climbs gently over the next 3 miles to Pleasant Creek. If you decide to go farther, plunge in and across the creek and continue on the dirt road that now mainly follows the wash bottom. The road continues to climb in a rolling fashion until at 6 miles it turns and begins the ascent of Boulder Mountain. Turn around here (or get ready for a steep, arduous pedal).

24. PLEASANT CREEK–SOUTH DRAW WASH (See map on page 121)

For mountain bikes. This ride is a moderately difficult 24-mile downhill from high on the flank of Boulder Mountain. You need either a drop-off or a car shuttle. The ride follows the Pleasant Creek drainage as it steps down off Boulder Mountain through forests of mixed evergreens, fluted sandstone canyons, high desert, and eventually redrock desert where it hits the South Draw Road inside the park. This road takes you to the end of the paved scenic drive, where you can pick up your shuttle vehicle. Although this ride is almost all downhill, dropping 3,000 feet in elevation, it is a long day requiring a good amount of stamina and technical riding ability.

Starting point: Larb Hollow Overlook (also identified as the Tantalus Overlook on some maps), approximately 15 miles south of Torrey, Utah, on UT 12. You first have to drop a car at the parking lot at the end of the paved scenic drive inside the park, 8 miles from the park entrance. Driving into the park and leaving a car here requires that you pay a park entrance fee. If you can't leave a car here you need to arrange a shuttle that can take you back to your vehicle on Boulder Mountain. To get to the start of this ride, drive west from the park visitors center 11 miles to Torrey. Go left onto UT 12 and drive approximately 15 miles to the Larb Hollow Overlook. Park here.

Length: 24 miles point to point. Allow at least 4 hours.

Riding surface: Pavement, dirt road, doubletrack, rough four-wheel-drive jeep road; loose broken rock, sections of sand.

Difficulty: Moderately difficult. Parts of the trail require focus and experience. There are a few uphill sections and a few stretches of sand.

Scenery/highlights: This is a ride of epic proportions, covering long distances, dropping substantially in elevation, and passing through at least three different life zones. The views from the overlook and along the ride into Capitol Reef and the Waterpocket Fold to the east and south, and to Thousand Lakes Mountain in the north, are superb.

Best time to ride: Spring and fall, provided that the ground is dry and the higher elevations are free of snow. Summer temperatures are delightful up high, but about 15 degrees hotter in the park.

Special considerations: You pass the Wildcat Ranger Station on your way to the start of the Pleasant Creek Road. You can stop in here, look at maps, talk to the ranger, and ask questions. Rest rooms are available at Pleasant Creek Campground, but not water. Bring plenty of your own; you're going to need it.

From the Larb Hollow Overlook (Tantalus Overlook) go south on UT 12 and ride approximately 2.5 miles to the Wildcat Ranger Station. From there, ride another 0.5 mile to the dirt road marked for Lower Bowns Reservoir. This is also Forest Road 181. You descend quickly on this packed dirt and gravel road for 3.5 miles to an intersection; bear left onto FR 168. (The right fork goes to the reservoir.) In another mile you begin

Millions of years of the earth's history are exposed in the vertical relief of the cliffs that flank Capitol Reef's Scenic Drive.

SARAH BENNETT ALLEY

pedaling across Jorgensen Flat, a wide-open sage- and grass-covered plain rimmed by ponderosa pines. The flat gently slopes away downhill and is dotted with piñon and juniper by the time you descend its lower end. You've already dropped about 1,000 feet at this point, and left the cool, moist alpine environment of the Aquarius Plateau behind.

Another mile or so along the route Pleasant Creek drops down through a gracefully fluted series of potholes and pour-overs in the rock. As you begin to make a steep descent down a jeep road with loose, broken rock, be looking over your left shoulder for a spur road taking off to Pleasant Creek. This is a short, 0.7-mile spur down to the creek where it courses over buff-colored sandstone and plunges into several deep pockets big enough for taking a dip. Several giant ponderosas stand guard over this little Eden, providing welcome shade. Take a break here, have a snack, and get ready for the grunt back to the main road.

Back on the main route, the steep descent over broken, rocky trail surfaces continues for 1.3 miles before emerging onto Tantalus Flat, almost 12 miles from your start. Within the next mile the route crosses Tantalus Creek, and then stretches across sage-dotted red flats for the next 2 miles. Unless it has rained recently, this stretch is bound to be sandy. After passing through Tantalus Flat the route climbs gently at first, and then more steeply over more broken, loose rock to a low pass where the route crosses into Capitol Reef National Park (14 miles from the start). Dropping off this pass, the route enters the head of South Draw, the drainage bisecting the monocline which is partially responsible for the formation of the features in Capitol Reef. Riding down through South Wash is a super-fun, fast-paced 6.5 miles to Pleasant Creek. Now it's time to get wet. You can attempt to ride through the creek at the ford but the bottom isn't always solid. You may be able to scout a way across stepping on rocks but chances are you will get wet in the end. Past the creek it is another 3.5 miles down a graded dirt road to the parking lot at Capitol Gorge and the end of the scenic drive.

Option: If you think you'll have it in you at the end of the day, you can leave your vehicle at the visitors center and ride the 8 miles out the rolling scenic drive to end your ride there. Some of the hills between the end of the scenic drive and the visitors center help inform you that riding all that way downhill is hard work. Shuttling from the center gives you a total distance of 32 miles.

For mountain bikes. The trip around the Cathedral Valley Loop is a magical 58-mile adventure that requires a sturdy four-wheel-drive vehicle, good weather, and planning. Riders willing to carry their camping equipment in panniers can do this tour without a vehicle, although most enjoy it as a vehicle-supported ride. Steep grades, rough jeep roads, long distances, and only one established campground at the halfway point all make for a loop best suited for experienced riders in excellent condition. The River Ford at the beginning of the Cathedral Valley Loop and several other washes along the way can become impassable due to weather.

Starting point: River Ford—the spot where the Cathedral Valley Loop Road crosses the Fremont River and heads north—is 4 miles east of the park's eastern boundary, or about 13 miles east of the visitors center.

Length: 60 miles round trip without spur roads. Allow 2 days and 1 night.

Riding surface: Dirt road, four-wheel-drive jeep roads; sections of broken rock, deep sand. Wash crossings can become muddy and impassable after rains.

Difficulty: Strenuous for all but very experienced, very fit mountain bikers. Using a shuttle vehicle, however, allows you to adjust the difficulty of the ride to some degree.

Scenery/highlights: The desert is awash with color out here, beginning with the blues, purples, grays, and greens of the banded Bentonite Hills just north of River Ford. As you head north the desert flames up into the deep reds and oranges of Entrada sandstone. The Waterpocket Fold is not the most notable feature along this route; instead, the freestanding monoliths of Cathedral Valley take center stage. Extensive erosion has carved the temples, castles, and cathedrals of this valley out of Entrada sandstone, with some capped by thin beds of greenish gray marine sandstone characteristic of the Curtis formation. Gypsum, a fine white calcium sulfate that flows and dissolves like toothpaste, has also had a hand in the creation of the features you see in Cathedral Valley. Glass Mountain is an exposed plug of gypsum, while Gypsum Sinkhole is what formed when a gypsum plug dissolved. Views into the South Desert from the Hartnet Road are wonderful.

Best time to ride: Strictly spring and fall; summertime is simply too hot. Fall sometimes sees monsoonlike moisture flows from the Gulf of Mexico that billow into heavy afternoon thunderstorms when they meet the hot air rising off the desert. Do not head into this backcountry if such a weather pattern is predicted.

Special considerations: Check with the ranger before you head out to get a full report on road and weather conditions. Don't even consider heading out this way if heavy rain is in the forecast. The slick, sticky mud that coats the roads after a rain makes progress almost impossible for bicycle and vehicle alike.

The park offers a road guide for a nominal fee with good information about the many sites along the way. A permit is required for camping in the backcountry but it is free. There is no fee for staying at the campground. There are only five sites at the Cathedral Valley Campground, and they are awarded on a first-come, first-served basis. There are pit toilets at the campground but you must bring all your own water. Make sure you have plenty of food and gas before you drive out this way. There is no firewood; bring a camp stove or charcoal and a firepan for cooking.

Just east of mile marker 91 on UT 24 you will find a small sign marking the short road taking you to River Ford. The road comes to a fork in about 0.5 mile leading to two different fords across the river. The left fork is usually shallower. Bikers will have to walk their bikes through the river here; riding is not recommended. Once on the other side traverse the sandy bottomlands along the river before climbing a switchback taking you into a colorful blue, gray, and purple landscape. The road then heads northwest through a dry wash, crossing back and forth over the wash before emerging onto the broad plain of North Blue Flats. The road traverses these flats for the next 4 miles before climbing into the beautiful, yet barren, Bentonite Hills. After descending out of these hills, the road crosses another broad flat and then climbs to a low saddle.

Approximately 14 miles from the start you come to the spur road for the Lower South Desert Overlook. This is a 1.2-mile road taking you to sweeping views of the long valley that parallels the Waterpocket Fold.

Jailhouse Rock, an enormous monolith of Entrada sandstone, towers above the valley floor beyond the overlook to the west. An old road descends into the valley here, but it is now designated as a foot and horse trail only. A little farther ahead the road drops into the narrow valley of Hartnet Draw, named for Dave Hartnet, a hearty fellow credited with pioneering this route between Fremont and Cainville in the early 1880s.

At 16 miles you pass a sign marking the park boundary. A sign indicating the 1-mile hiking trail to the Lower Cathedral Valley Overlook comes up on your right just over a mile later. At the end of this trail you can take in views to the Temples of the Sun, Moon, and Stars. Please be careful near the cliff edges at this overlook. The road crosses several more washes over the next 3 miles as it heads northwest. A sign for the developed Ackland Spring is on your right 20 miles from the start. The road crosses back and forth over Hartnet Wash, climbing over some rough, rocky terrain that will be challenging for a high clearance vehicle in spots, and arrives at the short spur road for the Upper South Desert Overlook 7 miles later. About 0.25 mile past this spur and overlook is South Desert Spring on your left. Another 0.25 mile beyond that is a spur road on the right that takes you to another overlook.

At mile 27.5 you come to Hartnet Junction, where the Hartnet, Cainville Wash, and Polk Creek Roads intersect. The Polk Creek Road leaves the park in 1 mile and winds its way up, up, up onto Thousand Lakes Mountain inside the Fish Lake National Forest. Your route instead turns right onto the Cainville Wash Road and heads north 0.5 mile to Cathedral Campground. This is your stopover for the night.

In the morning the first point of interest is the Morrell Cabin, 1.5 miles from camp, a testament to the pioneers' efforts in this area. Now 30 miles into the journey, you come to a turnoff and hiking trail to Upper Cathedral Valley Overlook. A collection of red Entrada sandstone monoliths, some 500 feet tall and capped with greenish gray layers of the Curtis formation, stand out in the desert like fairy-tale castles. This 2-mile hiking trail takes you to the base of some of these formations. An old daguerreotype photograph only recently discovered reveals that John C. Fremont's fifth expedition came through the upper Cathedral Valley in 1853. The picture shows the scene before you.

At 33 miles you come to the junction of the Cainville Wash and Baker Ranch Roads, where plugs, dikes, and sills of black lava that oozed into this landscape 3 to 6 million years ago become visible. (The Baker Ranch Road continues 27 miles north to I-70.) Just beyond you will come to the spur road for the Gypsum Sinkhole, a large hole that formed after a plug of gypsum dissolved away. The pit it left behind is 200 feet deep and 50 feet across. The road now descends through a region called the the Middle Desert, intermittently following a wash, over terrain that is again, quite rough in places. Approximately 9.5 miles past the Gypsum Sinkhole road you will come to the Lower Cathedral Valley spur road (42.5 miles from the start). This 1.5-mile spur road takes you to a bizarre mound of selenite crystals called Glass Mountain, as well as to the base of Temple of the Sun and Temple of the Moon.

Over the next 10 miles the road traverses broad stretches of open desert colored in pastel hues. Mounded formations characteristic of Morrison formation sandstone and shales abound. To the north is Black Mountain. At 53 miles the gray and black slopes of the Cainville Mesas begin to dominate. These are composed mainly of Mancos shale and Mesa Verde sandstone which make for poor soils and the stark, treeless landscape. The Cainville Road meets UT 24 approximately 60 miles from the start of this trip at River Ford, 5 miles south.

CAMPING

There are three campgrounds in Capitol Reef National Park, but only one that offers any amenities. **Fruita Campground** is located 1 mile from the visitors center on the scenic drive, has 70 sites, is managed on a first-come, first-served basis, and offers rest rooms, drinking water, and a dump station. There is a per-night fee and a stay limit of 14 days a year. Up to eight people may stay at one campsite. Presentations are offered nightly at the nearby amphitheater.

Fruita Campground has one group site that can be reserved from April 1 until October 20. Only mailed or faxed requests are accepted. The maximum group size is 40, with a limit of 10 vehicles. The maximum stay is 5 days, and there is per-night fee. Children under five are free but are included in the group count. Contact the park superintendent or send a fax to (435) 425-3026.

Wood collection is not permitted in the park, nor are ground fires. You must use fire grates or a gas camp stove.

The other two campgrounds are in the backcountry at least 30 miles from the visitors center. **Cathedral Valley Campground** has five sites, is approximately 25 miles north of UT 24, and can be reached via the Hartnet Road or the Cainville Wash Road. **Cedar Mesa Campground** has six sites and is located approximately 23 miles south of UT 24 on the Notom Road. Both are managed on a first-come, first-served basis.

There are several private campgrounds in the area. **Thousand Lakes RV Park** (1 mile west of town on UT 24). It has tent sites and RV sites with hook-ups, showers, laundry, and a store.

There are numerous choices for campgrounds and wilderness camping in the nearby Dixie National Forest. Stop in at the forest service office in Teasdale for more information.

LODGING

There are now a few chain hotels in Torrey: a **Days Inn,** a **Super 8,** and the **Best Western Capitol Reef Resort,** featuring luxury accommodations, a pool, and a restaurant. There is also a brand-new fancy **Holiday Inn** immediately outside the park that has all of same. The **Chuck Wagon Lodge** is right in town and has both new and old rooms, and the **Torrey Trading Post,** also in town, has cabins. The **Wonderland Inn** just east of town has reasonable rooms, as does the **Capitol Reef Inn and Café,** which also serves breakfast and dinner.

Between Bicknell and Torrey you'll find two B&Bs—the **SkyRidge** and the **Cockscomb Inn**—and a nice place called the **Lodge at Red River Ranch.** If you're looking for something really special, try the **Boulder Mountain Lodge** on UT 12 right in the town of Boulder, about 35 miles south of Torrey. There are also a handful of reasonable motels to choose from in Bicknell, 8 miles west of Torrey.

FOOD

Other than the restaurants found at the Torrey hotels, there are few choices. One of the very best is **Café Diablo,** with southwestern dishes and desserts every day. They are open for lunch and dinner May through October. **Robber's Roost Books and Beverages** is the place for a good

IT'S INTERESTING TO KNOW . . .

Archaeologists believe that people were farming the valleys and streambanks in the Capitol Reef area as early as A.D. 700. They grew corn and beans to supplement a diet that depended on hunting and the gathering of wild plants. They left few artifacts behind, but among them are distinctive petroglyphs like the ones found along the Fremont River inside the park. Intriguing images of human shapes adorned with jewelry, breastplates, sashes, and headdresses are attributed to the Fremont, though their meaning remains unclear. The Fremont culture was first identified by a young Harvard anthropology student working along the Fremont River in 1931 in what is now Capitol Reef National Park.

cup of coffee. You can browse its new and used book selection and peruse the collection of handmade gifts there. If you're after a burger and a good shake, **Brinks Drive-In** is the spot.

You can do a few loads of laundry at the **Chuck Wagon General Store** in Torrey and have an ice cream while you wait. The **Thousand Lakes RV Park** also has laundry facilities.

There are no real bike shops in the area surrounding Capitol Reef—or for miles around. Panguitch has **Mountain Bike**

DON'T MISS

Wonderful hiking opportunities abound in Capitol Reef National park. Several hikes traverse narrow slot canyons that should be avoided if there is a chance of flash flooding due to heavy summer thunderstorms.

Gooseneck Point (0.2 mile round-trip) and Sunset Point (0.6 mile round-trip) are both short, easy hikes on the west side of the park that overlook Sulphur Creek below. A wonderful one-way trip can be made through Sulphur Creek (6.2 miles one-way with a shuttle) and its narrow canyon, starting at the Chimney Rock trailhead and ending at the visitors center. Both Grand Wash (2.2 miles with shuttle) and Capitol Gorge (1.6 miles round-trip) offer great short hikes through deep canyons with towering sandstone walls that hikers of all sizes and abilities can enjoy. The lower section of Pleasant Creek makes for a superb day or overnight hike (9 miles round-trip) along a beautiful stream. The all-day hike through the Waterpocket Fold via Burro Wash (11.2 miles round-trip) is an excellent adventure for those with more stamina. The Rim Overlook Trail (4.6 miles round-trip), the Golden Throne Trail (3.4 miles round-trip), and the Fremont River Trail to the Fremont Overlook (2 miles round-trip) all access commanding views of Capitol Reef and make good day hikes. The hike to Hickman Bridge (1.9 miles round-trip) is always very popular, providing some of the best views anywhere of the greenbelt along the Fremont River, the entire Fremont River Canyon, and surrounding rock formations.

Heaven (435-676-2880) if you are coming this way from Bryce Canyon, and there are at least half a dozen in Moab. Make sure you come to this area supplied with spare tubes, a few tools, and some chain lubricant.

FOR FURTHER INFORMATION

Capitol Reef National Park—Superintendent, H.C. 70, Box 15, Torrey, UT 84775; (435) 425-3791; http://www.capitol.reef.national-park.com/

Dixie National Forest, Supervisor's Office, 82 N. 100 E., Cedar City, UT 84720; (435) 865-3700

Dixie National Forest, Teasdale Ranger District, P.O. Box 99, Teasdale, UT 84773; (435) 425-3702

Bureau of Land Management, Escalante Resource Area, Box 225, Escalante, UT 84726; (435) 826-4291

5

Cedar Breaks is an enormous, brilliantly hued amphitheater carved out of the western edge of the 10,300-foot-high Markagunt Plateau. The same intensely orange and pink strata found in Bryce Canyon National Park have been revealed at Cedar Breaks, only here they are 2,000 feet higher and set off by the lush greens of the surrounding high-alpine environment. The bowl—full of ridges, spires, and craggy rock formations that fall away from the rim of the plateau—drops 2,500 feet to the bottom of Ashdown Gorge and is more than 3 miles across. The same geologic formation and processes responsible for the wonderland of colorful pinnacles and hoodoos inside Bryce Canyon have created the stunning beauty of the landscape at Cedar Breaks.

The siltstone, limestone, and sandstone layers, tinted by iron, manganese, and other minerals, were deposited across this region close to 65 million years ago in a Paleocene lake about the size of Lake Erie. Limestone sediments from an earlier period, when shallow seas encroached and then receded from the area, washed into the lake and settled on top of other sediments. Volcanic activity followed, covering much of this region with lava. Later, the deeply faulted country throughout southern and central Utah uplifted into blocks that remain as today's enormous plateaus. The protective layer of lava that caps these uplifted fault blocks prevented their tablelike tops from being worn down, while their unpro-

141

tected flanks have experienced extensive erosion. The soft rock layers at Cedar Breaks, like those at Bryce Canyon, have yielded to eons of rain, hail, and wind, and are sensitive to the extended periods of freeze-thaw cycles that take place at these elevations.

The Markagunt, a Paiute Indian word meaning "highland of trees," hosts stunning wildflowers each spring and summer, as well as verdant spruce and pine forests intermingled with quaking aspens. Ancient bristlecone and limber pines clinging to the plateau's rim are fascinating trees whose twisted, weathered shapes add to the unique beauty of the monument. The lofty climes of the Markagunt constitute a beautiful oasis of cooler temperatures and greenery above the fiery desert.

Cycling in the Park

The awesome display of salmon and pink pinnacles inside the Cedar Breaks amphitheater is just one of the popular attractions atop the Markagunt Plateau. Another is the fantastic recreational possibilities awaiting outdoor-oriented folks year-round. In the summer season that means biking. Although the season is short, it is as sweet as they come. The high elevations, cool temperatures, and gorgeous alpine scenery make for a welcome getaway from the broiling temperatures that dominate in the Southwest most of the summer. The plateau is incredibly well suited for mountain biking, with its expanse of level, rolling terrain, network of trails, and wealth of overlooks and scenic views. If you have just arrived from out of state and are not used to the high altitudes here, you may want to take a day to acclimate to the thin, dry air before exerting yourself on a bike. The visitors center usually opens on June 1, or when the ground is free of snow. Temperatures are ideal for riding up here during the hottest part of the summer.

Brian Head is a sleepy little town that first made a name as its winter ski resort—which has now expanded to cater to summer mountain bikers. Riding the main road through the park, cruising around town on the Brian Head town trails, and making the trip out to the old pioneer cabins are great cycling adventures the entire family can enjoy. Pedaling out to the Twisted Forest to visit a stand of ancient bristlecone pines and taking in the view of Cedar Breaks from High Mountain is a good intermediate adventure, while swooping downhill on the trails at the Brian Head Mountain Bike Park has something for everybody. The supertechnical,

CYCLING OPTIONS

There are six rides listed in this chapter, one a road-bike ride, the other five for mountain bikes. The Cedar Breaks Scenic Drive is a 10-mile (total) out-and-back pedal on a paved road with shoulders along the rim of the Cedar Breaks amphitheater. The riding is easy but elevations are over 10,000 feet. The Brian Head Town Trail is an easy 5.5 miles of wide dirt path suitable for bike trailers and little folks that loops around town accessing restaurants, shops, and some beautiful scenery. The Pioneer Cabins Loop (5 miles total) is another easier ride suitable for beginning-level riders; it takes you through woodlands and meadows on mostly dirt roads and singletrack.

Riding out to High Mountain is a super 12.5-mile intermediate mountain-biking adventure that follows dirt roads and sections of doubletrack. Brian Head Mountain Bike Park has over 16 miles of single-track trails that wind around the resort's ski mountain. You can purchase a single-ride or all-day pass for the Giant Steps Lift to the top of the mountain, or you can ride uphill on the trails, many of which are steep and difficult. The ride off Blowhard Mountain is a classic among southern Utah mountain-bike rides, but it's not for everyone. This route, comprised mostly of singletrack, is a 7.5-mile one-way fat-tire odyssey that involves steep descents across knife-edge ridges, narrow trails, rocky switchbacks, drop-offs, and heart-stopping vistas.

superexposed descent off Blowhard Mountain is one of the most scenic rides in the area, but it isn't for the acrophobic. The rides listed here are just brief sampling, an appetizer if you will, of dozens more scrumptious trails in the Cedar Breaks and Brian Head area.

---

26. CEDAR BREAKS SCENIC DRIVE (See map on page 145)

For road and mountain bikes. This ride takes you along the very rim of the plateau at elevations that range between 10,350 and 10,440 feet. There are four main overlooks along the route, each providing a unique perspective on the brilliant maze of canyons and pinnacles below. While there are few hills and no requirements for technical riding ability, the extremely high elevations require a solid base of physical fitness and a good-sized pair of lungs. The scenic drive is also UT 148 and 143, and although speed limits are kept low through the park, you will be sharing the road with vehicles.

Starting point: Cedar Breaks Visitors Center, a small log-cabin structure that has many interesting displays and information available on the life and geology of the monument.

Length: 5 miles one-way (10 miles total). An option takes you to the town of Brian Head and back for a total distance of 16 miles.

Riding surface: Pavement. Unlike most parks, the scenic drive through Cedar Breaks is a state road with some shoulder to ride on.

Difficulty: Easy, except for the high elevations.

Scenery/highlights: From the overlooks along this route you can take in the whole amphitheater that is Cedar Breaks. Every stop along the way will give you another astounding perspective on this wondrous display.

Best time to ride: Late spring through fall. Because the amphitheater faces west, the best time for viewing is from midday to evening.

Special considerations: Do not ride out this way or approach any of the lookouts if thunderstorms are in the area. Warm air rising off the surrounding desert often combines with moisture evaporating off the plateau to blossom into storm clouds. The rim of the plateau and the high points of the plateau itself are very susceptible to lightning strikes.

From the visitors center ride out the short loop drive you came in on and go left. Pedal northward, bending east away from the rim through fragrant stands of spruce-fir evergreen forests, passing the short spur road to the amphitheater, campground, and a picnic area about 0.3 mile from the start. Just over 1 mile from the visitors center is Sunset View, where you can peer down into Arch Creek drainage. Jericho Ridge and Bristlecone Ridge flank this drainage immediately to each side.

You head east from here, riding away from the rim again, before doubling back and climbing just over another mile to the short spur road taking you out to Chessmen Ridge Overlook. You look into Chessmen Canyon and along the incredible wall of formations along Chessmen

Ride 26 • Cedar Breaks Scenic Drive
Ride 27 • Twisted Forest–High Mountain
Ride 28 • Blowhard Mountain

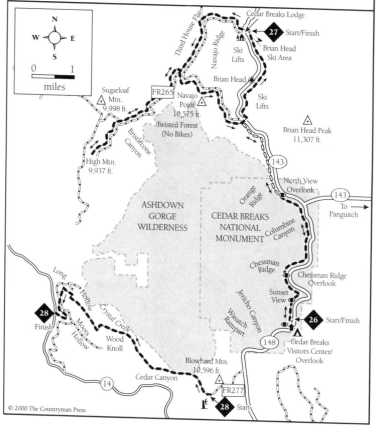

Ridge—the main ridge separating the two major drainages of the amphitheater, Ashdown and Rattlesnake Creeks. A short trail (0.6 mile one-way) leaves from here and traces the rim of the amphitheater, taking you to Alpine Pond. The next overlook is another 1.3 miles beyond, providing views into Rattlesnake Creek. A mile beyond this overlook is the junction with UT 143, which heads east to Panguitch. As you approach this junction you catch glimpses of the vibrant orange and pink of the cliffs through the trees.

Stunning views in all directions await riders who pedal the highest peaks of the Markagunt Plateau, home to Cedar Breaks National Monument.

LEE COHEN

Another 0.6 mile brings you to North View Overlook, the last view (and turnaround) point on this ride. From here you look down into Lavender Canyon and Highleap Canyon on either side, and beyond to Columbine Ridge (south) and Orange Ridge (north). When you've had a chance to catch your breath and take in the view, pedal back through the trees and flower-filled meadows, glancing every now and then over your shoulder to take in the view to the west.

Option: For serious road riders looking for more of a challenge, you can ride beyond North View Overlook another 4 miles to the town of Brian Head. You drop about 800 feet on your way there—elevation loss that will have to be regained on your way back. The steep climbs on the return challenge even the most fit rider. You may want to begin this ride in Brian Head, riding out to the visitors center, so you will not have to face the climb on the way back. From the center to Brian Head and back is 16 miles.

---

27. TWISTED FOREST–HIGH MOUNTAIN (See map on page 145)

For mountain bikes. This 12.5-mile intermediate biking adventure takes you through the gorgeous undulating terrain southwest of Brian Head. The route skirts the Ashdown Wilderness Area, taking you to a magical forest of pygmy bristlecone pines, and finally climbs to High Mountain, where some spectacular views into neighboring Cedar Breaks National Monument await. Although you won't need a lot of technical skills for this ride, good amounts of physical fitness and stamina are required.

Starting point: Cedar Breaks Lodge at the north end of Brian Head. The lodge is located just off UT 143 on Hunter Ridge Drive. As you head north through town, it is just past the turnoff to Navajo Lodge on your left. Brian Head is 2 miles north of the monument's boundary and about 8 miles north of the visitors center.

Length: 12.5 miles (total) out and back. Allow at least 4 hours to do the ride, make the short hike into the Twisted Forest, and take in the view from High Mountain.

Riding surface: Graded dirt road, doubletrack.

Difficulty: Moderate. The steep hills, distance, and high elevations tax even the fit rider.

Scenery/highlights: The combination of redrock and mountain scenery is spectacular. The hike through the eons-old bristlecone pines and the views from High Mountain are bonuses that give this ride a five-star rating. Bristlecone pines prefer to live in areas of poor, usually limy soils that are exposed to the full brunt of wind and weather. The views from High Mountain warrant bringing a camera along on this ride.

Best time to ride: Anytime mid-May through October, provided the ground is dry and free of snow. Be aware of hunt locations and schedules in the fall.

Special considerations: Drinking water and rest rooms are available at the lodge but not along the trail. Make sure you bring plenty of water and something to snack on while you take in the view.

From Cedar Breaks Lodge head out onto UT 143 and go left. Go approximately 0.3 mile north, toward Parowan, turning left onto Aspen Drive. Bear right onto Fir Street and begin the steep climb over Navajo Ridge on this graded road. You crest the ridge in about 0.7 mile, and descend the other side into an area called Third House Flat. In just under 2 miles you come to the junction with Dry Lakes Road. Turn left, pedaling south on Dry Lakes Road as it crosses a meadow and enters a glade of aspens. Continue heading south on this road for 1 mile to where it meets and merges with the Sugar Loaf Mountain Road coming in from the left at a junction.

Keep heading straight on the Sugar Loaf Mountain Road (also Forest Road 265) for another mile to where a spur road leaves to the left. Go left onto this doubletrack and follow it 0.25 mile to where it ends at the wilderness area boundary and the Twisted Forest Trailhead. Leave your bike to make the short hike among these craggy, old trees. The glowing pink cliffs beyond make a stunning backdrop to the wonderful shape of the pines. An overlook another 0.5 mile along the trail provides for fantastic views into the monument.

When you're ready to continue, head back to the main road and go left (south). Just over 1 mile from the Twisted Forest spur, the road climbs and then forks. The right fork is on a well-traveled road to Sugar

LEE COHEN

A cyclist enjoys a fast-paced section of singletrack across one of the many meadows that dot southern Utah's high plateaus.

Loaf Mountain. Your route bears left onto the jeep road, which now heads up into the aspens. Another 0.7 mile further you emerge from the trees and the spur taking you to a viewpoint appears on the left. Go left to take in some fantastic scenery or continue up the main jeep road another 0.5 mile to the summit of High Mountain. When you can tear yourself away, head back the way you came, saving enough energy to get back over Navajo Ridge.

Option: To vary your route on the return trip, consider heading back to town via the Sugar Loaf Mountain Road. To do this, head back the way you came for 2.3 miles, past the turnoff for Sugar Loaf Mountain, past the trailhead out to Twisted Forest, to where the Sugar Loaf Mountain Road branches off to the right (east) toward Navajo Ridge and the town of Brian Head. This road climbs steeply over Navajo Ridge, traverses a logged area, and comes out at the south end of town. Go left and coast back to Cedar Breaks Lodge, arriving at your car near the north end of town approximately 4 miles from where you turned onto the Sugar Loaf Mountain Road.

---

28. BLOWHARD MOUNTAIN (See map on page 145)

For mountain bikes. There are several world-class descents from the high country around the Brian Head area, and from the peak itself, into the surrounding valleys below. One of these is the ride off Blowhard Mountain. The thrilling white-knuckle terrain, heart-stopping vistas into Cedar Breaks and the Ashdown Gorge Wilderness Area, and 3,000 feet of vertical drop have earned fat-tire fans from around the country and attention from several glossy cycling magazines. These 7.5 miles of singletrack feature steep, narrow trails, rocky switchbacks, root drop-offs, and loose gravel; they're not for the skittish or faint of heart. Even experienced riders with expert handling skills find sections of this trail that force them to dismount. This route requires a shuttle, which can be done with your own vehicle or arranged through one of the shops in town.

Starting point: Blowhard Mountain trailhead. To get there drive approximately 1.5 miles south of Cedar Breaks National Monument Visitors Center on UT 148, and go right onto an unmarked dirt road (which is FR 277). Drive 1 mile to the signed trailhead on the right-hand side of the road. Park here alongside the road.

If you have two vehicles in your group and are doing your own shuttle, you will first have to leave a car below at the Moots Hollow trailhead. To get there continue driving south on UT 148 to UT 14. Go west on UT 14 approximately 8.5 miles and park just past milepost 9 at a turnout on the right side of the road. There are no signs marking this trailhead, but the trail drops out here through a cut in the cliffs.

FLORA

The majority of Cedar Breaks National Monument falls into the Canadian (8,500 to 10,000 feet) and subalpine (10,000 to 11,000 feet) life zones. A small part of the park at the bottom of Ashdown Gorge lies within the transitional life zone (6,000 to 8,500 feet). Engelmann spruce, subalpine fir, and Douglas fir are found in abundance through the monument, as is quaking aspen. Growing near the rim of the plateau are limber and bristlecone pines. Their twisted, contorted shapes make them easy to recognize and give them wonderful character. Bristlecone pines are thought to be among some of the oldest creatures on earth, some living to be 2,000 years old. They're also extremely drought tolerant, waiting for moist years in a 25- to 30-year cycle to shed their needles. You can see a stand of these ancient trees at Spectra Point inside the monument, or in the Twisted Forest, found along the ride of the same name.

Prickly currant, gooseberry, and wax currant are a few of the shrubs that can be found here, and are favored by resident and migratory birds for their summer fruits. Many of the wildflowers you would expect to find in a high, mountainous setting can be found here, including Indian paintbrush, Colorado columbine, green gentian, silver lupine, beard-tongue penstemon, elephant's-head, shooting-star, larkspur, marsh marigold, Parry's primrose, orange sneezeweed, and little sunflower. Cinquefoil, fleabane, wild rose, and—in rockier places and low to the ground—cushion phlox and subalpine phlox can also be found.

Length: 7.5 miles one-way. Allow 3 to 4 hours to complete this ride.

Riding surface: Wild and woolly singletrack, doubletrack.

Difficulty: Very difficult. Very technical throughout the first third of this ride, with another hairy section toward the end.

Scenery/highlights: The views into Ashdown Gorge Wilderness Area, and north into the glowing cliffs and pinnacles inside Cedar Breaks amphitheater, are stupendous. Make sure you look up from your wheel every now and then to see the impressive natural spectacle before you.

Best time to ride: Anytime June through early October, provided the ground is dry and free of snow. Sections of this trail can become a gooey, muddy mess when the ground is saturated. Be aware of summer forecasts that predict afternoon buildups; you are very exposed up here and do not want to get stuck in a lightning storm.

Special considerations: The shops that commonly run shuttles in this area are Brian Head Sports, Georg's Ski and Bike Shop, and High Mountain Outfitters. Their addresses and phone numbers are listed in the Trip Planning Appendix on page 165.

Water and rest rooms are available at the monument visitors center.

Follow the trail as it wraps around the northern side of the peak. The first stretch of trail contours the top of the mountain, ending 0.4 mile from the start to where it drops off the side of Blowhard Mountain into a series of steep switchbacks. Please use caution: The next section of trail is extremely steep with some nerve-racking exposures. The trail follows a knife-edge ridge as it drops down through the Pink Cliffs. Make sure you pause and secure your footing while taking in the unbelievable views before you—you don't want to topple over through here, where there is nothing to stop you. There is little letup in this trail's pitch and attitude for 1.5 miles until it finally, thankfully, mellows and levels at an intersection with the hiking trail to Potato Bottom inside the wilderness area.

For the next mile the trail winds around through thick, fragrant forests of mixed conifers, then picks up a doubletrack that crosses under a power line. Follow this doubletrack down to where it crosses the Crystal Springs Road (FR 1015), approximately halfway through the ride. To the left is UT 14; to the right is the wilderness boundary. Cross over the road and stay heading straight. Climb up Wood Knoll, skirting around its northern flank for almost 1 mile, and then descend the ridge between Long Hollow on your right and Moots Hollow on your left for another mile before the trail switches back and begins its descent into Cedar Canyon. Views to the south into Cedar Canyon and beyond to the Kolob Plateau are great along this stretch. To the north is Ashdown Gorge.

The trail descends off the ridge via several steep switchbacks above Long Hollow, and then wraps around and continues its descent on a doubletrack into Moots Hollow. This doubletrack crosses over a dirt road and traces the edge of the hollow along a rock ledge. Please check your speed and use caution both here and where the road finally turns and descends steeply through the bottom of Moots Hollow. The trail spits you out right onto the side road as you reach the canyon bottom. Climb into the shuttle vehicle and enjoy the ride back up.

29. BRIAN HEAD TOWN TRAIL (See map on page 154)

For mountain bikes. Besides the many Lycra-clad bikers zipping around town, a good indication of a bike-friendly community is a town trail system that is both functional and fun—and Brian Head has a good one. Ride from your lodge to dinner, to the bike shop, or simply to have a look around. These are wide dirt paths that can even accommodate a trailer, so the little ones can go along too. You'll find 5.5 miles of trail looping around Brian Head, and just over 400 feet of elevation change between the north and south ends of town. These trails offer a good opportunity to ease into being in the saddle at high altitude.

Starting point: The town of Brian Head, just 2 miles north of the monument boundary, or about 8 miles north of the visitors center. There are numerous places in town to pick up the trail, but one of the best is at the base of the lifts at the north end of town near Navajo Lodge. This is the lower end of town, and a good place to coast back to on your return.

Length: 5.5 miles round-trip. Plan on an hour or two—or three—to make your way around town on these trails, depending on how much eating, shopping, and sight-seeing you want to do.

Riding surface: Trails are dirt, sections of road linking them are paved.

Difficulty: Easy. The only element of difficulty is the elevations, which range between 9,500 and almost 10,000 feet here.

Scenery/highlights: These town trails allow you to access bike shops, restaurants, and all the lodges, while looping through quiet woods on your way back and forth. The tweet and banter of birds, the burble of Parowan Creek, and the gentle flutter of aspen leaves overhead, not the roar of car and truck traffic, serenade you on these trails.

Ride 29 • Brian Head Town Trail

Best time to ride: Anytime spring through fall, provided the ground is dry and free of snow. Riding on these trails when they are wet creates ugly ruts and will coat you with muddy splatter on your way to dinner.

Special considerations: A lot of folks commute to work and play on these trails in summer. Whether you're using them to get somewhere, or using them just to get out and have a look around, follow the rules of the road and stay to the right, allowing faster riders to pass you on the left.

Evening sun bathes the brilliant pink and orange cliffs of Cedar Breaks while thunderheads loom over Brian Head Peak.

The trails on the east side of UT 143 (the main route through Brian Head) climb at a gentler grade as they head south. If you're pulling a trailer or want an easier time of it heading out, ride back out on the drive you came in on, cross over UT 143—watching carefully for traffic—go left onto the highway, and pedal a short distance up the road to the Mountain View Market and Café to pick up the trail there. If you don't care which way you go, then head up past the Navajo Lodge and across the beginner hill south. The trail crosses Ridge View Street and then follows alongside Pinehurst Road behind Chalet Village, Brian Head Village, and the Edge Restaurant and Club. A little farther along the trail passes behind Georg's Ski and Bike Shop, and then crosses a meadow by the highway before intersecting Sugar Loaf Mountain Road.

Cross over the highway and begin your return journey here, again being careful to look for traffic before crossing the road. Pick up the trail directly across the highway from Sugar Loaf Road, and follow it as it winds around through an area that has been recently logged. A little insect called a bark beetle has taken a heavy toll on the evergreens atop the Markagunt in recent decades, prompting foresters to take down stands of both sick and healthy trees as a way of controlling further infestation.

Emerging from the trees, you pick up South Loop Road and follow it until you reach Chairlift 2 and the Giant Steps Lodge. Next you wind around behind Brian Head Sports and the Mall before crossing over Bear Flat Road. Continue past the town offices, cross over Burts Road, and enjoy a last trip through the trees and across Parowan Creek before encountering civilization once again near the Mountain View Market and Café and Timberline Condominiums. Head out onto UT 143, go left, and ride the short distance to Navajo Lodge, where you left your car.

---

30. PIONEER CABINS LOOP (See map on page 157)

For mountain bikes. This easy 5-mile loop takes you through evergreen forests and open meadows to two old cabins built and occupied by hearty homesteaders in the late 1870s. This route serves as a good introduction to riding the backcountry around the Brian Head area, and it's one that the smaller mountain bikers in the family will like, too. There is just a few hundred feet of elevation change and a couple of rocky spots, but nothing that requires a lot of bike-handling skills.

Starting point: Near Giant Steps Lodge at the base of the Brian Head Ski Resort at the main parking lot. (This is also where the lift that services Brian Head Resort Mountain Bike Park is headquartered.) To get there drive approximately 8 miles north on UT 148 and 143 from the monument visitors center. The parking lot is on your right.

Length: Just over 5 miles. Allow at least 2 hours to complete this loop.

Riding surface: Pavement, dirt road, doubletrack, singletrack.

Difficulty: Easy. Elevation change is minimal but altitudes are already quite high. A day to acclimate to the thin air up here before you head out to ride is recommended.

Scenery/highlights: Mixed spruce-fir and aspen forests, open meadows, and the charming pioneer cabins make this a great alpine outing.

Best time to ride: Anytime late spring through fall, provided the ground is dry and free of snow. In the fall, check with the forest service for schedules and locations of deer and elk hunts, and try to avoid them.

Ride 30 • Pioneer Cabins Loop

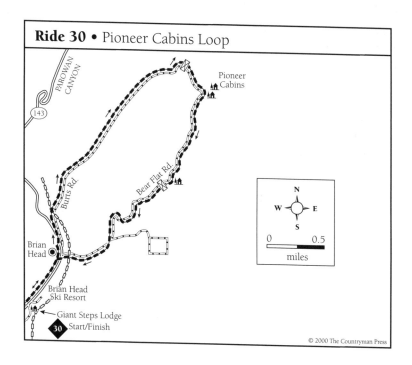

© 2000 The Countryman Press

Special considerations: Drinking water and rest rooms can be found at the facilities at the base of Brian Head Ski Resort.

Begin this ride by pedaling out onto UT 143 and heading north. Follow the highway downhill approximately 0.5 mile, past the town hall, and go right onto Burts Road. Follow this road for approximately 1 mile as it rolls along before ending at the start of a doubletrack. Go through a gate and follow this doubletrack as it descends to a creek crossing and heads into a meadow, where it becomes a singletrack. Continue to an intersection of trails at the top of the meadow. The log cabins are just beyond (2.6 miles from the start) in the aspens at the east end of the meadow. Leave your bike here and walk over to have a look. These cabins were built sometime in the late 1870s by two dairy farmers who brought their cows up to feed on the lush green grass of these meadows during summer. By the early 1900s both the dairy and the cabins were abandoned.

Back at the trail junction, go right and head south across the meadow, following the trail as it winds through the woods, climbs over a few small rocky hills, and past a marsh-rimmed pond (3.5 miles from the start). Just past the pond the trail emerges into another meadow. You'll find more remnants of pioneer efforts here. Next you come to two steel gates identifying private property; please stay on the main road. Now the route heads through an area logged because of beetle infestation, and downhill past several groups of summer homes. Bear left at two intersections, staying on the main road, and go right when you reach the intersection with the Bear Flat Road (4.5 miles from the start). The route soon turns into pavement and continues down to UT 143 near the town hall. Go left and ride the highway back to the parking lot at Giant Steps Lodge where you left your car.

---

31. BRIAN HEAD RESORT MOUNTAIN BIKE PARK
(See map on page 159)

For mountain bikes. If the thrill of the downhill is why you mountain bike, then you'll need to spend some time at the Brian Head Resort Mountain Bike Park. Here you can buy a single-ride or an all-day pass good for the Giant Steps Lift. This takes you up to 10,625 feet, just below the summit of Brian Head Peak, where you can choose among eight different singletrack trails ranging from easy to expert in difficulty. There are 16 miles of trails and many options for creating your own routes. Granted, you don't have to do much work going uphill, but there are enough twists, turns, and technical sections along some of these trails to keep you on your toes. The park is open through the summer and early fall on Friday, Saturday, Sunday, and holidays.

Starting point: Giant Steps Lodge and base facility, located in the town of Brian Head, 2 miles north of Cedar Breaks National Monument boundary and 8 miles north of the visitors center.

Length: There are 16 miles of trails ranging between 2.5 and 7 miles in length. Take a couple of hours or take all day.

Riding surface: Singletrack; some smooth, some rocky, some studded with roots.

Difficulty: Easy to very difficult. While two of these trails are easier than the rest, none is really suitable for rank beginners or kids with no riding

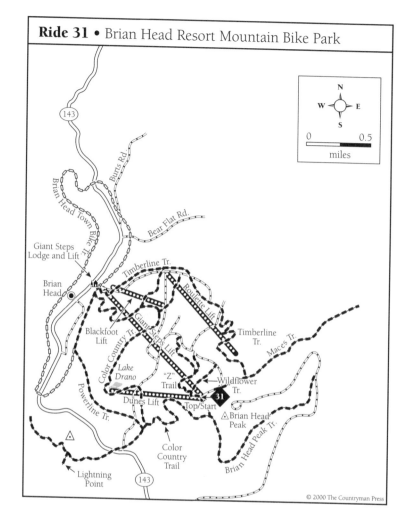

experience or bike-handling skills. Many of these descents are fast with tight turns and require some technical riding ability. Although you'll be riding downhill most of the time, it still takes some upper-body strength and forearm muscles (for braking) to safely negotiate these trails.

Scenery/highlights: The graceful brow of Brian Head Peak—rising to a lofty 11,307 feet above sea level, the highest point on the Markagunt Plateau—seems to look down approvingly on happy cyclists below. The singletrack at Brian Head Resort Mountain Bike Park is world class, as are the scenery and incredible panoramas into the surrounding country. The flaming pinks and oranges of Cedar Breaks and nearby canyons are set off by the verdant carpet of green atop the plateau.

Best time to ride: Anytime during the summer and fall. The mountain bike park opens sometime in early June. If afternoon thunderstorms are in the forecast, however, you may want to save it for another day. The lift towers, cables, and other facilities on this peak are the frequent targets of lightning.

You may want to visit during one of the special events held here. In the second week of July it's the Brian Header Intermountain Cup, a mountain-bike race featuring downhill and cross-country events. In August it's the Brian Head Bash Fat Tire Festival, with guided rides and parties. In September the park hosts another fat-tire race—this time a 12-hour relay—and the Red Rock Drop Downhill Race.

Special considerations: A fee is required for riding the chairs that access these trails. The mountain bike park also rents bikes and has a shuttle service; it offers special combination rates for a pass, a rental, and a shuttle. Call the park headquarters at (435) 677-2035 for more information.

Water, food, and rest rooms are available at the Giant Steps base facility.

A trail guide is available at the time you purchase your pass. There are two trails for beginning and intermediate riders, three for solid intermediate bikers, and three that advanced-level riders will love. The Color Country (3.8 miles) and Wildflower (3 miles) Trails have few requirements for technical maneuvering, but trail surfaces require caution. The Lightning Point Trail (4.5 miles) heads west, taking intermediate riders across UT 143 to a fantastic viewpoint, looping back to the resort base via the town trail. The Power Line Trail (2.4 miles) also descends the park's west side and offers some hair-raising sections. The Z Trail (3.5 miles) makes a wild descent underneath the lift at the top and then offers a choice of routes for the rest of the way down. The Timberline Trail (2.4 miles) traverses out underneath the rocky face of Brian Head Peak and then makes a technical descent through the ski area via several switch-

Technical descents off some of the higher peaks around Cedar Breaks require skill, quick reflexes, and a lot of concentration.

LEE COHEN

FAUNA

The ever-present raven is perhaps the most noticeable avian resident of the monument. Along the edges of the plateaus violet-green swallows perform acrobatic maneuvers in pursuit of insects. Clark's nutcrackers, chickadees, white-crowned sparrows, hairy woodpeckers, three-toed woodpeckers, and red-shafted flickers are also quite common. Golden eagles sometimes hunt for rabbits and other small mammals as do great horned owls. American kestrels and red-tailed hawks are some of the other raptor species that make their homes here. Migratory residents are many, but those that come to spend most of the summer are rufous and broad-tailed hummingbirds.

Porcupines, marmots, chipmunks, and weasels reside here, as does the golden-mantled ground squirrel. Mule deer and elk are found atop the plateau in summer, and are sometimes the quarry of cougars within the park. Bobcats and black bears have been sighted but are not common. Coyotes are occasionally spotted in the park.

backs, getting even more technical as it nears the bottom. The Timberline Trail also serves as the course for several races held here every summer.

If you're hungry for an uphill challenge before spending the day swooping down, pedal up the supertechnical Brian Head Peak Trail (2.2 miles). It will deliver you onto the graded dirt road that accesses the peak, which waits 2 miles beyond. The Maces Run Trail (7 miles) is the longest and perhaps the most technical trail in the park, crossing under Brian Head Peak and over sections of trail studded with rocks, roots, and boulders. Some sections of this trail are unridable. If you start feeling a little sheepish about all the downhill fun you're having and think maybe you should earn your gravity points for a change, try riding uphill through the park via the Color Country and Wildflower Trails. While they might be easy going down, they're anything but easy on the way up.

CAMPING

There is one campground inside Cedar Breaks National Monument, north and east of the visitors center on the east side of the road. It has 30 sites and is managed on a first-come, first-served basis. The campground has drinking water, rest rooms, picnic tables, fire grills, and an outdoor amphitheater where evening programs are given. The fee is $10 per night. The campground opens as soon as the ground is free of snow—generally sometime between the middle of June and July 4. Nighttime lows frequently dip down into the 30s and 40s at this elevation.

There are many possibilities for camping in the surrounding Dixie National Forest. Two developed forest service campgrounds can be found at Navajo Lake. **Spruces, Navajo,** and **Te-Ah Campgrounds** all have tent sites, water, rest rooms, and fire grills; they're managed on a first-come, first-served basis. **Duck Creek Campground** east of the Navajo Lake area is another good option.

Inquire at the Dixie National Forest Service Supervisor's Office in Cedar City for more ideas about camping in the area.

You'll also find the **Cedar City KOA** and the **Country Aire RV Park** (no tent sites); both have showers and pools and are located on North Main Street. There are at least three private campgrounds in the Panguitch area, including the **Big Fish KOA** and the **Hitch-n-Post Campground,** both on Main Street, and **Sportsman's Paradise RV Park** north of town on US 89. All have sites for tents, laundry, and showers.

LODGING

The closest and best option for lodging is just up the road in the town of Brian Head. **The Lodge at Brian Head** and the **Brian Head Hotel** are both affiliated with the resort and offer some good deals during summer. You can inquire about staying at one of these places or about renting a condominium unit through central reservations at Brian Head; call (435) 677-3000 or (800) 272-7426

or (435) 677-3000. For information about other condo rentals in
the area call **Brian Head Condo
Reservations** at (800) 722-4742 or
(435)677-2405. **Cedar Breaks
Lodge** in Brian Head offers accommodations that range from rooms
and studio apartments to three-
bedroom condos, plus a pool, hot
tubs, day spa, two restaurants, and
biking packages. Call (435) 677-
3000 or (888) AT-CEDAR. The
Chalet Village is another option in
Brian Head, offering hotel rooms
and condos; call (435) 677-2025 or
(800)-942-8908. Most of these
resort-type accommodations have
swimming pools and Jacuzzis, and

are geared up to serve cyclists in
the summer.

Around Panguitch Lake try
the **Rustic Lodge** on the west
shore of the lake (435-726-2627
or 800-427-8345), the **Deer Trail
Lodge Resort** on the northwest
side of the lake on Clearcreek
Canyon Road (435-676-2211),
or **Beaver Dam Lodge** (with a
restaurant serving three meals
a day) on the north shore (435-
676-8339). In Duck Creek try
the **Falcon's Nest at Duck Creek
Village** (800-240-4930), the
Pinewoods Resort (435-682-2512
or 800-848-2525), or the **Mea-
deau View Lodge B&B** (435-682-
2495).

The town of Panguitch,
about 20 miles northeast of Cedar
Breaks and Brian Head, has a
handful of reasonably priced
motels. You'll find more options in
Cedar City (about 20 miles west of
the monument), which has a good
selection of hotels, motels, and
B&Bs. Several of the big chains are
represented here, including **Best
Western, Holiday Inn, Comfort
Inn, Quality Inn,** and **Rodeway
Inn.** The accommodations in
Cedar City can fill up fast during
the summer because of the popular Shakespearean Festival that
runs from June through early
September, so call ahead.

FOOD

For a cup of coffee and a pastry try the **Bump & Grind** at the Brian Head Mall. **Espresso Express** in the Giant Steps Lodge also has the goods when it comes to java. The **Mountain View Café** is a good choice if you are looking for a hearty breakfast. It's located across from the Cedar Breaks Lodge in Brian Head and serves three good meals a day. The **Black Diamond Deli & Grill** also serves three meals and is always a good choice for a sandwich. Inside the Cedar Breaks Lodge you'll find the **Columbine Café** and the **Summit Dining Room,** featuring steaks, wild game, and daily specials. The **Steakhouse at the Lodge** (in the Lodge at Brian Head) serves steak, seafood, and pasta and is open for three meals a day. There are several clubs in town (a "club" in Utah is similar to a bar anywhere else), offering appetizers, drinks, and live entertainment.

DON'T MISS

Although the visitors center closes by 6 p.m. in the summer, there are still plenty of hours of sunlight to enjoy an evening hike along one of the rim trails in the park. A walk after dinner along the Ramparts Trail or Alpine Pond Trail is when Cedar Breaks is made even more dramatic by the long, slanting rays of the sun. This is also one of the best times of day to catch wildlife out and about. A picnic dinner out at one of the overlooks or along the trail is a great way to take in the scenery and spend an evening. Please be careful anytime you're near the cliff rims; the soils are soft and can give way under foot. Be especially careful if you are out along the cliffs in the evening when visibility is low.

LAUNDRY

There aren't too many choices close by. Check with some of the private campgrounds in the area, or try this one in Cedar City:

Raindance Laundromat & Car Wash, 430 S. Main St.; (435) 586-6964

BIKE SHOP/BIKE RENTAL

IN BRIAN HEAD

Brian Head Cross Country Ski & Mountain Bike Center, 223 Hunter Ridge Dr., (435) 677-2012

Brian Head Resort Rentals, 223 W. Hunter Ridge Dr.; (435) 677-2035

Brian Head Sports Inc., 269 S.

Brianhead Blvd.; (435) 677-2014

Georg's Ski & Bike Shop, 612 UT
143; (435) 677-2013

High Mountain Outfitters (shuttle service), 365 N. Hwy 143; (435)
677-2920.

IN CEDAR CITY

Cedar Cycle, 38 E. 200 S.; (435)
586-5210

Color Country Cyclery, 491 S.
Main St.; (435) 586-7433

Bike Route, 70 W. Center, (435)
586-4242

IN PANGUITCH

Mountain Bike Heaven, 25 E.
Center St.; (435) 676-2880

FOR FURTHER INFORMATION

Cedar Breaks National Monument—Superintendent, 82 N. 100
E., Cedar City, UT 84720-2606;
(435) 586-9451; http://www.nps.
gov/cebr/

**Brian Head Chamber of
Commerce,** Box 190068, Brian
Head, UT 84719; (435) 677-
2810

Cedar City Chamber of Commerce, 286 N. Main St., Box 220,
Cedar City, UT 84721; (435) 586-
4484

Dixie National Forest, Supervisor's Office, 82 N. 100 E.,
Cedar City, UT 84720; (435) 865-
3700

**Dixie National Forest, Powell
Ranger District,** Box 80,
Panguitch, UT 84759; (435) 673-
3431

Bureau of Land Management,
176 E. DL Sergeant Dr. (north
end of town on Main St.), Cedar
City, UT 84720; (435) 586-2401

6

It is hard to overestimate the significance of what took place in the desolate desert of northern Utah on May 10, 1869. With the final blows to the last, ceremonial golden spike that secured rail lines from east and west, shock waves of change rippled across the United States and beyond. America's perceptions of time and space convulsively collapsed into a fraction of what they had been: A trip across the open lands of the West was cut from 6 months by ox team and wagon to 6 days by rail. But with the meeting of the Central Pacific and Union Pacific rail lines also came a newly invigorated era of western settlement, and the beginning of the end of a way of life enjoyed by Native Americans for thousands of years.

Spanning the vast deserts and towering mountain ranges of the West to build America's first transcontinental railroad required enormous sums of money, millions of hours of brute labor, congressional endorsement, and the fantastic ambitions of a few businessmen. The dream was first envisioned when railroads began operating in the eastern states in the 1830s. It all began with a young engineer named Theodore Judah, who surveyed a potential route over the Sierra Nevada Mountains in 1862. Convinced that such a route was possible, Judah approached a group of wealthy Sacramento-area businessmen and persuaded them to form the Central Pacific Railroad. That same year Congress authorized

CYCLING OPTIONS

There are four rides listed in this chapter; one is a fairly long road ride and the other three are mountain-bike rides. Two rides taking cyclists along the old Central Pacific and Union Pacific Railroad grades on the Promontory Auto Tour route are relatively easy. The East Grade Tour is 9 miles long (total), and the West Grade Tour is 14 miles (total). A third ride follows the old railroad grades to the Big Fill and Big Trestle sites on a trail open to both bikers and hikers called the Big Fill Walk. Total distance for the Big Fill ride is 8 miles; it is easy to moderate. A fourth option for road riders takes them south on a seldom-traveled road toward Promontory Point.

legislation giving them the rights—along with cash subsidies and land grants—to begin building a rail line east from California.

At the same time the Union Pacific Railroad of New York was authorized to begin building westward from Omaha, Nebraska. Although work was begun the next year, it was not until the end of the Civil War that it began in earnest. A route closely paralleling the one that Mormon pioneers took west was agreed upon after the South lost its voice in the decision. Unemployed immigrants recently arrived from Europe, Civil War veterans, ex-slaves, and as many as 10,000 Chinese immigrants (who were shipped to California to replace the fortune seekers lured away to the Gold Rush) labored side by side for endless hours and pitiful pay in the service of two powerful rail barons, each intent on being the first to cross the vast lands of the West. The drive to be the first to connect east and west was so great that the two rail companies actually bypassed each other, laying parallel grades for 250 miles through Utah before Congress mandated that the rails meet at Promontory Point.

With the joining of the Central Pacific and Union Pacific rail lines, the political and economic life of the country transformed almost overnight. Politicians could now campaign across the country, raw goods could be shipped east to manufacturers, and finished products could be sent west. The rails also brought westward a flood of immigrants hungry for their chance at the American Dream. New towns and supply centers sprouted up quickly along the lines and beyond, deep into Indian territory. The lives of Native Americans were also radically transformed in a very short time. Rail cars brought soldiers who quickly put down their resistance to settlers. Hunters came, too, slaughtering herds of bison numbering in the millions, knowingly destroying the mainstay of the Indian way of life and economy. Indian removal onto reservations came quickly on the heels of the railroad, and was nearly complete by the turn of the century.

The energy, planning, and personalities involved—as well as the incredible cost in both dollars and human lives, not to mention the immense changes brought to this country—make the story of bridging this country by rail a fascinating chapter in American history.

Cycling in the Park

At Golden Spike National Historic Site you will find a small visitors center with some interesting exhibits, displays, and a good bookstore, as well as 1.7 miles of relaid track with impressive replicas of the two steam engines that met here in 1869, the *119* and the *Jupiter*. Also included in the site are more than 15 miles of graded railroad bed, ideal for seeing by bike while imagining the scene that took place here over a century ago. As you cruise along, perhaps hearing a rhythmic striking of metal on metal over a jumble of men's voices in the breeze, you can gaze out over the sage- and grass-covered slopes of the Great Basin Desert to the sparkling blue of the Great Salt Lake. Along the West Grade of the Promontory Auto Tour you'll ride past numerous blast zones, cut-and-fill sites, and culverts frantically dug by exhausted laborers, as well as the sign commemorating the completion of 10 miles of railway in a single day. This feat was achieved by 1,000 Central Pacific workers hauling, laying, and pounding rails in a continuous line far into the night.

Riding out on the East Grade Tour you'll follow a portion of the old Central Pacific grade and then branch off to the Union Pacific's Last Cut, where the final climb up to Promontory Summit was completed. Unlike most parks, you can bike here along a hiking trail known as the Big Fill Walk. Just south of the Big Fill is the site of Union Pacific's Big Trestle, spanning a 405-foot ravine.

A route for road riders that heads south from the park toward Promontory Point traces the shore of the Great Salt Lake and provides stunning views over critical marshlands to the Wasatch Mountains in the east, and to the Great Salt Lake and its mountainous islands to the south. Riding around Golden Spike is not technically difficult or too physically challenging, but it's a wonderful chance to get out of the car, take in some beautiful scenery, and pedal through time.

32. EAST GRADE TOUR (See map on page 174)

For mountain bikes. Riding from the visitors center out along the East Grade Tour route is an easy 9-mile cruise that everyone can enjoy. The route follows a paved road, picks up the dirt railroad grade that makes a loop, and then returns on the pavement. There is almost no elevation loss or gain along this route, where elevations remain close to 5,000 feet. If you would like to shorten this tour to suit the smallest bikers in your group you can drive the first 2.5 miles, park where the dirt road begins, and start riding the loop portion of the ride there.

Starting point: Visitors center. To do the shorter version of this ride, drive north and east from the visitors center on the road you came in on for 3 miles to where the Central Pacific Railroad grade crosses the road. Park off to the side of the road here.

Length: 9 miles. Allow at least 2 hours to ride this cherry-stem loop.

Riding surface: Pavement, dirt railroad grades.

Difficulty: Easy. There are a few very mellow grades, but otherwise this route is mostly level.

Scenery/highlights: At the visitors center, be sure to pick up the guide explaining various sites along the way. It costs a nominal fee but will greatly enrich your understanding of what you are going to see. The Last Cut site was the last summit Union Pacific workers had to make before ending their work at Promontory Point. You will also pass Chinaman's Arch, a limestone formation named for the thousands of Chinese workers who helped build the Central Pacific portion of the railroad. This route also passes by the trailhead for the Big Fill Walk, a trail that follows the railroad grade and is open to bikes. If you're interested, you can make a side trip out to see the Big Fill and Big Trestle sites on the grade. The empty, open country of the Great Basin Desert, the gentle peaks of the

Chinaman's Arch, a limestone formation along the East Grade Tour, was named in honor of the thousands of Chinese railroad laborers.

Promontory Mountains, views to the Great Salt Lake in the south, and the massive wall of the Wasatch Mountains that rise in the east all make this ride a scenic pleasure as well as an interesting historical tour.

Best time to ride: Almost anytime spring through fall. Summer temperatures can be hot, commonly reaching well into the 90s. Consider riding morning or evening if you're out here during the summer.

Special considerations: Water and rest rooms are available at the visitors center but at no other place along this route. You will be sharing the road with vehicles along the most of this ride, so please stay in single file and ride on the right-hand side of the road.

From the visitors center head northeast on the paved road that accesses the park, and ride for 1 mile to the junction with County Road 504. Go right onto this road and ride for another 2 miles to the dirt road signed for the Last Cut site and the East Grade Auto Tour. You can either turn right here and ride this dirt road to the start of the tour, or continue straight for another few hundred feet to pick up the railroad grade there. Either way you arrive at the start of the East Grade Auto Tour route in approximately 0.6 mile. This is also where you will find the parking area for the Last Cut site.

Once you're on the railroad bed, you pedal around some low hills and pass the Chinaman's Arch formation in 0.5 mile. The grade wraps around to the north as it contours a group of low hills, intersecting paved County Road 504 almost 1 mile past the arch. The grade then continues heading northeast, becoming the route designated as the Big Fill Walk. If you would like to ride 1 mile out to see the Big Fill and Big Trestle sites, cross over the road and continue riding on the railroad bed. Otherwise, turn left and follow the paved route west and north, returning to the visitors center in 4 miles.

---

3 3 . B I G F I L L T R A I L (See map on page 174)

For mountain bikes. One of the best things about riding out to the Big Fill and Big Trestle sites, and beyond, is that you'll have the wide, easy grades almost all to yourself. You may see a few hikers but you'll have no cars to worry about. Beginning and intermediate riders will have little problem negotiating this route. Although riding on the grades is easy there are a few hills to contend with here, demanding good physical fitness. An option lets you ride back to the visitors center via sections of the grade that parallels UT 83 and the paved CR 504. This option gives you a slightly longer total distance of 10 miles.

Starting point: The parking area near the Big Fill Walk trailhead. To get there from the visitors center drive north, then east on CR 504 for 4 miles to the signed parking area.

Length: 8 miles. Allow at least 3 hours.

Riding surface: Dirt, gravel railroad bed built in 1869.

Difficulty: Easy to moderate. Grades are a constant 2 percent, meaning there is only 20 feet of rise for every 1,000 feet of grade. There are steeper grades on the paved road to the park than there are on the railroad grades.

Scenery/highlights: The Big Fill is an enormous 170-foot-high, 500-foot-long mound that took 500 Central Pacific workers and 250 teams of animals 2 months to complete. Directly across from the Big Fill is Union Pacific's answer to spanning the deep ravine—the Big Trestle, spanning 405 feet. Beyond the ravine the grade drops gently toward the highway as it winds through the foothills of the Promontory Mountains.

Best time to ride: Anytime spring through fall. If you are visiting in summer plan on an early-morning or evening ride to avoid the hottest part of the day.

Special considerations: Rest rooms and water are available at the visitors center. Be sure to bring plenty of water, as none is available along the way.

As you head out onto the railroad grade you will immediately see a plaque commemorating the *Orange Special* wreck. This wreck occurred because of the steep grades that continue on the other side of the paved road. A few hundred yards from the start of the trail you'll find a crossover trail to the Union Pacific grade. At this point you can choose to pedal either grade as you head east. For the next mile you see evidence of several cuts and fills that sometimes required that additional fill material be quarried out of adjacent hillsides. As you rise around the hill you

Ride 32 • East Grade Tour
Ride 33 • Big Fill Trail
Ride 34 • West Grade Tour

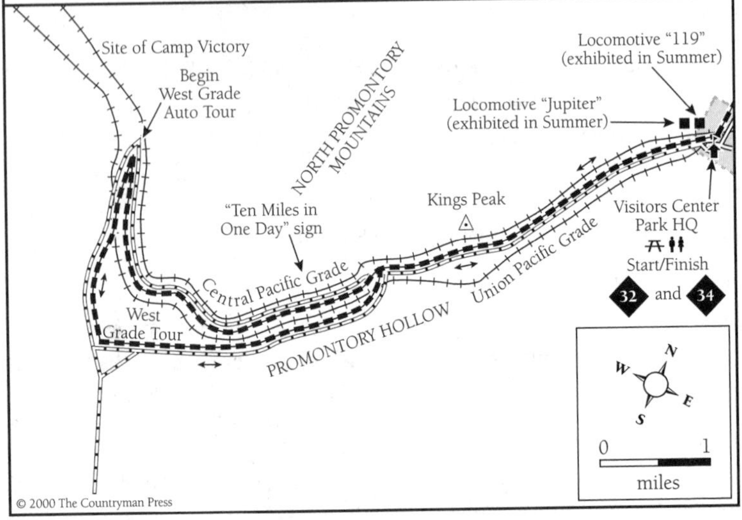

Site of Camp Victory

Begin
West Grade
Auto Tour

NORTH PROMONTORY MOUNTAINS

Locomotive "119"
(exhibited in Summer)

Locomotive "Jupiter"
(exhibited in Summer)

"Ten Miles in
One Day" sign

Kings Peak

Visitors Center
Park HQ
Start/Finish

32 and 34

Central Pacific Grade

West
Grade Tour

Union Pacific Grade

PROMONTORY HOLLOW

N
W E
S

0   1
miles

© 2000 The Countryman Press

can take in sweeping views of the Wasatch Mountains and the valley where the construction camps of both railroads were located. Junction City was situated where paved road intersects UT 83, directly across from Thiokol Corporation's Solid Rocket Motor manufacturing plant. The former site of Junction City is your destination and turnaround point. The Salt Creek Waterfowl Management Area, the Bear River Migratory Bird Refuge, the freshwater Willard Bay Reservoir, and the Great Salt Lake can also be seen stretching away to the east and south. From here you can see the grade as it angles its way east.

As you pedal along you may notice the caves that are quite common among the slopes of the Promontory Mountains. At marker 8 you can see a cave that was used as quarters for mine workers and their families. The caves undoubtedly made for sturdy and secure housing and were probably preferred to the tents that flapped constantly in the breeze.

As you approach the Big Fill and Big Trestle sites approximately 1 mile from the start, you can see that huge amounts of blasting and filling were

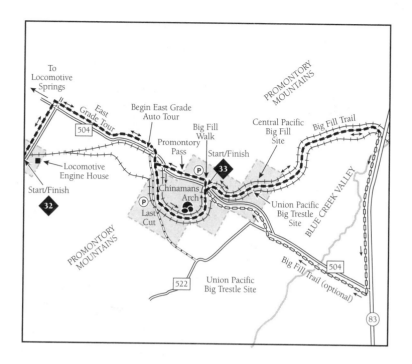

required to achieve these grades. Teams of two called double jackers drilled holes toward one another at various points up the slope, sometimes through solid rock. After the holes were drilled, a man dubbed the powder monkey would fill them with blasting powder, tamp in a fuse, and set off the charge. After the blast the rubble would be shoveled into mule dumpcarts and deposited at the fill sites. There were crews performing these tasks at several elevations along the slope, resulting in the stair-steps that you see.

Sites numbered 10 and 11 are the Big Fill and Big Trestle sites. While the Big Fill has remained usable for 130 years, little remains of the Big Trestle, which once stood 85 feet high and spanned 400 feet. Beyond these sites the route descends eastward, down the gentle angle of the grades to the turnaround point just under 4 miles from the start at UT 83. When you reach this point, reverse direction and head back.

Option: If you would like to make a loop route out of this ride, go right when you reach UT 83, onto the highway, and head south, parallel-

Setting up camp on BLM lands near Golden Spike National Historic Site where thousands of rail workers once lived in makeshift towns.

DENNIS COELLO

ing the deteriorating railroad grade that now resides on private property. Go south on this road for approximately 2.5 miles before turning right again onto CR 504. It is another 3.5 miles northwest on this road to the parking area at the Big Fill Walk trailhead. Total distance for this option is approximately 10 miles.

For mountain bikes. This ride follows a dirt road that runs between the two railroad beds, then makes a loop to return via the Central Pacific grade. The total distance for this out-and-back ride with a loop at the end is 14 miles. The route actually descends as you ride west, losing approximately 400 feet of elevation over the first 6 miles. Novice and intermediate riders in good physical condition should have little difficulty along this route, though, which requires no technical riding skills.

Starting point: Visitors center.

Length: 14 miles. Allow at least 3 hours to complete the ride.

Riding surface: Dirt road and old railroad bed.

Difficulty: Moderate to easy. A few hundred feet of elevation change and the longer distance make this ride slightly more difficult.

Scenery/highlights: This route wraps around the southern end of the North Promontory Mountains. The clean silhouettes of these barren Great Basin mountains, the solitude of wide-open country, and significant historical past of this area make for a rewarding biking experience. Along the way you'll pass the marker celebrating the point where 10 miles of finished track were laid in a single day by Central Pacific workers. You will also follow the final miles of grade built by thousands of immigrant hands during an era when work was scarce and life was cheap.

Best time to ride: Almost anytime spring through fall. Ride in the cooler hours of morning and evening to avoid the hottest part of the day.

Special considerations: Water and rest rooms are available at the visitors center. You will be sharing this route with vehicles, so stay to the right-hand side of the road and ride in single file.

From the visitors center ride out to your left, following the dirt road that runs between the two railroad grades. Pedal along in this direction, passing Kings Peak (5,666 feet) on your right. In 3.2 miles the road jogs south and crosses over the Union Pacific grade. Continue following this road west as it parallels the railroad grades for another 1.5 miles, and then heads straight while the railroad grades bend away and head north.

FLORA

The area surrounding Golden Spike National Historic Site is classified as Great Basin Desert. It is not as dry or as hot as many other deserts. Despite the 18 inches of annual precipitation, vegetation is exceedingly sparse. This is in part due to the saline content of the soils, which are generally poor, and the extremes of hot and cold in summer and winter. This kind of desert is actually salt–desert shrub.

The main types of vegetation in the park are sagebrush, saltbush, and grasses. A few Utah junipers grow on the slopes of the mountains. Indian rice grass and bluebunch wheat grass are quite common, as are four-wing saltbush, greasewood, and big sagebrush. Rabbitbrush, which erupts in a mass of golden blooms in fall, is also common.

In spring the small purple blooms of wild onion abound, as do those of the sagebrush bluebell. A small, endangered plant called the Pasley onion is similar to the purple onion, but its blooms are white. The exquisite creamy white cup-shaped flowers of the sego lily, Utah's state flower, grow low to the ground and are numerous in the park during spring. Later in the spring and summer you might see the blazing red skyrocket, or scarlet gilia, blooming, along with clumps of paintbrush, the yellow of threadleaf groundsel, a white or lavender morning glory, or the small yellow blooms of the fetid marigold. Woolly pod locoweed is a pinkish purple and globe mallow, which blooms later in the season, is orange. The western sunflower parades happy faces of brown and gold along roadsides in the park beginning in late July.

Follow the dirt road west-southwest for another mile past the spot where it leaves the railroad grade, passing a road that forks off to the left, to where the road makes an almost 90-degree turn and heads north.

Continue following the dirt road as it makes an almost 90-degree turn and heads north to rejoin the Union Pacific grade in 1.5 miles. Ride north on this grade for a few hundred feet to the start of the West Grade Auto Tour. Go right onto the tour route, doubling back and heading south on the Central Pacific grade. You follow the Central Pacific grade as it heads south, wraps around the southern end of the North Promontory Mountains, and turns east, toward the visitors center. Approximately 3 miles from the point where you doubled back on the Central Pacific grade you reach the sign marking the spot where 10 miles of track laid in a single day came to an end. From here it is approximately 3.6 miles back to the center.

---

35. PROMONTORY POINT ROAD (See map on page 180)

For road bikes. The ride out the Promontory Point Road is a wonderfully scenic, mostly level tour south along the eastern shore of a peninsula jutting into the Great Salt Lake. A branch of the Promontory Mountains forms the spine of the peninsula, which reaches almost 30 miles into the lake from the northern shore. Although this route is mostly level with only a few slight changes in elevation, the overall distance is long and will make the ride difficult for all but the seasoned road rider.

Starting point: Visitors center. If you would like to shorten this ride by 11 miles, drive to the start of the Promontory Point Road. To get there drive approximately 5.5 miles east on CR 504, the main road that accesses the park, to a Y intersection. The Promontory Point Road is also CR 522. Park off the road near this intersection.

Length: 54 miles total distance out and back; from the beginning of the Promontory Point Road, approximately 43 miles. Allow 4 to 5 hours.

Riding surface: Pavement.

Difficulty: Moderate to difficult.

Scenery/highlights: The views to the east across Bear River Bay to the Wasatch Range are wonderful, as are the vistas south across the lake to the mountainous desert islands that dot its surface. Fremont Island is just off the tip of the point; farther south is Antelope Island, now designated a state wildlife park, where a healthy herd of bison roams. Also to the east across Bear River Bay is the Bear River Migratory Bird Refuge, a critical stopover and nesting area for millions of birds. As many as 60 different bird species use the refuge. A visitors center for the refuge is located in Brigham City, where you can pick up a bird list before heading out to drive, or pedal, around a 4-mile gravel loop.

Ride 35 • Promontory Point Road Trail

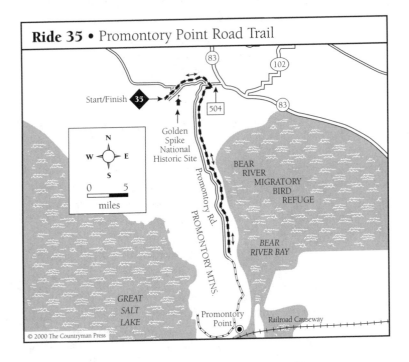

Best time to ride: Anytime spring through fall. Winds can be strong out of the south in the spring and also in late summer and fall. Summers are hot out here. If you are visiting anytime June through early September, you may want to plan on an early-morning or evening ride.

Special considerations: The nearest water and rest rooms are located at the visitors center inside the park. Be sure to bring plenty of water and some high-energy snacks to keep you going.

From the visitors center you ride north for 1 mile before going right onto CR 504, the main road that accesses the park from the east. Pedal approximately 4.5 miles to a Y intersection where CR 522 (Promontory Point Road) splits off and heads west, then south. Turn right onto this road, almost doubling back, and ride it as it continues west for less than a mile before swinging south toward Promontory Point. You pedal southward through open, desolate salt and mud flats for most of the next 10 miles before reaching the shore of the lake.

FAUNA

The Swainson's hawk is one of the most common resident raptors, but red-tailed and marsh hawks (also referred to as northern harriers) are quite common, too. Short-eared owls come out to hunt in the evening and are sometimes sighted in the morning, but the smaller burrowing owl can be seen almost anytime during the day. Around the visitors center you are likely to see both cliff and barn swallows, as well as ash-throated flycatchers, Brewer's blackbirds (which sometimes like to chase visitors), and sage thrashers. When you're out in the open away from the center you may hear and see meadowlarks, horned larks, gray partridges, sage grouse, sharp-tailed grouse, and chukars. Both the sage and the sharp-tailed grouse are considered endangered, as is the burrowing owl. Visitors regularly spot the California seagull, a year-round resident of northern Utah and the Utah state bird. The California seagull is honored by the state because flocks of them saved the Mormons' first harvest from the ravages of swarming grasshoppers.

Cottontails and black-tailed jackrabbits are very common in the country surrounding the park; less common are long-tailed weasels, badgers, and yellow-bellied marmots. Mule deer, coyotes, and pronghorn antelope are regularly seen in proximity to the park, and every now and then you might see a bobcat. Great Basin rattlesnakes are usually seen in the morning when they come out to sun themselves, while Great Basin gopher snakes can be seen almost anytime of day. Great Basin whiptail lizards are also fairly common around the park.

For the next 12 miles you ride between the steep eastern flank of the Promontory Mountains and the briny shores of the Great Salt Lake, pushing hard on your pedals only now and again where the road lifts you over a knoll. In springtime the lake level can rise to lap at the very edge of the road, but later in the fall you will be looking out across several hundred feet of mudflats to the water. Approximately 22 miles from the turn onto the Promontory Point Road the pavement turns to dirt and gravel. If you have wider touring tires and want to keep riding, the road continues another 17.5 miles to the tip and beyond, up the west side of the point a short distance. Otherwise, turn around when you reach the dirt road and head back the way you came.

CAMPING

There are no camping facilities located at Golden Spike National Historic Site, but you'll find two private campgrounds near Brigham City and almost unlimited camping in the nearby Wasatch-Cache National Forest. For private campgrounds in Brigham City, try the **Golden Spike RV Park** (435-723-8858), or the **Brigham City KOA** (435-723-5503) located 4 miles south on US 89. Both have a store, showers, and laundry facilities.

LODGING

There are a few options in Brigham City, including a **Crystal Inn** (where kids under 16 stay free), a **Howard Johnson,** and the **Galaxie Inn.** You have many more options 20 miles south in Ogden. Here you'll find a good selection of chain hotels including two **Best Westerns,** a **Holiday Inn,** a **Super 8,** and a **Motel 6.** Other options include the **Comfort Suites** of Ogden, the **Western Colony Inn,** and the bargain-rate **Millstream Inn.** One of the best options is the **Historic Radisson Suite Hotel** located directly across the street from the old Union Pacific Station, which also houses the Ogden-Weber Convention and Visitors Bureau Information Center. The architecture, ambience, location, and two good restaurants all make this an excellent choice for accommodations if you don't mind paying a little bit more.

FOOD

In Brigham City you'll find a handful of choices other than fast food, among them the **Idle Isle Restaurant** (24 S. Main St.), an ice cream parlor that serves sandwiches and soups for lunch and traditional American fare for dinner. The **Maddox Ranch House** (1900 S. US 89) is a steak-and-potatoes kind of place, and **Bert's Family Café** (89 S. Main St.) has got a little bit of everything American. **Old Ephraim's Grille, Hunan Village,** and the **Dixie Grill** are other possibilities all located on Main Street in Brigham City.

If you're staying in Ogden and looking for a hearty breakfast to get you going, try **Chick's Café** (319 24th St.) or the **Tamarack Restaurant** (1254 W. 21st St.). If you're in a hurry, you can get a great cup of coffee and a pastry to go at the **Daily Grind** (252 25th St.). The **Union Grill** (2501 Wall Ave.), **Rooster's 25th St. Brewing Company,** and the **Cajun Skillet** (2250 Washington Blvd.) are all great choices for a meal, but if you're looking for something special try the **Graycliff Lodge** (508 Ogden Canyon), which serves a variety of seafoods and steaks in a lovely setting. **La Ferrovia Ristorante** (210 25th St.) is the choice for Italian food.

IT'S INTERESTING TO KNOW . . .

Towns and tent cities sprang up along the tracks wherever the railroad passed through. The one-street towns that popped out of the desert at Promontory Summit, just outside the park, and at Junction City where the park's paved road intersects UT 83, were short lived. The town at Promontory Summit existed for only six months before railroad operations moved to Junction City, and then to Ogden. The majority of the many workers who followed the rails drifted away when the work was done, only a few staying to settle. Many of the people who rode the rails out West looking for a place to settle actually came with encouragement from the railroad companies.

As the dream of a transcontinental railroad was about to come true, the savvy businessmen who backed the project realized that the key to turning a profit in the future was creating a demand for their services. They needed goods and people to ship back and forth to make money once the railroad was completed, but they couldn't do it without land. Rail barons became land barons in the years immediately following the completion of the railroad, as they scooped up the land grants that were becoming available to the public. In this way they could offer cheap land, establish communities on the landscape, and guarantee themselves a demand for goods and travelers. All across the East and in Europe, they advertised arid desert lands as a fertile Eden, coaxing unknowing immigrants and yeoman farmers to come find their future. Many faced dreadful hardships as a result of such boosterism, but most survived to find their way in the West.

LAUNDRY

Other than the two private campgrounds in Brigham City try:

Hardy Enterprises, 249 N. Main St.; (435) 723-9000

In Ogden try:

Marta's Laundry, 2182 Pingree Ave.; (801) 625-0825

Ray's Coin-Op Laundromat, 2590 Monroe Blvd.; (801) 627-2197

BIKE SHOP/BIKE RENTAL

You can get most of your bicycle needs taken care of in Brigham City, but if you want to rent a bike you will need to go to Ogden, just 20 miles south.

IN BRIGHAM CITY

Loveland's Cycle, 352 N. Main St.; (435) 734-2666

Mountainland Outdoor, 80 S. Main St.; (435) 734-2660

IN OGDEN

Bingham Cyclery, 3259 Washington Blvd.; (801) 399-4981

The Bike Shoppe, 4390 Washington Blvd.; (801) 476-1600

Kent's Sports Store, 307 Washington Blvd.; (801) 394-8487

Miller's Ski & Cycle Haus, 834 Washington Blvd.; (801) 392-3911

DON'T MISS

Completed in 1924, the cavernous Union Station building saw as many as 120 trains a day by the mid-1940s. The station was restored in 1978 when several large murals were painted on the lobby walls. The South Mural depicts Chinese immigrant laborers working on the Central Pacific line, while the North Mural shows scenes of workers laying rail for the Union Pacific line from the east. You will also find the Ogden-Weber Convention and Visitors Bureau Information Center located here. The Wattis-Dumke Railroad Museum, found in the north end of Union Station, has several detailed exhibits and displays depicting how trestles, fills, and culverts were constructed, as well as eight model trains, a wonderful collection of old photographs, and a documentary film about the building of the transcontinental railroad. When you're done take a stroll down historic 25th Street.

FOR FURTHER INFORMATION

Golden Spike National Historic Site—Superintendent, P.O. Box 897, Brigham City, UT 84302; (435) 471-2209 (for visitors information, use extension 18 or 21); http://www.nps.gov/gosp/

Ogden-Weber Convention and Visitors Bureau Information Center, in Union Station at Wall Ave. and 25th St., Ogden, UT 84401; (801) 627-8288 or (800) ALL-UTAH

Wasatch-Cache National Forest, Forest Service Information Center at Union Station, or Ogden Ranger District Office, 507 25th St., Ogden, UT 84401; (435) 625-5112

7

In September 1996 President Bill Clinton set aside 1.9 million acres of south-central Utah's banded cliffs, high plateaus, wind- and time-worn pinnacles and buttes, and gracefully carved sandstone canyons and called it Grand Staircase–Escalante National Monument. Distinct topographies divide the monument into three parts: the cliffs of the Grand Staircase in the west, the massive Kaiparowits Plateau at center, and the canyons of the Escalante River to the east. Despite their differences they share several important qualities, including remoteness unrivaled in America's Lower 48 states, vast emptiness, and uncompromising wildness expressed in the enormous distances, exceedingly rough and unforgiving terrain, and the undisturbed habitats.

Stepping back and away to the north from the depths of the Grand Canyon are a series of cliff-rimmed terraces that rise to the Paunsaugunt and Markagunt Plateaus, home to Bryce Canyon National Park and Cedar Breaks National Monument. The Vermilion, White, Gray, and Pink Cliffs stack upon one another from south to north, exposing 200 million years of the earth's history in great swaths of color. The deep reds of Wingate sandstone form the ramparts of the Vermilion Cliffs, with aprons of pastel-hued Chinle formation flaring away from their bases. These Triassic-period deposits contain fossils from fish and dinosaurs when this area was tropical and covered with shallow seas. The Navajo sandstone of the White Cliffs above is composed of billions of frosted white sand grains deposited in great waves of blowing dunes. Above the Jurassic period's white Navajo sandstone cliffs are the younger, softer shales of the Gray Cliffs, deposited during the Cretaceous period when this region was an expanse of oceans and river deltas. Seashells, shark's teeth, and marsh plants preserved in beds of coal are routinely found in these layers. The Pink Cliffs form the crowning stair of the Grand Staircase and were created by limy siltstones that deposited in a freshwater lake, the same geologic happenstance that formed the brilliant pink amphitheaters at Cedar Breaks and Bryce Canyon. The Paria River, draining off the Paunsaugunt Plateau and flowing into the Colorado River in the Grand Canyon, has carved a series of narrow canyons, isolated buttes, and mesas into the staircase of cliffs.

Farther east the enormous gray-green Kaiparowits Plateau extends south in a triangle with the town of Escalante at its apex. The more than 800,000 acres of the plateau form the highest, driest, and most remote part of the monument. The rich fossil deposits of the Kaiparowits are regarded by many geologists as the best record of late Cretaceous life found anywhere in the world. The plateau is a land of twisted dry canyons, sheer cliffs, red hills of oxidized rock created by underground coal fires, and noxious salt- and lime-laden soils where plants refuse to grow.

The Straight Cliffs, stretching north and south for 42 miles, form the eastern boundary of the Kaiparowits Plateau. They step down to Fifty-Mile Bench and to the vast stretch of cream to pale peach-colored Navajo sandstone farther east, carved into a maze of canyons by the Escalante River. Among the beautifully water-sculpted twists and turns of these canyons you'll find lush riparian woodlands of cottonwoods, box elders, and willows, and hear only the sound of burbling water, desert breezes, and the lovely banter of songbirds.

There is much to see and do in Grand Staircase–Escalante National Monument, and no small amount of effort is required to become fully familiar with its many secrets, but even a short time spent appreciating these lands will reward you with a spirit refreshed and new appreciation of the power of wild places. This monument is managed not by the National Park Service, but by the Bureau of Land Management, which continues to allow hunting, grazing, and other traditional activities to take place on monument lands.

A cyclist enjoys the solitude and scenery along the Burr Trail.

Cycling in the Park

Because of the enormous size of this monument, the gargantuan proportions of the geographic features, and the tremendous distances between points, there are very few short, easy bike rides to take here, and no central location that provides access to the routes that do exist. There are five main routes that traverse the monument, four running north-south and one, the Burr Trail, running east-west through the northeast corner of the monument. These roads take the adventurous deep into the heart of the monument.

There are many opportunities for exploring the monument on two wheels, including the 78-mile-long Smoky Mountain Road, a graded dirt-and-gravel road with sections that requires a high-clearance vehicle and a good map. Traveling any of these routes as a multiday adventure, either by yourself or with a vehicle, requires that you come fully prepared to camp, bringing all the water, food, and equipment that you will need. Vehicles supporting cyclists should be in good working order and full of fuel before heading into the backcountry. Virtually all of these roads

CYCLING OPTIONS

There are six rides listed in this chapter; one is a road ride, and the other five are mountain-bike rides. An easy 12-mile (total) trip to the Paria movie set and the cemetery and old town site of Pahreah is suitable for the whole family. The road ride out to Kodachrome Basin and the fantastic rock pinnacles and spires found there (total distance 20 miles) and is a great beginning-to-intermediate road ride. The Wolverine Loop Road, off the Burr Trail, takes you to the Wolverine Petrified Wood Area and through a gorgeous circuit of desert surrounded by the Circle Cliffs. This is a 38-mile ride best suited for intermediate-to-advanced riders in good-to-excellent condition.

The last 18 miles of the Hole-in-the-Rock Road—the historic route traveled by Mormon pioneers in their push to cross the Colorado River and settle southeastern Utah—make a great 36-mile day trip that is also best for intermediate and advanced riders with good levels of fitness and stamina. The Cottonwood Canyon Road (47 miles) and the Johnson Canyon–Skutumpah Road (65 miles) are described as one-way routes for 1-day or multiday vehicle-supported rides. There are possibilities for riding out and back on these roads as simple day rides.

---

become impassable when wet due to the fine clay content in the soils. Drink plenty of fluids before, during, and after your ride to prevent the pounding headaches, fatigue, and sometimes nausea that result from exerting yourself in the desert.

---

36. PARIA CANYON MOVIE SET AND GHOST TOWN OF PAHREAH (See map on page 191)

For mountain bikes. This ride is a great adventure that takes you to the brilliantly colored formations of Paria Canyon and the picturesque set that has been featured in such films as Clint Eastwood's *The Outlaw Josey Wales*. A little farther up the canyon is the Pahreah town cemetery, and just across the river lie the meager remains of the town of Pahreah. This ride is well suited for beginning and intermediate riders in good physical condition, but riders of all abilities will enjoy the sights of Paria Canyon.

Starting point: The junction of the Paria Canyon Road and US 89. To get there drive approximately 45 miles east of Kanab on UT 89. Turn left on a well-marked dirt road. You will see a historical marker with a parking area on your left. Park here.

Length: 12 miles out-and-back. Allow at least 4 hours to pedal the distance and spend some time at the movie set and the town site.

Riding surface: Dirt road. The first 5 miles are graded and maintained but can become rough after rain. The last mile is a rougher jeep road.

Difficulty: Easy to moderate. For its first 5 miles the road is mostly level, but then it drops down a steep hill into Paria Canyon, adding an element of difficulty to an otherwise easy ride that requires little technical riding ability.

Scenery/highlights: Paria Canyon is a gorgeous, multicolored swath cut by the Paria River, which drains the Paunsaugunt and Table Cliff Plateaus to the north. Hoodoos and spires decorate the canyon rims in intriguing shapes and colors. *Paria* is a Paiute word meaning "muddy water," and when you see the river you'll know why. Where it flows into the Colorado River, just a few miles below Lees Ferry, it can sometimes turn that now clear, green stretch of water red, especially after heavy storms.

A plaque near the old movie set explains the history of the site, first built for a movie called *Sergeants Three* starring Frank Sinatra. The aura of the Old West is thick about the place. Continue on past the movie set to the Pahreah town cemetery to view the humble monuments to the hearty pioneers who struggled to eke out an existence here. What little remains of the town site lies across the river; please use caution when you cross the river.

Best time to ride: Spring and fall, when temperatures are more moderate. Avoid heading out here if the ground is saturated due to heavy rains; the sticky mud that results will adhere to everything it contacts.

Special considerations: Near the old movie set there are picnic tables and rest rooms but not running water. Be sure to bring plenty of water.

You must cross the river to get to the old town site It's not recommended that you ford the river on your bike to get to the ghost town,

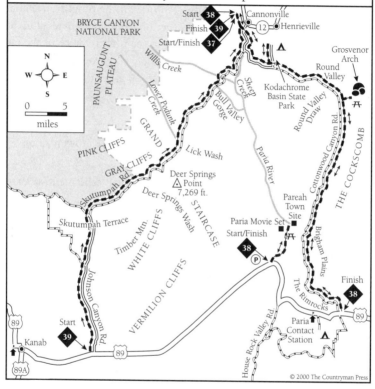

especially if thunderstorms are in the area or the river is swollen with spring runoff. Walk your bike across or, better yet, just leave it on the near side and walk over to see what's left of Pahreah.

From the parking area off US 89 ride out onto the dirt Paria Valley River Road and head north. For the first few miles you pedal north through wide-open country with sweeping views to the western edge of the

Kaiparowits on your right, and to the ramparts of the Vermilion Cliffs on your left. To the north the grayish promontory of Mollies Nipple (7,271 feet) rises above surrounding terrain. After 4 miles of mostly level north-ward progress, the road drops steeply into Paria Canyon.

Interesting rock formations in a multitude of hues abound. At the bottom of the hill on your left is the old Paria movie set. Stop there have a look around. When you are ready, continue on the rougher, unmaintained dirt road that continues for another mile past the movie set to the Pahreah town cemetery. If you are dying to see what remains of the old town site, you must cross the river. It is best to walk across and leave your bike behind. When you are done having a look around, head south . . . outta town.

---

37. KODACHROME BASIN STATE PARK (See map on page 191)

For road bikes. This ride takes you from the small settlement of Cannonville to geologic wonders found in Kodachrome Basin State Park. A mysterious series of geologic events took place to create the 67 brilliant-ly colored pillars that stand in this basin, some of which are 170 feet tall. The area is protected as a state park where you'll find a developed campground with a good complement of facilities. Beginning and intermediate road riders will enjoy this tour, which has a few hill climbs and some rolling terrain but is not very difficult.

Starting point: Cannonville, 5 miles south of Tropic on UT 12. Park in town.

Length: Just under 10 miles each way, approximately 20 miles total out-and-back. Allow 3 to 4 hours to ride the distance and spend some time hiking the trails in the park.

Riding surface: Pavement.

Difficulty: Easy to moderate. This route is mostly level with just a few changes in elevation.

Scenery/highlights: The 67 rock pinnacles found in and around Kodachrome Basin State Park are referred to in geologic terms as sand pipes. These strange yet beautiful pink-and-white-striped, candylike formations range in size from 6 to almost 170 feet. One of the most widely accepted theories holds that at some time in the distant past, possibly in Cretaceous or Tertiary times, shifting faults caused water and sediments deep underground to liquefy. Whether the intense pressure created when the faults moved forced the mixture upward into the shape of these columns, or they simply liquefied and then solidified in place, is uncertain. Particles of quartz, calcite, feldspar, and clay make up the sand pipes, which were left standing when surrounding rock eroded away. Most of the exposed rock in the park is Entrada sandstone; the lower orange layer is the Gunsight Butte Member of this group, while the white-and-orange-striped layer is called the Cannonville Member. Signs with fanciful names identify the permanent labels of some of these pinnacles.

Best time to ride: Spring and fall; if you have to ride around here in the summer, plan for a morning or evening ride.

Special considerations: There isn't much in Cannonville, but you will find most conveniences in Tropic. The campground at Kodachrome Basin State Park has bathrooms and drinking water. This is a good option for camping, as there are laundry and shower facilities available. There are also picnic tables and grills, making this a good place to have lunch.

Bring a lock along on this ride so you can secure your bike while you walk one of several trails taking you out among the rock chimneys.

From the town of Cannonville head south on the Cottonwood Canyon Road, following signs for Kodachrome Basin State Park. For the first 3 miles the road traces the upper Paria River drainage before reaching the junction with the dirt Skutumpah Road. Past this junction the road swings east, crossing over the stream course and climbing out of the Paria River drainage. For the next 4.5 miles the road rolls along gently through wide-open country, bringing you to the turnoff for Koda-chrome Basin. Go left to ride just over 2 miles to the park (the dirt Cottonwood Canyon Road continues straight ahead). After you've had some lunch and taken a walk among the bizarre forest of pinnacles here, mount up and head back the way you came.

FLORA

The canyons of the Escalante River harbor rich riparian habitats where several rare, endemic plants make their home. The upper Sonoran life zone (3,500 to 5,500 feet) and transition life zone (5,500 to 8,000 feet) are inclusive of the entire monument. As is true across most of Utah, piñon-juniper woodlands dominate in the upper Sonoran and parts of the transition life zones. Gambel oak and shrubs such as Oregon grape, ephedra (also called Mormon tea for its stimulating effects and its use by the pioneers), buffalo-berry, rabbitbrush, big sagebrush, and yucca are also common. Ponderosa and bristlecone pines can be found at the highest points of the Kaiparowits, and in the very northeastern corner of the monument high on the slopes of Boulder Mountain white fir, blue spruce, and Douglas fir exist.

Rocky Mountain maple and big-tooth maple occur in some of the moister areas while trees like box elder, water birch, velvet ash, and Fremont cottonwood inhabit the riparian corridors of the Escalante drainage system. In these wet riparian areas you can expect to find willows, pussy-toes, cattails, and perhaps even the spectacular helleborine orchid. The endemic Paria iris, delicate ladies'- tresses, and asparagus also grow along streambanks here. Sego lilies, the Utah state flower, and its orange cousin the golden mariposa lily can be found in spring, along with several species of wild onions, blooming purple to white. Arnica, slickrock paintbrush, several species of daisies, and blanketflowers are some of the showiest bloomers in early summer, but when fall rolls around rabbitbrush, snakeweed, aster, and sunflower steal the show.

Cryptobiotic crusts are another form of plant life ubiquitous in the monument. This knobby, black crust covering the soil is made up of fungi, lichens, algae, mosses, and bacteria living together in a symbiotic relationship, each benefiting from their mutual coexistence. Cryptobiotic crusts are the foundation of life in the desert due to their ability to prevent erosion, stabilize soils, retain moisture, and provide nutrients to plants struggling to survive. This living crust is extremely fragile; once it has been crushed by a footstep or bike tire, it turns to dust. Recovery and regrowth of cryptobiotic crusts takes decades. Although bikes are not permitted off established roads, there is no prohibition on where you can walk. Try to stay in washes, on slickrock, and on foot trails.

For mountain bikes. This road, one of the main north-south routes through the monument, is best ridden as a one-way vehicle-supported trip. The road extends between US 89 in the south and the town of Cannonville on UT 12 in the north for 47 miles. For much of the way it follows one of the most striking geologic features in the monument, the Cockscomb—an enormous double row of tilted rock that juts out of the desert like shark's teeth. Running parallel to these rock fins is Cottonwood Canyon, where an intermittent creek creates a corridor of lush vegetation that is a magnet for desert bird and animal life. The route through Cottonwood Canyon loses elevation from north to south. A high-clearance, four-wheel-drive vehicle is recommended for traveling this road.

Starting point: The town of Cannonville on UT 12, at the north end of the road. The road can be traversed in either direction, but going from north to south allows you to ride downhill.

Length: 47 miles one way. Take 1, 2, or even 3 days to travel this route.

Riding surface: Pavement, dirt road; sections can get very washboarded. There are many wash crossings that sometimes contain water.

Difficulty: Easy to strenuous, depending on how much of these 47 miles you choose to ride at a time. A few sections are lumpy and rocky, but very little of this route requires more than a beginning-to-intermediate level of technical riding ability.

Scenery/highlights: There are several interesting stops to make as you start out on this route. Kodachrome Basin State Park is home to a fantastic collection of pinnacles, geologically defined as sand pipes, created under pressure by shifting faults. The pink, orange, and white layers that color these pinnacles make many of them look like candy canes. Grosvenor Arch, located 17 miles from the start of the Cottonwood Canyon Road on UT 12, is a stunning double arch with the two spans spreading almost at right angles from one another. The larger of the two spans is 99 feet across. The Cockscomb is the northern extension of the East Kaibab monocline, a huge flexure in the earth's crust caused by faulting. Stretching all the way from Canaan Peak (9,293 feet) north of Henrieville to the Arizona border, the Cockscomb extends along this route for 15 miles. Cottonwood Canyon is lovely and has many good spots for camping along the creek beneath shady cottonwood trees.

Best time to ride: Spring or fall.

Special considerations: This road becomes impassable when wet, even for powerful, high-clearance, four-wheel-drive vehicles. The high clay content of the soils turns the surface of these roads into a slimy mess. Do not head out this way if the ground is saturated or if heavy rains are forecast. If you do get stuck out here in a storm, stay put and wait until the road surface has had a chance to dry out. Also, be very careful crossing washes if water is in them; vehicles often become stuck in wash sediments that can turn into a quicksandlike substance.

Be sure to come prepared for this remote and rugged backcountry. It's always a good idea to start out with more fuel, water, and food than you think you'll need. There are no facilities of any kind once you pass Kodachrome Basin State Park. Drinking water, rest rooms, showers, and laundry facilities are available at the park.

The first 7.5 miles of this route as you head south are paved. Past the turnoff for Kodachrome Basin State Park, the Cottonwood Canyon Road becomes dirt. As the road continues east, it traverses the yawning expanse of Round Valley, climbs up Slickrock Bench, and dips across Round Valley Draw and into Butler Valley as it begins to swing south and drop into Cottonwood Canyon. Almost 13 miles from Kodachrome Basin you come to the turnoff for Grosvenor Arch. It is 1 mile from the main road to see the arch.

Back en route the road drops into Cottonwood Canyon, which it follows in almost a straight line for the next 15 miles. At the end of the canyon the Paria River comes in from the west, cutting across the spine of the Cockscomb. For the next 8 miles the road follows the river south between its east bank and the eroded slopes of a low terrace called the Brigham Plains. For the last 5 miles of the route the road swings southeast and traces the outline of a bench called the Rimrocks through somewhat bleak badlands before dropping down to US 89, 10 miles west of the town of Big Water.

39. JOHNSON CANYON–SKUTUMPAH ROAD (See map on page 191)

For mountain bikes. This road can be ridden in either direction but is described here traveling south to north, primarily because of the fantastic views you'll get of Utah's forested high plateaus and salmon-colored rock amphitheaters. Although the grades are steady and the surface good, the road gains almost 1,400 feet in this direction. Skutumpah Road (pronounced "Skoot-UM-pah") is dirt and can be rough in places as it nears UT 12. The total distance of this route makes it best suited for a vehicle-supported 1-day or multiday trip. Using a vehicle as support allows you to tailor the difficulty of the ride to suit each cyclist's age, ability, and fitness level. Suggestions for shorter rides are given.

Starting point: The start of the Johnson Canyon Road east of Kanab, Utah. To get there drive east on US 89 from Kanab 15 miles and turn north onto the well-marked Johnson Canyon Road.

Length: Approximately 65 miles one way.

Riding surface: Pavement, sometimes-maintained dirt road; rough and washboarded in spots. The Skutumpah Road becomes extremely slippery when wet due to the high content of clays in the soil. Do not head out this way if the ground is saturated or heavy thunderstorms are forecast.

Difficulty: Easy to strenuous. Very little in the way of technical riding ability is required on this route, although sections of the Skutumpah Road roll up and down through washes and drainages, presenting several steep climbs. Be sure to slow down on descents where washboard is present; the bouncing and vibration can send your bike skidding out of control. If you use a vehicle for support, you can make the ride as easy or as strenuous as you like by adjusting the distance you ride. If you are supporting yourself with panniers, it will be strenuous.

Scenery/highlights: Just over 5 miles up the canyon you will encounter the old movie set for the series *Gunsmoke* on the right-hand side of the road. The set is fenced off and not open to the public, but nonetheless makes for a wonderful trip down memory lane. As you pedal up the Johnson Canyon Road you ride out of the reds of the Vermilion Cliffs and traverse country bathed in the light buff-to-peach hues of Navajo sandstone. The route then climbs up through the White Cliffs and turns northeast, traversing the bench between the White and Gray Cliffs. The Pink Cliffs that rim the Paunsaugunt in brilliant peach limestones become visible to the west as you travel north, while the vast complex of drainages feeding the Paria River, terminating at the definitive boundary of the Cockscomb formation, spread away to the east.

Best time to ride: Spring and fall.

Special considerations: Sections of the Skutumpah Road can be rough and washboarded. There are several steep climbs and portions of the road where your view of oncoming traffic is poor. Please be aware of vehicle traffic and obey the rules of the road.

You'll find no facilities and nowhere to get drinking water along this route. Come prepared; make sure you start out hydrated with plenty of snacks and fluids. Your vehicle should have a full tank of gas and carry more food and water than you think you'll need. It will come in handy in the event of a breakdown or bad weather that has to be waited out.

Hiking the slot canyon known as Bull Valley Gorge is an excellent diversion from a long day in the saddle. Getting into the slot canyon is somewhat tricky, though, and might not be suitable for everybody. Do not enter the gorge if thunderstorms are in the area: A heavy storm up above can send torrents of water crashing down through this canyon with little warning. You may want to bring along a lock so you can explore the canyon without worrying about your bike.

From US 89 at Johnson Canyon begin pedaling the paved road up the canyon. Just over 2 miles from the start look for a small but elegant arch in the white cliffs of Navajo sandstone. The road winds up through light, buff-colored country dotted by piñon and juniper as you climb through Johnson Canyon. At 5 miles is the old Gunsmoke set; the 12-mile out-and-back trip to the set is a great outing for the whole family. The road gains steadily as it climbs toward the junction with the Skutumpah and Glendale Roads on the Skutumpah Terrace, 24 miles from US 89. You can end your trip here for a great road ride.

To continue, go right at this intersection, leaving the pavement, and

FAUNA

Despite the often barren appearance of the landscape inside Grand Staircase–Escalante National Monument, it is home to an impressive number of animals. An extensive bird list identifies 290 bird species living in the monument. One of the most significant is the recently reintroduced California condor, a species that is slowly making its way back from the brink of extinction. The bald eagle, peregrine falcon, Mexican spotted owl, and southwestern willow flycatcher are some of the other rare or endangered birds found here. Prairie falcons, northern harriers, and numerous hawk species, including Cooper's, ferruginous, red-tailed, rough-legged, sharp-shinned, and Swainson's, have all been sighted. Four species of hummingbirds are here: black-chinned, broad-tailed, Calliope, and rufous. The riparian areas of the Paria and the Escalante provide a haven for migrating songbirds, including bluebirds, buntings, finches, some 9 species of flycatchers, 15 species of sparrows, 6 species of vireos, 11 species of warblers, and 5 species of wrens. An incredible array of water-loving birds has been sighted in the park, including American avocets, cormorants, sandpipers, Sandhill cranes, great blue herons, white-faced ibises, tundra swans, and numerous varieties of ducks, coots, and grebes.

Small rodents, squirrels, and rabbits serve as a food source for birds, reptiles, and larger mammals. Badgers, bobcats, gray foxes, coyotes, and weasels depend on these smaller animals, while skunks, ringtail cats, raccoons, marmots, porcupines, and pikas prefer more vegetarian fare. Minks, muskrats, and beavers can all be found along river corridors. Rocky Mountain elk have been known to come down from Boulder Mountain but usually prefer higher, greener environments. Black bears sometimes come down from adjacent high country in the fall to feast on acorns. Desert bighorn sheep are among the most agile and mobile animals within the monument. There are also three species of rattlesnakes here, the Great Basin, Hopi, and midget faded. The resident Glen Canyon chuckwalla lizard, California kingsnake, Utah Mountain kingsnake, Utah night lizard, southwestern black-headed snake, Painted Desert glossy snake, Mojave patch-nosed snake, and plateau striped whiptail lizard are all listed in Utah as species of special consideration because of habitat decline.

begin the northeastern leg of your journey that will take you through high desert with expansive views, piñon-juniper forests, and ranchland. The White Cliffs drop away to their Vermilion counterpart to the south; to the north the Gray Cliffs step back to Pink Cliffs. This is the "Grand Staircase," and here it is awash in color. Timber Mountain, perched atop the White Cliffs, lies like a dark brow atop the light landscape to the southeast as you make your way north and east.

For the first 20 miles of the Skutumpah Road the route stays fairly level, dipping through Skutumpah Creek, Slide Canyon, Meadow Canyon, and Lower Podunk Creek. Where each of these drainages crosses the terrace you'll find evidence of small ranching operations, dependent on the meager amount of water and grass found in this country. At Lower Podunk Creek, an often dry wash almost 45 miles from the start, the road starts dropping toward Bull Valley Gorge and begins to twist and turn, rising and dropping over downcut ridges. Nine miles farther a narrow bridge spans the gorge and Papoose Creek that worked to form it, allowing vehicles and cyclists to cross over. The bottom of the gorge can be accessed by hiking alongside the drainage upstream a short distance to the point where you can scramble down into the canyon. Do not enter this slot canyon if thunderstorms are anywhere in the area. Slot canyons can flood with a crushing volume of water in seconds with no advance warning.

At a high point beyond Bull Valley Gorge you get a fantastic view of the lofty 10,189-foot Powell Point on the Table Cliff Plateau, one of the highest and most spectacular viewpoints in southern Utah's plateau country. From here the road drops toward Willis Creek, climbs again, and then drops to the Paria River Valley, reaching the paved road to Kodachrome Basin State Park about 4 miles south of Cannonville and UT 12. When you reach the paved road go left following the Paria River upstream through the top of Cottonwood Canyon to Cannonville.

If you are in the Tropic-Cannonville area, or perhaps coming from Bryce Canyon National Park, and looking for a mountain-bike ride that you can do as a simple day trip, consider riding from Cannonville out to Bull Valley Gorge. It is approximately 15 miles from UT 12 to the gorge, where you can hike in the slot canyon. The route twists, turns, and rolls and makes for a good intermediate-mountain-bike adventure.

For mountain bikes. This is a moderately difficult but fast-paced circuit through the northeastern portion of the monument. Besides stunning redrock scenery and breathtaking views into surrounding country, the Wolverine Loop Road takes you to the Wolverine Petrified Wood Natural Area, where you can see broken branches, partial rounds, and numerous fragments of ancient trees lying about the desert—solid stone reminders of the ancient environments that once blanketed this country. The longer distance, rolling terrain, and overall elevation gain make this ride suitable for riders in good to excellent physical condition who have some stamina. The entire route is on dirt roads, posing little in the way of technical challenges for cyclists. This route is a good candidate for an overnight self- or vehicle-supported trip. There are many good campgrounds along the way.

Starting point: The junction of the Burr Trail (Bullfrog Scenic Backway) and the Wolverine Road. To get there from the town of Boulder on UT 12, drive east on the Burr Trail for 19 miles to the western junction of the Wolverine Road. Park at this junction.

Length: 37-mile loop. Allow a day to ride this loop and spend time hiking out around the Wolverine Petrified Wood Natural Area.

Riding surface: Dirt road, pavement; stretches of sand through the washes.

Difficulty: Moderately difficult to strenuous. Although no real technical riding skills are required for this route, good physical conditioning and stamina are. Some technical riding ability will come in handy over the sections of sand near the mouth of the canyons.

Scenery/highlights: This road makes a circuit of a basin defined on the north, west, and south by the Circle Cliffs. The cliffs give way at the side canyons that coax water west to join the Escalante. To the east the basin is defined by a massive flexure in the earth's crust known as the Waterpocket Fold, existing just inside the shared boundary with Capitol Reef National Park. The hike out to the eroded band of rock where pieces

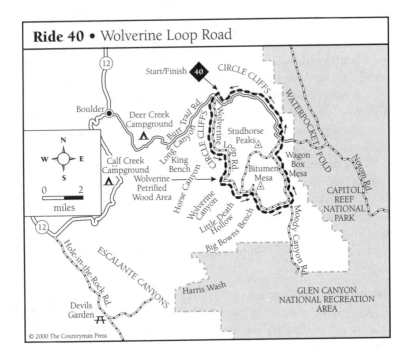

of petrified trees litter the ground is a wonderful momentary diversion from the many miles in the saddle.

Best time to ride: Spring and fall. Do not head out this way if the ground is saturated due to recent rains; the mud will adhere to your tires and bike parts, making them unusable. If you get caught out here in a storm, wait for a few hours until some evaporation has occurred.

Special considerations: There are no facilities out here of any kind, so come prepared. Make sure you have plenty of water, high-energy snacks, and fuel for your vehicle if you are doing this as a support trip.

Although you don't generally see a lot of people out here, you may want to bring a lock along this ride so you can secure your bike while you hike out to see the petrified wood area. Bikes are not allowed off developed roads and must be left at the parking area.

If you are interested in camping along this route, check in at the BLM offices in Escalante to get a list of areas suitable for camping.

From the junction with the Burr Trail head south on the Wolverine Loop Road. You will make good progress at first as the road slips gently off the flank of Boulder Mountain and into the desert. In 5.5 miles you cross a gulch marked as Horse Canyon. The road dips and rolls through several washes, continuing on a gentle descent for another 5 miles to the pullout for Wolverine Petrified Wood Area at the top of the Wolverine Canyon drainage. Park your bike, walk through a fence, and follow the lightly trod 1-mile trail through lumpy scrub-covered terrain as it parallels Wolverine Creek. Along the base of a multicolored, slope-forming layer belonging to the Chinle formation, you'll find broken pieces of an ancient forest lying all about. Please remember that removing or disturbing any naturally occurring or archaeological object on public lands is illegal.

Back on your bike, pedal eastward as the road begins to climb out of the Wolverine Creek drainage. After about a mile the road dips southward again as it heads toward the mouth of Death Hollow. As you cross over Death Hollow Wash the road again swings eastward and climbs. Two roads take off to your left over the next few miles, one of them striking out for Bitumen Mesa before you. The road climbs gradually from here to the intersection with the Moody Canyon Road approximately 18 miles from the start. This road accesses some of the spectacular lower canyons of the Escalante River, including Silver Falls Canyon. Stay left at this junction and pedal north toward the Burr Trail.

For the next 8 miles the road makes its way north along the base of Wagon Box Mesa, dipping through numerous wash depressions. You will arrive at the junction with the Burr Trail approximately 26 miles from the start. From here it is a relatively easy 11-mile downhill pedal to the junction where you left your car. As you ride west on the Burr Trail you first pass the modest forms of the Studhorse Peaks to your left, glide across the open expanse of White Canyon Flat, and descend toward the junction at Long Canyon to your vehicle.

Option: The Burr Trail is one of the most scenic backways through southern Utah and makes for a great vehicle-supported trip. The road is paved but primitive and narrow (no painted stripes) from where it leaves Capitol Reef National Park to the town of Boulder. Between these points it is approximately 34 miles of rolling terrain, spectacular views, and memorable desert scenery.

41. HOLE-IN-THE-ROCK ROAD (See map on page 205)

For mountain bikes. The Hole-in-the-Rock Road is the route taken in 1879 by 236 Mormon pioneers, 1,000 cattle, and 80 wagons on their way to settle southeastern Utah. Men were lowered in barrels over the edge of the cliff at the end of the road to blast a way through the rock down to the Colorado River, where they ferried across and began the same process to get up the other side. Miraculously, not a single animal, wagon, or life was lost on the 6-month journey. The entire length of the Hole-in-the-Rock Road—from where it leaves UT 12 just 5 miles east of the town of Escalante to a notch in the rock where Lake Powell sparkles below—is 57 miles. The first 38 miles are well-maintained dirt road easily driven by passenger cars. The last 18 miles, beginning at Dance Hall Rock, are rougher, and a good place to begin a cycling adventure. This is the route described here, although there are many options for making this a longer or shorter vehicle- or self-supported trip on the Hole-in-the-Rock Road. There are many good places to camp along the way. Intermediate-level riders with a good-to-excellent level of physical fitness can pedal this route with little difficulty provided they come prepared and have the stamina to endure a long day in the saddle.

Starting point: Dance Hall Rock, a large freestanding mound of sandstone on the left-hand side of Hole-in-the-Rock Road with one side hollowed out into a large cavern. Here, the story goes, pioneers danced to the music of fiddle players days before the harrowing descent through the "hole-in-the-rock." To get there drive UT 12 east from the town of Escalante 5 miles to the start of the Hole-in-the-Rock Road. Go right and drive south 38 miles to Dance Hall Rock. Park there.

Length: 37 miles out-and-back. This is an all-day affair if you are not camping along the way.

Riding surface: Dirt road; sections of washboard and sand.

Difficulty: Moderate to strenuous. The distance is by far the most challenging aspect, although there are several sections over slickrock near the end of this ride that require a good amount of technical skill.

Scenery/highlights: When you try to imagine a caravan of 80 wagons and 1,000 head of cattle bumping along this road, you begin to appreci-

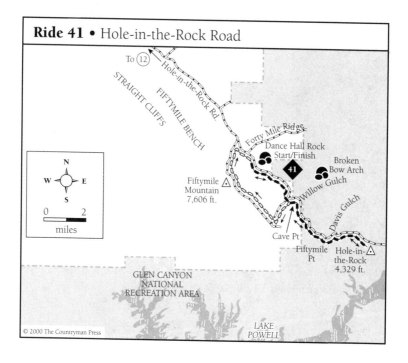

ate the tenacity and toughness of the early Mormon settlers. Given a directive, or order, from church headquarters in Salt Lake City to settle the fertile lands of southeastern Utah along the San Juan River, they dutifully began preparing for a journey they thought would take 6 weeks. In the fall of 1879 they struck out from the town of Escalante southward for lands unknown. They moved quickly over the first 50 miles but crept over the last 6. Sections of rough slickrock and sand slowed them down considerably. A 45-foot drop and almost three-quarters of a mile of steep slickrock down to the Colorado River awaited them at the end of the road. Men with picks and blasting powder lowered over the side opened a notch through the rock just wide enough for the wagons to fit through. It took 6 weeks of backbreaking labor to complete the road down to the river. The group then ferried across the Colorado River without incident on a large raft that had been built upstream and floated down to the crossing. After struggling up the far side of the canyon, they arrived at the future town site of Bluff, where they dug in and began the work of establishing a new city in the land of Zion.

Dennis Coello

A cyclist approaches the old movie set in Paria Canyon.

The vast expanse of desert that surrounds you as you travel south on this road is much the same as it was when the pioneers came through here 120 years ago, with the exception of the view at the end of the road: Where the silt-laden Colorado River once burbled along toward the Gulf of California stands now the quiet blue waters of Lake Powell. To the east extends a great expanse of pale rock—Navajo sandstone, sculpted by the canyon-forming rivulets feeding the Escalante River. To the west the Kaiparowits Plateau sprawls across the horizon, terminating in a well-defined band of rock jutting southward called the Straight Cliffs.

Best time to ride: Spring or fall. This road, and many of the side roads that access camping areas, become impassable in wet weather. Do not attempt to ride or drive on the Hole-in-the-Rock Road if there has been rain or if heavy thunderstorms are forecast.

Special considerations: This is very remote country, and you will find little in the way of facilities along the way. There are picnic tables and vault toilets at the Devils Garden pullout and parking area 12.5 miles south of UT 12, but that's it. Make sure you come prepared: Start out with a full gas tank, and enough food and water to last for several days.

As you head south along the Hole-in-the-Rock Road you'll want to stop at Devils Garden and make the short hike to see the fantastic shapes and colors of the hoodoos found there. Park at Dance Hall Rock, 26 miles farther down the road, and pedal southward on an easygoing dirt road. The phalanx of the Straight Cliffs accompanies you southward to the west, while pale peachy orange slickrock stretches away to the east. The road undulates as it dips through numerous sand washes, descending over the first 4 miles to the domed shapes of Sooner Rocks. At Sooner Rocks and again at Cave Point, another 4-plus miles down the road, the road actually forms the boundary between Grand Staircase–Escalante National Monument and adjoining Glen Canyon National Recreation Area.

The road continues to roll and dip over the terrain, becoming decidedly rougher in another 4 miles past Fifty-Mile Point. Here the road drops steeply over a ledge and the riding becomes more technical as the road crosses over sections of slickrock, drops off ledges, and traverses sections of loose, broken rock. At the end of the road in another 6 miles, where the cut drops away through the rock, you'll find a visitors registration box. Sign your name as proof you made the journey and then carefully make your way down through the blasted cut—you can still see drill holes, steps, and wagon-wheel marks—for a quick plunge in the lake. When you're properly refreshed head back the way you came.

Option: If you have a couple of days to ride, you might want to consider pedaling the Fifty-Mile Bench Road. You can make a 27-mile loop by connecting the Fifty-Mile Bench Road with the Hole-in-the-Rock Road. This loop can be ridden in either direction, but either way Dance Hall Rock makes a good starting point. You can pedal south, beyond Dance Hall Rock, approximately 6.5 miles and go right on the Fifty-Mile Bench Road. The route then climbs almost 2,000 feet on dirt and jeep roads up the Sooner Slide (a slide is an apron of eroded material) and contours the slopes below the Straight Cliffs as you head north. Fabulous views of the Escalante River drainage system, the Henry Mountains, and the sprawl of Glen Canyon National Recreation Area abound. The road then drops down Willow Tank Slide to rejoin the Hole-in-the-Rock Road, where you go right to ride back to Dance Hall Rock.

CAMPING

There are only two developed campgrounds within the monument; Calf Creek, along UT 12 between Escalante and Boulder, and Deer Creek, 6 miles east of Boulder on the Burr Trail Road. Picnic tables, grills, rest rooms, and water are available at each. **Calf Creek Campground** has 13 sites and is at the head of the Lower Calf Creek Falls Trail. There is a per-night fee and a separate day-use fee. **Deer Creek Campground** has 4 sites; a per-night camping fee is charged. The campgrounds are managed on a first-come, first-served basis. There is a 14-day stay limit at both.

Primitive camping is the most popular kind of camping in the monument but takes more planning and know-how. Driving and riding the back roads here make for very long days if you are not camping—which is also one of the best ways to experience what the monument has to offer. If you plan to travel any of the roads in the monument and are interested in camping, visit one of the monument's offices (Escalante or Kanab) to get information on backcountry camping techniques and requirements, a list of primitive campground locations, and updates about weather and road conditions.

The **Triple-S RV Park** on Main Street in Escalante has sites for tents and small cabins, plus a laundry and showers. The **Hitch'n Post RV Park** and the **Crazy Horse Campark,** both in downtown Kanab, have tent sites and showers. There are at least three private campgrounds in the Panguitch area, including the **Big Fish KOA,** the **Hitch-n-Post Campground,** both on Main Street in town, and **Sportsman's Paradise RV Park** north of town on US 89. All have sites for tents, plus laundry and showers. The **Bryce Pioneer Village Motel** in Tropic has tent sites and showers.

Kodachrome Basin State Park, south of UT 12 and Cannonville, has rest rooms and showers, and takes reservations. For more information call (435) 679-8562; for reservations, (800) 322-3770.

There are also many excellent

options for camping in the Dixie National Forest, adjacent to the monument. You'll find developed and primitive campgrounds, some at higher elevations where it is much cooler during summer.

LODGING

There is no lodging available inside the monument and never will be. In Escalante there's a handful of motels, including the **Prospector Inn,** which has a lounge and a restaurant; the **Moqui Motel,** with kitchenettes; and the **Circle D Motel,** where there is a restaurant and pets are welcome. The **Rainbow B&B** is another option in Escalante. In Boulder you'll find good, basic rooms at the **Cliff Palace Motel** or **Poole's Place,** but if you want something really special try the **Boulder Mountain Lodge.** The grounds, location, hospitality, and excellent food make this one of southeastern Utah's few destination lodges. There are several inns, motels, and at least half a dozen B&Bs in the little town of Tropic. The **World Host Bryce Valley Inn** has a restaurant that serves Mexican and American food three meals a day and has a liquor license. **Doug's Place Country Inn,** the **Bryce Pioneer Village Motel** (which also

has cabins), the **Under the Rim Inn,** and two B&Bs are your other choices in Tropic. In Kanab there is a **Super 8,** a **Holiday Inn Express,** and the **Red Hills Motel,** which is managed as a Best Western.

FOOD

The **Hell's Backbone Grill** inside the Boulder Mountain Lodge offers the best food you'll find anywhere in this neck of the woods. Summer through fall you can get a meal at the **Burr Trail Café** at the intersection of the Burr Trail and UT 12 in Boulder. In Escalante the **Cowboy Blues Diner and Bakery** serves three western-style meals a day, as does the **Circle D Restaurant,** but with a Mexican flair. The **Golden Loop Café** also serves three meals a day. The motels and inns in Tropic are where you can get a meal served to you, but you'll have to get your groceries in Boulder, Escalante, or Kanab. There are more options for places to eat in Kanab, including **Parry's Lodge,** which serves steaks, seafood, and continental fare three meals a day and while you eat you can look at hundreds of pictures of Hollywood's former greats. The **Chef's Palace Restaurant** offers prime rib, seafood, and American fare; it's also open to serve three meals a day. **Nedra's Too** serves both Mexican and American food in a friendly atmosphere, or you can try the **Wok Inn** if Szechuan cuisine is more your style. One of the best choices for a good, healthy home-cooked meal is **Best Friends Café,** associated with the internationally known animal shelter nearby. **Willow Creek Books & Coffee & Outdoor Gear** is a great place to get a cup of java; pick up a good book, field guide, or map; and get some advice.

LAUNDRY

Kanab Laundry & Car Wash, 260 E. 300 S., Kanab; (435) 644-5626

BIKE SHOP/BIKE RENTAL

In the small towns that surround the monument you won't find much in the way of bike shops.

Mountain Bike Heaven, 25 E. Center St., Panguitch; (435) 676-2880

IT'S INTERESTING TO KNOW . . .

The region that now includes Grand Staircase–Escalante National Monument has been the scene of some of the most bitter and hotly contested environmental debates in the West over the last 20 years. It began in the early 1980s with a fight over the Burr Trail, arguably one of the most scenic back roads in America. Local boosters wanted the road paved for boat-towing RVs heading to Bullfrog Marina on Lake Powell. Environmentalists argued that keeping the road in a more primitive condition was the key to preserving the wild and scenic qualities of the area—qualities that in the end would bring more stable economic health to local communities than the mining, logging, farming, and cattle ranching that had always sustained them. Conservative interests looking out for the rights and livelihood of local communities won that round, but local and national environmental organizations consistently work to curtail the traditional resource-extractive industries that impact the landscape, earning the ire of those who have made their living off the land for generations. Over the years increasing pressure on land managers by the most vocal and well-organized environmental groups have resulted in restrictions on timber sales, cutbacks in grazing allotments, and limitations on ORV (off-road vehicle) use.

Bike Zion, 445 Zion Park Blvd., Springdale; (435) 772-3929; http://www.bikezion.com/

FOR FURTHER INFORMATION

Grand Staircase–Escalante National Monument—Supervisor's Office, 337 S. Main St., Suite 010, Cedar City, UT 84720; (435) 865-5100; fax (435) 865-5170; http://www.ut.blm.gov/monument/

Grand Staircase–Escalante National Monument, Escalante Interagency Visitors Center, 755 W. Main St., Escalante, UT 84726; (435) 826-5499; escalant@ut.blm.gov (for information specific to the Escalante Canyons area)

Grand Staircase–Escalante National Monument, Kanab BLM Field Office, 318 N. First E., Kanab, UT 84741; (435) 644-2672

Garfield County Travel Council, P.O. Box 200, Panguitch, UT 84759; (800) 444-6689; http://www.escalante-cc.com

Kane County Travel Council, 78 S. 100 E., Kanab, UT 84741; (800) 733-5263; http://www.kaneutah.com

Dixie National Forest, Supervisor's Office, 82 N. 100 E., Cedar City, UT 84720; (435) 865-3700; www.fs.fed.us/dxnf

Dixie National Forest, Escalante Ranger District, 755 W. Main St., P.O. Box 246, Escalante, UT 84726; (801) 826-5400

DON'T MISS

Anasazi Village State Park, located just outside the town of Boulder, has an excavated ruin site and a museum full of interesting artifacts and exhibits explaining the life of the creative and highly religious ancient people who thrived in the area. For more than 700 years the Ancestral Puebloans farmed corn, beans, and squash in nearby fields before disappearing entirely between A.D. 1200 and 1300. Calf Creek Falls Recreation Area and the hike up to the 126-foot Lower Calf Creek Falls are a good introduction to hiking the canyons of the Escalante River. On the way to the falls you walk between high canyon walls of Navajo sandstone streaked with desert varnish, see ancient Indian petroglyphs and ruins, and cool off while the desert sun blazes overhead.

8

NATURAL BRIDGES NATIONAL MONUMENT

Unlike the famed stone arches that rise out of the redrock desert in Arches National Park, the natural stone spans found inside Natural Bridges National Monument connect chasms that drop away from a sandstone terrace into twisting canyons. Arches are created out of free-standing fins or bulges of rock that fracture and spall due to moisture and frost, whereas natural bridges are created by the forces of stream erosion. The three main bridges celebrated in this monument span the entrenched meanders of White and Armstrong Creeks and have been carved out of the beautiful buff-colored Cedar Mesa sandstone. While the streambeds that course beneath Sipapu, Kachina, and Owachomo Bridges remain dry most of the year, they can become raging torrents during heavy summer thunderstorms and spring runoff.

Some 260 million years ago the area that is now Natural Bridges was at the edge of a vast sea that covered most of eastern Utah. Constant breezes blowing off the sea carried sand up one side of the dunes where it then cascaded down the back. The pattern of this deposition is evident in the cross-bedding of the Permian period's Cedar Mesa sandstone found throughout the park. Layers of silt and clay deposited in the low-lying areas between the dunes became pockets of weaker material that have helped undermine overlying sandstone layers. As streams became entrenched, it worked hardest against the rock walls that separated

beyond which lies the Dark Canyon Wilderness Area. To the south you'll be looking out over the Grand Gulch Plateau, draining into Grand Gulch and eventually the San Juan River. To the southwest rises Moss Back Butte and the Tables of the Sun. White Canyon stretches away to the northwest, draining into what is now Lake Powell but was formerly the Colorado River.

Best time to ride: Spring and fall. Ride in the early morning or evening to avoid the hottest time of day as well as tourist traffic that can become busy in spring and fall.

Special considerations: Please be careful on the cliff rims here; very little is fenced, and there are sheer drop-offs in many places. Climbing on the bridges is strictly prohibited. Afternoon thunderstorms are common in the late summer and fall; be wary of lightning, and do not stand on open or exposed points if a storm is coming your way. Do not enter the canyons if heavy thunderstorms are nearby, due to the danger of flash flooding.

Water and rest rooms are available at the visitors center but nowhere else along the way. Bring plenty of water with you.

From the visitors center go right onto Bridge View Drive and ride approximately 0.7 mile to the start of the one-way loop. Bear right onto the loop and roll along for just over a mile to the view of Sipapu Bridge. Past this viewpoint the road descends and then climbs across a shallow drainage, taking you by a picnic area and to another pullout and trailhead for Sipapu Bridge 0.4 mile beyond. Another third of a mile beyond the Sipapu trailhead is a parking area and trailhead for Horsecollar Ruin. From here the road dips again and then turns south, winding its way southwestward along the rim of White Canyon for another 1.7 miles before arriving at the view for Kachina Bridge, situated above the confluence of White and Armstrong Canyons. The trail down to Kachina Bridge also leaves from this viewpoint pullout.

From the Kachina Bridge viewpoint the road turns and heads east, climbing gently before turning south again toward the Owachomo Bridge view. You reach this pullout approximately 1.8 miles beyond the Kachina Bridge view. A short hiking trail takes you down to the foot of Owachomo Bridge. From here the road rolls and then climbs gently in a northeasterly direction for the next 2.5 miles to the start of the one-way loop. It is another 0.7 mile back to the visitors center from there.

---

43. BURCH CANYON–DEER FLAT ROAD (See map on page 216)

For mountain bikes. The ride out around the head of White and Burch Canyons on the Deer Flat Road is a fun trip into the backcountry surrounding the park that has no requirements for time or distance. Whether you are a beginning or advanced rider, you can adjust the length of this ride to suit your schedule and energy. The trail requires some technical bike-handling skills in places along this route, which dips and rolls quite a bit.

Starting point: Approximately 3 miles east of the visitors center near the junction of UT 275 and a dirt road signed for Deer Flat. This road is often identified as the Burch Canyon Road and/or BLM Road 254 on maps, but is commonly known as the Deer Flat Road. Turn north onto this road and park where you can find space to pull off.

Length: 8 miles out-and-back to head of Burch Canyon; 18 miles out-and-back to start of climb to Deer Flat; 30-mile loop to Woodenshoe Buttes via Bears Ears Road.

Riding surface: Dirt road; hard-packed and fast in places, sections of broken rock and loose sand. Be wary of loose sand and gravel where the road dips through drainages.

Difficulty: Moderate to difficult. Trail surfaces and the rolling terrain make this route best suited for riders of intermediate skill and fitness, though novices should not be put off. If you are going for the big distance you will need strength and stamina more than you will technical skills. Route-finding skills will come in handy, too.

Scenery/highlights: Riding out around the head of the White and Burch Canyon drainages is a wonderful pedal into the breathtakingly beautiful color country that surrounds Natural Bridges. The light, buff-colored Cedar Mesa sandstone defines the edge of the canyon drainages loosely paralleled by this road. The road itself traverses the dark red overlying layers of the Triassic Moenkopi formation. Another light-colored layer above the Moenkopi appears shadowed by greens and purples character-istic of Chinle formation shales. The layer responsible for the cliffs that rim the mesas above is the red-to-orange wall-forming Wingate sand-stone. The dark, reddish brown Kayenta formation is responsible for the distinctive formations of the Bears Ears and Woodenshoe Buttes.

Best time to ride: Spring and fall. During the summer months, get an early start to avoid the hottest hours of the day. Do not ride out this way if the ground is wet or thunderstorms are predicted. The gooey red mud that results will make concrete doughnuts out of your tires.

Special considerations: Water and rest rooms are available 3 miles west of the beginning of this ride at the monument's visitors center.

There are many roads heading off in all directions once you reach the top of Dry Mesa. If you are interested in riding the long loop option—and even if you're not—it is recommended that you have a map.

From the start of the dirt Deer Flats Road pedal north into the brilliant reds of the Moenkopi formation. The road wraps around the base of Maverick Point 1 mile from the start, plunges across upper White Canyon, and then climbs out again, traversing woodlands of piñon, juniper, and big sagebrush. The road continues to roll for another mile before dipping into the south fork of Burch Canyon. Once you have climbed out of this dip you climb intermittently over the next 2 miles, gaining approximately 500 feet before crossing over the middle fork of the Burch Canyon drainage. Along this portion of the trail the landscape seems to funnel away into White Canyon.

The road zigs and zags where it crosses over the middle fork of the drainage which novice riders may want to turn around before they are committed to more uphill riding on the return trip. Beginning at the middle fork and extending westward, the light-colored Cedar Mesa sandstone laps at the edge of the road, then bends around and heads west, following the contour of the slope for another mile. It then makes a gradual descent toward the northernmost fork of the drainage that drops into White Canyon.

Approximately 2.5 miles after crossing the middle fork you cross over the North Fork of Burch Canyon. The road then follows the contour of the slope around the foot of a mesa another 2.5 miles into yet another

Looking back toward the brilliant band of red rocks that cap a set of twin peaks known as the Bears Ears.

drainage, Deer Canyon, a tributary of White Canyon that drains the area around Woodenshoe Buttes. Just beyond Deer Canyon the road climbs; this is a good turnaround point for intermediate riders. Heading back from here gives you an out-and-back total of 18 miles.

Option: The very fit and adventurous rider may want to continue from here. On the other side of the canyon the road climbs steeply for almost 700 feet onto the top of the mesa and Deer Flat. The road then travels northeast along the edge of the mesa, staying mostly level for the next 2 miles. Over the next mile the road climbs steeply, arriving between the Heel and Toe Buttes of Woodenshoe Buttes 12 miles from your starting point. Between these buttes you come to an intersection where you must make a decision about your return trip. You can either go back the way you came, or go right onto Forest Road 181 (Woodenshoe Road). This road traverses the edge of Dry Mesa heading southeasterly for approximately 7.5 miles to the intersection with FR 088 (Elk Ridge Road). Go right onto this road and pedal 2 miles to the Bears Ears, at which point the road begins a steep, winding 6-mile descent back to UT 275. You emerge onto this paved road 0.5 mile east of the start of the Deer Flat Road. Turn right and ride back to your vehicle.

44. BEARS EARS TO WOODENSHOE BUTTES (See map on page 216)

For mountain bikes. This ride is a magical out-and-back adventure that begins near the distinctive twin butte formation of the Bears Ears in the high country north of the monument. Mountain and desert come together here as deep stands of mixed conifer flank the glowing red buttes of the Bears Ears and cloak the tablelands of Dry Mesa. The Woodenshoe Buttes, at the edge of the Dark Canyon Wilderness Area, are separate heel and toe buttes. While this route is mostly nontechnical, the overall distance and elevations may make it more difficult for some; it's best suited for beginning and intermediate riders in good physical condition. An option allows superfit riders to tackle this ride from the start of the Bears Ears Road and loop back to the start via the Deer Flat (Burch Canyon) Road (approximately 30 miles round-trip).

Starting point: The intersection of FR 088 and 184 just past the Bears Ears. To get there drive 3.5 miles east of the visitors center on UT 275, past the turnoff for the Deer Flats Road, to FR 088 (signed as the Elk Ridge Road). Drive approximately 6.5 miles on the Elk Ridge Road to the junction with FR 184, taking off to the right toward South Long Point. Park at this intersection.

Note: Although this road is graded and maintained seasonally, it features steep grades and can be rough in places. A high-clearance, four-wheel-drive vehicle is recommended to access the start of this ride. Do not head up this way if the ground is wet or thunderstorms are forecast; the sticky mud that results is to be avoided at all costs.

Length: 8 miles one way, 16 miles out-and-back. Allow at least 4 hours to complete this ride.

Riding surface: Graded dirt road; sections of loose rocks, washboard.

Difficulty: Easy to moderate. No real technical riding skills are required for this ride, but a solid base of physical fitness is recommended.

Scenery/highlights: Rolling open meadows, stands of evergreens and quaking aspens, and the redrock formations of the desert come together in breathtaking contrast. Views down into White Canyon and the mon-

Rabbitbrush, common to the Southwest, erupts in a profusion of yellow blooms every fall—a stunning contrast against deep, blue desert skies.

ument, across the Grand Gulch Plateau, and beyond to the Red House Cliffs are truly spectacular.

Best time to ride: Anytime spring through fall. Elevations along this route range between 8,000 and 8,500 feet, which means it is cooler up here in the summer, but likely to be wet and impassable in the early spring and late fall. Lower elevations are baking hot in summer. Avoid this area if the ground is wet and thunderstorms are forecast. You don't want to get caught out here during one of the region's violent summer thunderstorms, which can pack a fierce electrical punch.

Special considerations: Water and rest rooms are available at the monument visitors center 3.5 miles west of the Elk Ridge Road on UT 275. Stay hydrated; although temperatures may be cooler up here, the air is still dry and works to zap your body's fluids.

From the intersection of the Elk Ridge Road (FR 088) and the road out to South Long Point (FR 184), pedal due north through an open meadow and stands of spruce, fir, and aspen for 1 mile to an intersection with FR 108. Go left, pedaling west on FR 108 (Woodenshoe Road). This road begins to climb, reaching an intersection with a jeep road 3 miles from the start. Stay straight, heading past this junction on what is now FR 181

FLORA

Natural Bridges National Monument exists at elevations between 5,500 and 6,500 feet and falls into the transition life zone. Piñon and juniper trees dominate here, and are accompanied by an abundance of big sagebrush. Other shrubs include rabbitbrush, round-leaf buffalo berry, cliffrose, and, on certain north-facing exposures, manzanita. In the slightly wetter areas of the park, near seeps or springs, communities of Gambel oak and Utah serviceberry thrive.

In the spring you might see the yellow blooms of western wallflower, so named because it likes to grow in the shelter of rocks and other plants, particularly sagebrush. Yellow cryptantha, scarlet gilia (also called skyrocket), and the lovely yellow-to-peach blooms of prickly pear cactus are common throughout the park in spring. The deep red claret cup cactus blossoms are stunning. Evening primroses wave large tissue-like petals in both white and yellow later in spring and early summer, and by midsummer yellow stalks of prince's-plume, purple locoweed, and as many as six different species of penstemons show their colors.

but is still referred to as the Woodenshoe Road. Just beyond this intersection the road crosses over a low saddle and then descends in a southwesterly direction over the next 1.5 miles, providing glimpses of the sprawl of redrock desert and White Canyon below.

The road next intersects the jeep road that accesses Woodenshoe Canyon and the trail of the same name inside the Dark Canyon Wilderness Area. Stay on the graded Woodenshoe Road as it swings northwest and rolls along through gorgeous open country, reaching the toe portion of Woodenshoe Buttes in 2 miles. The road then skirts between the northeastern flank of the toe butte and the edge of Woodenshoe Canyon. Views into the canyon inside the wilderness area are spellbinding. The tabletop of Dry Mesa is directly across the canyon. You ride along the toe of Woodenshoe Buttes for approximately 1.5 miles until you reach an intersection between the toe and heel. This is your turnaround point. Ride back the way you came, enjoying the views and the scenery from the other direction as you go.

Option: If you rode up to the Bears Ears and left your car just off UT 275, or got dropped off or have a shuttle vehicle waiting for you, you can return via the Deer Flat (Burch Canyon) Road. From the intersection between Woodenshoe Buttes go left and descend onto Deer Flat. In just over 3 miles the road drops off Deer Flat into Deer Canyon, and then wraps around the head of the Burch and White Canyon drainages for the next 9 miles on a rolling jeep road. You emerge onto UT 275 0.5 mile west of the start of the Elk Ridge Road.

---

45. FRY CANYON (See map on page 216)

For road bikes. From the visitors center inside the monument to the small settlement of Fry Canyon is a gorgeous out-and-back tour through brilliantly colored rock formations layered in hues of red, white, and orange. As you head west the road descends gently toward Fry Canyon, following the White Canyon drainage as it seeks out the Colorado River to the north. Although this route does not see a lot of heavy traffic and is not technically demanding, good levels of physical fitness and stamina are recommended. Seasoned road riders will love this one.

Starting point: Visitors center.

Length: 24 miles one way; 48 out-and-back. Allow 4 hours to complete this ride.

Riding surface: Pavement; reasonably wide shoulders.

Difficulty: Moderate to strenuous. Intermediate riders in good-to-excellent condition will have little trouble with this route. The road descends gently toward the turnaround point, losing 1,200 feet in elevation. This will have to be regained on the return trip.

Scenery/highlights: The fantastic hues of the landscape set against the deep blue of the desert sky are something to marvel at along this route. The bright light-colored layers of Cedar Mesa sandstone, reds of the Moenkopi formation, and pastel-hued Chinle formation paint this wonderland in colors that are sometimes hard to believe.

Best time to ride: Anytime spring and fall. Summers are generally hot in these parts, with temperatures often reaching the century mark.

Securing your bike while you are taking in the sights or hiking is a good insurance policy against a bad ending to a cycling vacation.

Special considerations: Water and rest rooms are available at the visitors center. There is a small store and a café at the Fry Canyon Lodge.

From the visitors center pedal eastward on UT 275 for 4 miles to the intersection with UT 95. The road climbs slightly to this intersection. Go right onto UT 95 at this intersection and head southwesterly through rolling piñon and juniper woodlands. You remain on UT 95 for the duration of this ride. For the first 3 miles you traverse an area known as Harmony Flat, then the route parallels and gently descends along the south side of Armstrong Canyon. Just under 8 miles from where you turned onto UT 95 you pass an intersection with UT 276, which heads left toward Halls Crossing on Lake Powell, where a ferry crosses the lake. You will have dropped approximately 600 feet in elevation by this point.

One mile past this intersection the road passes over To-ke-chi Canyon and then wraps around the base of the Moss Back portion of the House Cliffs. Moss Back Butte caps these cliffs at 7,736 feet. The matrix of canyons inside the monument stretches away to your right. You flank the House Cliffs as you head north for approximately 3 miles, at which point the road takes a more northwesterly direction paralleling White Canyon as it begins its descent toward the Colorado. As you descend alongside the canyon toward your final destination you enjoy sweeping views up Deer,

FAUNA

Ravens and scrub-jays are two of the most common residents of the monument, but white-throated swifts and violet-green swallows can also be found in abundance. One or possibly two pairs of peregrine falcons are known to be nesting inside the monument, which is also home to red-tailed hawks, great horned owls, kestrels, and nighthawks. Rufous-sided towhees, black-throated and white-crowned sparrows, dark-eyed juncos, and yellow warblers pass through Natural Bridges.

A variety of pocket mice, chipmunks, and rats are some of the smaller mammals in the monument, and the elusive ringtail cat is also found here. Bobcats, mountain lions, and black bears are also seen in the monument; bears fairly regularly in the fall when they come down from the high country to the north to feed on the rich meat of acorn nuts. The monument and the area surrounding it are also known as a hot spot for bats. Some 15 species of bats come to feed on the insects that are drawn to the seeps and the springs of the canyons.

Hideout, and Cheesebox Canyons, which drain the high country to the north. All flow into the ever-widening White Canyon. The colorful butte midway between Hideout and Cheesebox Canyons is known as the Cheesebox. Approximately 10 miles from the intersection with UT 276 the road bends around and heads southwest, dropping 2 more miles into Fry Canyon and the settlement of the same name. When you've had a rest and something to drink, head back the way you came.

Options: There are many more miles of fantastic scenery along UT 95, which stretches another 35 miles to Hite. You may want to consider starting at Fry Canyon and riding from there toward Hite. There are also possibilities for riding east on UT 95 toward Blanding. This is an option for very fit, experienced riders, though, because the road rolls up and down a considerable amount with several steep pitches. Another option is to head south on UT 261 across the Grand Gulch Plateau until the road drops over the edge via several hair-raising switchbacks known as the Mokee Dugway. The switchbacks themselves are dirt; the pavement ends a few hundred yards before the road plunges over the cliffs. Views from the edge of the plateau into Valley of the Gods are spectacular.

CAMPING

There is one campground at Natural Bridges National Monument, located 0.3 mile past the visitors center on the right. It has 13 sites, is operated on a first-come, first-served basis, is shaded, has vault toilets, picnic tables, and fire grills, and is open all year. There is no water at the campground, but you will find a faucet at the visitors center. The campground fills up quickly May through September. It is best to arrive by noon, if not earlier, to secure a campsite. A per-night fee is charged. Wood gathering is prohibited, so bring a cookstove or charcoal for cooking. A designated overflow camping area is located at the intersection of UT 95 and UT 261. There are no facilities available here.

Kampark Campground in Blanding is the closest private campground with both tent and RV sites. It's on the south edge of town and has showers as well as a small store. **Devils Canyon Campground** and **Nizhoni Campground** are both located in the Manti–La Sal National Forest outside Blanding and have limited services. There are two campgrounds near Hanksville 100 miles west of the monument, and at least one in Mexican Hat 45 miles to the south. There are also campsites available near Hite Marina on Lake Powell for a fee (no facilities).

There are endless opportunities for wilderness camping on the BLM lands surrounding the park and in the nearby Manti–La Sal National Forest.

LODGING

Options for lodging are few and far between out here. The closest is the **Fry Canyon Lodge** (435-259-5334). Rooms are moderately priced, and you'll find a small café and a store where picnic and camping items can be purchased. The lodge is open seasonally, so call ahead. Blanding has a couple of motels, a couple of B&Bs, a **Comfort Inn,** and a **Super 8 Motel.** Hanksville and Mexican Hat both have at least two motels but are pretty sparse on services.

Monticello, north of Blanding, also has a handful of choices.

FOOD

It is a good idea to bring a cooler full of food and drinks when you come to Natural Bridges, because restaurants and grocery stores are hard to find. In Hanksville the **Red Rock Restaurant** serves American food three meals a day; otherwise it's burgers and shakes at **Blondies Eatery** or **Stan's Burger Shack.** In Blanding it's the **4 C's Restaurant** for sandwiches and Mexican food, the **Elk Ridge Restaurant** for Mexican and American food, or the **Old Tymer Restaurant** for fried chicken and prime rib. Blanding is a completely dry town in case you were hoping for a beer. In Mexican Hat the **Olde Bridge Bar and Grill** serves American, Mexican, and Navajo food three meals a day, along with beer. Both the **Mexican Hat Lodge** and **Burch's Motel** have small cafés serving meals.

LAUNDRY

There simply aren't any laundry facilities within a reasonable distance. The towns of Moab and Torrey, Utah (see chapters 1 and 4), both several hours away, have places to do laundry.

IT'S INTERESTING TO KNOW . . .

Geologists agree that 10 million years ago the Colorado Plateau was a featureless plain, and that the erosional processes responsible for the fantastic rock formations and deep canyons that now cleave the plateau did not begin until after the last glacial period ended 18,000 years ago. Melting ice sheets and increased rainfall produced abundant runoff as the glaciers that covered North America began their retreat. Another relatively wet climatic period beginning 4,000 years ago and ending close to 900 years ago was most likely the period when the bridges began forming. The largest of the spans is believed to be 5,000 years old, and the youngest may be less than 1,000—very young by geologic standards, but the aging process continues through spalling due to freeze and thaw cycles and the ever-present effects of wind and weather. Someday all of these bridges will collapse.

BIKE SHOP/BIKE RENTAL

The nearest bike shop in this corner of the state is found in Moab, where there are several, but that is almost 135 miles away. There is also a shop in Cortez, Colorado, which is almost as close.

FOR FURTHER INFORMATION

Natural Bridges National Monument—Superintendent, P.O. Box 1, Lake Powell, UT 84533; (435) 692-1234; http://www.nps.gov/nabr/

San Juan County Multi-Agency Visitors Center, 117 S. Main St. (at the San Juan County Courthouse), P.O. Box 490, Monticello, UT 84535; (800) 574-4FUN

Manti–La Sal National Forest, Monticello Ranger District (offices in Price and Moab also), 496 E. Central, P.O. Box 820, Monticello, UT 84535; (435) 587-2041

BLM San Juan Resource Area, 435 N. Main, Monticello, UT 84535; (435) 587-2141

DON'T MISS

The short, 0.6-mile hike down to the Horsecollar Ruin takes you to one of the most beautifully constructed and well-preserved Ancestral Puebloan ruins in southeastern Utah. Although it was abandoned more than 700 years ago, a large kiva with its original roof still exists. A ladder leading down into the kiva was also in place when the ruin was rediscovered by Zeke Johnson, the first curator of the monument, who stumbled upon the site some 20 years after coming here. The ladder has been removed to prevent people from climbing down into the kiva. You can still peer into the kiva from the side and see the original firepit, a small hole called a *sipapu* where the Hopi believe spirits come into and leave the world, and a bench at the back. The horsecollar shapes of the ruin doorways at the far end of the alcove are very distinctive. The round shape of the rooms is also unique among Ancestral Puebloan ruins.

9

At Timpanogos Cave National Monument you'll find an eerie underground wonderland of hanging stalactites, ghostly stalagmites and rock draperies, mounded flowstone, craggy fingers of helictites, and something called "cave popcorn." These formations are the combined handiwork of geologic forces deep within the earth, water, gravity, and time.

Timpanogos Cave is actually a complex of three limestone caverns now connected by constructed passageways. The caverns are located high on the side of the almost sheer-walled American Fork Canyon, deep in northern Utah's Wasatch Mountains. The first of the three caves was discovered in 1887 by Martin Hansen, a Mormon settler from American Fork. Hansen was in the canyon cutting timber when he came upon a set of cougar tracks. He followed the tracks to a ledge, where he stumbled upon a small cave opening. Word quickly spread of the fantastic formations inside the cave, most of which were soon looted by souvenir hunters. The other two caves were discovered in 1915 and 1921; a year later, in 1922, the caves and the astonishing natural features inside them were declared a national monument by President Warren G. Harding.

Clues to the formation of these caves can be seen along the 1.5-mile trail that ascends to their entrance, beginning with the billion-year-old Precambrian sedimentary rocks at the bottom. Near the end of the trail, at the cave entrance 1,000 feet higher, are Mississippian rocks only 330 million years old. This layer is composed of soft limestones deposited when shallow seas covered northern Utah. A dramatic period of mountain building about 20 million years ago lifted these sedimentary layers skyward along the Wasatch Fault. It is thought that the caves began to form during Pleistocene times, 1 to 2 million years ago, a period of receding glaciers, increased snowmelt, and bountiful precipitation. Water trickling down through the rock layers found a fault and began to dissolve the weaker limestones. Weak carbonic acids—created when rain and snow absorb naturally occurring carbon dioxide in the air—helped enlarge joints and faults in the rock, increasing the size of the caves. After the caves formed, water bearing calcium carbonate continued to seep in, dripping off the ceilings, coating the walls, and creating the beautiful cave decorations found here.

Cycling in the Park

Because of the small size of this park, its location on an extremely steep slope, and the fact that its main scenic resource is underground, there are no roads or trails in Timpanogos Cave National Monument on which you can ride a bike. The surrounding country, however, offers some of the best road- and mountain-biking routes in the Wasatch. The steep, mountainous terrain of the Wasatch Mountains means that most of the trails in the area gain and lose in elevation; none is completely flat. Families of strong beginning-to-intermediate riders who favor knobby tires can explore the upper reaches of American Fork Canyon on a dirt road and see the remnants of the silver mines that once thrived there. Beginning and intermediate cyclists might also want to venture out to the Timpooneke Road, trying their skills on the Great Western Trail along the way. The ride up to Silver Lake Flat Reservoir is another good intermediate-level outing and rewards you with beautiful lakeside views after a short but challenging climb. A trail from the reservoir takes the adventurous to a gorgeous alpine setting.

The singletrack riding out along the Ridge Trail and its many connecting trails will thrill advanced-level mountain bikers, who could spend several days creating their own routes out here. The Alpine Loop, an incredibly scenic circuit of Mount Timpanogos Wilderness Area via American Fork and Provo Canyons, is a classic road tour for the seasoned

There are five rides listed in this chapter, one for road bikes and the other four for mountain bikes. A 9-mile mountain-bike trip up to Dutchman Flat and some old mine workings in the upper reaches of American Fork Canyon, and a 7-mile ride up to Silver Lake Flat Reservoir, offer moderate riding options for beginning and intermediate riders on dirt and gravel road surfaces. A 16-mile (total) out-and-back tour on the dirt Timpooneke Road around the north and west flanks of Mount Timpanogos is longer, involves a significant amount of climbing, and is better suited for solid intermediate riders in excellent condition. A section of the Great Western Trail that parallels this route provides an opportunity for trying out some singletrack.

The Ridge Trail offers experienced riders in excellent condition several possibilities for exploring singletrack trails. The ride written up here is a 6-mile descent that intermediate riders can try. A 17-mile optional loop eliminates the need for a shuttle on this ride and gives advanced riders looking for a longer, more challenging ride something to sink their teeth into. The 40-mile circuit of Mount Timpanogos via the Alpine Loop is a road ride perfectly tailored to the serious road biker who loves monster climbs and long distances.

skinny-tire enthusiast. Please be aware that you will need to pay an access fee at a toll booth near the mouth of American Fork Canyon.

46. AMERICAN FORK CANYON ROAD TO DUTCHMAN FLAT (See map on page 234)

For mountain bikes. The ride up American Fork Canyon beyond Tibble Fork Reservoir takes you to the old Dutchman Mine site. Beginning and intermediate riders who are in good physical condition and aren't afraid of some climbing and a few stretches of loose rock will really enjoy this trip up one of the Wasatch Mountains' most scenic canyons.

Starting point: Tibble Fork Reservoir. To get there from the Timpanogos Cave Visitors Center drive approximately 2.5 miles up American Fork

Canyon on UT 92, bearing left onto UT 144 at the North Fork junction (signed for Tibble Fork Reservoir). Drive another 2 miles to the parking lot just across from the reservoir.

Length: 9 miles out-and-back. Allow 3 hours to complete this ride.

Riding surface: Dirt road, gravel road; sections of loose rock and washboard.

Difficulty: Easy to moderate. Although this ride is relatively short and not much technical riding skill is required, the 1,000 feet of elevation change and higher altitudes will make it more difficult for some.

Scenery/highlights: American Fork Canyon is alpine scenery at its best. Fall is beautiful up here; stands of quaking aspens turn brilliant gold while Rocky Mountain maples add hues of red and orange to the hillsides. On the way up you will pass by the Old Glory Mine, and at the turnaround point at Dutchman Flat you'll see the workings of the Dutchman Mine. Both mines brought silver ore out of the ground in profitable amounts during the 1880s and 1890s. During this era the Wasatch Mountains were abuzz with mining camps and mine workers hoping to strike it rich. The peaks and ridges of this canyon, and Little Cottonwood Canyon to the north, are honeycombed with old mines and tunnels from this area's mining heyday. Be careful around old mines, as they can collapse. Never enter an old mine shaft or tunnel; the air inside is often laden with noxious gases that can cause injury and even death.

Best time to ride: May through October; before that it is likely to be muddy with snowmelt and spring runoff.

Special considerations: You'll find vault toilets and a water spigot at the Tibble Fork Reservoir parking area. No drinking water is available along the trail, so bring plenty of your own. Never drink from an open stream unless you are carrying a water purifier or can first boil your water.

From the parking area at Tibble Fork Reservoir go left onto the dirt road heading up American Fork Canyon. This is Forest Road 085. You climb gently at first through a steep-walled canyon, passing the point where Silver Creek flows into the American Fork drainage just over 1 mile from your start. In another mile you pass the remains of the Old Glory Mine

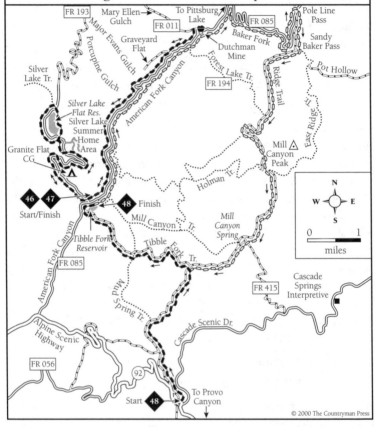

Ride 46 • American Fork Canyon Road to Dutchman Flat
Ride 47 • Silver Lake Flat Reservoir
Ride 48 • Ridge Trail–Tibble Fork Loop

FR 193 Mary Ellen To Pittsburg
Gulch Lake
FR 011 FR 085 Pole Line
Pass
Major Evans Gulch Baker Fork Sandy
Graveyard Baker Pass
Flat Dutchman
Mine Pot Hollow
Porcupine Gulch Forest Lake Tr.
Silver FR 194
Lake Tr.
American Fork Canyon Ridge Trail
Silver Lake
Flat Res. East Ridge Tr.
Silver Lake
Summer Mill
Home Canyon
Area Peak
Granite Flat
CG
Holman Tr.
46 47 48 Finish
Start/Finish Mill Canyon Tr. Mill
Canyon
Spring
Tibble Fork
Reservoir Tibble Fork Tr.
FR 085
Mud Spring Tr. Cascade
Springs
FR 415 Interpretive
Alpine Scenic
Highway Cascade Scenic Dr.
FR 056
92
Start 48 To Provo
Canyon

N
W—E
S

0   1
miles

© 2000 The Countryman Press

site on your left. Over the next mile the road climbs steeply at times, makes a couple of switchbacks at the base of Major Evans Gulch, and then continues its upcanyon progress at a steady grade. Just before you reach the spur road to Graveyard Flat the road climbs steeply again, but then levels off as you pass the right-hand spur up to Forest Lake and roll into Dutchman's Flat. The mine workings are against a slope at the north

Mighty Mount Timpanogos fills the sky above this cyclist frolicking on the singletrack trails that criss-cross its flanks.

end of the flat. When you've had a good look around and had time to enjoy your surroundings, saddle up and head back the way you came.

Option: If you're game, you can continue another 3.5 miles up to Pole Line Pass on FR 085, or ride up to the very end of American Fork Canyon to the Pittsburgh Lake trailhead on FR 007. A very steep road also takes off right out of Dutchman Flat and heads up Mary Ellen Gulch to the Yankee Mine site, but it will be too steep for most.

---

47. SILVER LAKE FLAT RESERVOIR (See map on page 234)

For mountain bikes. The ride up to Silver Lake Flat Reservoir is a relatively short but steep climb to a beautiful, sparkling blue body of water rimmed by high mountain peaks, lush alpine scenery, and wildflowers. If you're up here in the fall you'll find hues of gold, crimson, and bronze. This route climbs approximately 1,000 feet over 3.5 miles, makes a circuit of the reservoir, and then descends the same way. It's appropriate for novice and intermediate riders in good physical condition.

Starting point: Tibble Fork Reservoir. To get there from the Timpanogos Cave Visitors Center drive approximately 2.5 miles up American Fork Canyon on UT 92, bearing left onto UT 144 at the North Fork junction (signed for Tibble Fork Reservoir). Drive another 2 miles to the parking lot just across from the reservoir.

Length: 7 miles round trip. Allow 3 hours to do the ride and spend a little time by the reservoir cooling your heels.

Riding surface: Pavement, dirt road.

Difficulty: Moderate. Although the distance is relatively short, you'll gain 1,000 feet up to the reservoir.

Scenery/highlights: Wonderful alpine scenery abounds up here. To the south you'll be looking at the massive Mount Timpanogos with its glacially sculpted basins and jagged peaks and ridges. To the west looms Box Elder Peak (11,101 feet) inside the Lone Peak Wilderness Area.

Best time to ride: Anytime May through October, provided the ground is dry and snow free. Summer is delightfully cool at these altitudes.

Special considerations: Vault toilets and water are available at the Tibble Fork Reservoir parking lot and at Granite Campground.

If you have the time, the legs, the proper footwear, and a bicycle lock, consider hiking 1.5 miles beyond the reservoir up to the gorgeous peak-rimmed Silver Lake.

From the parking lot at Tibble Fork Reservoir begin by pedaling up paved FR 010 approximately 0.7 mile to Granite Flat Campground. Bear right on the road as it turns to dirt and begins to climb toward Silver Lake Flat Reservoir. Once the road turns to dirt it becomes FR 008 and begins climbing around many sharp turns and curves. You'll gain a significant amount of elevation over the next mile until you reach a ridge. Once you are on top of the ridge follow the road as it doubles back and climbs a little more gently, passes the access to the Silver Lake Summer Home Area, and then reaches the south end of the reservoir.

Follow the road as it as it heads north along the west shore of the reservoir and then circles around, following the shore the entire way. Stop anywhere you like as you make your way around the reservoir and take time to enjoy the incredible scenery that surrounds you. Toward the south end of the lake the road crosses over on top of the dam and then rejoins the main road you came up on. When you're ready to go, check that your helmet is on snugly and your front wheel is firmly clamped into the fork of your bike, and get ready for a fast-paced descent. Please stay to the right and be aware of uphill vehicle traffic.

---

48. RIDGE TRAIL–TIBBLE FORK LOOP (See map on page 234)

For mountain bikes. There are many options for creating loops that include the Ridge Trail in the area just north of the Alpine Loop Scenic Drive (also UT 92) not far from the park. Most require a solid base of physical fitness and an advanced-to-expert level of technical riding skills. One of the easier options is described here. It leaves from the Ridge Trail access along the Alpine Scenic Loop, traverses a series of ridgelines, and then descends the Tibble Fork Trail. This route of just over 6 miles requires a car shuttle. If you have the time and stamina, a longer ride that takes you in a loop the other direction does not require a shuttle.

Starting point: The trailhead and parking area found at the highest point along the Alpine Loop Scenic Drive. First drop a shuttle vehicle at Tibble Fork Reservoir (unless you are willing to ride the 9 miles back up on the pavement). To get to Tibble Fork Reservoir from the Timpanogos Cave Visitors Center drive approximately 2.5 miles up American Fork Canyon on UT 92, bearing left onto UT 144 at the North Fork junction (signed for Tibble Fork Reservoir). Drive another 2 miles to the parking lot just across from the reservoir and leave the shuttle vehicle there. (Start here for the longer ride.)

Return to UT 92, turn right at the North Fork intersection, and continue driving up on the Alpine Scenic Loop another 7 miles to the summit parking area. This is also the trailhead and access for the Ridge Trail. Park here.

Length: 6 miles point to point; allow 2 to 3 hours. The longer version is a loop just over 18 miles; allow 5 hours or a half a day.

Riding surface: Singletrack. The longer ride also has graded dirt road. The usual obstacles found along singletrack trails in the mountains (roots and rocks); very loose with powdery dirt late in summer when ground is dry and trails have seen a lot of traffic; aspen roots and knob.

Difficulty: Moderate to difficult. The longer version is more challenging, plus longer, making it strenuous for even advanced-level riders in good condition. Elevations along the short version of the trail peak at about 8,200 feet. The longer route reaches 9,600 feet.

Scenery/highlights: The views in all directions are spectacular from the Ridge Trail. Most immediately to the northwest is Box Elder Peak (11,101 feet). Beyond it is Lone Peak (11,253 feet) and the dramatic spine of Alpine Ridge. Mill Canyon Peak looms up ahead as you're heading north along the Ridge Trail; it rises to an elevation of 10,349 feet. To the south the massive outline of Timpanogos dominates the skyline. In midsummer wildflowers bloom in great swaths of color.

Best time to ride: June 1 or later until mid- to late October. Afternoon thunderstorms are quite common in the late summer and early fall. If you see dark clouds approaching and hear the rumble of thunder, stay well off high places and exposed ridgelines. If thunderstorms are pre-

Stream crossings are a common obstacle when biking in the mountains in summer. It is safer to wade in and secure your footing as you cross.

dicted for the afternoon, you may want to choose another day for this ride, or be sure to get an early start.

Special considerations: Vault toilets and a water spigot can be found at Tibble Fork Reservoir, but there are no other facilities along the route. Be sure to bring plenty of fluids and snacks.

From the Ridge Trail (Forest Trail 157) access at the summit of the Alpine Loop Scenic Drive, begin pedaling northward, descending at first and then rolling up and over several knolls along the ridge. You reach the Pine Hollow Trail (FT 047), taking off to your left, 1 mile from the start. For the next 0.5 mile the trail contours around the side of a knoll above Pine Hollow, arriving at Mud Spring and the Mud Spring Trail (FT 173).

For the next 1.5 miles the trail traverses the ridge separating Tibble Fork and Deer Creek drainages at elevations between 8,000 and 8,200 feet, arriving at the Tibble Fork Trail (FT 041) after a short climb. Pause here to make sure that your helmet is on tightly, your brakes are properly adjusted, and your front wheel is snugly locked into your front fork. Go left onto the Tibble Fork Trail and get ready for a wild ride. The trail descends steeply for most of the first mile, dropping through rocky slots among aspen trees, crossing, flower-filled meadows, and then diving into the trees again as it twists and winds downhill. The second mile of the descent gives you some reprieve as you hit more level terrain and contour the slope before being sent headlong through the steep bottom portion of the drainage. The Tibble Fork Trail ends at the reservoir dam on an access road to a group of summer homes. Go right on this dirt road, ride across the dam, and turn left when you reach the pavement. Ride approximately 0.4 mile to your shuttle vehicle at the parking lot.

Option: If you are interested in an epic all-day adventure, begin at the Tibble Fork Reservoir parking lot and head north on FR 085 up the north fork of American Fork Canyon. You ride this dirt-and-gravel road 4.5 miles to Dutchman Flat. Beyond Dutchman Flat is another mile of pedaling up the canyon before reaching a junction. Go right at this junction and continue following FR 085 up another fork to Pole Line Pass. It is 3 miles and almost 1,300 feet up to this pass from this junction. The road is steep, rocky, and loose in places; it crests the summit in a clearing where the Ridge Trail (FT 157) takes off to the south.

Over the first 0.5 mile you skirt the west side of a knoll and then

This keyhole, like thousands of others in southern Utah, is technically an arch, and was created by erosion of an isolated rock fin that does not bridge a watercourse. *(Photo by Lee Cohen)*

A cyclist pauses along the White Rim Trail to take in a spectacular view over the Colorado River to the La Sal Mountains beyond. *(Photo by Dennis Coello)*

Far right: A group of cyclists hike into one of many slot canyons in Canyonlands National Park—always a good place to escape the sun and heat of midday. *(Photo by Dennis Coello)*

Right: In the canyon and plateau country of southern Utah, landscapes and views like this one at Bryce Canyon are often a mixture of vertical and horizontal elements. *(Photo by Sarah Bennett Alley)*

Bottom: A touring cyclist stops to take in the stunning kaleidoscope of colors inside Cedar Breaks National Monument. *(Photo by Dennis Coello)*

A cyclist negotiates the Burr Trail as it winds its way through massive rock formations near Capitol Reef National Park. *(Photo by Dennis Coello)*

Mountain bikers using a vehicle for support somewhere between Natural Bridges and the Needles District of Canyonlands National Park. *(Photo by Dennis Coello)*

The scenery of southern Utah is constantly changing. In lower elevations red rock abounds, but at higher elevations you will find stands of quaking aspen and a variety of plants and animals common to alpine environments. *(Photos by Dennis Coello)*

A cyclist takes time out of the saddle to explore a mountain of slickrock inside Zion National Park. *(Photo by Dennis Coello)*

Springs, or "seeps," emerge between rock layers and create lush micro-environments critical to the survival of desert wildlife. They're often associated with caverns or overhangs such as this. *(Photo by Dennis Coello)*

A cyclist breaks from riding Rim Rock Drive to gaze out toward Independence Monument and the Colorado River valley beyond. *(Photo by Sarah Bennett Alley)*

The cliff dwellings of the ancient Puebloan Indians, also called the *Anasazi*, who thrived atop Mesa Verde some 800 years ago, are visually striking and hauntingly serene. *(Photo by Dennis Coello)*

The shifting sands of Colorado's Great Sand Dunes make for a fascinating study of light, shadow, and texture. The patterns that blowing grasses and animals leave in the sand are also intriguing, but are swept away by the wind almost as soon as they appear. *(Photo by Dennis Coello)*

A fully-loaded mountain bike and rider crest the Trail Ridge Road above the clouds at almost 12,000 feet above sea level. The Trail Ridge Road in Rocky Mountain National Park is the highest paved road in the continental United States. *(Photo by Dennis Coello)*

FLORA

Timpanogos Cave National Monument falls within the transition life zone. Cone-bearing evergreens dominate on the north-facing slopes of the monument, especially firs. Douglas fir, white fir, and limber pine are the most common trees along the trail, but you will also see Rocky Mountain juniper, curly-leaved mountain mahogany, Rocky Mountain maple, and Gambel oak. Chokecherry, Utah serviceberry, and elderberry are several fruit-bearing shrubby trees that can be found here. Well-known shrubs such as wild rose and raspberry are commonly found at Timpanogos, as are the less familiar ninebark and ocean-spray. Both have small white flowers and small leaves and are members of the rose family. Wildflowers are abundant in the monument by midsummer and include such species as Leonard's violet and Eaton's red penstemon, stemless goldenweed, Indian paintbrush, blue chiming bell, and Colorado columbine. Pennyroyal, Solomon's seal, evening primrose (which blooms pink to white), yellow stonecrop, and yellow sweet clover are less easily recognized but also bloom in the monument.

descend to Sandy Baker Pass. Stay right on the Ridge Trail at the junction on the pass. This is the West Side Ridge Trail, and it takes you around the western flank of Mill Canyon Peak. (The trail to the left contours around the eastern side of the peak.) For the next 1.7 miles the trail courses through stands of mixed conifers and aspens, and crosses a talus slope before arriving at the junction with the Lake Trail (FT 171) heading away on your right. Beyond this junction the trail climbs, steeply at times, for the next 0.6 mile. After the trail comes around a ridge, there is another trail dropping away to your right; ignore it and follow the Ridge Trail as it contours the slopes just below Mill Canyon Peak for the next mile. Views to mighty Timpanogos are breathtaking from here.

As you round another ridge the Holman Trail (FT 039) takes off to the right. Just beyond is Rock Springs, where the East Ridge Trail, wrapping around the eastern flank of Mill Canyon Peak, rejoins the main Ridge Trail. It is a rough, rocky descent from Rock Springs to Mill Canyon Spring, where the Mill Canyon Trail takes off to the right. Just before you reach this junction you pass a jeep road that drops off the east side of the ridge to the Cascade Scenic Drive. Past this junction is just over another mile of fun, rolling ridgeline traverse to the Tibble Fork Trail. Go right onto the Tibble Fork Trail (FT 041) and continue back down to the reservoir as described above.

---

49. TIMPOONEKE ROAD–GREAT WESTERN TRAIL
(See map on page 243)

For mountain bikes. The Timpooneke Road is a spectacularly scenic route that wraps around the northern and western flanks of majestic Mount Timpanogos and the Mount Timpanogos Wilderness Area. From where the road begins at Timpooneke Campground to its end at the Dry Canyon trailhead is 8 miles. Novice riders in good condition may want to ride out to just the high point along the route, about halfway along the outbound leg. Intermediate riders will probably want to stick to the road, but some riders, including those with excellent bike-handling skills, will want to try sections of the Great Western Trail that parallels the road for the first 2 miles of the route.

Starting point: Timpooneke Campground. To get there from Timpanogos Cave National Monument drive up American Fork Canyon on UT 92 (Alpine Scenic Loop), bearing right in 2.5 miles at the North Fork junction. Continue on UT 92 for another 3 miles to Timpooneke Campground. Park here.

Length: 16 miles (total) out-and-back. Allow at least 4 hours to complete this ride.

Riding surface: Dirt, gravel road. The singletrack of the Great Western Trail, which parallels the road, is root and rock studded and quite technical in places.

Difficulty: Moderate. You can make this ride a little bit easier or very difficult, depending on your skill and fitness level. There is a fairly significant amount of elevation change along this route. Your starting elevation is approximately 7,200 feet at Timpooneke Campground, the high point about halfway along the outbound portion of the ride is about 8,600 feet, and the elevation at the turnaround point is approximately 7,600 feet. A

Ride 49 • Timpooneke Road–Great Western Trail
Ride 50 • Alpine Scenic Loop

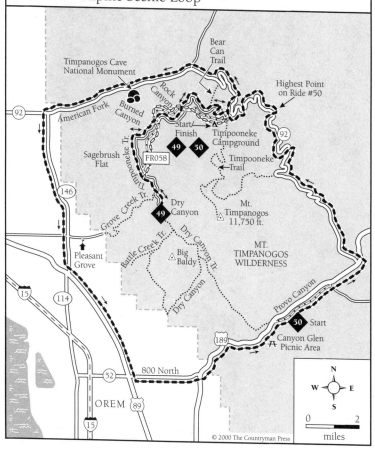

total of 2,400 feet of elevation gain is possible if you ride out to the end of the road and back.

Scenery/highlights: As you pedal your way around this 11,750-foot giant, you can gaze upward into the glacier-carved bowls and buttresses of this mountain's massive peak and ridgeline system. In the other direction you will enjoy sweeping views over the Utah Valley and Utah Lake. The alpine scenery is fantastic. Keep an eye out for hawks soaring at eye

Handlebar-high wildflowers add to the fantastic riding found in the high peaks of the Wasatch on a summer's day.

level, deer grazing at the edge of a meadow, or the stout white figure of a mountain goat scrambling across the top of a high ravine.

Best time to ride: Mid- to late May until fall. If afternoon thunderstorms are predicted, save this one for another day. Heavy rain, lightning, and hail can lash this mountain during summer thunderstorms. Stay away from high, exposed areas if lightning is nearby.

Special considerations: Water and vault toilets are available at Timpooneke Campground and the trailhead area, but not along the way. Be sure to stay hydrated and bring plenty of high-energy snacks.

From the Timpooneke Campground ride out of the parking lot and pick up the dirt-and-gravel road that heads north labeled FR 056 (Timpooneke Road). The road begins climbing, making several switchbacks below the Woolly Hole Basin before contouring around a narrow ridge and heading west. Just over a mile from the start you pass the Bear Canyon trailhead on your right. Beyond this trailhead the road heads north for about 0.5 mile before switching back and heading south as it contours around another sharp ridge. Views of Utah Valley emerge as you round the corner of this ridge and can look west. To the north are spectacular views of Box Elder Peak and Lone Peak. For the next mile the road heads south and west as it contours around the head of Rock Canyon. Views up to the north-facing buttresses of Timpanogos are also quite good here.

After the road bends around another ridge, exiting the Rock Canyon drainage, it climbs steadily in a southwesterly direction for another mile, around the top of Burned Canyon, reaching the high point in the ride in a clearing near a corral at approximately 8,600 feet. This is a good turnaround point for beginning or intermediate riders who do not want to commit themselves to more climbing on the return trip. Past the corral the road descends for about 0.5 mile before passing a small pond and turning south. Now heading due south, the road continues to descend gradually across an area called Sage Flat. You descend along the western flank of Mount Timpanogos for approximately 3 miles before encountering Grove Creek trailhead. Another 0.6 mile beyond this trailhead the road skirts the edge of a clearing and ends at the Dry Canyon trailhead. From the clearing at the end of the road you can look up and see the jagged ridgelines and 11,750-foot summit of Mount Timpanogos. After you've had a break, a snack, and a good long drink of water, get back on your bike and return the way you came.

Option: The Great Western Trail is a singletrack that parallels the Timpooneke Road for most of this route. You can pick up this singletrack approximately 0.3 mile from the start of this ride at the start of the Timpooneke hiking trail on the left-hand side of the road. For the first 2 miles the trail traverses the head of the Bear Canyon drainage above the road, and then drops down and crosses the road, continuing west across the top of Rock Canyon. At the western ridge defining Rock Canyon the trail again crosses the road and parallels it closely for the next mile as it makes its way across the top of Burned Canyon. The trail continues above the road as it heads south into Sagebrush Flat. The trail ends in Sagebrush Flat, where it meets the road just over a mile from where the road ends at Dry Canyon trailhead. The Great Western Trail route follows the road from where the trail ends, and then continues along the Dry Canyon Trail, which extends all the way into Provo Canyon. This section of the trail is extremely rough and is not recommended for cyclists.

---

50. ALPINE SCENIC LOOP (See map on page 243)

For road bikes. The 42.5-mile Alpine Scenic Loop traverses both American Fork and Provo Canyons, wraps around the eastern flank of Mount Timpanogos—climbing an 8,000-foot pass—and skirts the foot of the massive mountain to the west through the towns of Orem and Pleasant Grove. This is a strenuous, all-day tour that seasoned road riders looking for a serious challenge won't want to miss. The loop can be ridden in either direction, but is slightly less grueling going counter-clockwise up Provo Canyon and down American Fork Canyon.

Starting point: Canyon Glen Picnic Area just beyond the mouth of Provo Canyon. You can park at the mouth of American Fork Canyon near the intersection of UT 92 and UT 146 and have the flat section of the ride to warm up on first. A third starting point in the town of Pleasant Grove splits the flat riding between the beginning and end of your ride.

Length: Approximately 42.5 miles. This will take the better part of a day.

Riding surface: Pavement.

FAUNA

Steller's jay and pinyon jays are quite common in the monument. In the summer a variety of hummingbirds, including rufous and broad-tailed, are drawn to the abundant wildflowers. At least seven species of warblers, including Virginia's, orange-crowned, Wilson's, and the Nashville warbler, all make their way here. Evening, black-headed, and pine grosbeaks are regulars in the monument, as are Cassin's finches and their more common cousin the house finch. The flashy yellow bird with an orange head is none other than a western tanager, and the bright blue streak you see is most likely a mountain bluebird. Many different species of hawks have been sighted in the monument, including the sparrow, red-tailed, gos, sharp-shinned, and Cooper's. Both golden eagles and bald eagles have also been seen here.

An abundance of small mammals that includes chipmunks, squirrels, skunks, raccoons, and beavers live in the monument and its environs. Larger mammals regularly seen in and around the monument are mule deer, elk, moose, and mountain goats. The latter are often seen above the Timpooneke Road. Black bears have been seen in the monument but are very rare. Several kinds of reptiles are found here, including western diamondback rattlers, garter snakes, gopher snakes, and a small 8- to 10-inch snake called a rubber boa that looks more like a giant earthworm than a snake.

Difficulty: Strenuous. This is a long ride over a high mountain pass that even experienced road riders will find very challenging. Near the town of Pleasant Grove you reach the lowest elevation of the ride, about 4,600 feet, and as you pass over the ridge separating the American Fork and Provo drainages your elevation is just over 8,000 feet. US 189 through Provo Canyon regularly sees heavy traffic.

Scenery/highlights: The stunning alpine scenery through American Fork and Provo Canyons is as good as it gets. This route makes a complete circuit of the mighty Mount Timpanogos, allowing you to look up to its dramatic ridgelines, gracefully carved glacial cirques, and luxuriant green slopes as you pedal your way around the massive mountain.

Best time to ride: May through September. If afternoon thunderstorms are forecast, save this ride for another day. Afternoon buildups can lash these peaks with heavy rain, hail, high winds, and lightning. Stay off the pass if one of these storms is lurking nearby.

Special considerations: Bathrooms and drinking water are available at almost all the campgrounds and picnic areas along the way. Eat and drink frequently—*before* you experience hunger or thirst. Drink more water than you think you need; exerting yourself in the thin air and strong sun of high altitudes rapidly depletes your body of its fluids.

Please use caution while pedaling along these canyon roads; most of this route is narrow and winding and, during the summer, busy with tourists who are looking at the scenery. A bright or white piece of clothing will help alert motorists to your presence.

Beginning this loop by riding up Provo Canyon is a good choice, because the grades tend to be more gradual. It is approximately 7 miles from the mouth of Provo Canyon to the junction with UT 92 (Alpine Scenic Loop Road). After turning left onto UT 92 you climb more steeply, gaining over 1,000 feet in 3 miles as the road follows the North Fork of the Provo River skyward to its headwaters on the eastern flank of Mount Timpanogos. Views into the glacially carved cirques and basins below the jagged ridgelines of Timpanogos are spectacular along the next 2 miles of the route, which makes several switchbacks before arriving at the Brigham Young University Alpine Summer School facilities. The road levels between here and Timpanogos Campground, but only momentarily; another series of switchbacks climb another 1,000 feet over the next 4 miles to arrive at the 8,000-foot pass marking the end of your climbing.

Descending the north side of the pass into the American Fork drainage is a fast, hair-raising ride with many sharp curves and turns. You drop 2,000 feet over the first 7 miles to North Fork Junction, and another 1,000 feet over the next 5 miles to the mouth of American Fork Canyon. As you exit the canyon take your first left, heading south on UT 146 toward Pleasant Grove. It is approximately 5 miles to Pleasant Grove on UT 146 and another 0.5 mile to US 89. Go left onto US 89 and continue south for approximately 4 miles to 800 North in Orem. Go left onto 800 North and ride another 5.5 miles to Canyon Glen Picnic Area or where you left your vehicle near the mouth of Provo Canyon.

Just another day on the Ridge Trail, near Timpanogos Cave National Monument.

CAMPING

There are no campgrounds inside Timpanogos Cave National Monument, but you'll find some great campgrounds very close by under the management of the Uinta National Forest. There are 10 excellent campgrounds in American Fork Canyon and 4 off the Alpine Scenic Loop. Almost all of them have vault toilets, picnic tables, and fire grates, but not drinking water.

If you need an RV site, try the **American Campground** (801-756-5502) in American Fork located at 418 East and 620 South. There are several private campgrounds in Provo Canyon offering tent and RV sites. **Frazier Park (801-225-**5346) is 5 miles up Provo Canyon, and the **Riverbend Trailer Park** (801-225-1863) another mile beyond. Frazier Park has showers, and Riverbend has both showers and laundry facilities.

Plenty of wilderness camping is available in the Uinta National Forest.

LODGING

You will find a **Quality Inn** in American Fork and a handful of chain motels in Orem, including a **Marriott Fairfield Inn,** a **Hampton Inn,** and **La Quinta** and **Rodeway Inns.** The **Hillcrest Motel** is another option in Orem. In Provo, just a few minutes south, you'll have many more choices for accommodations. If you want to be in the mountains and don't mind paying a bit more, give the **Sundance Resort** a try. This is actor Robert Redford's home as well as the home of the Sundance Summer Theater and the Sundance Institute, a think tank and laboratory for independent filmmakers that hosts the Sundance Film Festival every year. The resort has cottages in a beautiful alpine setting and two restaurants that serve delicious nouveau cuisine.

FOOD

There is a snack bar at the visitors center inside the monument serving mostly snack foods and a few lunch items. Just 7 miles away in American Fork you can have your choice of a few dozen fast-food restaurants, or you can try something else quick and easy like **Niko's Teriyaki Express, Taybo's Wraps, Mi Ranchito** Mexican food, or the **China Light Café,** all found along State Street. In Orem there are hundreds of restaurants to choose from. Try **Café del Sol** (530 E. 1400 S.), **Chevy's Fresh Mex** (539 W. University Pkwy.), or **El Azteca Mexican Taco Shop** (78 S. State St.) for Mexican, or **Fresh Food Junkies Café** (500 S. State St.) for something light and healthy. You can get a great smoothie at **Mayberries Fresh Fruit Creations** (1468 N. State St.). For something different try **La Carretta Peruvian Restaurant** (1605 S. State St.). The **Sundance Grill** at Sundance Resort serves three good meals a day, and the **Tree Room** (also at the resort) offers a more sophisticated dining experience for dinner and brunch on Sunday.

LAUNDRY

There are many possibilities for doing laundry in the city of Provo. Here a couple in the smaller towns of Orem at the mouth of Provo Canyon:

The Soap Box, 353 S. State St.; (801) 225-9914

Wash-N-Dry, 588 N. State St.; (801) 225-5148

BIKE SHOP/BIKE RENTAL

IN AMERICAN FORK:

Bike Peddler, 24 E. Main St.; (801) 756-5014

BMC Bikes, 99 N. 100 W.; (801) 756-8300

IN OREM:

Adams Bicycles, 230 N. State St.; (801) 255-0280

Mad Dog Cycles (rentals), 736 S. State St.; (801) 222-9577

Wasatch Bicycle Co., 948 N. State St.; (801) 226-2388

FOR FURTHER INFORMATION

Timpanogos Cave National Monument—Superintendent, R.R. 3, Box 200, American Fork, UT 84003; (801) 756-5238; http://www.nps.gov/tica/

DON'T MISS

Cascade Springs, located just north and east of the monument off the Alpine Scenic Loop Road (UT 92), bubbles cool and clear right out of the ground, and has created an incredibly rich habitat for birds, animals, and native species of trout. A boardwalk lets you walk around the spring and peer down into its crystalline waters. To get there drive 2.5 miles to North Fork Junction, bear right on UT 92, and drive another 7 miles to the Cascade Springs Road.

Utah County Travel Council, Suite 111, 51 S. University Ave. (in the old county courthouse), Box 912, Provo, UT 84601; (801) 370-8393 or (800) 222-UTAH

Uinta National Forest, 88 W. 100 N., Provo, UT 84601; (801) 377-5780

Uinta National Forest, Pleasant Grove Ranger District, 390 N. 100 E., Pleasant Grove, UT 84062; (801) 785-3563

10

Geologist Clarence E. Dutton, poetic chronicler of John Wesley Powell's famous Colorado Plateau explorations, perhaps said it best when he described the fantastic buttes and chasms of Zion in 1880: "There is an eloquence to their forms which stirs the imagination with a singular power and kindles in the mind . . . a glowing response. . . . Nothing can exceed the wondrous beauty of Zion . . . in the nobility and beauty of the sculptures there is no comparison." Sheer canyon walls over 2,000 feet high, soaring rock monoliths or thrones, and beautifully etched mesas all painted in exquisite hues of buff, gold, peach, and salmon, as well as the peacefully burbling Virgin River, lush hanging gardens, and numerous waterfalls that pour off the cliffs after a rainstorm, all contribute to the magnificent natural beauty of this park.

The amazing formations of Zion exist at the western edge of the Colorado Plateau, an enormous raft of layered sedimentary rock covering all of southeastern Utah and parts of the other Four Corners states. The landscape of the plateau has been dramatically shaped by rivers carving down through its surface, most notably by the one that shares its name with the plateau: the Colorado. The usually placid North Fork of the Virgin, which looks to be little more than a stream most of the time, can turn into a crashing, angry torrent carrying trees and boulders like tiny bits of flotsam during heavy summer thunderstorms. This small stream is almost solely responsible for the downcutting that has resulted in the 2,000- to 3,000-foot sheer walls of Zion Canyon.

Navajo sandstone is almost 2,000 feet thick here, thicker than anywhere else in the Colorado Plateau, and forms most of the towering monoliths and sheer walls in the canyons. The frosted quartz grains and sweeping cross-bedded design of the Jurassic's Navajo sandstone tell the story of a time 150 to 200 million years ago when most of what is now western North America was a Sahara-like desert, covered by enormous dunes that moved back and forth across the land as prevailing winds shifted. The Jurassic's Kayenta formation, lying below the Navajo sandstone, is made up of softer mudstones, siltstones, and sandstones deposited across a broad floodplain or river delta. This layer has eroded away more easily, undermining the Navajo sandstone standing above it, which then falls away from existing walls in great vertical sheets. The park is large and extends far beyond Zion Canyon into a wilderness of still more outstanding natural wonders and stunning beauty.

Cycling in the Park

Whether you're a hard-core mountain biker, a skinny-tire fan, or still on training wheels, you'll love the pedal up through Zion Canyon. Families with little folks will want to stick to the paved Pa'rus Trail, a 2-mile stretch beginning in Watchman Campground and traversing the lower end of the canyon. There is no better way to take in the scenery along the entire 7-mile length of this canyon than from the seat of your bike.

Beginning in the year 2000, bikers will no longer have to share the road with endless streams of camper and car traffic. In a move aimed at decreasing traffic and parking problems that have caused headaches for park personnel and impacted the park experience for visitors, Zion will require anyone who wants to see the upper canyon and doesn't have a bike or is willing to walk to ride a shuttle bus. This will make pedaling the park's main road far more enjoyable. Traffic is almost never a problem on the Kolob Terrace Road or Kolob Canyons Road, but it can be on the Zion–Mount Carmel Highway (UT 9). Unfortunately, bikes are not allowed in the long tunnel along the incredibly scenic Zion–Mount Carmel, because it is so constricted and dangerous. The 5-mile road from the Kolob Canyons entrance at the north end of the park up to Kolob Canyons Viewpoint is paved and a fairly good climb. There are

CYCLING OPTIONS

There are seven rides listed in this chapter; two are suitable for either road or mountain bikes, two are designated road-bike rides, and three are designated for mountain bikes. Two of the rides described here are suitable for families: the Pa'rus Trail and the ride to Grafton Ghost Town. Another possible ride for families or beginning cyclists heads out to the Virgin Overlook on Gooseberry Mesa and is listed at the end of the Gooseberry Mesa ride. The ride up to the Kolob Canyons is short but steep and suitable for intermediate-level road or mountain bikers.

A moderately difficult road ride on the Kolob Terrace Road takes skinny-tire fans to Kolob Reservoir. Serious intermediate and advanced mountain bikers will love both the JEM Loop and the riding possibilities atop Gooseberry Mesa. Here you can take your pick of an easy cruise on a dirt road out to the Virgin Overlook; a fun, moderately challenging doubletrack that reaches the tip of the mesa and accesses a trail taking you to a heart-pounding overlook; or almost 10 miles of superchallenging slickrock singletrack trails that wind around the top of the mesa.

several good hiking opportunities off this road, as well as along the main park road through Zion Canyon. (It is a good idea to carry a lock while biking anywhere in the park so you can feel free to adventure up any of the trails without having to worry about your bike while you're gone.) The short ride out to the ghost town and old movie set of Grafton, where parts of the classic 1970s film *Butch Cassidy and the Sundance Kid* were filmed, is also very scenic and a great ride for families. The JEM Loop is great off-road adventure well suited for intermediate-level riders with good route-finding skills, and almost all levels of mountain bikers will be thrilled with riding opportunities atop Gooseberry Mesa—especially very accomplished technical riders who love the challenge of slickrock.

51. PA'RUS TRAIL (See map on page 257)

For road and mountain bikes. The recently opened Pa'rus (pronounced "PAH-roos") Trail is the first phase of a transportation plan for nonmo-

Gazing toward Kolob Terrace and the formations of Zion from Hurricane Mesa.

torized means of travel along the park's main road through Zion Canyon. The trail parallels the main road through the lower canyon, winding its way along the North Fork of the Virgin River for almost 2 miles (one-way). This paved trail provides a wonderful, car-free cycling environment for bikers of all ages, and can accommodate bike trailers as well. While pedaling along the Pa'rus Trail, remember to stay to the right and obey all traffic signs where the trail crosses park roads.

Starting point: Watchman Campground, just up and across the road from the park's main visitors center. Park in the amphitheater parking lot.

Length: Just under 2 miles each way, 4 miles round-trip. Allow at least 1½ hours to pedal the route and enjoy the scenery.

Riding surface: Pavement.

Difficulty: Easy. This trail makes for a perfect family outing.

Scenery/highlights: *Pa'rus* is a Paiute word meaning "bubbling, tumbling water," and as you pedal along this trail to the serenades of the Virgin River, as well as Oak and Pine Creeks, you'll know how the trail earned its name. The lush vegetation that flourishes along their banks is dominated by the majestic Fremont cottonwood, which turns a beauti-

Ride 51 • Pa'rus Trail
Ride 52 • Zion Canyon Trail

ful gold in autumn. You'll see Moenave and Kayenta formations, with the towering white cliffs of Navajo sandstone standing above. Ponderosa pines appear in miniature high on the cliff rims and in the chinks of the canyon walls where they have managed to get a foothold.

From the more open lower reaches of the canyon you'll enjoy broad views of the graceful monoliths that flank the canyon higher up. As you head up the canyon the Watchman and Bridge Mountain are immediately to your right; the West Temple, Altar of Sacrifice, and Meridian Tower are on your left. Toward the end of the trail you'll be looking at the East Temple, Twin Brothers, and Mountain of the Sun upcanyon to your right. The Streaked Wall and the Sentinel are on your left.

Best time to ride: Anytime, provided temperatures are comfortable. Summers get too hot to really enjoy exerting yourself in the middle of the day. An early-morning or evening ride is always a great time to be out in the canyon: The light plays dramatically on the cliff walls and monoliths, temperatures are cooler, and you are most likely to see wildlife. While the tops of the surrounding plateaus can remain snow covered throughout the winter, the canyon floor usually stays free of snow.

Special considerations: Rest rooms and water are available at both the visitors center and Watchman Campground. Please stay to the right as you ride along the trail and obey all traffic signs. Be wary where the trail crosses over park roads: Motorists might not see you.

From the amphitheater parking lot turn onto the access road to head out the way you came in. After crossing over the Virgin River on a bridge, immediately go right onto the trail. You skirt the edge of South Campground as you pedal northward, up the canyon. Just past the campground you cross over a service road. From here simply continue heading north along the river, through an open meadow and over another bridge. Pine Creek comes in from the right just before the trail reaches an intersection with the Zion–Mount Carmel Highway (UT 9) heading east through the park, and the Zion Canyon Scenic Drive that heads into the upper canyon. The trail continues to parallel the scenic drive for a short distance beyond this intersection, and then ends at 2 miles where it joins the drive. This is the turnaround point for a completely car-free cycling adventure.

---

52. ZION CANYON (See map on page 257)

For road and mountain bikes. The ride up Zion Canyon on the park's main road is undoubtedly one of the most scenic bike rides you will ever take. You can begin by pedaling 2 traffic-free miles along the Pa'rus Trail (ride 51) before hitting the main road at the intersection of UT 9 and

The massive formation known as Mountain of the Sun dwarfs a cyclist enjoying a peaceful pedal through Zion Canyon.

the scenic drive taking you another 5 miles into the upper canyon. Beginning-to-advanced riders in good physical condition will have little trouble negotiating the mostly level terrain along the canyon floor. You can add 2 miles by beginning your ride in the town of Springdale.

Starting point: Visitors center. Beginning in Springdale is also a good option. Another possible starting point is from the amphitheater at Watchman Campground.

Length: 14 miles out-and-back; 18 miles out-and-back from Springdale.

Riding surface: Pavement. The Pa'rus Trail is also paved.

Difficulty: Easy to moderate. The distance and few rolling hills at the start of this route will make it more difficult for some. Elevation change is negligible.

Scenery/highlights: The farthest reaches of the lower canyon extend to the town of Springdale. From there, and for the first few miles of the route, the canyon is broad with views that take in the Towers of the Virgin to the west, and Johnston Mountain, the Watchman, and Bridge Mountain to the east. Beyond the junction of UT 9 and the park's main road you enter the middle canyon. The massive vertical relief of the Streaked Wall is directly west of the junction, and it's followed by the Sentinel, Court of the Patriarchs, Mount Moroni, and Lady Mountain on the left (west). To the east stand the East Temple, Twin Brothers, and Mountain of the Sun.

Past Zion Lodge, which sits at about the canyon's halfway point, you enter the cool, shadowy depths of the upper canyon. Here the walls seem to lean in, towering above the tree-lined river and the road. A short hike from the lodge takes you to Emerald Pools, where Heaps Canyon pours over into Zion Canyon. Lady Mountain, Castle Dome, Behunin Canyon, Mount Majestic, and the Spearhead encircle the pools to the west, while the Great White Throne looms over the canyon to the east. The river and the road make a great sweeping curve around the formation known as Angels Landing, and the smaller monolith in front of it known as the Organ. Across the road from Angels Landing, Echo Canyon comes in from the east. Beyond Big Bend the canyon gets even narrower and deeper as it approaches the turnaround point at the Temple of Sinawava. A short trail at the end of the road allows hikers to approach a section of

FLORA

Elevations in Zion National Park range between 3,666 feet and 8,740 feet and span three life zones. In the lower Sonoran life zone, found below 3,500 feet, desert scrub communities dominate. Blackbrush, four-wing saltbush, the Utah yucca, and prickly pear, beavertail, claret cup, and Whipple cholla cacti favor the lower, warmer altitudes. In the upper Sonoran life zone (3,500 to 5,500 feet) single-leaved piñon and Utah juniper woodlands dominate, along with Gambel oak, little-leaved mountain mahogany, and shrubs such as buffalo berry, Utah serviceberry, shrub live oak, broom snakeweed, and rabbitbrush. In the transition life zone (5,500 to 8,000 feet) towering ruddy-barked ponderosa pines are easy to spot. Mexican manzanita is a common shrub, as are big sagebrush, mountain mahogany, and snowberry. Rocky Mountain or big-tooth maple turns brilliant red or orange, while quaking aspens glow golden.

The Canadian life zone is found in the highest elevations of the park near Lava Point and on the buttes above the Kolob Canyons, where the dominant trees are white and Douglas firs. In the riparian zones along river corridors the majestic Fremont cottonwood is king, but is attended by velvet ash, box elder, water birch, and netleaf hackberry. Hanging gardens around seeps are oases unhampered by the desert environment that surrounds them. Here you are likely to find several varieties of mosses, maidenhair fern, alcove columbine, scarlet monkey flower, clumps of Jones reed grass, and sometimes the giant helleborine orchid.

There are over 670 species of flowering plants in Zion; they include narrow leaf balsamroot, golden columbine, desert marigold, western wallflower, and prickly pear cacti. Shrubs such as cliffrose, bitterbrush, blackbrush, and Oregon grape bloom yellow, while four different species of penstemons bloom red to pink, joined by scarlet gilias, claret cup cactus, and slickrock paintbrush in their preference for crimson. Pinks include common rock cress, Zion sweet pea, desert phlox, shooting-star, and wood rose. Two varieties of lupines, desert sage, larkspur, indigo bush, and the tri-petaled spiderwort all bloom purple. Utah daisies, evening primroses, and prickly poppies bloom bright white to cream. White blossoms of the sacred datura unfold in the evening to a breathtaking 5 to 8 inches in diameter.

Late afternoon sun illuminates the Towers of the Virgin as a rider slips along the Pa'rus Trail.

the canyon called the Narrows. Here the canyon walls close in to a distance that barely allows the river to pass.

Best time to ride: Year-round, anytime temperatures are comfortable for riding. Summers are very hot, with the mercury often rising past the century mark. During mornings and evenings you are most likely to avoid the bulk of daytime traffic, and have cooler temperatures. These are also the times of day when the lighting on the canyon walls and monoliths is the most dramatic, and wildlife tends to be most active.

Special considerations: Water and bathrooms are available at the visitors center, Watchman Campground, and Zion Lodge about halfway up the canyon. Don't forget to bring a bike lock; there are several great short hikes to take advantage of on this ride.

From the visitors center head out of the parking lot and go left. Turn left again at the junction with UT 9 (Zion–Mount Carmel Highway). If you want to start out on the Pa'rus Trail from Watchman Campground, follow ride 51 to the junction with UT 9. From Springdale, ride the main road into the park and follow either the road or the Pa'rus Trail north until it ends, where you continue on the park's main road.

From here the route follows the scenic drive through the middle and upper canyon, rolling along through the shadowy depths of the canyon toward its eventual end at the Temple of Sinawava. As you pedal through the canyon, cool breezes born out of the constant shadows and water of the creek create pockets of refreshment. After you've taken some time to admire the Temple of Sinawava and made the hike up along the river toward the Narrows, remount and reverse direction, enjoying a totally new perspective on the scenic delights of Zion Canyon on your way back.

---

53. KOLOB CANYONS VIEWPOINT (See map on page 264)

For road and mountain bikes. The ride up to Kolob Canyons Viewpoint is a short but fairly strenuous pedal up to a lookout where you can take in stunning views of the Finger Canyons of the Kolob. The walls of these canyons, which drain the upper Kolob Plateau to the east, stand in almost vertical pinkish red ramparts streaked with desert varnish. This ride climbs at a steady grade into the far northwestern corner of the park, an area bypassed by most visitors. Although the route does not require technical riding skills, it will take a strong pair of legs and a good pair of lungs to negotiate the 1,000-foot-plus climb to the viewpoint. The road is narrow and winding, and traffic can be heavy at times.

Starting point: Kolob Canyons Visitors Center, just off I-15 as you head north toward Cedar City. It is approximately 35 miles from the main park entrance and visitors center at Zion Canyon.

Length: 5.5 miles each way, 11 miles total out and back.

Riding surface: Pavement; narrow and winding—please use caution.

Difficulty: Moderate to strenuous. Although the route is short, the almost 1,200 feet of elevation gain will make this ride difficult for all but the very fit. A mountain bike with lower gearing will be helpful on this ride.

Scenery/highlights: The Finger Canyons of the Kolob feature the same towering buttes, vertical walls, and beautiful redrock hues of red, pink, salmon, and buff found to the south in Zion Canyon, but here the country is higher and the slopes and valleys at the base of the red cliffs are cloaked in the greens of junipers, firs, and pines. Many would argue that the scenery and wilderness character of Kolob Canyons make this area

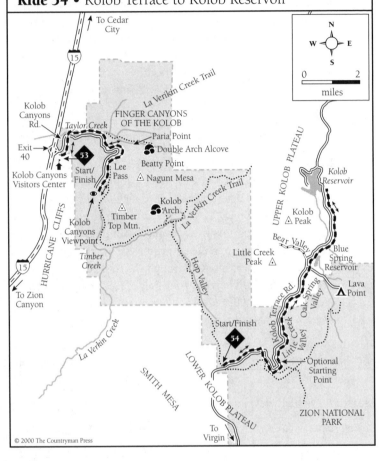

Ride 53 • Kolob Canyons Viewpoint
Ride 54 • Kolob Terrace to Kolob Reservoir

To Cedar City

Kolob Canyons Rd.

Exit 40

Kolob Canyons Visitors Center

Kolob Canyons Viewpoint

To Zion Canyon

HURRICANE CLIFFS

Taylor Creek

Start/Finish

Lee Pass

Timber Creek

Timber Top Mtn.

La Verkin Creek Trail

FINGER CANYONS OF THE KOLOB

Paria Point

Double Arch Alcove

Beatty Point

Nagunt Mesa

Kolob Arch

La Verkin Creek Trail

Hop Valley

Little Creek Peak

Bear Valley

UPPER KOLOB PLATEAU

Kolob Reservoir

Kolob Peak

Blue Spring Reservoir

Lava Point

Kolob Terrace Rd

Little Creek Valley

Oak Spring Valley

Start/Finish

Optional Starting Point

LOWER KOLOB PLATEAU

ZION NATIONAL PARK

SMITH MESA

La Verkin Creek

To Virgin

N
W — E
S

0   2
miles

© 2000 The Countryman Press

even more spectacularly beautiful than the more heavily visited canyon to the south. A short 0.5-mile hike from the end of the road takes you to still more great views over the Timber Creek drainage, and across to the canyons and Timber Top Mountain.

A 5.5-mile out-and-back hike from the Taylor Creek trailhead, approximately 2.5 miles from the visitors center, takes you up the Middle Fork of Taylor Creek with numerous stream crossings to the Double Arch Alcove.

Enjoying the JEM Loop just west of Zion National Park.

The La Verkin Creek Trail leaves from the road at Lee Pass about 4 miles from the start and penetrates deep into the backcountry of the park.

Best time to ride: Anytime the road is dry and free of snow. The Kolob Canyons Visitors Center is more than 1,000 feet higher than the Zion Canyon Visitors Center, and the high country of the plateaus above can remain covered with snow well into spring. Be aware of weather forecasts; if afternoon thunderstorms are predicted, plan this ride for another day or make sure you get an early start.

Special considerations: Water and rest rooms are located at the Kolob Canyons Visitors Center. This road is very narrow and winding; please stay to the right, ride in single file, and use caution.

From the Kolob Canyons Visitors Center mount up and ride out to your right. Breathe deeply and get ready for 5.5 miles of steady grades taking you to the lookout. The road first bends north to traverse the face of the Hurricane Cliffs, which mark the western edge of the Markagunt Plateau and the larger geologic region of the Colorado Plateau. As you cross the face of the cliffs, you can look out westward to the mass of high peaks belonging to the Pine Valley Mountains at the eastern edge of the basin and range region. After 1 mile the road turns east and heads up Taylor Creek drainage, climbing steadily for the next 1.5 miles through piñon and juniper, interspersed with Gambel oak, before turning south and climbing along the South Fork drainage of Taylor Creek.

As you climb out of the South Fork drainage the road curves west and heads up across the slopes of Beatty Point. Just over 4 miles from the start you reach Lee Pass (6,060 feet), which divides the Taylor Creek and Timber Creek drainages. Here breathtaking views into the canyons flood the eastern horizon—and only get better as you reach the end of the road. Make the short hike out the end of the road when you get there, or simply spend your time gazing out into the spectacular redrock scenery before you. When you're ready to go, head back the way you came.

---

54. KOLOB TERRACE TO KOLOB RESERVOIR (See map on page 264)

For road bikes. Like the Kolob Canyons Road, the twisting ribbon of pavement that climbs up and across the lower Kolob Plateau, known as the Kolob Terrace Road, offers some fantastic scenery in an area that sees very few of the thousands of visitors who throng Zion Canyon each year. The road begins in the town of Virgin at an elevation of 3,550 feet and climbs more than 25 miles through several life zones to the reservoir, at an elevation of 8,131 feet. The ride described here begins more than halfway up the road at the Hop Valley trailhead near Spendlove Knoll. From here it is approximately 11 miles and 1,800 feet to Kolob Reservoir, a blue jewel set among evergreens crowning the redrock formations of the Kolob Plateau. Intermediate and advanced road riders in good-to-excellent condition will be best equipped to handle the distance and climbing on this ride. Options for shorter, easier rides are possible here. If you just want to get out with the kids and pedal around a bit, drive all the way to the reservoir and ride the road that makes its way around the shore.

Starting point: Hop Valley trailhead on the Kolob Terrace Road. To get there from the park's main visitors center in Zion Canyon, drive 14 miles west on UT 9 to the town of Virgin. Go right onto this road (on the east side of Virgin) and drive 15 miles up, up, up to a pullout and trailhead on the left-hand side of the road. Park here.

FAUNA

Hummingbirds, including black-chinned, Costa's, and broad-tailed, come to feed on the bounty of blooms in the park. Cliff swallows, violet-green swallows, and white-throated swifts delight in the vertical environments the canyons provide. Green-tailed and rufous-sided towhees; vesper, song, and black-throated sparrows; and five different warblers—yellow, yellow-rumped, Virginia's, black-throated gray, and Grace's—are commonly found in the park during summer. Solitary and warbling vireos are also found here, as is the lovely lazuli bunting. Rock wrens, house wrens, and the canyon wren are more of the many birds that visit the park seasonally. In the riparian areas you are likely to see mallards, grebes, and the great blue heron, as well as spotted sandpipers, American dippers, and water ouzels. Turkey vultures are commonly seen pinwheeling in the sky, while red-tailed hawks tend to soar in a straighter line. Golden eagles have been known to nest in the park, as have peregrine falcons. American kestrels are also quite common around Zion. Wild turkeys have recently made a comeback in Zion.

Mule deer are quite common in the park. Far less visible are the desert bighorn sheep, reintroduced into the park in stages beginning in the 1960s. Every now and again elk wander into the park from the higher reaches of the Markagunt Plateau to the north. Mountain lions thrive throughout. Desert cottontails, pocket gophers, cliff chipmunks, striped and spotted skunks, and muskrats are found in a variety of habitats in the park. Ringtail cats, gray foxes, and raccoons tend to keep a low profile.

Reptiles are probably the most commonly seen animal in the park and include eastern fence lizards, short-horned lizards, and western skinks as well as gopher snakes, whipsnakes, and garter snakes. The only poisonous reptile in the park is the western rattlesnake, which would much rather slither away and hide than have to bite anybody. Besides the seven different amphibious species that live in the waters of Zion, there is also a tiny snail, about the size of a pinhead. This minuscule creature, called the Zion snail, is endemic to the seeps and springs of Zion and found nowhere else in the world. Cutthroat trout and bluehead suckers are known to live in the streams of Zion, but the fishing is notoriously poor.

Singletrack along the Virgin River near Zion.

You can also park 3 miles farther up the road at a pullout and parking area at the top of a steep hill, at the intersection with the road to Lava Point Campground, another 4.5 miles along the road.

Length: 22 miles. Allow at least 4 hours to complete this ride. Shorter options: 16 miles out-and-back; 7 miles out-and-back.

Riding surface: Pavement; narrow and winding.

Difficulty: Moderate to strenuous. There is one steep hill with about a 9 percent grade 2 miles into the trip (the two shorter options avoid this), but the rest of the elevation gain is gradual.

Scenery/highlights: Just inside the park boundary near Spendlove Knoll, you will see several cinder cones—evidence of a fairly recent era of volcanism on the plateau. After crossing over a lava field the road climbs through ponderosa pine and Gambel oak before emerging onto the plateau itself. You'll roll through a series of beautiful, open meadows dotted with grazing cattle before reaching Kolob Reservoir, a popular recreation spot and a good place to cool your heels.

Best time to ride: May through September; beginning in October and running through April this road can be closed due to snow. You can plan on temperatures being anywhere from 15 to 20 degrees cooler up here in summer than in the valleys and lower canyons of the park.

Special considerations: There is little in the way of amenities along this route so be sure to come prepared. Bring plenty of your own water. Pit toilets are available at the Lava Point Campground, located 1.5 miles from the paved road on a rough dirt road, and at the reservoir.

The Kolob Terrace Road has no shoulders and is very narrow and winding. Please use caution, staying to the right and riding in single file.

From the parking area at the Hop Valley trailhead and pullout directly west of Spendlove Knoll, go left onto the Kolob Terrace Road and follow it as it climbs east toward Firepit Knoll. The road climbs to a saddle between the two cinder cones and then skirts the southern flank of Firepit Knoll. As you pedal these few miles, you'll see the Lee Valley stretching away to your right. The road then descends into Pine Spring Wash before making a switchback and beginning its climb through tall stands of ponderosa pines to the plateau. Pine Valley Peak (7,428 feet) is to the south as you climb toward the top of the plateau. Shortly after gaining the plateau you come to a parking area that serves as a good optional starting point. From here the road doubles back and heads north, climbing between an unnamed peak to the north and Pocket Mesa to the south before picking up Little Creek drainage and heading across Little Creek Valley.

For the next 3 miles the road climbs gently through the open ranch country of Little Creek Valley, encountering the turnoff for the primitive Lava Point Campground 7.5 miles from the start. It is over a mile on a dirt road to reach the campground, which might serve as another optional starting point if you are on mountain bikes. Just beyond the turnoff to the campground is Blue Springs Reservoir. A jeep road directly across the road from the reservoir heads up Bear Valley. The Bear Valley is flanked by Little Creek Peak and Kolob Peak on either side. The road heads north for 3 miles, descending and then climbing gently toward Kolob Reservoir through a valley between Kolob Peak and the higher reaches of the Kolob Plateau. When you get to the reservoir take a break, enjoy the incredible transformation of the scenery, and have a snack before heading back the way you came.

55. GRAFTON GHOST TOWN (See map on page 271)

For mountain bikes. The out-and-back adventure to the old town site of Grafton is an easy off-road adventure the little bikers are sure to enjoy. The picturesque ruins of Grafton were made famous in the 1970s film *Butch Cassidy and the Sundance Kid.* Although the ruins of the church, a home, and several other outbuildings are in worse shape now than they were then, they're well worth seeing.

Starting point: The small town of Rockville, 3.5 miles west of Springdale on UT 9. Park along UT 9 near Bridge Road (200 East).

Length: 3.75 miles each way, 7.5 miles out-and-back. Allow at least 2 hours to ride out to Grafton and poke around the ruins.

Riding surface: Mostly dirt road, short section of paved road.

Difficulty: Easy. There are several small hills along this route, which is otherwise level.

Scenery/highlights: The ghost town of Grafton, the graveyard, and the fabulous scenery all make this outing a wonderful trip back in time. Mormon pioneers originally founded the town of Grafton a mile downstream on the banks of the Virgin River in 1859, but a flood two years later destroyed much of it and the decision was made to move the town to its present location. The new site at the mouth of South Wash, however, was also prone to flash flooding from the wash that drained the mesa behind the town. Floods, combined with hostilities from neighboring Paiutes, forced the residents of Grafton to relocate from 1866 to 1868. Further hardships resulted in the abandonment of the settlement by 1900. A schoolhouse and most of a home are still standing with the help of reinforcements, many of which were installed during the making of the movie in the late 1970s.

Best time to ride: Spring and fall; if you are here in the summer a morning or evening ride to Grafton is recommended.

Special considerations: There are no facilities along this route. The closest water, rest rooms, and other refreshments are in the nearby town of Springdale.

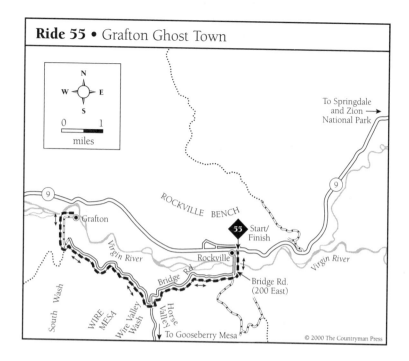

From where you parked in Rockville find the Bridge Road (200 East). Go south over the bridge and the Virgin River, and follow this paved road to the right as it makes a 45-degree turn to the west. It soon turns to dirt. Green fields stretch away from the road down to the river on your right, interrupted now and again by stretches of desert. There are also several interesting sculptures to the right as you ride along; don't miss the Cadillac out in the field. To the left the redrock flank of Gooseberry Mesa rises almost vertically out of the valley floor.

At 1.5 miles into the ride you come to an intersection with the Smithsonian Butte Scenic Byway, which accesses Gooseberry Mesa. Go right, continuing on the Grafton Road to ride out of Horse Valley and Wire Valley Wash west along the foot of Wire Mesa. Soon after South Wash comes in from the left, the road makes another sharp turn to the right and heads north toward the town of Grafton. After you've taken some time to walk around and see the ruins, head back the way you came.

56. THE JEM LOOP (See map on page 273)

For mountain bikes. This is an easy-to-moderate mountain-bike adventure that traverses some of the rolling red hills south of the town of Virgin and north of Gooseberry Mesa. The route crosses wide-open terrain, but the trail is not well marked. Although it is difficult to get truly lost on this ride, having a good sense of direction and good route-finding skills will come in handy. Riders of all abilities will enjoy the red desert scenery, fast-paced singletrack, and spectacular views.

Starting point: A pullout on a dirt road just southwest of the town of Virgin. To get there from Virgin drive west just out of town on UT 9, turning left (south) onto a dirt road just before milepost 17. Drive south over a bridge, continue past a sign and a turnoff for a park and picnic area on your left, and go over a cattle guard. Go a few hundred feet past the cattle guard to a rocky jeep road sloping away to the right. Turn right onto this road and follow it a short distance to where it ends in a looped turnaround just above the Virgin River. Park here.

The short jeep road to the parking area should be passable to most cars, but if you are in a low-slung passenger vehicle you may want to park back at the park and picnic area you passed on your way in.

Length: 13-mile loop. Allow at least 3 hours to complete this loop.

Riding surface: Singletrack, dirt road; a few rocky sections, otherwise hard-packed.

Difficulty: Easy to moderate. A few of the rocky sections require some technical riding skills. A section of trail that traverses the Virgin River along a rock ledge has a good deal of exposure. Novice riders who aren't completely sure of their bike-handling skills should dismount and walk.

Scenery/highlights: This is a great pedal through the sage-dotted red hills southwest of the park. Gooseberry Mesa fills the southern horizon, while the mass of red, pink, and white cliffs, buttes, and monoliths of Hurricane Mesa and Zion dominate the scene to the north and east.

Best time to ride: Spring and fall. If you're here during the summer months, an early-morning or evening start is strongly recommended.

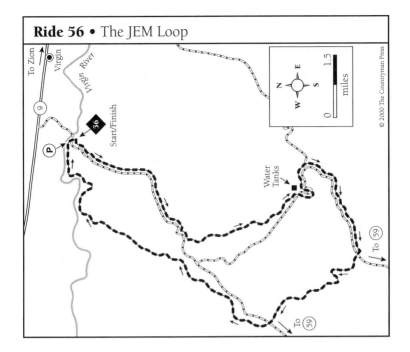

Ride 56 • The JEM Loop

Special considerations: There are no facilities out here, so come pre-pared and bring plenty of your own water. Rest rooms and other conve-niences can be found in the towns of Virgin and Springdale.

Take note of geographic markers as you head out on this trail; they will help orient you. A section of this trail is very exposed along the edge of a canyon. Riders who are not absolutely confident of their bike-han-dling skills should dismount and walk their bikes.

Begin by pedaling back out the short jeep road you drove on down to the parking area. Go right when you reach the dirt road and pedal southwest on this road for approximately 2 miles to where it dips through a large wash. Go past this wash another 0.5 mile until another wash comes in from your left. Turn left into this drainage and pedal for just under a mile to where a singletrack starts on the left side of the wash. (A cairn, or stack of rocks, marks the point where the singletrack begins.) Follow this singletrack as it rolls along for 1.5 miles to its end at a dirt road near some water tanks.

Dismounting and negotiating dangerous sections of trail on foot is a good way to ensure a safe and happy cycling adventure.

Go left on the dirt road, continuing in a southeasterly direction, for 0.5 mile to a junction approximately 4.5 miles from the start. Turn right at this intersection and ride this dirt road for just over 2 miles to the start of another singletrack on the right-hand side of the road. (The start of this section of trail may be marked with another stone cairn, or possibly some flagging.) Follow this fast, rolling section of singletrack northwesterly for 0.5 mile to where it enters a rocky wash. Ride down the wash for a short distance, picking up the singletrack where it leaves the wash and then returns before hitting another dirt road about a mile later; you're now approximately 8.5 miles from the start.

Cross over the road and follow the trail as it swings north, then northeast. In 0.5 mile you encounter a less-used road in a clearing. Follow this road for a short distance to the left, bearing right when it forks. Look for the start of a singletrack marked by flagging and old tires. Follow this singletrack as it dips and rolls for the next 3 miles through the desert scrub, crossing several washes. You cross through a rocky wash and then follow along its southern edge as it drops away to become a shallow canyon. The trail follows the edge of the canyon for the rest of the way, rolling and dipping across several side drainages and coming very close to the edge in places. Please be careful traversing this last section of trail. The trail ends at the loop where you parked your vehicle, 13 miles from the start.

---

57. GOOSEBERRY MESA (See map on page 277)

For mountain bikes. There is something for everyone on Gooseberry Mesa, from the person who simply wants to get out for an invigorating pedal in some stunning redrock desert scenery, to the superexperienced techno-wizard looking for singletrack trails and a serious challenge. The recently constructed singletrack trails make several loops that traverse miles of rolling slickrock atop the mesa, and have been gaining the respect and admiration of fat-tire fans from all over the West. Some of these routes are extremely difficult, requiring balance, skills, and steely nerves. Others are less intimidating but offer plenty of thrills and opportunities for improving your bike-handling technique. Total mileages vary, depending on how many of the singletrack loops you decide to ride. Novice and intermediate riders are sure to enjoy the rolling doubletrack and spur out to a mind-bending overlook (8 miles total), and even families towing trailers or with little folks can have a good time pedaling the dirt road out to Virgin Overlook (just over 3 miles total).

Note: The map and description of the Gooseberry Mesa Trails were provided courtesy of Bike Zion, the only full-service bike shop in Springdale, just outside of Zion National Park. Owner Dean Williamson and a dedicated following of fat-tire fanatics built many of the trails atop Gooseberry Mesa and have many other projects in the works. Stop and see them for any of your bike-related needs, or to get some ideas on where to find more great riding possibilities in the Zion area.

Starting point: At the Y intersection of the Gooseberry Mesa Road and the road out to Virgin Overlook. To get there from Springdale, just outside Zion National Park's south entrance, drive west 2.7 miles on UT 9 to the town of Rockville. Go south on Bridge Road (200 East) in Rockville and drive over the bridge, following the paved section of road as it makes a 45-degree turn to the right. The road soon turns to dirt. Continue 1.5 miles to an intersection and go left on the Smithsonian Butte Scenic Byway. This is a graded and maintained dirt road that accesses UT 59 and the town of Hurricane. It is passable to passenger vehicles except when wet. Do not drive out this way if the ground is saturated; the mud will be a slippery, sticky mess. Drive up a steep hill and continue on this dirt road for approximately 5 miles to the Gooseberry Mesa Road. Turn right and drive another 3.5 miles to the Y intersection of the Left Fork Road, the road that goes out to the end of Gooseberry Mesa, and the main road, which continues out to Virgin Overlook. Park here.

If you are interested in riding only the singletrack or want to shorten your ride out to the point of the mesa, drive 1 more mile on the Left Fork Road to a pullout just beyond a cattle grate.

Length: 4 miles out-and-back to the Virgin Overlook. Five-mile loop to the Virgin Overlook on Steve's Rim Job trail. Approximately 8 miles out-and-back to the point. Ten different singletrack trails varying between 0.5 and 2.5 miles; total of 10 miles.

Riding surface: Dirt road, doubletrack jeep road with sections of sand and rock, singletrack primarily over slickrock with pockets of sand and broken rock.

Difficulty: Easy to very strenuous. While riding the road out to the point of the mesa or to Virgin Overlook requires very little technical riding ability, most of the singletrack riding out here requires strength, skill, and a lot of riding experience. You must honestly judge your riding ability and be sure of your ability to dismount quickly, or be prepared to suffer the consequences. You are not totally committed on these singletrack loops; most are short, and it's easy to bail out and ride on the road.

None of these singletrack trails is easy, but most agree that the Slikrok 101 Loop and Steve's Rim Job, the trail that traverses the northwest edge of the mesa, are slightly easier than some of the rest. The Cattle Grate Trail is harder, and some of the others, including God's Skateboard Park, the Rattlesnake Rim Trail, and That Dam Trail, are extremely difficult.

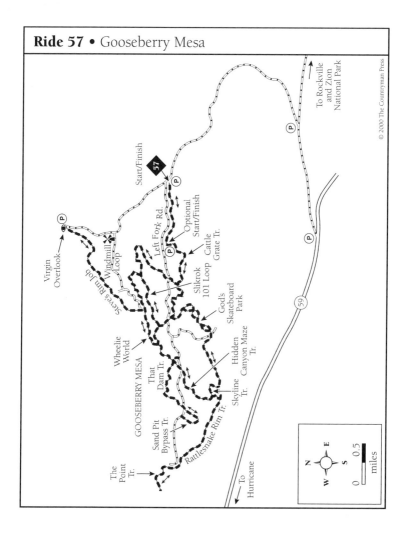

Ride 57 • Gooseberry Mesa

© 2000 The Countryman Press

To Rockville
and Zion
National Park

Start/Finish

57

Left Fork Rd.

Optional
Start/Finish

Cattle
Grate Tr.

Virgin
Overlook

Windmill
Loop

Steve's Rim Job

Slikrok
101 Loop

God's
Skateboard
Park

Wheelie
World

Hidden
Canyon Maze
Tr.

GOOSEBERRY MESA

That
Dam Tr.

Skyline
Tr.

Sand Pit
Bypass Tr.

Rattlesnake Rim Tr.

The
Point
Tr.

To
Hurricane

59

N
W   E
S

0   0.5
miles

God's Skateboard Park and the Sand Pit Bypass Trail are the most technical of the trails out here. Several new trails, including Wheelie World, Hidden Canyon Maze, and the Skyline Trail, provide even more slickrock thrills. The Skyline Trail, by all accounts, is the most difficult of all.

Scenery/highlights: This is gorgeous desert terrain. Smooth rounded humps of peach-to-beige slickrock are interspersed with pygmy forests of piñon and juniper, sagebrush, and manzanita, as well as numerous desert wildflowers that bloom in spring. Sweeping views to the north of Hurricane Mesa and the Kolob Plateau, northeast into the formations of the park (best seen from the Virgin Overlook), and directly east to the Smithsonian Butte and the Eagle Crags are superb. From the end of Gooseberry Mesa you look across to an isolated butte, Sand Mountain, and the valley that cradles St. George beyond to the west. To the northwest is the clump of peaks known as the Pine Valley Mountains.

Of course if you're a technically accomplished mountain biker who likes to use a bike like a pogo stick, then the rollicking, hair-raising singletracks that crisscross the lumpy slickrock of Gooseberry Mesa will be the highlight of this ride for you.

Best time to ride: Spring until mid-June; fall until mid-September. It is awfully hot up here in the summer months, but the mesa is slightly higher than the valley floor. You don't want to ride up here if the ground is wet or heavy thunderstorms are in the forecast. Any part of the ground that is dirt will turn into a muddy mess that sticks to your tires and shoes like cement.

Special considerations: You'll find no facilities or drinking water along this route. Be sure to bring plenty of fluids to consume before, during, and after this ride, especially if you plan on spending the day wrestling your bike along these slickrock trails.

Many of these routes are extremely challenging. Please use your judgment and ride safely!

For an easy ride with the kids out to the Virgin Overlook, go right at the Y intersection and follow the main Gooseberry Mesa Road approximately 1.6 miles to the lookout. Reverse your route on your return. (If you want to make this a longer ride, you can park at the turnoff from the Smithsonian Scenic Byway for Gooseberry Mesa and ride the main road to the overlook from there. This adds 3.5 miles each way and gives you a total trip distance of almost 11 miles.) To ride Steve's Rim Job, one of the less difficult singletrack trails featuring heart-stopping views of the Virgin River Valley and Zion, start by pedaling out toward the Virgin Overlook. Approximately 1 mile from the Y intersection and 0.5 mile before you get to the overlook, a jeep road takes off on the west side of the road. This is

A cyclist zips along fast-paced singletrack atop Gooseberry Mesa through forests of juniper and piñon pine.

Windmill Road. Go left onto this road and ride past a windmill, the namesake of both the road and this trail—the Windmill Loop (approx. 3.5 miles total). Follow the Windmill Road approximately 1 mile until it comes to a junction with another old jeep road. Bear left and follow this road a short distance as it winds back and forth. Bear right where the road meets slickrock and ride along the edge of the formation until you see some rock cairns. Here the trail is marked with sticks and rocks, leading

Sarah Bennett Alley

A hand-carved headstone in the Grafton cemetery is testament to the many hardships, including hostile Indians and repeated floods, that settlers faced here.

you to a trail that traverses the north rim of the mesa. Follow the trail along the north rim until reaching the main Gooseberry Mesa Road at Virgin Overlook. Go right and ride the road back to the Y intersection and your car.

For the singletrack trails, there is not space enough here to describe each and every dip, turn, and drop-off in great detail. Although painted dots and dashes on the rocks serve as markers, many of the trails are hard to follow. Most of these trails can be linked together and ridden in a large loop using part of the dirt doubletrack road (the Left Fork Road) that accesses the point of the mesa. The places where particular trails take off from and emerge onto the Left Fork Road, ending near the tip of the mesa, are identified in the description below of the east-west ride along the Left Fork Road to the end of the mesa.

From the Y intersection ride out on the Left Fork road toward the tip of Gooseberry Mesa. In approximately 1 mile you cross over a cattle grate and observe a pullout and parking area immediately to your left. On the far (south) side of the parking area you can pick up the singletrack called the Cattle Grate Trail. If you do so, follow this singletrack south then west to a junction in 1 mile where you can turn left to continue riding the trail, or right to return to the road.

Just under 2 miles from the start the Cattle Grate Trail returns to the Left Fork Road and the point where the most technical trail of all, God's Skateboard Park, takes off on the left-hand (south) side of the road. Just beyond this junction on the main Left Fork Road, you come to several S turns. The access trail to both the Slikrok 101 Loop and That Dam Trail leaves on the north side of the road from the top of the first turn. This access trail is an old jeep trail that heads due north for just a few hundred feet before ending where the Slikrok 101 Loop takes off to the right and heads east, and That Dam Trail heads off to the left and west. The Wheelie World Trail connects with That Dam Trail about 0.3 mile from its start and parallels both That Dam Trail and Slikrok 101 as it heads east. Wheelie World cuts through the parking area at the end of the Windmill Road and continues east for another 0.5 mile before rejoining the Slikrok 101 Loop.

If you were brave enough to try God's Skateboard Park and survived, you emerge in about a mile onto an old jeep road that rejoins the Left Fork Road just beyond the S turns. Go right and follow the jeep road north past a series of strangely humped rock formations known as the Elephants. You can take this jeep road all the way back to the Left Fork road (about 1 mile), or look for another singletrack trail taking off to your left shortly after you hit the jeep road. The 2.5-mile Rattlesnake Rim Trail leaves from the jeep road on the left as you head north, just after the elephant formations subside. This trail traces the southern rim of the mesa and then rejoins the Left Fork Road just before the trail leading out to the very tip of the mesa.

Just over a mile from the start of the Rattlesnake Rim Trail you find the 1-mile Hidden Canyon Maze Trail taking off to your right and heading north. A little farther along the Rattlesnake Rim Trail another slickrock route called the 0.4-mile Skyline Trail takes off on your right. The Skyline Trail is extremely difficult and dangerous and should not be attempted except by those with the most polished technical skills. It winds its way north to join the Hidden Canyon Maze Trail.

The Left Fork Road continues rolling past the intersection with the jeep trail that accesses God's Skateboard Park and the Rattlesnake Rim Trail, across stretches that are sometimes rocky, sometimes sandy, toward the end of the mesa. Approximately 1 mile beyond that junction with the jeep road, you encounter one of two sand pits. Just beyond the first sand pit That Dam Trail rejoins the Left Fork Road on your right. You can pick up this trail here on your way back. Another, longer sand pit awaits ahead, but just in case you haven't had enough technical slickrock riding by now, you can take the ultratechnical Sand Pit Bypass Trail, which makes a loop around the sand pit on the south side of the road. Once you get past the second sand pit, it is approximately 0.6 mile to the spot where the Rattlesnake Rim Trail rejoins the road on the left. Just beyond, the doubletrack of the Left Fork Road comes to an end and the Point Trail, accessing the very tip of the mesa, begins.

Only the first half of the trail is ridable for most. At a certain point you will have to leave your bike and scramble out to the end of the mesa, where the world drops away below you. Please be careful out here and do not approach the edge. There is almost 2,000 vertical feet of nothing below you. Make your way back either on road or trails.

CAMPING

There are two developed and one undeveloped campgrounds in Zion National Park. Both **South Campground** and **Watchman Campground** are located near the park's south entrance across from the visitors center. Both are managed on a first-come, first-served basis. Between the two of them there are 250 campsites. Facilities include rest rooms, drinking water, picnic tables, fire grates, RV dump stations, and utility sinks. A per-night fee is required at both. Sites with RV hook-ups are available at Watchman Campground for a slightly higher fee. Group campsites are available by reservation to organized groups of 9 to 40 people. A per-person, per-night fee is charged, along with a campsite fee. Reservations can be made for either campground by calling (800) 365-2267 or by visiting the park's reservation Web page (http://www.reservations.nps.gov/)

The **Lava Point Campground** is located 20 miles into the park's backcountry on the Kolob Terrace Road. It has six shaded sites and sits on a lava-capped mesa at an elevation of 7,900 feet. This is a primitive campground with vault toilets and no other facilities. You must bring your own drinking water. The campground is managed on a first-come, first-served basis, and no fee is charged. The maximum vehicle size allowed is 19 feet.

There are many options for camping on BLM lands surrounding the park. Talk to a park ranger or stop in at the BLM offices in St. George.

Zion Canyon Campground (479 Zion Park Blvd.) in the town of Springdale can accommodate RVs and has laundry and shower facilities. Call (435) 772-3237. There are many choices for private campgrounds in St. George, a favorite wintering ground for the snow-weary, about 45 miles away.

LODGING

The **Zion Lodge** is a charming structure that offers rustic accommodations in the heart of Zion

Canyon. You can hike right out the front door, listen to the Virgin River burbling by, or just enjoy the way the light plays on the canyon walls as the sun moves overhead. The lodge is open year-round and offers western-style cabins, motel rooms, and suites. A restaurant in the lodge will pack a picnic lunch if notified in advance. Lodge accommodations book up months in advance, so it is recommended that you make reservations at least 6 months ahead.

There are a good number of options in Springdale. The **Best Western Driftwood Lodge,** the **Zion Park Inn,** and the **Zion Desert Peal Inn** all offer all the amenities. **The Cliffrose Inn** (435-772-3234 or 800-243-8824) and **Flanigan's Inn** (435-772-3244 or 800-765-7787) are other good choices. The **Canyon Ranch Motel** (435-772-3357) offers cottages with kitchenettes, and the private **Zion Canyon Campground** (435-772-3237) has both cabins and motel rooms. The **Pioneer Lodge Motel** (435-772-3233) and the **El Rio Lodge** (435-772-3905) are older but tried and true. All these lodging options are located on Zion Park Boulevard, the main road through town.

There are more than half a dozen B&Bs located in Springdale and Rockville. Stop in at the Tourist Information Center in Springdale to see what appeals to you.

FOOD

The **Zion Lodge Dining Room** in the park is a moderately priced restaurant serving American fare three meals a day. A snack bar at the lodge serves fast-food items.

There are several great options for a meal in Springdale, the most noteworthy being a Mexican/nouveau southwestern restaurant called the **Bit & Spur** (1212 Zion Park Blvd.). The food is as spicy as you like and delicious. It's open for dinner only. You can get breakfast at the **Bumbleberry Restaurant** (897 Zion Park Blvd.), at the **Shonesburg Restaurant** (897 Zion Park Blvd.), or at **Flanigan's Inn & Restaurant** (428 Zion Park Blvd.), which also serves a great lunch and dinner. There's the **Panda Garden Chinese Restaurant** (805 Zion Park Blvd.), the **Pioneer Restaurant** (828 Zion Park Blvd.) serving American food and some vegetarian dishes, and the **Switchback Grille & Trading Co.** (1215 Zion Park Blvd.), which offers steaks, seafood, wood-oven pizzas, and rotisserie chicken in a trendy atmosphere.

LAUNDRY

Several of the hotels in Springdale offer a laundry service or have laundry facilities. Other than St. George, the nearest Laundromat about 22 miles from the park is

Heritage Valley Laundromat, 55 E. State St., Hurricane; (435) 635-3642

BIKE SHOP/BIKE RENTAL

IN SPRINGDALE:

Bike Zion, 445 Zion Park Blvd.; (435) 772-3929; http://www. bikezion.com/

DON'T MISS

Don't miss the chance to hike one of the trails in Zion Canyon when visiting the park. While trips to the Emerald Pools, Hidden Canyon, Weeping Rock, or the approach to the Narrows are all wonderfully scenic hikes to beautiful parts of the canyon, none can compare to the experience of hiking up to Angels Landing. This stunning monolith of Navajo sandstone juts out into Zion Canyon, forcing the Virgin River to make a great bend around it and its lower companion rock, known as the Organ. The masterfully engineered trail to the top of Angels Landing was finished in 1926 and was one of the first trails built in the canyon. Parts are etched into the almost sheer rock face of the formation, while others traverse razor-sharp ridges. Sections of chain have been bolted to the rock for safety along the most dangerous parts of the trail. Heart-stopping views to the canyon floor 1,000 feet below and directly across the canyon to the enormous bulk of one of the park's most famous features, the Great White Throne, await those who have both the nerve and the legs to get themselves to the top. This hike is not for everyone; the big exposure, steep trail, and overall length of the hike make it suitable for those in good-to-excellent condition who are confident of their ability to make it to the cliff rim and descend safely. This is not a good hike for small children, and it should be avoided completely if there is a chance of a thunderstorm or if the rock surface is wet or may be covered with snow and ice.

Bicycles Unlimited, 90 S. 100 E.; (435) 673-4492

The Bicycle Warehouse, 1060 E. Tabernacle; (435) 673-0878

Red Rock Bicycle Co., 146 N. 300 E.; (435) 674-3185

IN CEDAR CITY:

Bike Route, 70 W. Center; (435) 586-4242

Cedar Cycle, 38 E. 200 S.; (435) 586-5210

Color Country Cyclery, 491 S. Main St.; (435) 586-7433

FOR FURTHER INFORMATION

Zion National Park— Superintendent, Springdale, UT 84767; (435) 772-3256; **Tourist**

Information, Town Center Old Church, 868 Zion Park Blvd., Springdale, UT 84767

St. George Chamber of Commerce (in the historic county courthouse), 97 E. Saint George Blvd., St. George, UT 84770; (435) 628-1658

Bureau of Land Management (BLM) (good selection of maps and field guides), Dixie Resource Area, 225 N. Bluff St., St. George, UT 84770; (801) 673-4654

Dixie National Forest— Supervisor's Office, 82 N. 100 E., Box 627, Cedar City, UT 84721; (435) 865-3200

Dixie National Forest, Pine Valley Ranger District, 289 E. Riverside Dr., St. George, UT 84770; (435) 652-3100

IT'S INTERESTING TO KNOW . . .

The first human visitors to Zion Canyon were most likely Archaic Indians who came here seasonally to hunt and gather. They were followed by Ancestral Puebloans, also called the Anasazi, who left behind images hidden among the canyon walls. The seminomadic Southern Paiute were the next to inhabit the region; they hunted and gathered seeds and plants in the area but never took up permanent residence.

The first documented full-time resident in the canyon was Isaac Behunin, a Mormon pioneer. He built a cabin and tilled the rich river soils near the present site of Zion Canyon Lodge. Thinking that the place was his promised land and a refuge from persecution he had suffered elsewhere, he named the canyon Zion.

Part Two COLORADO

11

On a quiet country road just outside a small agricultural community on the plains of southeastern Colorado lies Bent's Old Fort, arguably one of the most significant sites in the history of the American West. The fort was first built in 1833 on the banks of the Arkansas River as a trade and rest stop along the Santa Fe Trail by Bent, St. Vrain & Company. Because timber was scarce, it was built mainly of adobe mud with the labor of Mexican women. It was later destroyed by fire but has been beautifully re-created on the original site with genuine historic artifacts. Knowledgeable volunteers dressed in period garb demonstrate the crafts and activities of the era, as well as provide interesting insight to the life and history of the fort.

Brothers William and Charles Bent, along with Ceran St. Vrain, were all from St. Louis and participated in the fur trade as young men, but saw the opportunity for profit in trade with Mexicans to the south and the wealthy and highly mobile Plains Indians. As the only opportunity for rest, resupply, and repairs between Independence, Missouri, and Santa Fe, Bent's Fort was a welcome stopover for many weary travelers. Trade flourished with the Mexicans, who sought silver, furs, and horses in exchange for goods such as cloth, glassware, and tobacco. Thousands of beaver pelts moved through the fort in its first years. When the beaver population later declined, buffalo hides and horses became the most

Dropping down into Picket Wire Canyon from the prairie that surrounds Bent's Old Fort and the area around La Junta, Colorado.

common trade currency. These were supplied by the tribes of southern plains, which included the Kiowa, Comanche, and Cheyenne. The Indians brought buffalo hides that were pressed into bales at the fort, and horses, many of which were taken in raids. In return they sought blankets, guns, axes, tobacco, pipes, tools, bells, and beads.

The Bents' reputation as traders gave them access to many Indian villages, and their knowledge of Indian languages and customs enabled them to dominate trade on the southern plains. Their work to keep peace between tribes further benefited their business and helped establish their fort as headquarters for the Upper Platte and Arkansas Indian Agency in 1846. Next door to the trade room at the fort is the council room, where terms of trade were agreed upon and peace talks conducted among warring tribes.

During the Mexican-American War the military took over the fort, packing its storerooms with munitions and soldiers. Later an unending flow of gold seekers and settlers disrupted relations with the Indians, polluted surrounding water sources, and stripped the landscape of its grass and trees. The disappearance of the bison, increasing tensions between settlers and Indians, and a particularly severe cholera epidemic finally killed trade at the fort. St. Vrain tried unsuccessfully to sell the fort to the U.S. Army in 1847, and it is thought that William Bent himself burned the place down in 1849 before moving his operations downriver.

During its heyday the fort hosted trappers, traders, and adventurers such as Jim Bridger and Kit Carson; it was a magnet for both the curious and the scholarly exploring the West. Bent's Fort also played an important role in the pursuit of Manifest Destiny by serving as a gateway for settlement and the eventual annexation of Mexico's northern territories. And by introducing Native Americans to firearms, durable goods, alcohol, and disease, the fort changed their cultures forever, weakening their ties to the land and so facilitating settlement of the surrounding country.

Cycling in the Park

Because this historic site sits on only a few acres, there is no cycling inside the park. The gentle prairie that stretches away from Bent's Fort in all directions, however, offers a great opportunity for both avid road riders and pleasure riders to get out of the car, breathe in the friendly prairie air, and imagine the bustle of activity that once existed here. You can ride the old Santa Fe Trail along CO 194 from either La Junta or Las Animas to get to Bent's Fort, or ride it out to the south and west toward the settlement of Timpas inside the boundaries of the Comanche National Grassland before looping back to La Junta. Also south of La Junta you'll find the Picket Wire Canyonlands, a break in the prairie's surface where the Purgatoire River has eroded down through layers of pastel-colored sandstone. This area offers a fantastic opportunity to do some exploring on your mountain bike. The hidden valleys and beautiful rock walls created by the river are the site of several homesteads, most of which now lie in ruins. Prehistoric rock art thought to have been left by nomadic hunter-gatherers moving through the area possibly as long as 4,500 years ago can also be seen along the canyon walls. Still, the most interesting attractions in the canyonlands are the dinosaur tracks found in the sandstone along the river. These prints, laid down 150 million years ago in Morrison formation sand- and mudstone, constitute what is considered the largest track site in America.

Bent's Old Fort and surrounding areas see most of their visitor traffic in spring and fall, when the temperatures are more reasonable. The fort itself sees a scant 45,000 visitors a year, the bulk during the spring months. Summers are scorching in this area, with midday temperatures frequently rising over the century mark, and winters in this part of Colorado are characterized by ground blizzards and freezing temperatures making, it unsuitable for any kind of biking adventure. Your best bet for riding in the Picket Wire Canyonlands is spring, when vegetation has not yet choked the trails and temperatures aren't too hot. Nevertheless, it can be buggy this time of year, and the wind blows steadily. Fall—which sees fewer visitors and less wind—is also a good time for visiting the fort.

---

58. THE SANTA FE TRAIL—HIGHWAY 194 (See map on page 292)

For road bikes. This route follows the old Santa Fe Trail and can be ridden from La Junta to Bent's Old Fort (7 miles one-way), and from the fort to Las Animas (13 miles one-way). This section of the Santa Fe Trail—known as the Mountain Branch—followed the Arkansas River west before dropping south over Raton Pass to Taos. The Cimarron Cutoff branched off from the town in Kansas of the same name and headed directly southwest across a barren and waterless stretch of country to rejoin the main route near present-day Las Vegas, New Mexico. The Mountain Branch of the trail was considered one of the hardest sections, featuring slow going and plenty of danger. Wagon trains moved only about 15 miles a day across land the Kiowa and Comanche steadfastly defended as their own.

Ride 58 • The Santa Fe Trail–Highway 194
Ride 59 • Comanche National Grasslands Tour

Today the setting is rural; the terrain is mostly flat, with a few low rolling hills. Riders of all abilities will enjoy an hour or two cruising the mostly quiet backcountry roads of these sleepy farm towns. Be aware of farm trucks and equipment on these back roads. Work trucks barrel along these stretches at high speeds, and getting around slow-moving pieces of farm equipment requires special care.

Ruins of the Dolores Mission in Picket Wire Canyon dating from the mid-1800s.

Starting point: The Koshare Indian Museum, on the campus of Otero Community College located on 18th Street west of Santa Fe Avenue, or City Park, between 10th and 14th Streets and Park and Colorado Avenues, both in La Junta.

Length: Approximately 16 miles round-trip. 26 miles round-trip from Bent's Old Fort to Las Animas.

Riding surface: Pavement.

Difficulty: Moderate. The road surface and terrain are suited for beginners, but their traffic and length make make them better for intermediate riders.

Scenery/highlights: These are nice tours through peaceful farming country. The sweeping views, gentle breezes, and easy pedaling let your mind wander back to the days when this area was a busy hub for traders and travelers. The Koshare Indian Museum is well worth a visit.

Best time to ride: Spring and fall; wind can make this ride more difficult in spring. During the summer months it is probably wise to ride early or

Mounds of beautiful pink bush morning glory bloom midsummer in Picket Wire Canyonlands.

late in the day, when temperatures are cooler. You may find that there is more farm traffic at these times, however.

Special considerations: As noted, speeding farm trucks and slow-moving farm equipment may pose some risk on the road.

Water and bathrooms are available at Bent's Old Fort and in La Junta. You'll find there are very few spots along the way for fueling up, so be sure to bring plenty of your own water and a lunch or some snacks.

From the Koshare Indian Museum or the City Park in La Junta, ride north on Colorado Avenue to First Street (US 50). Go right onto US 50, ride east for 0.5 mile to the intersection with CO 109, then turn left across the railroad tracks and over the Arkansas River. Continue heading north on CO 109 for another 0.5 mile before turning right onto CO 194 (Trail Road). You now pedal east on CO 194 for approximately 7 miles to Bent's Old Fort National Historic Site. When you're ready, head back the way you came. If you're starting this ride at the fort, simply reverse these directions. If you are staying in Las Animas and riding to the fort from there, head north on US 50 and ride approximately 1 mile from downtown, across the Arkansas River, to the junction with CO 194. Go left on CO 194 and pedal westward approximately 8.5 miles to Holbrook Canal

Road. Go left onto this road and ride just over 1 mile to where you intersect CO 194 again. Go left onto CO 194 here and follow it another 3 miles to Bent's Old Fort. When you are ready to go head back the way you came.

59. COMANCHE NATIONAL GRASSLAND TOUR (See map on page 292)

For road bikes. This route follows the Santa Fe Trail southwest from La Junta to the small community of Timpas along Timpas Creek, where early travelers slaked their thirst. Because of its length, traffic, and gentle dips and rises, this is an intermediate-level road ride. There are options for making this a longer or shorter road tour.

Starting point: City Park in La Junta, between 10th and 14th Streets and Park and Colorado Avenues.

Length: Approximately 40-mile loop; 45-mile loop; approximately 60-mile loop.

Riding surface: Pavement; rough and buckled in places on back roads.

Difficulty: Moderate to difficult. Because of the length and the highway riding, this is an intermediate-to-advanced road ride. A good level of physical fitness is required to negotiate some of the rolling terrain.

Scenery/highlights: The Comanche National Grassland, managed by the U.S. Forest Service, was established in 1954. Almost half a million acres in three counties are included, and although there are more than 200 grazing allotments within its boundaries, this remains a great example of prairie ecosystems. The undulating prairie surface that gives way to the Purgatoire River drainage along with the broken sandstone ledges, broad valley floors, and riparian areas are home to a wealth of bird and animal species that depend on the habitats and geography found here.

Despite the barbed-wire fences, windmills, and occasional water trough, the sweeping outline of this country is much the same as it was during the era when thousands of immigrants, fortune seekers, and soldiers passed through here on foot and horseback. This stretch of the trail marks the transition from prairie to mountains, a significant milestone in the journey and one you can appreciate from the Sierra Vista Overlook

FLORA

Some of the showy spring bloomers you will see both in the canyon-lands and on the grasslands are yellow flax, pink locoweed or milk vetch, and pink and purple phlox. In the early-spring canyonlands you might be lucky enough to spot a white sand lily. Purple penstemon eventually gives way to the fiery red blooms of Indian paintbrush in summer, which is followed by gorgeous mounds of pink bush morning glories and dense patches of sunflowers.

Some of the species that comprise the grasslands include glue gramma, alkali sacaton, western wheat, and June grasses. Check in with the folks at the Comanche National Grassland office in La Junta for a more complete plant list.

just off CO 71. From here the Spanish Peaks come into view, a guiding marker along the Santa Fe Trail. From bluffs above Timpas Creek, reached by a short trail, you can take in a sweeping vista of the Rocky Mountains.

The Timpas Picnic Area just outside the settlement of the same name is a great place to stop and take a break. A 0.5-mile nature trail takes you to Timpas Creek and back; stone markers along the way reveal where the Santa Fe Trail came through. There are covered picnic tables and vault toilets here, but not water.

Best time to ride: Spring through fall, but beware of strong winds in springtime. Because this is an agricultural area, you're likely to find just as much traffic on the roads in the early morning and evening as in the middle of the day. In summer midday gets good and hot.

Special considerations: Water and bathrooms are available in La Junta. Bring plenty of water and snacks: This is a longer ride with no convenience stores along the way. There are no services in Timpas.

From the city park in La Junta, ride north on Colorado Avenue. When you reach Fifth Street turn left (west) to cross over the Anderson Arroyo, where you intersect Barnes Avenue. At Barnes Avenue Fifth Street becomes US 350, the main highway to the town of Trinidad.

Cyclists examining dinosaur tracks along the banks of the Purgatoire River.

To ride the 40-mile loop, head out of La Junta on US 350 and ride 16 miles southwest to the settlement of Timpas. When you get to Timpas, look for County Road 16.5 on your right. This takes you to the Timpas Picnic Area, where you can take a break in the shade, walk to the creek, or gear up for your ride back. When you are ready, ride back out onto US 350 heading northeast. After 3 miles you come to the intersection with CO 71. Turn left onto CO 71 and ride due north for 9 miles to the town of Hawley. There you turn right onto CO 10 and ride 10 miles to US 50. When you reach US 50 go right and ride approximately 1 mile back into La Junta.

Option 1: To ride the 45-mile loop, head out of La Junta on US 350 and ride approximately 4 miles to CR 26 (listed on some maps as CR 21). Turn left onto CR 26 and ride due south for 7 miles. At this point the road makes a 45-degree turn to the right; about a mile later it makes another to the left. Follow the road for another 2 miles as it bends around before turning into CR N. You follow this road for 9 miles to the town of Timpas. Cross over onto US 350 and find CR 16.5, which takes you to Timpas Picnic Area for a snack and a break. When you're ready to head back, ride back as directed in the preceding paragraph.

Option 2: To ride the 60-mile loop, follow the directions for option 1, but instead of heading back via CO 71 and 10, head out of Timpas on CR N, continuing west. You ride 5 miles west on this road before it makes a 45-degree turn and becomes CR 11. Ride 10 miles north on CR 11 to its intersection with CO 10. Turn right onto CO 10 and ride it for another 10 miles to the town of Hawley. Continue east on CO 10 for another 10 miles to US 50, where you go right, back into La Junta.

---

60. PICKET WIRE CANYONLANDS (See map on page 299)

For mountain bikes. This is a great intermediate-level, out-and-back mountain-bike adventure with plenty to see along the way: You'll drop down into the sandstone canyons of the Purgatoire River drainage and ride along the river where you will see ruins, dinosaur tracks, the old Rourke Ranch, and perhaps even ancient Indian petroglyphs. Mileages between 10 and almost 24 miles are possible, depending on where you choose to start and how far you decide to go. You can spend anywhere from a couple of hours to an entire day exploring the nooks and crannies of this beautiful river canyon.

Starting point: Approximately 25 miles south of La Junta. Drive out of town on US 350; after approximately 4 miles, bear left onto CR 26, following it as it makes several 90-degree turns. When you come to an intersection with CR N, continue heading due south, now on CR 25. Continue southbound on this road, passing the intersection with CR 802, until the road makes another 90-degree turn and heads west, becoming CR B. At the corner where CR 802 ends and CR B heads west, a dirt road takes off to your left. Follow this dirt road until you reach a bulletin board listing information about Picket Wire Canyonlands. Park here.

If you have a four-wheel-drive or high-clearance vehicle you may wish to drive the 3 miles on the dirt road to the pipe gate to begin this ride.

Length: 16.5 miles round-trip to the dinosaur tracks. 23.5 miles round-trip to the Rourke Ranch. Subtract 6 miles from these totals if you begin your ride at the pipe gate.

Riding surface: Rough dirt road with rocky sections, doubletrack, singletrack.

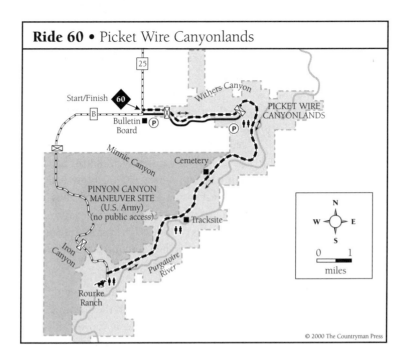

Start/Finish **60**

Bulletin Board

PICKET WIRE CANYONLANDS

Withers Canyon

Minnie Canyon

Cemetery

PINYON CANYON MANEUVER SITE (U.S. Army) (no public access)

Tracksite

Iron Canyon

Purgatoire River

Rourke Ranch

0 — 1 miles

© 2000 The Countryman Press

Difficulty: Moderate to difficult. There's one particularly steep, rocky section at the start that everyone but the most skilled technical riders will have to walk. Otherwise this is an intermediate ride requiring a good level of physical fitness.

Scenery/highlights: The canyon is lovely; pastel-hued layers of sandstone have been revealed by the work of the Purgatoire River, providing the vertical surfaces used by the ancients for their intriguing figures and symbols. Little archaeological research has been done in the area, so little is known about the people who left their mark here. Some of the glyphs are thought to be 4,500 years old, while others have been estimated to be only 350 years old.

The hidden valleys and beautiful rock walls created by the river are the site of several homesteads, most of which now lie in ruins. Among them you can find the remains of the Dolores Mission and Cemetery, built sometime between 1871 and 1889 when Mexican pioneers first established a permanent settlement. The Rourke Family Ranch, also known as the Wineglass Ranch, was established in 1871 to raises horses and cattle; originally it was only 40 acres. By the time the ranch was sold in 1971 it had accrued 52,000 acres and was one of the oldest and most successful ranches in southeastern Colorado. The land is now divided between the forest service and private interests. While the old ranch buildings are owned by the forest service, they are closed to the public.

The dinosaur tracks found in the sandstone along the river may be the highlight of this ride. More than 1,300 visible tracks and close to 100 different trackways stretch for a 0.25 mile along the river. Almost half were left by the enormous plant-eating Brontosaurs, while the other half were left by a ferocious two-footed, meat-eating scavenger called allosaurus. These tracks, laid down 150 million years ago in Morrison formation sand- and mudstone, constitute what is considered the largest track site in America. Some of them are hard to spot. When you find a print, dampen the impression with water and watch it come to life.

FAUNA

In Picket Wire Canyon and the surrounding area live approximately 275 different species of birds, 60 of mammals, 40 of reptiles, 11 of fish, and 9 of amphibians. Among the area's more famous bird inhabitants is the lesser prairie chicken. Other birds you might see in the area include ring-necked pheasants, bald eagles, and long-billed curlews. Pronghorn antelope prefer the wide-open spaces, while white-tailed deer are more likely to be spotted in the canyon. Mountain lion, bobcat, and coyote are among the predator species that survive here.

Best time to ride: Spring and fall. By midsummer the daytime temperatures soar. If you do ride here in the summer, make sure you get an early start and bring plenty of water. Mild days in the winter are ideal here, provided the trail is not snow covered or wet and muddy.

Special considerations: Because this area does not see a lot of traffic, portions of the trail along the river bottom can get very overgrown, at times making forward progress almost impossible. Put on bug spray before heading down this way spring through fall. Also, don't forget sunscreen. Vault toilets are located at the entrance to the canyon, the track site, and the ranch, but no drinking water is available, so be sure to bring plenty.

A hand-carved headstone belonging to the grave of a Mexican settler in the Dolores Mission cemetery.

From the bulletin board ride east on Forest Road 500A for approximately 3 miles until you come to a pipe gate. Go around the gate and head down the steep, rocky section into the bottom of the canyon. This section is treacherous; you'll probably want to dismount and walk your bike through it. When you reach the canyon floor, the jeep road turns into a doubletrack that sometimes becomes a singletrack. Approximately 3.5 miles from the pipe gate you come to the ruins of the mission and cemetery. At this point the trail traverses more river bottom, then begins to parallel the river more closely. From the mission ruins it is about 1.5 miles of rolling up-and-down along the river to the dinosaur tracks. Once you get past the tracks, the trail becomes less overgrown and more open. Another 3.5 miles from the tracksite you'll reach the Rourke Ranch. When you're ready to return, simply head back the way you came.

CAMPING

Camping is limited in this area. Tent camping is possible, and showers are available for registered campers only, at the **KOA** in La Junta. This campground has a swimming pool and accepts pets; it's located at 26680 W. US 50.

IT'S INTERESTING TO KNOW . . .

The Purgatoire River—which joins the Arkansas in La Junta—is so named because a group of Spanish soldiers was believed to have died in the valley without the benefit of clergy. The river, originally named El Rio de Las Animas Perdidas en Purgatorio (River of Lost Souls in Purgatory) by the Spanish, was later rechristened the Purgatoire, by the French who trapped and hunted in the early 18th century. Cowboys and ranchers living in the area corrupted this when they named the nearby canyon the Picket Wire. Today locals pronounce *Purgatoire* as "Purgatory."

LODGING

Holiday Inn Express, Quality Inn, and **Super 8** all have swimming pools (nice after a hot ride) and offer continental breakfast. The slightly thriftier **Stagecoach Inn** features a pool. There is also the **Travel Inn** of La Junta, which has kitchenettes. If you like B&Bs, try the **Jane-Ellen Inn**. Check with the La Junta Chamber of Commerce for more information. If you plan to stay in Las Animas, try the **Best Western Bent's Fort Inn.**

FOOD

As you might suspect, there are some pretty good Mexican restaurants in La Junta. Try **El Azteca** (710 W. Third St.), **Cristina's** (101 Dalton Ave.), or **El Cid** (1617 Raton Ave.). If Chinese is what you're after, try the **New China Restaurant** (414 W. First St.). **Carducci's** (114 Santa Fe Ave.) offers Italian fare, while **Chiaramonte's** (208 Santa Fe Ave.) and the **Capri Restaurant** in the Quality Inn (1325 W. Third St.)

offer slightly more upscale continental dining. **Café Grandmere** (401 W. Third St.) offers a good lunch and dinner menu and seems to be a favorite among locals.

LAUNDRY

Clothes Pin of La Junta, 717 E. Third St.; (719) 384-9812

Fifth St. Laundry (drop-off), 311 W. Fifth St.; (719) 384-9919

BIKE SHOP/BIKE RENTAL

Joey's Bike Shop, 112 W. First St.; (719) 384-6575

FOR FURTHER INFORMATION

Bent's Old Fort—Superintendent's Office, 35110 CO 194 E., La Junta, CO 81050-9523; (719) 383-5010; http://www.nps.gov/beol/

La Junta Chamber of Commerce, 110 Santa Fe Avenue, La Junta, CO 81050; (719) 384-7411

DON'T MISS

The Koshare Indian Museum has excellent collections of Plains Indian clothing, moccasins, and hide paintings, as well as pottery, baskets, and silverwork from such tribes as the Hopi, Zuni, and Navajo. An enormous, beautifully built kiva is the centerpiece of the museum and the site of Native American dances every Saturday evening in summer and on holidays. The dancers are a Boy Scout troop that's not Native American but is nationally known for its authentic dance routines.

Las Animas Chamber of Commerce, 332 Ambassador Thompson Blvd., Las Animas, CO 81054; (719) 456-0453

U.S. Forest Service—Comanche National Grasslands, 1420 E. Third St., La Junta, CO 81050; (719) 384-2181

12

The Black Canyon of the Gunnison, a jagged 53-mile tear in the earth's crust, is a testament to the powerful eroding forces of water. The 12 miles of Black Canyon set aside as a national park are the deepest and narrowest part. At its lowest point the canyon bottom lies 2,425 feet below the rim, and at its narrowest the canyon spans a mere 1,300 feet.

The story of the Gunnison River and its creation of Black Canyon began as much as a billion years ago with the uplift of the Rocky Mountains. More recently the Gunnison uplift pushed this region even higher, while volcanic activity in the West Elk Mountains (to the north) and San Juan Mountains (to the south) began to cover the region with soft lava and ash. With each eruption the course of the Gunnison changed, until finally the river ate its way down through the softer volcanic layers and etched its course into the extremely hard underlying Precambrian schist and gneiss. The squiggles and banding in the dark rocks are telltale signs of their metamorphosis deep below the earth's crust, where they were heated and compressed under enormous pressure before rising closer to the surface. This process separated the different kinds of rock crystals into the discernible bands you can see in the Painted Wall, and is what made the rock hard and strong enough to stand in nearly vertical ramparts for the estimated 2 million years it took for the river to cut down to its present elevation. Today the river rumbles and boils over polished boulders much as it has for eons, remaining a tantalizing lure for kayakers, anglers, hikers, and climbers.

A hundred years ago farmers and boosters started eying the Gunnison's water covetously. Eventually they hatched a plan to survey the river in search of a place to drill a tunnel and pipe water through the Vernal Mesa to the dry Uncompahgre Valley beyond. In the first attempt to float the river in 1900, after a month of mishaps, the five men had to abandon their effort. One man, Abraham Lincoln Fellows, was determined to try again, this time using a rubber mattress and orchestrated resupply efforts from the rim above. He was successful in navigating the river and finding a site for the tunnel. Construction was begun on the diversion tunnel in 1905 and completed four years later. The 5.8-mile-long tunnel still brings water through the earth to the Uncompahgre Valley at the Gunnison Diversion Dam near the East Portal.

Cycling in the Park

Both the North and South Rims of the canyon have roads that skirt the very edges of the gorge, featuring dizzying views into the chasm. Both make for excellent biking adventures, as does the road that accesses the East Portal area. The South Rim of the canyon receives close to 90 percent of the park's 230,000 annual visitors because of its proximity to major highways and the towns of Montrose and Grand Junction. Riding here during peak season can be frustrating because of car and camper congestion. The North Rim must be accessed via CO 92, which heads east and then south from the town of Delta, Colorado. It's much quieter and allows for more of a wilderness experience on two wheels. Along either rim it's a good idea to carry with you a lock to secure your bike so you can take advantage of the great hiking trails along the way.

If you want to get out of the park, road riding through the rural Uncompahgre Valley is a nice option for those who favor skinny-tire adventures. The Dry Creek Loop is a good introduction to the many great trails just outside Montrose, many of which connect to the 140-mile-long Tabeguache Trail. The trek up the Crystal Creek drainage is a wonderful fat-tire trip into the alpine country atop Black Mesa. This region, punctuated by the low, blue mass of the Uncompahgre Plateau to the west, is the transition zone between the larger geologic provinces of

CYCLING OPTIONS

There are six rides listed in this chapter, three road rides and three mountain-bike rides. Roads along both the North and South Rims are easy to moderate and offer excellent opportunities for hiking and seeing the canyon. The more heavily traveled South Rim Road is paved, while the North Rim Road is dirt; both are about 5 miles long one-way (10 to 11 miles total). A 14-mile road ride down to the bottom of the canyon via the East Portal Road is moderate to strenuous and good for strong riders who are comfortable sharing the road with cars. All the rides within the park are at fairly high elevations, which makes riding there more strenuous. Another road ride makes a 32-mile loop on back roads through the rolling agricultural country of the Uncompahgre Valley. The Dry Creek Loop is a moderate 14-mile mountain-bike ride that serves as an excellent introduction to the trail system on the Uncompahgre Plateau; the Crystal Creek Loop is a fairly long (28 miles), but not technically difficult, fat-tire adventure that climbs up through forested terrain atop Black Mesa.

the Colorado Plateau and the Rocky Mountains. It is beautiful, wild country where you can enjoy road and off-road riding most of the year.

---

61. SOUTH RIM DRIVE (See map on page 307)

For road bikes. This could be considered the premier ride inside Black Canyon of the Gunnison National Park. For just over 5 miles you wind along the rim of one of the most dramatic gorges in the world enjoying spectacular views of southwestern Colorado's high plateau country. Elevations along the South Rim are quite high, so a good level of physical fitness is recommended, but this ride is suitable for the whole family.

Starting point: South Rim Visitors Center. The South Rim is located 15 miles east of Montrose, via US 50 and CO 347.

Length: Approximately 5.5 miles one-way, 11 miles round-trip. Allow at least 2 hours for this ride, more if you take any of the hikes.

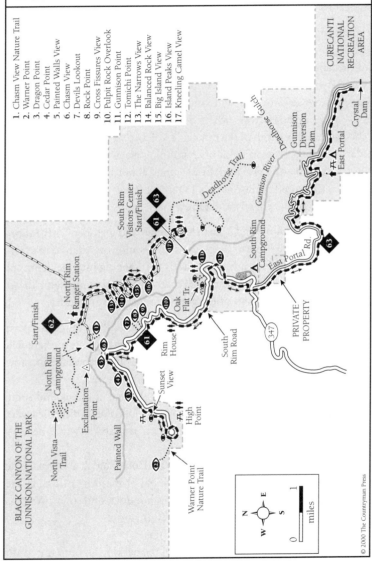

Ride 61 • South Rim Drive
Ride 62 • North Rim Road
Ride 63 • East Portal Road

1. Chasm View Nature Trail
2. Warner Point
3. Dragon Point
4. Cedar Point
5. Painted Walls View
6. Chasm View
7. Devils Lookout
8. Rock Point
9. Cross Fissures View
10. Pulpit Rock Overlook
11. Gunnison Point
12. Tomichi Point
13. The Narrows View
14. Balanced Rock View
15. Big Island View
16. Island Peaks View
17. Kneeling Camel View

BLACK CANYON OF THE GUNNISON NATIONAL PARK

CURECANTI NATIONAL RECREATION AREA

South Rim Visitors Center Start/Finish

Deadhorse Trail

Deadhorse Gulch

Gunnison River

Gunnison Diversion Dam

Crystal Dam

East Portal

South Rim Campground

East Portal Rd.

North Rim Ranger Station

Start/Finish

North Rim Campground

Exclamation Point

Painted Wall

North Vista Trail

Rim House

Oak Flat Tr.

South Rim Road

347

PRIVATE PROPERTY

Sunset View

High Point

Warner Point Nature Trail

N E S W

0   1
miles

© 2000 The Countryman Press

Riding surface: Pavement.

Difficulty: Easy to moderate. No technical skills are needed for this ride, but the elevations and rolling terrain require an intermediate level of physical fitness.

Scenery/highlights: The gently rolling terrain, overlooks into Black Canyon, and sweeping views to the Uncompahgre Plateau, Grand Mesa, and the jagged outline of the San Juan Mountains to the south make this a five-star ride. There are 12 overlooks along this route and several short hikes that are well worthwhile. From Rock Point and Devils Lookout you peer down into the Narrows, where the distance between rims (1,150 feet) is shorter than the depth of the canyon (1,725 feet). The short walks out to Cedar Point and Dragon Point offer stunning views of what is called the Painted Wall. You may also want to take time (about 1½ hours round-trip) to hike from the end of the road out to Warner Point—a great place to take in the view, beat the crowds, and have a snack before heading back.

Best time to ride: April and May to September and October. Early morning and evening are some of the prettiest times and you will find less traffic to contend with. The only drawback is that looking into the depths of the canyon is difficult at these times because of the slanting light. To get the best view of the bottom of the gorge, do this ride at midday.

Special considerations: Elevations on the South Rim range between 7,500 feet and 8,400 feet, so if you live at lower altitudes the air here will feel relatively thin. The area can also be dry and hot, especially in summer. Be sure to drink plenty of water and wear sunscreen.

Thunderstorms are common here in the summer and fall, and some can be quite violent with high winds, hail, and lots of lightning. Be aware of weather forecasts before heading out on your bike; you'll be very exposed along the canyon rims.

There are rest rooms available at the Rim House and at the end of the road at High Point. There is also a snack bar at the Rim House, at the Pulpit Rock pullout, that sells hamburgers, hot dogs, and sodas. Water is available at the visitors center and at the Rim House.

From the visitors center simply ride out of the parking lot onto the South Rim Road and head west. It's easy to pull over and take in the view from

The yawning depths of Black Canyon and the streaks and patterns of the canyon walls are truly something to marvel at.

the saddle, but make sure you watch for cars as you make your way into and out of pullouts. Make your way to the end of the road at High Point, and after you've had a snack or made the hike out to Warner Point, remount and head on back the way you came.

Option: If you're a hard-core road rider consider starting this ride from Montrose, which adds approximately 33 miles to your total distance. This is a popular route for cyclists living in the area, but it requires a good set of legs with lungs to match—you'll climb almost 3,000 feet from Montrose to the canyon rim.

62. NORTH RIM ROAD (See map on page 307)

For mountain bikes. This is an easy-to-moderate out-and-back cruise along Black Canyon's much quieter North Rim. While the North Rim is slightly lower than the South, its views are no less spectacular, and the remoteness and serenity you'll find are worth the extra effort it takes to get here. Riders of all abilities will enjoy this trip.

Starting point: North Rim Ranger Station. From Montrose, either take US 50 east and CO 92 west through the Curecanti National Recreation

FLORA

The high-desert environment atop the rims of Black Canyon features piñon pine, juniper, deciduous Gambel oak, or scrub oak, and service-berry. Studies have revealed that some of the oldest piñon pines in the West exist on the rims of Black Canyon. These trees, dated to between 800 and 900 years old, are extremely drought tolerant. The hike out to Warner Point on the South Rim, and up Green Mountain on the North Rim, are some of the best places to see these ancient trees.

In the spring the yellow sunflowerlike blossoms of narrow-leaved balsamroot are ubiquitous on the rims. Blue chiming bells can also be seen, as can the yellow-to-peach blossoms of prickly pear cactus. The deep red of claret cup cactus is rarer. Later in the summer the fiery red blooms of Indian paintbrush are easy to spot, as are the deep blues and purples of silvery lupine. Several varieties of penstemons also thrive here. In the fall the yellows of rabbitbrush and snakeweed dominate. A complete plant list is available at the visitors center.

Area to Crawford, or take US 50 west through Delta, then CO 92 to Crawford. From Crawford you follow a well-signed gravel road to the North Rim. Park at the North Rim Ranger Station.

Length: 5 miles one-way, 10 miles out-and-back. Allow 2 hours to complete this ride with time spent at the overlooks.

Riding surface: Graded gravel road.

Difficulty: Easy to moderate. There are some rolling hills on this ride, but none is very long or steep.

Scenery/highlights: The view into the Narrows is spectacular from this side of the canyon, as are the views from Balanced Rock, Big Island, and Kneeling Camel Overlooks. This side of the canyon has a much wilder feel; keep your eye out for grazing mule deer at dusk, or a golden eagle soaring along the canyon rim, enjoying the lift of the warm air currents rising out of the canyon. You may even be lucky enough to spot one of the endangered Gunnison sage grouse that live on the North Rim.

If you have enough energy when you get back to your car, there's a great hike that leaves from the ranger station. The North Vista Trail takes you in 1.5 miles to Exclamation Point—a fantastic view but still nowhere near the view you'll get by continuing 2 more somewhat strenuous miles to the top of Green Mountain with its dramatic vistas of the West Elk Mountains to the north.

Best time to ride: Anytime spring through fall. It's best to ride in the morning or evening, because summer midday can be hot. These are also the times you are most likely to see wildlife out and about, as well as the best times for avoiding the dust thrown up by sight-seeing vehicles.

Special considerations: Elevations along the North Rim are high enough (between 7,200 and 8,200 feet) to require some time to adjust to the thinner air. You'll also want to drink plenty of water and guard against the fierce rays of the sun by wearing sunblock or covering up. Also, thunderstorms tend to build up over the mountains here in the summer and fall, and they can turn a clear blue day dark and threatening in a matter of minutes.

There are rest rooms and water available at the North Rim Campground, and rest rooms at the end of the North Rim Road. Bring a lock if you plan to walk the Deadhorse Gulch Trail.

After you've stopped in at the station to talk to the ranger, look at the displays, and thumb through the information available there, head out onto the road and go left (east). Simply pedal along in this direction, pulling over to peer down into the canyon whenever the opportunity presents itself. In 5 miles you come to the end of the road. There is a 2.5-mile (one-way) hiking trail out to Deadhorse Gulch that offers some great views into the East Portal area of the canyon. There are six overlooks. After you've taken the easy hike out to Deadhorse Gulch or had your snack and some water, remount and head back the way you came.

---

63. EAST PORTAL ROAD (See map on page 307)

For road bikes. This is a more challenging route that drops down into the bottom of Black Canyon at the park's eastern boundary, and then contin-

A cyclist enjoys a late afternoon pedal along the north rim of Black Canyon.

ues along the banks of the Gunnison River to where the road ends at Crystal Dam inside the Curecanti National Recreation Area. You should be at a good-to-excellent level of physical fitness to make the climb back out of the canyon to the rim, which gains almost 2,000 feet in 5 miles.

Starting point: South Rim Visitors Center, 15 miles east of Montrose, via US 50 and CO 347.

Length: 7 miles one-way, 14 miles out-and-back. Allow 3 hours to complete this adventure.

Riding surface: Pavement.

Difficulty: Moderate to difficult. Sections of this road are curvy and steep, and in the summer you will be sharing it with a steady stream of car and camper traffic. The route's length and elevation changes require an intermediate-to-advanced level of physical fitness.

Scenery/highlights: This route traverses some really beautiful open country before dropping down to the river at East Portal and the Gunnison Diversion Dam. The park ends at East Portal, and if you continue you will be riding inside the Curecanti National Recreation Area. The 2 miles along the river between East Portal Campground and Crystal

Dam aren't much like the bottom of the canyon inside the park, but they're very pretty and provide several opportunities for a quick dip before making the climb back up to the rim.

Best time to ride: Spring and fall; the weather is gorgeous and the crowds aren't as thick. In the summer, an early-morning or evening start makes the trip cooler.

Special considerations: Sections of this road are packed with tight curves and, during peak visitation, see a fair number of cars and campers. Do not be overly concerned about giving vehicles space to pass on the curves; take up as much of the lane as you need to safely negotiate your turn. You can move over to the right on the straightaways, where it is easier and safer for vehicles to pass.

Rest rooms and water are available at the East Portal Campground.

From the South Rim Visitors Center head out onto the main road and go left, riding back out the way you came in. In approximately 1 mile, the East Portal Road takes off on your left. Prepare yourself for 4 miles of fun, winding road down to the ranger station and campground at the Gunnison Diversion Dam. Continue past the campground for another 2 miles to Crystal Dam. You can take a break here, cool your heels, take a dip, and get ready for the climb back to the rim. To return, simply turn around and head back the way you came.

---

64. HIGH MESA LOOP (See map on page 314)

For road bikes. This ride is a loop through part of the Uncompahgre River valley and the small agricultural communities that thrive there. The route rolls over some low mesas and is a classic that almost any level of road rider will enjoy. It follows most of the Fruit Loop, a longer route that is a favorite of local road riders and hosts a bike race every year.

Starting point: The Montrose County Historical Museum, in the town of Montrose, 15 miles west of the monument. To get to the museum, turn west onto Spring Creek Road at the intersection of Townsend Avenue (US 550) and Main Street. (Spring Creek Road is the western extension of Main Street as it crosses over Townsend Avenue.) The museum is about a block west of this central intersection on the right-hand side of the road.

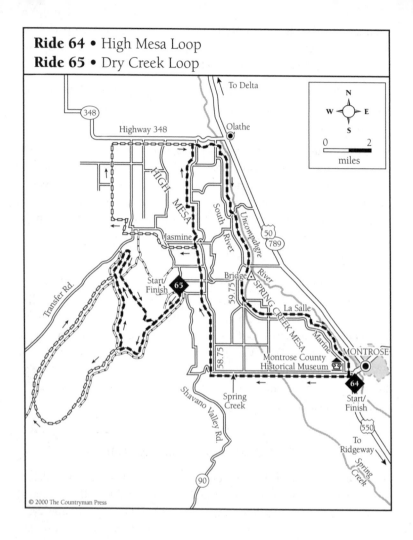

Ride 64 • High Mesa Loop
Ride 65 • Dry Creek Loop

To Delta

348

Highway 348

Olathe

N
W—E
S

0   2
miles

HIGH

MESA

South River

Uncompahgre

50
789

Jasmine

Bridge

River

SPRING CREEK MESA

La Salle

Transfer Rd.

Start/
Finish   65

59.75

Marine

MONTROSE

58.75

Montrose County
Historical Museum

64

Shavano Valley Rd.

Spring
Creek

Start/
Finish

550

To
Ridgeway

90

Spring Creek

© 2000 The Countryman Press

Length: 32-mile loop. Allow 3 hours to complete this loop.

Riding surface: Pavement.

Difficulty: Easy to moderate. Traffic is light on these back roads.

Scenery/highlights: The Montrose County Historical Museum at the start of this ride features many excellent displays providing insight into the history of the Uncompahgre Valley and the Western Slope of Colorado. This is a pleasant tour of the fields and fruit orchards of the fertile Uncompahgre Valley. Views up to Fruitland Mesa (to the north and east) and the Uncompahgre Plateau (to the west) are great.

Best time to ride: Anytime March through October; can be enjoyed almost year-round. At just over a mile in elevation, the summers stay reasonably cool and the winters are mild; with more than 250 days a year of sun, you have endless opportunities to get out and do some pedaling.

Special considerations: You may find some farm traffic on these back roads in the early morning and evening hours. Rest rooms and water are available at the Montrose County Historical Museum. The museum is open Memorial Day through September, Monday to Saturday during regular business hours. A nominal fee is required for visiting the museum.

From the museum ride west on Spring Creek Road for approximately 6 miles to CR 58.75, where you go right (north). After 3 miles CR 58.75 reaches Kiowa Road and becomes CR 58.50. Keep pedaling north, passing Jasmine Road about a mile after Kiowa, also on your left. At this point the road climbs up onto High Mesa, then continues for another 6 miles to CO 348 as High Mesa Road (CR 58.25). Turn right onto CO 348 and ride for 1 mile into the town of Olathe, looking for Church Road on your right. Turn right onto Church Road; 1 mile later, turn left (south) onto South River Road.

In 5 miles you come to an intersection with Jay Jay Road on your left. Continue straight; the road turns into CR 59.75. Keep heading south on this road until the intersection with LaSalle Road. Turn left (west) onto LaSalle Road and ride just under 4 miles to Marine Road. Go right onto Marine Road and pedal for approximately 3 miles to where it ends at Spring Creek Road. Go left on Spring Creek Road and ride about a mile back to your car at the museum.

Option: If you are interested in riding the slightly longer Fruit Loop, turn left onto Jasmine Road and ride it west and north to where it intersects CO 348 about 4 miles west of Olathe. Take CO 348 into Olathe and return to Montrose as described above. Total mileage for this option is 43 miles.

For mountain bikes. This cherry-stem route offers an introduction to the many trails in the area and a taste of the mesa and plateau country that makes mountain biking around here so great. This ride traverses just a small section on the north slope of the enormous Uncompahgre Plateau where adventurous mountain bikers can find weeks of worthwhile riding. Intermediate riders in good condition are best suited to this route.

Starting point: Shavano Valley trailhead. To get there, head west out of Montrose on the Spring Creek Road. You can pick up this road at the center of town at the intersection of Main Street and Townsend Avenue (US 550). (Spring Creek Road is the extension of Main Street on the west side of Townsend Avenue.) Drive west on Spring Creek Road for approximately 6 miles to CR 58.75. Go right, and drive north on CR 58.75 for about 3 miles to Kiowa Road. Go left onto Kiowa Road until it ends at the Shavano Valley trailhead for the Tabeguache Trail. Park here.

Length: 14 mile round-trip. Allow 2 to 3 hours' riding time.

Riding surface: Four-wheel-drive jeep roads.

Difficulty: Moderate. Intermediate riding skills and a good level of physical fitness make this ride most enjoyable, but it is one all types of riders will enjoy.

Scenery/highlights: This is a great cruise through some wild and pretty country. Riding through Dry Creek Canyon, negotiating stream crossings, and honing your skills under the deep blue Colorado sky make for a great way to spend the day.

Best time to ride: March through October.

Special considerations: It can be hot out here on a midsummer day. Be sure to bring plenty of water and some high-energy snacks. No water or bathrooms are available at the start of this route.

Whenever riding on public lands and through forests in the fall, be aware of hunting-season times and locations. A bright-colored jersey will help alert others to your presence during this time of year.

FAUNA

In the summer the sky is always busy along the rim; the large shapes of pin-wheeling turkey vultures are the most noticeable. But look carefully, because it may be a golden eagle soaring along the rim hunting up a meal. Both golden eagles and peregrine falcons nest in the niches of the canyon walls, where the updrafts make for easy soaring and good flight training. Corbids such as ravens, magpies, Steller's jays, and pinyon jays are common and among the most vocal inhabitants of the area. The bright yellow-and-orange western tanager spends a good part of the season here, as does the rufous-sided towhee. Violet-green swallows love the vertical environment of the canyon, as do white-throated swifts. Both of these birds can be seen, and heard, flying at the speed of jet fighters along the canyon rims.

Mule deer are the most common large mammal living around the rims of the canyon, but you might catch sight of a coyote at dusk. Mountain lions and black bears live in the proximity of the canyon but are rarely sighted. Badgers, marmots, and porcupines are much more common, and signs of their activity in the area are easy to spot.

From the Shavano Valley trailhead ride up the main Tabeguache Trail for 4 miles. At the end of an almost mile-long descent you are in Dry Creek Canyon; make a right turn. Ride north along the canyon bottom for another 4.5 miles, negotiating several stream crossings. You ride under some power lines as you cross the valley floor, and then cross the stream one more time before climbing a steep jeep road (0.5 mile) up to the power-line road. Once on top of the mesa, follow the power-line road for approximately 3 miles before rejoining the Tabeguache Trail. At the Tabeguache Trail, go left and ride close to 2 miles back to the trailhead.

Option: For a longer, more adventurous ride, continue up the Tabeguache Trail instead of turning onto the Dry Creek Canyon Road. When you reach the Dry Creek Canyon turnoff keep heading straight, crossing Dry Creek, and heading up onto Cushman Mesa. Pedal 4 miles past Dry

Ride 66 • Crystal Creek Loop

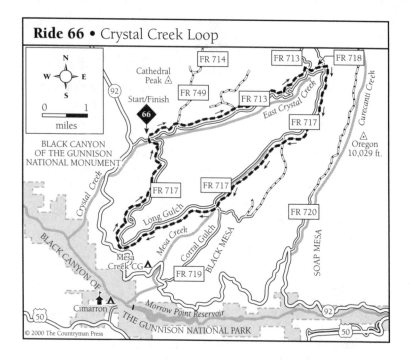

Creek, negotiate a short section of singletrack, and then another 0.5 mile of jeep road, following the Tabeguache Trail across the mesa to an intersection. Go right at this intersection and follow a jeep trail northeast for approximately 5 miles to where it rejoins the Dry Creek Canyon Road. Finish the ride as described above by crossing under the power line, crossing through the creek, climbing up the steep section that takes you back up on top of the mesa, and rejoining the Tabeguache Trail that will take you back to the Shavano Valley Trailhead.

66. CRYSTAL CREEK LOOP (See map above)

For mountain bikes. This is a tour of some of the really beautiful country atop Black Mesa, the heavily forested plateau that defines the northern rim of Black Canyon between Crystal and Curecanti Creeks. Riders in good shape with excellent stamina will relish the long, winding climb up Crystal Creek (almost 2,800 feet) to the top of the mesa at an eleva-

The view south over Uncompahgre country towards the San Juan Mountains from atop Black Mesa.

tion of 10,500 feet above sea level. From there you cruise along the top of the mesa, through deep stands of spruce, fir, and aspen, taking in some spectacular views of the San Juans to the south before dropping off the mesa via the Schmit Creek drainage.

Starting point: Begin this ride at the intersection of CR J82 and Forest Road 717. To get here take CO 92 south and east from Crawford about 10 miles to where CR J82 takes off to the left up the Crystal Creek drainage. Drive approximately 1.5 miles to the intersection of CR J82 and FR 717. Park here.

Length: 28 mile loop. Allow 4 to 5 hours to complete this loop.

Riding surface: Graded dirt, four-wheel-drive jeep roads.

Difficulty: Moderate. Not much technical skill is required for this ride, but its length, long climbs, and elevations demand at least a moderate level of physical fitness.

Scenery/highlights: From the lookout at the top of the Crystal Creek drainage, views of the San Juans, Black Canyon, Big Blue Wilderness Area, and Uncompahgre are superb. The deep, fragrant evergreen forests up here make a nice change from the drier piñon, cedar, and oak mix found along the canyon rims. Watch for a variety of wildflowers in summer, including columbine, Indian paintbrush, elephant-heads, and, along the creeks, chiming bells. In fall this plateau, like the Uncompahgre, is a favorite for Rocky Mountain elk.

Best time to ride: May through September. Because this plateau is high, it is not free of snow until later in the spring. In midsummer this area is nice and cool while lower climes are hot.

Special considerations: I do not recommend riding up here, or anywhere in the high plateau country, during the late-fall elk hunt. If you have to ride during these times, you must wear high-visibility clothing.

There are no bathrooms or water along this route. The town of Crawford is your nearest resource for food, water, and gas.

From the intersection where you parked your vehicle begin riding up the Crystal Creek drainage on CR J82. This road shortly becomes FR 713. Continue climbing up, up, up this graded dirt road for approximately 8 miles before reaching the intersection with FR 718 at almost 10,500 feet. At this intersection you find the Crystal Creek Ranger Station and Lookout. Go right onto FR 718 and ride it for about a mile before it intersects with FR 717. Turn right onto FR 717 and follow it as it rolls along through sweet-smelling pine forests atop Black Mesa. After about 4 miles of traveling along the top of the mesa the road picks up and gently descends along Mesa Creek. It follows the creek for close to 4 miles before hitting an intersection with FR 716. Bear right and stay on FR 717 as it wraps around the point of the mesa, directly above CO 92. The road then turns and heads north, descending all the way into Schmit Creek and coming out at the intersection where you left your vehicle. From the intersection with FR 716 back to your vehicle is close to 11 miles.

CAMPING

The park has two campgrounds, one on each rim. There are 102 sites at the **South Rim Campground** (which rarely fill up), and 13 sites at the **North Rim Campground** (which occasionally fill up). All campsites are available on a first-come, first-served basis and a fee per night is charged. Water is available at both campgrounds but must be used sparingly, because it has to be hauled in by truck. Campsites have a fireplace or charcoal grill and a picnic table. Wood gathering is not permitted and no wood is available at the campgrounds. It's a good idea to bring water, charcoal, and wood with you.

There are many possibilities for wilderness camping on the north side of the canyon and west of Montrose.

There are several campgrounds available in the Uncompahgre National Forest near Cimarron, about a half hour east of Montrose. **Big Cimarron Campground** along the Cimarron River has 16 sites. No fee is charged, but you must bring your own water. **Beaver Lake Campground** and **Silver Lake Campground** are farther up the road, with 16 and 60 sites, respectively. To get to all three take US 50 east from Montrose approximately 24 miles, go left onto the Owl Creek or Cimarron Road, and go south about 20 miles.

LODGING

There is a good selection of hotels and motels in Montrose to choose from. Most are located on the east end of town on Main Street (US 50). You'll find the usual assortment of chain hotels—a **Holiday**

IT'S INTERESTING TO KNOW . . .

The 2,300-foot Painted Wall inside the monument is the highest cliff in Colorado and is nearly twice as high as New York's Empire State Building.

Inn, a **Days Inn,** a **Super 8**—as well as at least a dozen motels. There are also a couple of B&Bs in town. Check the yellow pages or visit the Montrose Area Chamber of Commerce for more listings.

FOOD

There are many restaurants in Montrose to choose from. If you are up for Mexican try the **Whole Enchilada** (44 S. Grand Ave.), or if you're hungry for Italian try **Sicily's Italian Restaurant** (1135 E. Main St.). For steak and seafood try the **Backwoods Inn** (103 Rose Lane). **Valley Books and Coffee** (328 E. Main St.) makes a good cup of coffee and provides the opportunity to cruise the bookshelves. You can also get a cup of coffee and a bagel in the morning, or a bagel sandwich at lunch, at **Back Street Bagel and Deli** (1920 S. Townsend Ave.).

LAUNDRY

Highlander Laundry, 1347 E. Main St., Montrose; (970) 249-1741

Southside Laundry, 1918 S. Townsend Ave., Montrose; (970) 240-3419

BIKE SHOP/BIKE RENTAL

Cascade Cycles, 25 N. Cascade Ave., Montrose; (970) 249-7375

Grand Mesa Cyclery, 2015 S. Townsend Ave., Montrose; (970) 249-7515

KC's Cycles, 330 Meeker St., Delta; (970) 874-1563

FOR FURTHER INFORMATION

Black Canyon of the Gunnison National Park—Superintendent, 102 Elk Creek, Gunnison, CO 81230; (970) 641-2337, (970) 249-1914, ext. 23 (South Rim Visitors Center); http://www.nps.gov/blca/

Montrose Visitor and Convention Bureau, 1519 E. Main St., Montrose, CO 81401; (800) 873-0244

Delta Chamber of Commerce and Visitors Center, Third and Main Streets, Delta, CO 81416; (970) 874-8616

Uncompahgre National Forest—Headquarters, 2250 US 50, Delta, CO 81416; (970) 874-7691

Uncompahgre National Forest—Ouray District, 2505 S. Townsend Ave., Montrose, CO 81401; (970) 249-3711

Bureau of Land Management—
Uncompahgre Resource Area,
2505 S. Townsend Ave., Montrose,
CO 81401; (970) 249-6047

**Colorado Plateau Mountain Bike
Trail Association,** P.O. Box 4602,
Grand Junction, CO 81502; (970)
241-9561

DON'T MISS

The Ute Indian Museum actually sits on land once farmed by the infamous southern Ute Chief Ouray and his wife, Chipeta. The museum houses a good collection of ceremonial artifacts, some of which belonged to Chief Ouray. The grave of Chipeta, a monument to Ouray, and picnic facilities are also at the museum. The Montrose County Historical Museum has a wealth of old photos and displays that portray what life was like in the Uncompahgre Valley and along the Western Slope during the late 19th and early 20th centuries. You will find Ute Indian artifacts, collections of arrowheads, antique toys, medical equipment, a relocated homesteaders' cabin with all its original furnishings, and a library of old newspapers, journals, and books.

13

Colorado National Monument is a geologic wonderland of sheer-walled canyons, arches, windows, whalebacks, and massive rock spires, all colored in mixed hues of pink, peach, purple, red, and brown. The landscape is unmistakably Colorado Plateau country with its warm palette of rocks laid down in horizontal layers. Forced upward in a gigantic uplift, the plateau that is the centerpiece of the monument reveals 2,000 feet of the earth's geologic history. Some of these layers, like the Kayenta formation, are harder and have worked like a protective cap atop the cliffs and monoliths, while softer layers have eroded away underneath. Fractures in the rock, where water can seep in and wind can find a fingerhold, are what begins the process that leaves behind inspiring monoliths such as Sentinel Spire, the Kissing Couple, and Independence Monument. At its highest point the rim of this plateau, which is geologically part of the Uncompahgre uplift, is more than 2,000 feet above the Colorado River below. The views from Rim Rock Drive north to the purple-gray Book Cliffs and Grand Mesa beyond, and into the Grand Valley of the meandering mighty Colorado River, are truly spectacular.

Cycling in the Park
Running from northwest to southeast through the heart of the monument, the 23-mile Rim Rock Drive rises from the valley floor and climbs the plateau, tracing the edge of its rim before descending back to the

valley floor, providing a fantastic opportunity to get out of your car and do some pedaling. This route is regarded by road cyclists around the region as one of the premier rides in Colorado. The area around Grand Junction and Fruita is quickly becoming one of the hottest biking destinations in the West, especially for off-road enthusiasts who have grown weary of the crowds that flock to the original mountain-biking mecca of Moab, just a few hours southwest. The singletrack rides along the river, including Marys Loop, Lions Loop, and others, are fast becoming favorites for mountain bikers who crave desert scenery. The annual Fruita Fat Tire Festival, held the last week in April, draws hundreds of fat-tire fiends who participate in group rides, races, parties, and more.

A local proactive cycling community, the Colorado Plateau Mountain Bike Trail Association (COPMOBA), the Bureau of Land Management, and the Forest Service have created extensive trail networks through not just the immediate area but the entire region. Kokopelli's Trail, linking Grand Junction and Moab, Utah, and the Tabeguache and Paradox Trails, linking Montrose and Grand Junction, constitute hundreds of miles of off-road biking for hardy cyclists in search of adventure. Many more mountain-biking trails exist in the purplish gray hills of the Book Cliffs to the north of Grand Junction, a favorite area for local riders. Riding out to Rattlesnake Canyon via the Black Ridge Hunter Access Road is a fat-tire adventure that leaves just outside the park and provides more of a wilderness adventure than some of the more popular trails. You may want to take the family and ride around the Colorado River on the River Front Trail System, a network of paved trails that highlight the variety of life around this desert river. This is high desert with well over 250 days of sunshine a year.

---

67. RIM ROCK DRIVE (See map on page 328)

For road bikes. This route traverses the highest and most spectacular portion of Rim Rock Drive, allowing beginning and intermediate riders to avoid the harrowing grades and curves at either end of the road. After taking some time at the visitors center to look at the many interesting displays on the monument's geology, flora, and fauna, you can amble back outside, get on your bike, and enjoy some spectacular scenery. Adjust the length of your ride to suit your schedule, interests, or energy level. Be sure to pick up one of the park's brochures on the Rim Rock Drive, so that when you stop to take in the view you can read up on all the interesting facts about the monument.

Starting point: Colorado National Monument Visitors Center.

Length: 9 miles one-way; 18 miles out-and-back. Take the whole day or just a few hours to pedal this route.

Riding surface: Pavement.

Difficulty: Moderate to easy. The distance to the suggested turnaround point, the elevation gain (from 5,700 to 6,500 feet), and the rolling nature of the terrain make this a moderate ride.

Scenery/highlights: Views looking down into the canyons running away off the rim are fantastic. The spires and monoliths standing in the canyon bottoms and just off the rim are beautiful, strange, and great to marvel at while taking a break. Your perspectives on the views and scenery are quite different on the return trip.

Pausing to look up the Colorado River from a spot along Marys Loop near Colorado National Monument.

Best time to ride: Anytime between March and October. Hardier cyclists may want to ride this route when it's cooler and they can have the park to themselves.

You will encounter the bulk of the road's tourist traffic along the road during the middle of the day, so an early-morning or evening ride is recommended. Morning traffic along the southeast half of the monument road up to the turnoff for Black Ridge and Glade Park can become heavy due to commuters from the small town of Glade Park.

Special considerations: Traffic along Rim Rock Drive can get heavy during peak tourist season, so be sure to pay attention to vehicles pulling into and out of scenic overlooks; chances are they are looking at the scenery, not at you. Also, take up as much of the lane as you need to negotiate some of these sharp turns safely, then move over to the right on the straighter sections to allow cars to pass.

You are relatively high and exposed up here; beware if you see a thunderstorm threatening.

Water and rest rooms are available at the visitors center but nowhere else along the way.

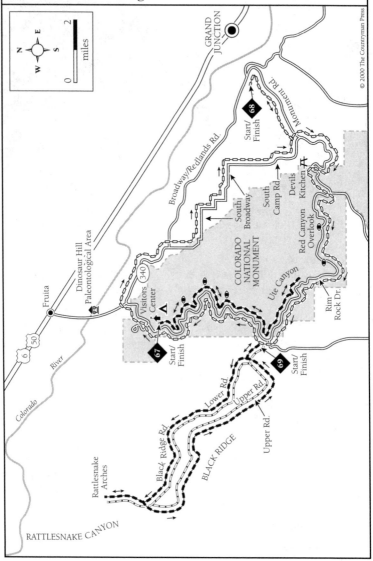

Ride 67 • Rim Rock Drive
Ride 68 • Monument Loop
Ride 69 • Black Ridge

© 2000 The Countryman Press

GRAND
JUNCTION

N
W · E
S

0   2
miles

68
Start/
Finish

Monument Rd.

Broadway/Redlands Rd.

South Broadway

South
Camp Rd.

Devils
Kitchen

Red Canyon
Overlook

COLORADO
NATIONAL
MONUMENT

Ute Canyon

Rim
Rock Dr.

Dinosaur Hill
Paleontological Area

340

Visitors
Center

Fruita

6
50

Colorado   River

67
Start/
Finish

69
Start/
Finish

Lower Rd.

Upper Rd.

Black Ridge Rd.

Upper Rd.

BLACK RIDGE

Rattlesnake
Arches

RATTLESNAKE CANYON

The singletrack trails of Mary's Loop, Lion's Loop, and others are becoming increasingly popular among mountain bikers.

From the visitors center simply ride out onto Rim Rock Drive heading south and east; go as far as suits your level of fitness and enthusiasm. Turnaround points include the Coke Ovens Overlook at 3.5 miles from the visitors center, Artists Point at 4.3 miles, Highland View at 5.5 miles, and Fallen Rock Overlook at 9 miles. When you have had enough, simply turn around and head back the way you came.

---

68. MONUMENT LOOP (See map on page 328)

For road bikes. This loop takes you along the base of the monument's redrock cliffs, up into the monument and along the rim of the plateau, and back down to the river valley. It is considered one of the best rides anywhere by serious road bikers, and it is this group who relish the 5 to 8 percent grades, the 2,000 feet of vertical gain, and the spine-tingling hairpin turns on the descent, not to mention the views.

Starting point: The intersection of CO 340 (Broadway) and Monument Road, the road that accesses the monument from Grand Junction. A shopping center at this intersection has plenty of parking.

Portions of the singletrack trails near the monument are part of the 142-mile-long Kokopelli's Trail that stretches between Fruita, Colorado, and Moab, Utah.

Length: Approximately 40-mile loop. Allow 3 to 4 hours to complete this loop—more if you want to spend time on the rim taking in the view.

Riding surface: Pavement; rough, loose gravel in spots.

Difficulty: Difficult. The ability to negotiate steep grades and sharp turns, as well as confidence riding with traffic, are all musts. A well-honed set of legs and a large set of lungs are also strongly recommended.

Scenery/highlights: Riding along the base of the cliffs and looking up into the canyons of the monument afford wonderful views of some really spectacular scenery. Riding up into the monument and along Rim Rock Drive gives you the chance to compare vistas.

Best time to ride: Almost year-round, although temperatures don't really start to warm up until sometime in March. Autumn is a great time, as the days are warm and much of the tourist traffic has abated.

You encounter the bulk of the road's tourist traffic during the middle of the day, so an early-morning or evening ride is recommended. Morning traffic along the southeast half of the monument road up to the

FLORA

In springtime look for the orange to red blooms of Indian paintbrush, purple four-o'clock, and pink and purple phlox in the monument. The creamy white blossoms of serviceberry shrubs also bloom in the spring and are followed by the stunning yellow blooms of cliffrose in June. The large, white blooms of evening primrose open only after the sun's damaging rays have faded. A number of different cacti can be seen blooming within the monument in the spring, including prickly pear, whose blossoms range from yellow to peach, fishhook cactus (pink), and claret cup (deep red). The summers are too hot and the sun too strong for flowers, but the fall signals another bloom. Yellows dominate in autumn, with rabbitbrush and snakeweed taking center stage.

turnoff for Black Ridge and Glade Park can become heavy due to commuters from the community of Glade Park.

Special considerations: This loop is described in a counterclockwise direction, but it may be ridden in the other direction. Entering the monument from the east, or Grand Junction, side makes the climb longer, although average grades are less than those coming up from the west entrance.

There are two short tunnels approximately 1.5 miles up the road from the west entrance. Because of these tunnels—and because you are likely to encounter a fair amount of car and camper traffic—it is a good idea to wear high-visibility clothing, carry a light for the tunnels, and try to ride in the morning and evenings when there is less traffic.

Check your brakes before you head down. Control your speed and expect sharp curves, rough pavement, and loose gravel in spots.

From the shopping center at the intersection of Broadway (CO 340) and Monument Road, begin riding west on Monument Road toward the entrance of the monument. In approximately 4 miles turn right onto South Camp Road, about 0.5 mile before the west entrance of the park. Ride north on South Camp Road for 2.5 miles to where the road ends at South Broadway. Go left onto South Broadway and follow it as it makes a series of jogs through some residential areas. In approximately 4 miles South Broadway intersects the Broadway/Redlands Road (also CO 340). Continue heading north and west on this road for another 3 miles until you reach the west entrance of the park.

Inside the park you immediately begin climbing. In 1.5 miles you reach a series of two short tunnels. You may want to time your passage through the tunnels between waves of traffic. In 4.5 miles from the entrance you reach the visitors center, having gained over 1,000 feet. From here you will roll along, continuing to gain in elevation, as you negotiate numerous curves along the rim. Seven miles from the visitors center you pass the turnoff for Glade Park, and another 4 miles beyond that you gain the highest point in the ride as you cross the top of Ute Canyon (6,640 feet). From here it is all downhill. It is approximately 8 miles from the high point in the ride to the east entrance of the monument, where you exit and ride 4 miles back to your vehicle via Monument Road.

---

69. BLACK RIDGE (See map on page 328)

For mountain bikes. This is an incredibly scenic, fast-paced ride on a four-wheel-drive road that accesses a trailhead leading into Rattlesnake Canyon and Rattlesnake Arches. This is redrock country at its best. The route out to the trailhead borders a Wilderness Study Area, so please stay on the main road. Intermediate and advanced riders will love this one. The short hike to the arches is highly recommended.

Starting point: Bulletin board where the Black Ridge Hunter Access Road leaves from the main road (Rim Rock Drive), 12 miles from the east entrance or 11 miles from the west entrance. Information is posted on road and trail closures, as well as hunting information. Park here.

Length: 25 miles out-and-back. This is at least a 4-hour ride, and an all-day affair if you are going to hike down into the canyon.

Riding surface: Four-wheel-drive jeep road; rough and rocky in spots.

Difficulty: Moderate. Intermediate riding skills, good fitness and stamina are recommended for negotiating the terrain and long distance.

Scenery/highlights: This is gorgeous redrock country. Views into Devils,

FAUNA

The monument is home to an impressive number of raptors, including turkey vultures, peregrine falcons, golden eagles, red-tailed hawks, and kestrels. Both peregrines and golden eagles successfully nest within the monument. Bald eagles visit the area in winter but remain close to the river, as their main food source is fish. White-throated swift or violet-green swallows love to play in the updrafts off the canyon walls. Atop the rim you are likely to see magpies, ravens, and pinyon and scrub-jays, while down below you might see a quail, a ring-necked pheasant, or even a meadowlark. The lovely cascading tune of the canyon wren is a sure sign you're in canyon country.

Cottontails, jackrabbits, rock squirrels, and chipmunks are common in the monument. Mule deer also make their home here, as do the rare but magnificent desert bighorn sheep. Coyote, gray fox, bobcat, and cougar also live in the monument but are not often seen.

Rattlesnake, and Mee Canyons and the jumble of side canyons from Black Ridge are stunning. The hike down to see the arches in Rattlesnake Canyon is well worth the time and effort.

Best time to ride: Anytime from March to October, provided the ground is dry. Midsummer can be sizzling in this country; if you have to ride, bring plenty of water and stay hydrated.

This area sees a lot of deer hunters in the fall. It is not recommended that you ride anytime the deer or elk hunt is on, but if you have to ride in the late fall take proper precautions: Find out when and where hunts are taking place, avoid those areas if you can, and wear high-visibility clothing.

Special considerations: You don't even want to consider riding out here if it has been snowing or raining and the ground is saturated. When wet, these soils turn into a clay-mud concoction that can wreak havoc on your chain and deraileurs and turn your day into an epic slog. Riding on this kind of surface when it's wet also leaves behind ugly ruts and gouges that are dangerous to bikers and take years to repair.

There are actually two roads that parallel each other for almost 9 miles of this route: The Upper Road is open from April 15 to August 15, and the Lower Road is open from August 15 to February 15. Only one road is open at any given time due to the BLM's efforts to try to minimize damage to the route caused by off-road traffic.

The nearest water and rest rooms can be found at the monument's visitors center 7 miles north on Rim Rock Drive.

Follow the Black Ridge Hunter Access Road as it rolls along, climbing gently then descending through beautiful, healthy stands of junipers to the intersection of Upper and Lower Roads just over a mile from the start. Depending on the time of year you will either go right onto the Lower Road that continues below the top of the ridge, or left onto the Upper Road that continues along the top of the ridge. Both roads come together again in approximately 8 miles. At the junction of these roads your elevation is about 6,500 feet. (For a shorter ride with less climbing, turn around at this intersection for a round-trip distance closer to 18 miles.) You descend over the next 3 miles to the beginning of the Rattlesnake Canyon trailhead at an elevation of 5,800 feet. After you have had a break, taken in the view, or returned from the 3.5-mile hike down to see the 11 arches, head back the way you came.

---

70. RIVERFRONT TRAIL SYSTEM (See map on page 335)

For road and mountain bikes. The Colorado Riverfront Trail System is a wonderful collection of paved trails that parallel the Colorado River near the center of Grand Junction. It's designed to highlight the rich habitat along the river corridor in an otherwise arid region. These trails pass through wetlands, cattail marshes, and cottonwood groves; over gravel bars; around ponds and lakes; and along canals. They provide an opportunity for the whole family to get out and enjoy the surroundings without worrying about car traffic.

Starting point: Riverside Park in downtown Grand Junction on West Street and Grand Avenue, on the east bank of the river.

Length: 8 miles total. Individual trails average between 0.5 mile and 1.5 miles in length. Ride for as long as you want.

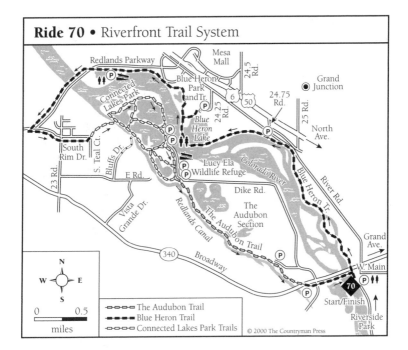

Ride 70 • Riverfront Trail System

Riding surface: Pavement.

Difficulty: Easy.

Scenery/highlights: The Colorado River corridor, including the junction with the Gunnison River just east of town, contains over 200 species of birds, 3 endangered fish species, and a variety of mammals that depend on this area's riparian habitat for survival. This is a great place for birding and becoming familiar with the character of desert wetlands. Views up into the redrock cliffs and canyons are great from here.

Best time to ride: Anytime weather permits.

Special considerations: Riverside Park is equipped with bathrooms, picnic tables, a playground, and many nice shade trees. To access the trails on the west side of the river, cross over on Broadway (CO 340) and ride approximately 0.5 mile to the start of the Audubon Trail. Be careful crossing traffic lanes.

A cyclist stops to take in the view of Independence Monument and Wedding Canyon from an overlook along Rim Rock Drive.

From Riverside Park you can begin by riding up the Blue Heron Trail (1.85 miles) along the east bank of the river, which takes you up to Blue Heron Lake and eventually routes you onto Redlands Parkway, across the river, and onto South Rim Drive, which feeds you into Connected Lakes State Park. At this park you can explore a number of loop options before heading back south via the Audubon Trail (1.53 miles), which winds its way along the Redlands Canal. When you reach the end of the Audubon Trail behind a shopping center on Broadway (CO 340), you need to ride east over the bridge on Broadway, turning onto the Blue Heron Trail to get back to the park.

---

71. MARYS LOOP (See map on page 337)

For mountain bikes. This loop and the others that adjoin it constitute some of the best singletrack riding in the area. Skilled mountain bikers, and intermediate riders who are looking for a challenge, love these trails. Portions of Marys Loop and adjoining Lions and Troy Built Loops all are part of the 142-mile Kokopelli's Trail that begins 5 miles west of Fruita

Ride 71 • Marys Loop

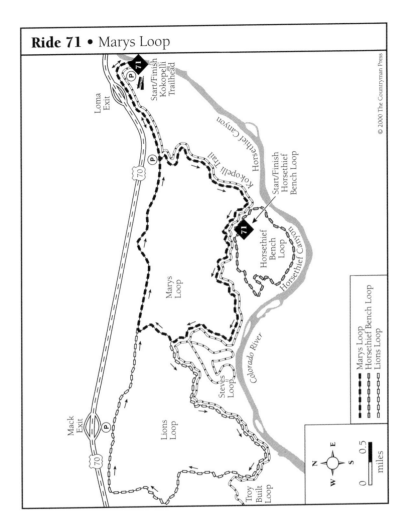

© 2000 The Countryman Press

at the Loma exit. These trails roll and bump along a scenic stretch of redrock terrain between I-70 and the Colorado River.

Starting point: Kokopelli's trailhead at the Loma boat-launch area. Take I-70 west from Grand Junction for 5 miles. Take the Loma exit (exit 15). Go left, then left again along a frontage road to the Loma boat-launch area. Park here. If this parking lot is full, go back toward the exit and continue past it to the Loop Parking Lot.

The outstanding views from the edge of the plateau make Rim Rock Drive one of the most popular road rides in Colorado.

Length: Approximately 11-mile loop. Allow 2 to 3 hours to complete this ride, more if you plan to do any of the optional loops.

Riding surface: Singletrack, short sections of gravel, four-wheel-drive roads.

Difficulty: Moderate to difficult. There are several steep climbs and some supertechnical sections that require all but the most skilled riders to dismount. Please use caution. A bruised ego heals a lot quicker than painful scrapes or broken bones.

Scenery/highlights: Views to the river and into surrounding canyons are great. This is some really beautiful redrock country.

Best time to ride: Spring and fall. If you are riding in the summer months, an early-morning or evening ride is recommended.

Special considerations: Please use caution on these trails. Steep, rocky sections and obstacles make this, and other trails in the area, very technical in spots. Dismount and walk your bike over these sections if you are unsure of your ability to negotiate them.

Begin by riding the pavement back toward the exit you drove in on. Just past the exit the road turns to gravel. Follow this road as it climbs west over the ridge. In just under a mile you come to a jeep road on your right. Go right and begin climbing on this jeep road. You emerge onto a rim above the river, which turns into singletrack approximately 3.5 miles from the start. Horsethief Bench is out to your left; a loop trail of the same name encircles that formation. (This is a short, fun loop that is not too technical and will add about 4 miles to your total distance.) The next section of the trail is dangerous—please use caution.

Approximately 4.5 miles into the ride you encounter a fence. Use the steps to go over the fence, or go through the open gate. Please leave the gate as you found it. Close to mile 5 you look into the mouth of scenic Rattlesnake Canyon. Approximately 5.5 miles from the start the single-track ends and becomes a dirt road. You begin to ride away from the river toward Mack Ridge. At 6.5 miles from the start you encounter another major intersection; stay right on Marys Loop (a left here picks up Lions Loop). Just over 7 miles from the start you will come to the frontage road. Turn right and follow it back to the trailhead where you parked.

Option: Lions Loop is close to 8 miles and adds 2 hours to your ride. Lions Loop is more technical and involves more climbing. Lions Loop makes a circuit of the next mesa to the west by climbing up, up, up first singletrack, then a jeep road that crosses the mesa (also called Mack Ridge), before descending a hair-raising stretch of trail to the frontage road. Go right on the frontage road and head back to the trailhead.

CAMPING

Saddlehorn Campground is situated near the monument's visitors center. Campsites are available on a first-come, first-served basis. Each site has a picnic table, charcoal grill, and access to drinking water. Backcountry camping is free and is permitted anyplace farther than 0.25 mile from a road or trail.

There are managed BLM campsites in Rabbit Valley almost 20 miles west of Fruita. You can get there by taking exit 2 off I-70, just before the Utah border. There is also a campground at Highline State Recreation Area (970-858-7208) at Highline Lake about 5 miles north of I-70 from the Loma exit on CO 139. Wilderness camping is available throughout the BLM lands surrounding Grand Junction and Fruita, and in the Grand Mesa National Forest.

There are a couple of private campgrounds in town with both hook-ups and tent sites. You can get a shower here and do some laundry as well. Try the **Grand Junction/Clifton KOA** just east of town (3238 East Business 70), or the **Fruita Junction RV Park and Campground** just off I-70 adjacent to the Welcome Center in Fruita.

LODGING

All the big hotel and motel chains are represented in Grand Junction; there are several neat B&Bs in the area. You'll find a handful of places to stay in Fruita: a **Super 8,** a couple of motels, and a couple of B&Bs. Stop in at the Colorado Welcome Center west of Grand Junction off I-70 at the Fruita exit to get a complete list of lodging choices in the area.

FOOD

If you are looking for a good cup of coffee in the morning, a pastry, or maybe a hot breakfast, try **Jitters Espresso Bar** (504 Main St.). **Common Grounds** (1230 N. 12th St.) also specializes in gourmet coffees. **Main Street Bagels** (Sixth and Main) or

Durango Bagels (2232 N. Seventh St.) is a good place to secure that famous food group with a hole in the middle. Try the **Rockslide Restaurant and Brewery** (401 Main St.) after your ride for an appetizer and beer.

LAUNDRY

There are at least eight Laundromats in Grand Junction. Here are just a few:

Easy Wash Laundra-Mat, 811 N. Ave.; (970) 242-9767

IT'S INTERESTING TO KNOW . . .

The rocky soils and sunny clime of the Grand Junction area have, in the last 30 years, found fans among grape growers and vintners who are now producing award-winning wines. There are six wineries in the Palisades area just 7 miles east of Grand Junction. Touring some of the wineries on your bike is a delightful way to spend an afternoon and take in some great scenery. If you are around in late September, be sure to check out the Winefest celebration, with wine-tasting tours and musical entertainment.

Wash 'N Clean World, 1916 N. 12th; (970) 243-4420

IN FRUITA:

Fruita Washeteria, 404 US 6 and 50; (970) 858-9950

BIKE SHOP/BIKE RENTAL

IN GRAND JUNCTION:

Bicycle Outfitters, 251 Colorado Ave.; (970) 245-2699

Bike Peddler, 710 N. First St.; (970) 243-5602

The Bike Shop, 10th and N. Ave.; (970) 243-0807

Tompkins Cycle Sports, 301 Main St.; (970) 241-0141

IN FRUITA:

Over the Edge Cycling & Adventure Sports, 202 E. Aspen Ave.; (970) 858-7220 or (800) 873-3068; www.gj.net/~edge

FOR FURTHER INFORMATION

Colorado National Monument— Superintendent, Fruita, CO 81521; (970) 858-3617; COLM_Superintendent@nps.gov; http:// www.nps.gov/colm/

Grand Junction Chamber of Commerce, 360 Grand Ave., Grand Junction, CO 81501; (970)

242-3214; http://grand-junction.net

Fruita Chamber of Commerce,
P.O. Box 1177, Fruita, CO 81521;
(970) 858-3894

Bureau of Land Management,
2815 H Road, Grand Junction,
CO 81506; (790) 244-3000

U .S. Forest Service—Grand Junction Ranger District, 2777
Crossroads, Unit A, Grand
Junction, CO 81506; (970) 242-8211

Colorado Plateau Mountain Bike Trail Association, P.O. Box 4602,
Grand Junction, CO 81502; (970)
241-9561

DON'T MISS

There are three museums in town collectively known as the Museum of Western Colorado, the Main Museum, Dinosaur Valley, and Cross Orchards Historic Site. At the small Main Museum (248 S. Fourth Street) you can see exhibits of Ute baskets, tools and jewelry from ancient Fremont digs, Mimbres pottery, and other interesting displays on the geology and history of western Colorado. Dinosaur Valley (Main St. Mall at 362 Main Street) offers lots of fascinating information and exhibits on paleontology and dinosaurs and is sure to be a hit with the kids. Enormous dinosaur models move and growl, and an almost life-sized *Tyrannosaurus rex* will surely terrify some. At the Cross Orchards Historic Site (3073 Patterson/F Rd.) you can take a tour of a working apple orchard that has been producing fruit and cider since the 1890s. The Cross operation was once the largest and most productive orchard in the region, supplying fruit to Denver and cities around the West. Demonstrations, antique farm implements, and a number of annual events such as a quilt show are delights.

14

CURECANTI NATIONAL RECREATION AREA

Three lakes created by three successive dams along the Gunnison River are the centerpiece of Curecanti National Recreation Area. These reservoirs have transformed the arid Gunnison Basin, providing hydroelectric power, water for agriculture, and one of the most popular recreation areas in Colorado. Blue Mesa is the easternmost and the largest, serving as the main storage reservoir. It is also the highest, with a surface elevation of 7,519 feet. Morrow Point Reservoir, west of Blue Mesa, snakes through steep canyon walls of dark Precambrian rock, marking the beginning of Black Canyon. The Morrow Point Dam produces the bulk of the hydroelectric power of the three. Crystal Lake Reservoir extends farther west into Black Canyon, terminating at Crystal Dam just outside the Black Canyon of the Gunnison National Monument.

The lava-covered mesas that come to an abrupt end at the canyon rims above Crystal Lake, and the rocky spires that flank the cliffs and buttes beyond, reveal the violent volcanic past of this region. Some 30 million years ago repeated volcanic eruptions created the West Elk Mountains to the north of the lakes. Later eruptions formed the San Juan Mountains to the south. The persistent flow of the Gunnison River eroded its way down through the softer volcanic materials, and through the eons etched its path into the hard Precambrian rock that was earlier transformed deep below the earth's surface under tremendous pressure and heat. As the rock cooled, its crystalline components separated into

CYCLING OPTIONS

There are five rides in this chapter, two road rides and three mountain-bike rides. Because the centerpiece of this park is a large body of water, riding within the recreation area is somewhat limited. Still, US 50 from the Elk Creek Visitors Center to Blue Mesa Dam is a wonderful 22-mile pedal along the shore of Blue Mesa Lake that road riders with experience will find easy to moderate. Two mountain-bike rides, one up Beaver Creek and the other up Soap Creek, are both 10-mile easy-to-moderate routes up nearby drainages that feed the lake. The road ride up to Black Mesa on CO 92 gains over 2,000 cumulative feet and is very strenuous for all but seasoned road riders. Views from along this route are spectacular and make up for some of the difficulty. The mountain-bike ride out through the Hartman Rocks area is sure to thrill avid fat-tire fans. Singletracks take off in all directions, offering the chance to create a variety of routes. The loop described here is 18 miles long and features sections that are moderate to technically challenging.

the bands you see in the rock walls of the canyons. The rock became extremely hard in this process, allowing for the nearly vertical canyon walls. Softer volcanic mudflow materials and layers of ash eroded more easily, forming the more open basins that now cradle the waters of Blue Mesa.

Cycling in the Park

Boating and fishing bring the most visitors to the park, but increasingly people who come to enjoy the lakes with their bikes in tow are finding that there are some exceptional riding opportunities nearby. Because the boundaries of the recreation area correlate to the shoreline of the lakes, there is very little biking inside the park. The highways that skirt the shore of the lake and the rim atop the canyon, however, make for some excellent road tours that serious road riders will relish. Shorter excursions along the road offer options for recreational riders, and for mountain bikers the foothills and mesas just outside Gunnison provide some classic off-road riding. In fact, in recent years this area has produced some of this country's best mountain-bike racers, who love to train here because of the high altitudes, good weather, and great terrain.

Crested Butte, the hip ski town just 35 miles north of Gunnison, is a mountain biker's paradise, especially in the summer when the lower-elevation rides are hot and dusty. The towns of Montrose and Gunnison are both outdoor-oriented communities with healthy populations of cyclists, good bike shops, and public-land managers who are receptive to bikers' needs. The camping facilities inside the park make a great base for exploring the fantastic biking and other recreational opportunities this area offers. Returning to camp by the lake where you can enjoy a refreshing dip after a long, hot day in the saddle is just about as good as it gets.

---

72. US 50–ELK CREEK TO BLUE MESA DAM
(See map on page 346)

For road bikes. US 50 runs east-west through Curecanti, and as of this writing was freshly repaved with a nice, wide shoulder, making it bike friendly and a great way to take in views of the lake and surrounding scenery. The route described here is from the Elk Creek Visitors Center to the Blue Mesa Dam Overlook, although many options exist for making this a shorter, or longer, ride.

Starting point: Elk Creek Visitors Center. If you want to shorten this ride, begin from one of the campgrounds or picnic areas along the route to the west of the visitors center.

Length: 22 miles out-and-back. Allow at least 3 hours for this ride—more if you want to spend time at the overlook or take one of several great hikes along the way.

Riding surface: Pavement.

Difficulty: Easy to moderate. Although this route is mostly flat, a few rolling hills and the overall distance make the ride more demanding.

Scenery/highlights: This is a beautiful trip along the shore of Blue Mesa Lake. While pedaling you can take in sweeping views of the surrounding country while enjoying the sparkle of the sun on the water and the deep blue of the Colorado sky. Just before you cross over the Middle Bridge you pass the pullout and trailhead for the hike to Dillon Pinnacles. This is an easy 4-mile round-trip hike up to the strangely eroded volcanic for-

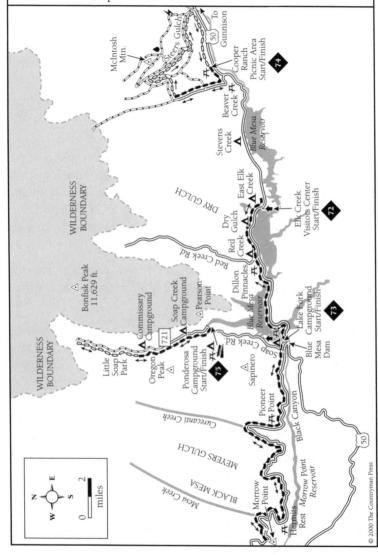

Ride 72 • US 50–Elk Creek to Blue Mesa Dam
Ride 73 • Black Mesa
Ride 74 • Beaver Creek
Ride 75 • Soap Creek Road

To Gunnison
50
Steers Gulch
McIntosh Mtn.
Cooper Ranch
Picnic Area
Start/Finish
74
Beaver Creek
Stevens Creek
Blue Mesa Reservoir
WILDERNESS BOUNDARY
East Elk Creek
DRY GULCH
Dry Gulch
Elk Creek
Visitors Center
Start/Finish
72
Red Creek Rd
Red Creek
Bonfisk Peak
11,629 ft.
Commissary Campground
Soap Creek Campground
721
Pearson Point
Dillon Pinnacles
Blue Mesa Reservoir
Lake Fork
Campground
Start/Finish
73
WILDERNESS BOUNDARY
Little Soap Park
Oregon Peak
Ponderosa Campground
Start/Finish
75
Soap Creek Rd
Sapinero
Blue Mesa Dam
Curecanti Creek
Pioneer Point
Black Canyon
BLACK MESA
MEYERS GULCH
Morrow Point Reservoir
Mesa Creek
Morrow Point
Hermits Rest
50

N
W E
S
0   2
miles

© 2000 The Countryman Press

346 BICYCLING COLORADO

Playing on singletrack trails in the Hartman Rocks area.

mations that define the geologic history of the area. At the Blue Mesa Dam Overlook you can marvel at human tinkering with the natural world and gain some sense of Black Canyon as it continues to carve its way west.

Best time to ride: Spring through fall. US 50 can see a lot of traffic, however, during peak vacation times in the summer; an early-morning start or an evening ride is recommended.

Special considerations: Car and camper traffic can be heavy on this road. Keep well off to the side and ride in single file. A good pair of shatter-resistant glasses is essential for protecting your eyes from sun and flying debris whenever you ride your bike. Of course you should be wearing a helmet as well. Water and rest rooms are available at all the campgrounds and information centers along this route.

From the Elk Creek Visitors Center ride out onto US 50 and head west along the north shore of Blue Mesa Lake. You cross over the Bay of Chickens in about a mile and then hug the shore for the next 4.5 miles before reaching Middle Bridge. Cross the bridge and continue heading west along the southern shore of the lake. The road passes through the small settlement of Sapinero as you turn and head south along the Lake Fork Arm of the reservoir. You then follow the highway as it crosses over this arm on the Lake Fork Bridge, turning right onto CO 92 about 0.5 mile after the bridge. You pass the Lake Fork Information Center on your right, cross over the dam, and ride another 0.7 mile to the Blue Mesa Dam Overlook. After you have absorbed the view and had a good rest, a drink of water, and maybe a snack, head back the way you came.

---

73. BLACK MESA (See map on page 346)

For road bikes. This road ride is a classic, well loved by skinny-tire enthusiasts near and far, but it is not for the faint of heart, lungs, or legs. Beginning at the Blue Mesa Dam Overlook at an elevation of 7,720 feet, you climb to approximately 9,000 feet, then roll along the south flank of Black Mesa over unending 300-foot pitches to Morrow Point. The views from along CO 92 are unparalleled. Sweeping vistas of the Uncompahgre Plateau, the jagged peaks of the San Juans, the lakes, and Fossil Ridge to the east are spellbinding.

Note: This ride was suggested by Chris Haas, resident road-riding guru based at Tuneup Ski & Bike Shop in Gunnison. Chris and his dirt-loving counterpart Greg Morin are committed to the growth and spirit of cycling. They and all the friendly folks at Tuneup are full of great suggestions for riding in the area, so stop in and see them.

Starting point: Blue Mesa Dam Overlook. An alternate starting point that gives you a few miles of flat to warm up on is in the small town of Sapinero. There is a lodge and restaurant with a good-sized parking lot; you can park here if you ask inside first.

Length: 22 miles one-way; 44 miles out-and-back. Beginning at Sapinero will add 3 miles each way to your total distance.

Riding surface: Pavement.

Difficulty: Difficult.

Scenery/highlights: The views! Don't forget to look up and out as you are bent over your handlebars pedaling yourself silly. This is truly one of the most scenic routes in Colorado.

FLORA

The low country surrounding Blue Mesa Lake is an arid high-desert environment that supports plant types termed *sagebrush communities*. As the label implies, this life zone is dominated by sagebrush, but in wind-sheltered areas you find Gambel oak and serviceberry taking hold. As you go higher you encounter forests of piñon pine and Utah juniper—the short, round evergreens that distinguish much of the West's high deserts. Above that on certain slopes you begin to see ponderosa pines, easy to identify because of their height, long needles, and reddish bark. Then you enter into an alpine life zone where quaking aspen and mixed stands of spruce and fir dominate.

The spring bloomers include Indian paintbrush, white to pink cushion phlox, yellow stonecrop, and the pink blooms of hedgehog cactus. Bitterbrush (yellow) and serviceberry (white) are common shrubs that bloom in May. Scarlet gilia, also called shooting-star, is bright red and blooms in June, as does the pale orange globe mallow. Toward August the purple-blue blossoms of lupine emerge, followed by the blazing yellows of rabbitbrush and snakeweed in the fall.

Along the tributaries coming into the lakes you find a variety of cottonwood trees, dominated by the narrow leaf cottonwood. Several types of willows also grow along streams here; most common is the coyote willow. Chokecherry, alder, and dogwood are some of the other species of trees and shrubs commonly found near water here.

Best time to ride: Anytime spring through fall. CO 92 from Curecanti over to Crawford really doesn't see too much traffic, so a midday ride is fine. Keep an eye out for those cloud buildups in summer and fall. You are pretty exposed along this route and don't want to get caught out here in a lightning storm.

Special considerations: Water and rest rooms are available at the Lake Fork Information Center just before you cross over the dam. There are no other conveniences along this route. This is a grueling test of strength and endurance even for those in peak condition, so it's probably not for everyone. You may, however, want to test yourself and see how far you

The rolling terrain and interesting rock formations of the Hartman Rocks area makes it a favorite among mountain bikers.

can go. That's fine—just make sure you are well rested and well hydrated before you go. You may want to recruit a support vehicle so you can travel the whole route and enjoy the view when you decide you've had enough.

From the Blue Mesa Dam Overlook ride west on CO 92. You roll along, climbing gently for the first 6 miles, until you reach Pioneer Point and the Curecanti Needle Overlook. At this point the road bends around into Curecanti drainage and heads north, descending slightly until reaching the hairpin turn that swings back southeast and starts you up the biggest climb of the ride. For the next 4.5 miles you climb 7 to 8 percent grades until you reach the crest of a ridge just over 1,000 feet from your starting elevation. While the worst climb is behind you, there are many short, tortuous ones ahead. The road now rolls and pitches between 8,700 and 9,000 feet for the next 11 miles. Press onward. You eventually reach Morrow Point just before a power line crosses over the road. This is as good a turnaround point as any. (The highest point in the ride is at Mesa Creek, another high point lurks 4 miles beyond Morrow Point, and from there it is all downhill if you are continuing on to Crawford.)

For mountain bikes. This up-and-back adventure takes you up the beautiful Beaver Creek drainage on a gently climbing dirt road. The road becomes rougher past a gate and some homes and continues up and over the ridge to the west, where it connects with other jeep roads coming out of Gunnison, making a loop route possible for the adventurous who have the legs and energy. The ride is well suited for intermediate and beginning riders in good physical condition.

Starting point: Cooper Ranch Picnic Area and trailhead, at the far eastern end of the park, 5 miles west of Gunnison. If parking here is limited, try the Neversink Picnic Area and trailhead. This is a mile farther east of the Cooper Ranch Picnic Area and has a great hike to do after your bike ride.

Length: 10 miles out-and-back. Add 2 miles total if you start from Neversink Picnic Area. Allow at least 2 hours for this ride.

Riding surface: Graded dirt road, jeep road.

Difficulty: Easy to moderate.

Scenery/highlights: This is a pretty creek valley that drains off the southeastern slope of the West Elk Mountains. The vegetation and terrain are a good introduction to the country surrounding the incredibly scenic Gunnison Basin.

Don't miss the short hike along the north shore of the Gunnison River out of Neversink Picnic Area about a mile up the road from the start of this ride. This easy 1.5-mile streamside walk takes you through prime bird habitat where many year-round and migratory species can be identified. It is also in the vicinity of a great blue heron rookery.

Best time to ride: Anytime spring through fall, provided the ground is dry.

Special considerations: Be careful when crossing US 50 from the picnic area to the start of the Beaver Creek Road: Cars and campers travel at a high rate of speed through here.

Stevens Creek Campground, just a few miles west of the starting point for this ride, has vault toilets and drinking water.

Blue Mesa Reservoir and the connecting bodies of water of Curecanti National Recreation Area are one of Colorado's most popular recreation destinations.

From the Cooper Ranch Picnic Area ride out onto US 50 and go east for a few hundred feet to where the Beaver Creek Road (Forest Road 3113) leaves from the opposite side of the road. Cross over, go around the gate, and begin riding up Beaver Creek Road. You encounter at least two gates on this road; please leave them as you found them. You immediately climb up around the toe of a hill before dropping into the Beaver Creek drainage.

Approximately 2 miles from the start you see a jeep road taking off to your right. Continue on the main road. From here you climb gently along Beaver Creek, going through another gate and past some homes, to where the road becomes rougher. Continue until the canyon narrows and the road makes an abrupt switchback before climbing up and over the ridge. Unless you are ready to negotiate the steep, rough terrain that lies ahead, turn around here and head back the way you came.

Option: If you want to continue, keep following this road as it climbs onto a ridge. In approximately 2 miles you come to an intersection. Go left and continue climbing the ridge another 1.5 miles, until the road turns right and drops into Steers Gulch. Ride the Steers Gulch Road downhill in a southeasterly direction for approximately 6 miles, then make a right-hand turn onto an improved road that takes you back to US

50 and your car, another 4 miles west. This option adds at least 15 miles to your day and no doubt makes for an epic adventure.

---

75. SOAP CREEK ROAD (See map on page 346)

For mountain bikes. This out-and-back fat-tire adventure begins at the end of the Soap Creek Arm of Blue Mesa Lake and climbs into the aspens and evergreens of the West Elk Mountains, leaving the dry sagebrush and scrub country behind. Beginning and intermediate riders will enjoy this dirt road as it winds its way up a scenic drainage, gaining only a few hundred feet over the length of the ride. More advanced riders looking for a longer, more challenging ride can continue up this road as it becomes a rough-and-tumble jeep trail leading to the edge of the West Elk Wilderness Area.

Starting point: Ponderosa Campground, 7 miles up the Soap Creek Road. This road leaves CO 92 almost directly across from the Blue Mesa Dam Overlook and heads north, paralleling the Soap Creek Arm of Blue Mesa Lake.

Length: Approximately 4.5 miles one-way; 9 miles out-and-back. Allow 3 hours for this ride. From Commissary Campground to Big Soap Park at the wilderness area boundary is another 5 miles.

Riding surface: Dirt road, some jeep road.

Difficulty: Easy to moderate. Although not much technical riding ability is required, a good level of physical fitness is recommended to feel comfortable exerting yourself at these elevations (7,900 to 8,100 feet). Rougher sections of road beyond Commissary Campground require intermediate technical skills.

Scenery/highlights: This ride takes you up out of the desert environment that surrounds the lake into the cooler, heavily forested alpine environment of the West Elk Mountains. Climbing along Soap Creek you see many of the trees and wildflowers you would expect to find in the mountains of Colorado. Immediately to the west is Soap Mesa, capped by 10,029-foot Oregon Peak. To the east are the Coal Creek and West Elk drainages, which are protected inside the West Elk Wilderness Area.

FAUNA

Some of the larger mammals you are likely to see are mule deer, Rocky Mountain elk in winter and early spring, and bighorn sheep, which favor the lower elevations around the east end of Blue Mesa Lake's southern shore. Up in some of the tributaries that feed the lakes you may see signs of beaver; if you're really lucky, you may spot a river otter.

Great blue herons, with their enormous wingspans and telltale legs trailing out behind them in flight, are fairly common in the area. Ospreys, peregrine falcons, and golden and bald eagles all thrive on the fish of Curecanti's reservoirs. Numerous hawk species find there are plenty of small rodents to keep them happy, like the Gunnison prairie dog, jackrabbits, and cottontails. If you catch a flash of blue along one of the trails, it is most likely a mountain bluebird; a yellow flash is probably a yellow warbler. A variety of warblers are known to visit here during the spring and fall. In October the lake and rivers of the region are an important stopover for numerous waterfowl and shorebirds.

Best time to ride: Anytime spring through fall, but beware of wet, muddy surfaces in the spring. In the fall you need to be aware of hunting-season times and locations. It is a good idea to stay out of the backcountry if a hunt is under way.

Special considerations: The bugs can get irritating up here in the warmer months. It's not a bad idea to put on some bug spray before you go. There are vault toilets and drinking water available at Ponderosa Campground.

From the Ponderosa Campground and Picnic Area head back out onto the main Soap Creek Road (FR 721). Simply follow this road as it makes its way up into the Soap Creek drainage. Approximately 1 mile after you start out you come to a gate. Go through, making sure you leave it as you found it. You descend from here another mile past the gate to a fork in the road. To the right takes you to Soap Creek Campground, to the left keeps you on the main road; take whichever you like, because they rejoin about 0.5 mile past the campground. Continue riding up toward Commissary Campground—and beyond if you have the energy. If you don't, take a break here, drink some water, enjoy your surroundings, and ride back out the way you came in.

---

76. HARTMAN ROCKS LOOP (See map on page 356)

For mountain bikes. Also known as the Rage in the Sage, this is the Gunnison area's most famous mountain-bike ride and the scene of several off-road races every year. The rolling terrain, beautiful sandstone fins and knobs, and spectacular views—not to mention the smooth jeep roads and sections of wild, lugelike singletrack—make this loop ride and the many trails that crisscross the area a real playground for intermediate and advanced riders. Even beginning or intermediate riders will really enjoy pedaling around out here, as long as they are willing to get off their bikes for a steep hill or two.

Starting point: Hartman Rocks parking area. To get here, drive west out of Gunnison on US 50, turning south (left) just as you pass the airport onto Gold Basin Road. Wind around the airport, cross over Tomichi Creek, and continue for about a mile to a dirt road taking off west (right) that's signed for the Hartman Rocks area. Turn here and drive a short distance to a sign for Hartman Rocks and a bulletin board. Park here.

Length: 18-mile loop. There are many options for creating longer and shorter routes. Allow 3 to 4 hours to complete this ride.

Riding surface: Four-wheel-drive jeep road, singletrack.

Difficulty: Moderate to difficult. Some sections are easy but others are steep, with loose rock, and very technical. Use caution. If you are unsure about your ability to negotiate any section of the trail, dismount and walk your bike.

Scenery/highlights: This is lovely rolling sagebrush country dotted by a few junipers. The rock formations make for fun knobs and hills to ride around. The views from up on this plateau are wonderful. To the north lie the West Elk Mountains, and beyond to the east is nestled Crested Butte. More directly east is Fossil Ridge, and to the south and west are the rugged peaks of the San Juan Mountains. To the northwest is the heavily forested brow of Black Mesa, forming the northern rim of Black

Ride 76 • Hartman Rocks Loop

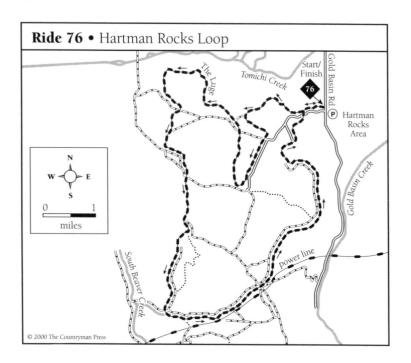

Gold Basin Rd

Start/
Finish

76

P Hartman
Rocks
Area

Tomichi Creek

The Luge

Gold Basin Creek

N
W E
S

0   1
miles

South Beaver Creek

power line

© 2000 The Countryman Press

Canyon. About halfway through this route, near Beaver Creek, you encounter the remains of the old Aberdeen Quarry. Granite from this quarry was used in the construction of the Colorado capitol in 1890.

Best time to ride: Anytime between April and October, provided the ground is not saturated. Riding on these trails when wet will coat your bike with a thick, gooey substance and leave unsightly ruts behind. In the summer plan an early-morning or early-evening ride.

Special considerations: Prickly pear cactus thrives out among the sagebrush in these hills, and while its gorgeous yellow-to-peach blooms are pleasing to the eye, its thorns can be a nightmare for a biker. Stay on trails and roads to avoid tangling with one of these prickly critters.

You will likely encounter other off-road enthusiasts of the motorized variety. While the jeeps are easy to spot and don't move that fast, motorcycles travel at a high rate of speed along some of these trails. If you hear them coming up behind you, get off the trail and give them plenty of room. This area gets a lot of attention from recreationalists of all kinds, and often trash and broken glass get left in their wake; be aware of broken glass along certain portions of this trail.

Late-summer thunderstorms frequently blossom over the mountains and then move on to lash these foothills with rain and lightning. Be aware of storm clouds brewing before you head out this way.

You'll find no drinking water or bathrooms at the trailhead or anywhere along this route. Acquire everything you'll need for this ride in the town of Gunnison.

From the parking area head west, go around a fence and climb a steep hill. At the top of the hill (0.7 mile) go right, onto a singletrack, cross through an open meadow, over a jeep road (1.3 miles), following the trail as it swings south and climbs. Ignore a trail taking off on the right (1.8 miles), and continue, crossing another open stretch before coming to an intersection with several jeep roads and trails (2.2 miles). Go straight onto the dirt road ahead, pedaling due south for just under a mile to where a single track bears off to the right (3 miles). Take this singletrack that soon swings around and heads due north. The trail climbs and then descends, crosses over another jeep road (4 miles) and then gets wild with lots of tight turns and obstacles—a section locals call "The Luge." After making a circuit of some low hills the trail swings south again and follows a fence line (6 miles). It then crosses over another dirt road, goes through several gates, picks up a jeep trail (7 miles), and then joins a more major route known as McCabe Lane (7.5 miles) as it continues southward. Follow a series of double and singletrack sections of trail to the most southern point in the loop (11 miles) before turning left to head up a gully and through another gate. The trail heads due east up a drainage, picking up a powerline service road (11.8 miles), crossing over sections of singletrack, and then intersecting another dirt road (12.8 miles). Cross over this road as the trail heads north via stretches of intermingled singletrack and jeep road. A short spur road (14.7 miles) takes off on the right to an overlook of the Gold Bar Creek drainage. For the next mile the trail parallels this drainage as it heads north. There are many side trails along this section. Soon the trail drops over the edge (16 miles). Several singletracks wind around through gullies, around rock outcroppings, and over slick rock to deliver you back to the parking lot 2 miles later.

CAMPING

There are well over 400 campsites among 10 different campgrounds at Curecanti, some more secluded than others. The bigger campgrounds tend to have the most facilities. There are campgrounds with many sites and some with just a few; check at one of the park's information centers to see which might be right for you. Camping is on a first-come, first-served basis. Length of stay at most sites is unlimited, though some specify a 14-day limit. **East Elk Creek Group Campground** requires reservations; call (970) 641-2337.

Camping is also available at **Soap Creek** and **Commissary Campgrounds** above **Ponderosa Campground** in the Gunnison National Forest. **Red Bridge Campground** in the Gunnison Resource Area of the BLM is available above **Gateview Campground.** There are many possibilities for wilderness camping on surrounding public lands; inquire at local offices of the BLM and forest service.

A handful of private RV campgrounds in the area offer amenities such as showers, convenience stores, and laundry.

IT'S INTERESTING TO KNOW . . .

Curecanti is named for Chief Curicata of the Ute tribe, who formerly lived in this area. The first nonnative people who ventured into the region were the Friars Dominguez and Escalante, who came through in 1776 following the Gunnison River in search of an overland route connecting the missions of New Mexico and California. The town and the river are named for Captain John W. Gunnison, a government surveyor who camped along the river here in September 1853 while searching for a transcontinental railroad route. A month later, while making winter camp in Utah, Gunnison and his men were attacked by Indians. Save for four souls, the entire party was killed.

LODGING

There at least two dozen hotels and motels in Gunnison. Several of the big chains are represented here, including **Best Western, Days Inn, Super 8, Econo Lodge,** and **Holiday Inn.** There are also many guest lodges, cabins, and B&Bs, some located on the outskirts of town or on mountain streams. Check out the accommodations guide at the Gunnison Chamber of Commerce.

DON'T MISS

You can rent boats at either of the marinas, or take a boat tour guided by a naturalist who will provide a wealth of fascinating information about the area's geology, wildlife, and history. Call the Elk Creek Marina to make reservations: (970) 641-0402. If you'd like to wet a line, inquire at one of the local fishing shops or guide services in Gunnison.

FOOD

A restaurant at Elk Creek serves diner-type food: sandwiches, hamburgers, pasta, and the like. There are also small grocery stores at each of the marinas offering snack foods and drinks. The **Ley-Z-B** restaurant in Sapinero offers hearty, western-style fare.

You'll find a number of good, reasonably priced restaurants in Gunnison, partly because it is a college town. For those in need of a good cup of coffee in the morning, try the **Bean, Cottonwoods,** the **Perfect Blend,** or **Mocha's Drive-Through Coffeehouse,** all on Main Street. **The Firebrand Delicatessen** (108 N. Main St.) is a great place to get some breakfast or a really good sandwich. For a Mexican meal try the **Blue Iguana** (303 East Tomichi Ave.); for Chinese try **House of China** (405 W. Tomichi). There are a number of places to get a steak in town, including the **Cattlemen Inn** (301 W. Tomichi).

LAUNDRY

High Country Services, 700 N. Main St.; (970) 641-3894

BIKE SHOP/BIKE RENTAL

Rock N Roll Sports, 608 W., Tomichi Ave.; (970) 641-9150

Tomichi Cycles, 134 Tomichi Ave.; (970) 641-0285

Tuneup Ski & Bike, 222 N. Main St.; (970) 641-0285

Curecanti National Recreation Area—Superintendent, 102 Elk Creek, Gunnison, CO 81230; (970) 641-2337, Elk Creek Visitors Center, ext. 205; http://www.nps.gov/cure/

Gunnison Country Chamber of Commerce, 500 E. Tomichi, Box 36, Gunnison, CO 81230; (970) 641-1501

Gunnison National Forest and **Bureau of Land Management,** Gunnison Resource Area, 216 N. Main, Gunnison, CO 81230; (970) 641-0471

15

Inside the boundaries of Dinosaur National Monument lie one of the richest fossil beds ever discovered and more than 325 miles of sprawling canyon- and plateau-country wilderness straddling parts of Utah and Colorado. Included in the park are the Green River, the westernmost section of the Yampa River, and the two rivers' confluence at Echo Park.

About 145 million years ago enormous rivers swept across a broad plain, depositing their rich loads of silt and organic matter across wide-mouthed deltas. The landscape was covered by a dense jungle of tree ferns and club mosses and home to a fantastic variety of giant reptiles, creatures we have come to know as dinosaurs. They died and the bodies of hundreds of dinosaurs were deposited on a sandbar near here to be later covered by the sediments of an encroaching sea. Remains of the enormous vegetarian known as brontosaurus, the spiny-tailed stegosaurus, the small but fleet-footed camptosaurus, and the fierce meat-eating allosaurus have all been found here among the fossils of other riparian creatures such as turtles and alligators. Eleven species of dinosaurs have been identified here. The skeletons of these reptiles were slowly replaced over the eons by dissolved silica percolating down through the sediments, taking the shape of the bones before hardening into stone.

As the Rocky Mountains began to rise to the east this area was dragged upward, then later squeezed from either side by faulting and

Returning from an evening reconnaissance ride just outside Dinosaur National Monument.

uplifting. Eventually, the rock layer containing the dinosaur bones made its way to the surface and was exposed along the top of a ridge. In 1909 the paleontologist Earl Douglas spotted the perfectly preserved tailbones of an apatosaurus—more commonly called the brontosaurus—on the same ridge that is now housed inside the Dinosaur Quarry building and visitors center.

The rivers, canyons, and plateaus that comprise the wild country beyond the quarry, painted in hues of peach, salmon, pink, and brown, are just as spectacular as the fossil riches here. As the Green and Yampa Rivers cut down through the layers of stone they left behind breathtaking chasms and nearly vertical rock walls, many of which bear the mark of the ancient Fremont Indians who etched the many intriguing figures and symbols found here. Together the eras that the fossils, petroglyphs, and scenery represent, and the stunning beauty of the park, make a visit to Dinosaur National Monument a magical experience.

Cycling in the Park

Dinosaur National Monument is a large park surrounded by big, empty country; as a result the mileages of the roads and trails within and around the park are significant. Any of these routes can be amended to suit your schedule and ability by simply driving to a different starting point. All of the dirt roads in and around the park become impassable for bikes and cars when wet and require a high-clearance vehicle, preferably four-wheel drive, when dry. Using a support vehicle is a good way for cyclists to negotiate longer distances.

One of the best back-road adventures here is an east-west traverse of the monument via the Yampa Bench Road. This road can be accessed in the east from Elk Springs, or from park headquarters at the south boundary of the park. The Yampa Bench Road snakes its way along the terrace, or bench, between the Yampa River Canyon and Blue Mountain, accessing some incredibly wild and scenic country. The Echo Park Road is a thrilling descent through winding sandstone canyons to the confluence of the Green and Yampa Rivers, while the paved Harpers Corner Scenic Drive climbs up onto the Yampa Plateau from the main southern entrance, providing stunning views north into the Canyon of Lodore and east up the Yampa River Canyon. The Blue Mountain and Cub Creek Roads leave from the Dinosaur Quarry and traverse the gorgeous tilted rocks and canyons of the Green River to take you to some fascinating archaeological and prehistoric petroglyph sites. At the end of the road you'll come to the cabin where homesteader Josie Morris lived for almost

CYCLING OPTIONS

There are four rides in this chapter; one is a road ride and the other three are mountain-bike rides. The ride west through the park on the Cub Creek Road is a 23-mile mixed pavement-and-dirt ride well suited for beginning and intermediate riders on mountain bikes. The Harpers Corner Road is a road tour with several possible starting points for rides from 12 to 28 miles. The ride down to Echo Park and back is a 26-mile mountain-biking adventure best suited for fit riders who can tackle the long climb on the way out. If you have a sturdy, high-clearance vehicle (four-wheel drive is optimal), you can drive to another starting point that allows you to shorten the ride to 10 miles total. The Yampa Bench Road stretches for 46 miles through the park's backcountry, and is combined with county roads for a 72-mile loop, is recommended as a vehicle-supported day or overnight trip.

50 years raising her own livestock, fruits, and vegetables. The town of Vernal, Utah, just 15 miles from the park's west entrance, is another western mountain town becoming known for its bike trails; it hosts the Dinotrax Fat Tire Festival every August. There are two bike shops in Vernal to attend to all your biking needs.

---

77. CUB CREEK ROAD (See map on page 365)

For mountain bikes. Although most of this route is paved, the road is extremely narrow and rough in spots. The last 2.5 miles, which take you out to a rock art panel and the Josie Morris cabin, are dirt. This is a spectacular adventure almost all riders will enjoy. Except for a few short hills, it follows the mostly flat terrain along the Green River. Views to Split Mountain, wildlife along the river, and other interesting things to see make this a great two-wheeled adventure.

Starting point: Dinosaur Quarry Visitors Center. To shorten your total distance by 8 miles, drive the Blue Mountain Road to the Green River Campground and Ranger Station and begin here.

Length: 11.5 miles each way, 23 miles out-and-back; 7.5 miles each way if you start at the Green River Campground. Allow at least 3 hours to ride straight out and back. You can take half a day out here if you spend time along the way to enjoy the sights and sounds of this canyon country.

Riding surface: Pavement, dirt road; rough in spots.

Difficulty: Easy to moderate. Although no technical riding skills are required, the slightly rolling terrain and overall distance may make this ride more challenging for some.

Scenery/highlights: As you begin riding east on the Blue Mountain Road (which turns into the Cub Creek Road past the Green River Ranger Station), you will be looking into the geologically fascinating Split Mountain Canyon. Here the river had already begun carving its path down into the soft Tertiary sediments before they uplifted into an enormous anticline. The river continued to carve its way down through the mountain, creating the appearance of a mountain split down the middle. Near the start of this ride you come to one of the oldest known archaeological sites in the park.

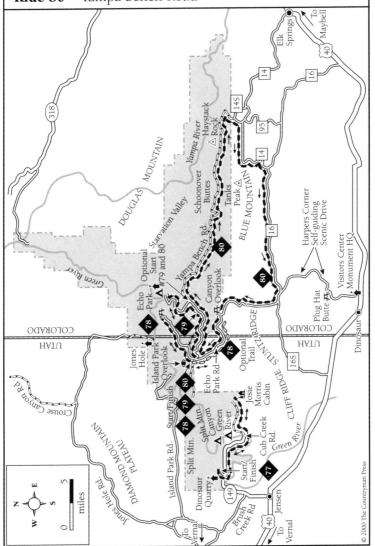

Ride 77 • Cub Creek Road
Ride 78 • Harpers Corner Road
Ride 79 • Echo Park
Ride 80 • Yampa Bench Road

Once you are past the Split Mountain Campground turnoff, your main view as you head east is into Cub Creek Valley. To the right are the purple-and-gray-banded hills that distinguish the Morrison formation, the group of rock layers where so many incredible fossil discoveries have been made. Almost 11 miles from the start begin looking up to your left in the dark patches of desert varnish, where the ancients left their fascinating images long ago. Among them you might see lizards, three princesses, trapezoidal figures wearing necklaces, and the flute player known as Kokopelli. Please do not touch these rock art drawings.

Best time to ride: Spring through fall. In midsummer plan a morning or early-evening ride, when it is cooler and there is less traffic.

Special considerations: Be aware of car and camper traffic. There are bathrooms, water, and phones at both the Dinosaur Quarry Visitors Center and at the Green River Campground and Ranger Station.

From the visitors center at the Dinosaur Quarry ride out of the parking lot and down the hill to the main road. Go left onto what is called the Blue Mountain Road. You climb gently before turning south and paralleling the river. At approximately 1.5 miles is the Swelter Shelter, so named because it was excavated in the heat of summer, contained projectile points that date from 7000 to 4000 B.C. Petroglyphs (images etched into the stone) and pictographs (images painted onto the stone) near the site were probably left by people of the Fremont culture, who lived in the area about 1,000 years ago. Take the short spur into Split Mountain Campground and make the short hike out onto the Desert Voices Trail to get an even better look into Split Mountain.

In approximately 4 miles you come to the turnoff for the Green River Campground and Ranger Station. Past the ranger station the road begins to swing around to the east again, crosses the river, and continues up into Cub Creek Canyon. At 9 miles the road turns to dirt. About 0.5 mile after you come to a fork. Stay left to get to the rock panel and the old cabin. If you are up for it, hike up the very short Hog Canyon Trail that leaves from the far side of the parking area. Beyond, the road offers some interesting exploring but soon begins climbing at steep grades to the top of Cliff Ridge. Whenever you're ready you can head back the way you came.

The views from Harper's Corner Scenic Drive are expansive, as is this one looking north to the Uinta Mountain range of northeastern Utah.

78. HARPERS CORNER ROAD (See map on page 365)

For road bikes. The entire Harpers Corner Scenic Drive is 31 miles. Experienced and superfit road riders might want to tackle this 60-miler as an epic all-day excursion, but most will want to do the shorter rides well suited to beginning and intermediate-level riders. As you roll along the top of the Yampa Plateau, high above the boiling and churning river below, fantastic views and wide-open country surround you.

Starting point: Island Park Overlook, approximately 28 miles from the start of the scenic drive at the southern boundary of the park. For a more challenging ride begin at Canyon Overlook, 8 miles before you reach Island Park Overlook, 20 miles from the start of the drive.

Length: 6 miles each way, 12 miles out-and-back. The longer ride starting at Canyon Overlook adds 8 miles each way resulting in a total out-and-back distance of 28 miles.

Riding surface: Pavement; rough in spots, narrow with *no* shoulders.

FLORA

Four life zones are found within Dinosaur National Monument: riparian along the river; upper Sonoran from the river up to about 5,500 feet; transition between 5,500 and 7,000 feet; and Canadian from 7,000 feet to the top of Blue Mountain at 8,500 feet. Cottonwoods and box elders are the dominant tree species along the river, but you will also find thickets of willows, some alders, and a variety of grasses favored by birds and deer. The upper Sonoran life zone is dominated by sagebrush communities where you'll also find shrubs such as greasewood and shadscale. Bunch wheat grass and June or "cheat" grass (a European import) also exist at this life zone, as does rabbitbrush, which blooms a brilliant yellow in fall. If you are lucky in spring you might stumble upon the delicate creamy white blooms of the sego lily, the Utah state flower that grows close to the ground and has little in the way of foliage. Purple aster, scarlet gilia, and in some places orange globe mallow dot the desert. Utah juniper and piñon pine begin to appear along the higher regions of this life zone, and dominate in the transition life zone. Other woody shrubs and trees found in the transition zone include Gambel oak, mountain mahogany, and (in some of the wetter drainages) big-tooth maple. Ponderosa and yellow pines begin to appear at the northern edge of this life zone. Some of the bloomers you will find here include pink and purple milk vetch, the yellow daisylike balsamroot, showy goldeneye, and silvery lupine. At the very top of Blue Mountain you'll find many of the same trees in the transition zone, with the addition of Douglas fir, blue spruce, white fir, limber and lodgepole pines, and quaking aspen. Shrubs that appear here include elderberry, mountain ash, chokecherry, and currant. Willows can be found in wet areas, and you may also see a mountain lilac.

Difficulty: Easy to moderate. No technical skills are needed for negotiating this route, but a good level of physical fitness is recommended. The elevations atop the plateau are around 7,500 feet, so the air is a little thinner. Make sure you are comfortable sharing the road with vehicles.

Scenery/highlights: The views up here are spectacular. To the east you look up the Yampa River, flanked to the south by Blue Mountain and to

The vibrant yellow blooms of rabbitbrush delight the eye but can tickle the nose.

SARAH BENNETT ALLEY

the north by Douglas Mountain. To the southwest lies Split Mountain. To the north is Diamond Mountain Plateau and beyond that the peaks of the Uinta Mountains, the only east-west range in the country.

Also, don't miss the short 1-mile hike out to the very edge of the canyon via the Harpers Corner Nature Trail at the end of the road.

Best time to ride: Anytime spring through fall. The summer months see the most traffic, and it can get pretty darn hot around then. Starting early or late in the day is recommended as a way of avoiding the bulk of tourist traffic. The light at these times of day is also ideal for viewing the canyons, and wildlife tends to be more active.

Special considerations: Be sure to pick up the informative pamphlet on the Harpers Corner Scenic Drive, with numbers and mileages that correspond to specific sights along the way, before heading out to start your ride. It's available at the visitors center for a nominal fee. The roads are awfully narrow up here; ride in single file and as far to the right as you feel comfortable. Be extra wary of cars, as the people behind the wheel are probably as captivated by the scenery as you are. Cars often come to an abrupt stop without warning. In the morning or evening watch also for wildlife darting across the road.

Water and rest rooms are available at the visitors center at the start of the drive. Pit toilets are available at Canyon Overlook and at the end of road at Harpers Corner. Have plenty of gas in your car, water, and food with you before you head up this way. Stay hydrated; the climate, elevation, and heat will work to sap your body's moisture and energy.

Check with the ranger at park headquarters for an update on expected weather conditions and be aware of potential afternoon thunderstorms. You are extremely exposed along this plateau.

From the Island Park Overlook ride out onto Harpers Corner Road and go left. You roll gently up and down, reaching the Iron Springs Overlook just over a mile from the start. From there you descend and climb again, passing Harper Peak, the highest point on the plateau at 7,786 feet above sea level. Approximately 4.5 miles from the start of your ride you come to the Echo Park Overlook. Echo Park is a natural amphitheater surrounded by sheer canyon walls and where the Yampa and Green Rivers come together. In the middle stands the beautifully sculpted Steamboat Rock. This was once the site of a proposed dam, but public outcry defeated the plan and the dam was moved upstream to Flaming Gorge. At 6 miles you reach Harpers Corner, named for a rancher who used to corral his cattle out here. Take an hour or so and walk out to the point—you won't be disappointed. When you are ready to go just head back the way you came. If you begin at Canyon Overlook you must first ride the 0.8 mile of graded gravel road from the overlook to the main road. If you would rather not ride this section, park off to the side of the gravel road near its junction with the paved scenic drive and begin pedaling there. From here it is an enjoyable 8 miles of gently rolling, grassy terrain atop the Yampa Plateau and sweeping views before reaching Island Park Overlook.

---

79. ECHO PARK (See map on page 365)

For mountain bikes. Riding in canyon country often requires that you ride downhill on the way out and up on the way back in order to get to the best places. This is true of the ride down to Echo Park and back.

A cyclist slips between towering sandstone walls as she nears Echo Park and the confluence of the Green and Yampa Rivers.

Beginning riders who are up to the physical challenge of climbing the 2,500 feet back out of the canyon, and intermediate as well advanced riders, will love the thrill of the descent. Almost everyone will enjoy the incredible beauty of the terrain. Several possibilities exist for making this a shorter, easier ride.

Starting point: Island Park Overlook, approximately 25 miles from park headquarters at the south end of the park. If there is no parking room available, you can pull out on the dirt road directly across from the start of the Echo Park Road, or park at any of the other pullouts along the main road. If you want to shorten this ride by driving the 8 miles down Echo Park Road and parking at its intersection with the Yampa Bench Road, you must have a high-clearance four-wheel-drive vehicle.

Length: 13 miles one-way, 26 miles out-and-back. The shorter version starting at Yampa Bench is 5 miles one-way, 10 miles out-and-back. Allow at least 4 hours to complete this ride.

Riding surface: Graded, maintained dirt road; pretty rough in spots, especially after rain.

Difficulty: Moderate to difficult. This route requires few technical skills. The ride down requires caution and a lot of braking but not much energy. The ride up, however, requires a solid base of physical fitness.

Scenery/highlights: Dropping down Iron Springs Wash, crossing the open Pearl Park, and then heading into Sand Canyon and eventually Pool Creek Canyon, which deposits you at the shore of the river at Echo Park, is a thrilling descent through some gorgeous country. On your way down you pass the old buildings of the Chew Ranch, established by Jack Chew in 1910. A little farther is the homestead of Ralph Chew, Jack's brother, built by hand between 1920 to 1940. Be sure to stop at Whispering Cave, where you can cool off in the breezes drawn through the cavernous opening. Just across the road and the creek from the cave are the Pool Creek petroglyphs, haunting images of godlike humanoid figures. Echo Park is an incredibly beautiful opening in the canyon where the Yampa, the last free-flowing river in the Colorado River system, comes in to meet the Green River. The prow of Steamboat Rock towers over the emerald green waters of the river. The canyon and the habitat created by the river are home to several endangered species (including five species of fish) and to the majestic peregrine falcon. It was here that a dam was planned in the 1950s, but public protest resulted in the dam being constructed upstream at Flaming Gorge.

Best time to ride: Spring through fall. Temperatures can get sizzling out here in the summer, so bring plenty of water and an energy snack.

Special considerations: This road becomes virtually impassable when wet, though the slippery mud dries out in a few hours. If a storm breaks when you are in the canyon, wait for a while before heading back up.

To shorten this ride, you can bring along a support vehicle and take turns at the wheel. Remember, you must have a sturdy, high-clearance vehicle, preferably four-wheel drive, to negotiate these roads.

There is a campground at Echo Park; water is available there only in the summer.

From the Island Park Overlook head out onto the main road and go right, riding for approximately 0.7 mile to the start of the Echo Park Road. You may want to pause here, observe the route of your descent, and make sure your wheels are snug in your forks and your brakes work

A rider pauses to examine one of several old buildings built by the Chew brothers, who ranched this area in the early 1900s.

properly. You begin at an elevation of approximately 7,600 feet. The road starts by descending Iron Springs Wash. The Chews, who homesteaded in the canyon in the early 1900s, did not have engineered switchbacks and simply dropped straight down this wash, hitching their animals to the rear of their wagons to act as brakes. You will have to use the muscles in your hands and forearms to slow your progress down this road, which emerges onto a bench of level terrain called Pearl Park just over 3 miles from the start.

It is 1.5 miles across this flat before the road descends again, dropping into the top of Sand Canyon. The road winds down through upper Sand Canyon for 2.5 miles, eventually emerging onto another flat called the Yampa Bench. Approximately 8 miles from the start of the ride you come to the junction with the Yampa Bench Road; bear left to head down to Echo Park. At this junction your elevation is 5,576 feet. After another 1.5 miles of pedaling you arrive at some of the old ranch ruins left behind by the Chew brothers. Another 2.5 miles along the route, in Pool Creek Canyon, you'll come to Whispering Cave, a long, low opening in the cliff wall where cool air from fissures in the rock above comes rushing out. There are petroglyphs across the road and a creek hiding behind the trees. In another mile you arrive at Echo Park, just over 5,000 feet. You may want to take a dip in the mingled waters of the Green and Yampa Rivers in preparation for your big climb on the return trip. The toughest stretch is the last few miles up Iron Springs Wash.

80. YAMPA BENCH ROAD (See map on page 365)

For mountain bikes. This dirt road traverses some of the more remote backcountry of the park, winding its way east and west along the bench between the steep slopes of Blue Mountain and the river canyon below. Portions of the 46-mile Yampa Bench Road can be ridden out-and-back as a one-day outing, or a 72-mile loop can be ridden as a self-supported or vehicle supported two-day adventure by linking county roads just outside the park. Elevations along the route vary between 5,500 feet, at the junction with the Echo Park Road, and almost 7,000 feet where the road climbs the toe of Blue Mountain in the east and crosses the park boundary.

Starting point: Island Park Overlook 0.7 mile from the start of the Echo Park Road. If you have a high-clearance, four-wheel-drive vehicle, you can to drive 8 miles down the Echo Park Road to Yampa Bench Road and park there.

If you begin from the east end you can park in the town of Elk Springs, or drive in via County Roads 14 and 14N approximately 18 miles over the toe of Blue Mountain and down to the bench to begin your ride. That way you avoid the climb back up and over the eastern end of Blue Mountain.

Length: 72-mile loop. Even riding out along portions of this route make for an all-day adventure. If you are going to ride the entire loop, plan on 2 days out and a night camping.

Riding surface: Graded dirt, jeep roads.

Difficulty: Easy to very difficult. You can make this ride as easy or as hard as you like if you have a vehicle that can negotiate these backcountry roads. Otherwise this ride is long and difficult for all but the most seasoned long-distance riders.

These fascinating images were likely left by people of the Fremont culture who lived in this area between 700 and 1,000 years ago.

Scenery/highlights: Simply being out here in this rugged, wild country with hawks soaring overhead and the river crashing among the boulders below is the highlight of this ride. Castle Park Overlook, Harding Hole, and Wagon Wheel Point provide dizzying views into the depths of the canyon and panoramic vistas beyond. From Castle Park Overlook you can see 250 feet down to the Mantle family's 1919 homestead. Also below is Mantle Cave, an alcove in a box canyon where storage sites held grain grown by the Fremont Indians in the canyon bottom. The ruins of the old Baker Cabin, and Haystack Rock where peregrine falcons nest, are other points of interest along this route. The road out to Haystack Rock is closed between April and mid-July while the disturbance-sensitive peregrines are fledging their chicks.

Best time to ride: Spring or fall; however, these are the times of year that rain is more likely. When wet, these backcountry roads are impassable due to the greasy texture of the mud. Despite the elevations along the Yampa Bench Road, temperatures during midsummer reach well into the 90s and sometimes hit the century mark.

Special considerations: When exerting yourself in the desert, plan on drinking at least a gallon of water per day. No water is available along this

FAUNA

A wide variety of mammals, birds, and fish inhabit the region in and around Dinosaur National Monument, some common, some rare and endangered. Among the most endangered are the five species of fish found in the murky waters of the Yampa and the Green Rivers. Highly adapted to thrive in the warm, silt-laden waters of the Colorado River system, the humpback chub, bonytail chub, roundtail chub, razorback sucker, and Colorado squawfish have suffered from the cold, clear waters that numerous dams spill back into the river.

Common along the banks of the river is the elegant great blue heron. Other avian residents along the river include common mergansers, spotted sandpipers, dippers, and mallard ducks. Bald eagles have been known to spend part of the year here, and peregrine falcons have several aeries in the cliffs above the river.

Beaver, river otter, and muskrat are some of the furry creatures that like the water. You might get to see some bighorn sheep. They spend most of their time higher up in the transition life zone, as do mule deer, coyote, red fox, and mountain lion. Black-tailed jackrabbits, white-tailed jackrabbits, chipmunks, kangaroo rats, and cottontails thrive at these elevations, which is why you will find the majority of hawks living here. Redtails, marsh hawks, and the common nighthawk, which primarily feeds on insects, are just a few of the hawk species found here. You may see a wandering garter snake, a desert striped whipsnake, a Great Basin whiptail, or maybe a timber or a western rattlesnake.

Black bears, Rocky Mountain elk, and the occasional moose visit the higher reaches of the park, which is also home to porcupines and yellow-bellied marmots. Blue grouse and sage grouse are secretive, ground-loving birds that you might see here, as opposed to the pinyon jays, Steller's jays, and magpies that are constantly heard and seen.

route, so bring not only plenty of water but also plenty of food, gasoline, and all the proper equipment if you plan to stay overnight.

Also, bicycles are not allowed off established roadways anywhere in national parks. Please leave your bikes at the parking areas provided and do not ride the short trails to the overlooks or other points of interest.

Camping in the backcountry of the park is allowed, but you must first

A cyclist contemplates the reflection of towering sandstone walls across the placid waters of the Green River.

obtain a free backcountry camping permit. These are available at the visitors centers located at the east, west, and south entrances to the park. You must camp at least 0.25 mile away from the road, but your vehicle is not allowed off the road. This means you must park on the roadside and carry your camping equipment to the place you wish to camp. Bikes are similarly restricted to roadways and so must be either left with your vehicle or carried to your camp. There are plans afoot at Dinosaur National Monument to create one or more vehicle-friendly camps along the Yampa Bench Road, but as of this writing none exist.

Before you head out this way be sure to check in with a park ranger to get a weather forecast, an update on road conditions, a backcountry camping permit if you need one, and any other information that will help make your trip an informed and enjoyable one.

From the Island Park Overlook ride approximately 0.7 mile south to the start of the Echo Park Road. This road drops dramatically off the rim down through Iron Springs Wash, then crosses the open piñon and juniper flats of Pearl Park before dropping into upper Sand Canyon (see ride 79). At 8 miles you come to the intersection with the Yampa Bench Road at 5,576 feet. Turn right and roll along within a few hundred feet of that elevation for most of the next 10 miles.

Approximately 6 miles from the start of the Yampa Bench Road is Castle Park Overlook (m. 14), where you can look down on the Mantle Ranch and see Mantle Cave. Hells Canyon and the road down to the Mantle Ranch come up in another mile. This is a private road and the ranch is off-limits to the public. As the road climbs out of Hells Canyon it becomes rougher. Another 1.5 miles past Hells Canyon you come to Harding Hole Overlook and, 1.5 miles beyond that, to Wagon Wheel Point (18 miles from the start). From here the road begins to climb around the flank of Blue Mountain.

About 3.5 miles past Wagon Wheel Point you come to Baker Cabin, where the Baker family homesteaded for 12 years beginning in 1918. The combination of drought, poor livestock prices, and overgrazing of the area drove them out by the 1930s. The road continues to climb gently for another 7 miles to the spur road leading out to Haystack Rock. About 1.5 miles past this turnoff (30 miles from the start) the road heads southward and begins its climb over the eastern edge of Blue Mountain. From a high point of about 7,200 feet you'll begin your descent into Bear Valley.

As you begin your descent down the southern slope of Blue Mountain into Bear Valley you come to a fork in the road 32 miles from the start. CR 14N goes to the left (east) and CR 95 continues south. These roads are graded and maintained the rest of the way. A left onto CR 14N goes to CR 14 and US 40 at Elk Springs. To make a loop and head back to your starting point, bear right onto CR 95, picking up CR 14 westbound in just over a mile. Head due west on CR 14 for approximately 5 miles, following it as it turns south reaching CR 16 in another 3 miles (m. 41). Head west on CR 16, across some open, desolate country where you'll have only vultures circling overhead for company. After approximately 16 miles this county road meets Harpers Scenic Drive. Go right, if you need to go back to your starting point, and ride another 17 miles to Island Park Overlook.

CAMPING

All campgrounds are managed on a first-come, first-served basis. The stay limit at all campgrounds is 14 days.

Green River Campground, located 6 miles east of the Dinosaur Quarry, has 88 sites, drinking water, flush toilets, tables, and fireplaces; it is well shaded and has firewood for sale. Open April to October. Fee required.

Split Mountain Campground, 4 miles east of Dinosaur Quarry, has four sites for group camping only (eight people or more), drinking water, flush toilets, fireplaces, and firewood for sale. Fee required. Open all year. Call (435) 789-8277 for reservations.

Rainbow Park Campground, located 26 miles from the Dinosaur Quarry via the Island Park Road (unpaved), has two sites, no water, vault toilets, tables, no fires. No fee. Open all year.

Echo Park Campground, 38 miles north of park headquarters, has 13 sites, plenty of shade, drinking water, vault toilets, tables, and fireplaces. Fee required. Open all year. The road requires a high-clearance vehicle—four-wheel drive is recommended—and is impassable when wet.

Deerlodge Park Campground, 53 miles east of headquarters, has eight sites, no drinking water, vault toilets, tables, fireplaces, and shade. No fees. Open all year.

Gates of Lodore Campground, 106 miles north of park headquarters at the very north end of the park, has 10 sites, drinking water, vault toilets, tables, fireplaces, and some shade. Fee required. Open all year.

There are several private campgrounds in the vicinity of Vernal, Utah. The **Vernal KOA** on the west side of town and has a pool, store, showers, laundry, and playground. Both tent and RV sites are available. The same is true for **Campground Dina** on the north side of town. It has showers, laundry, and a store, as does **Fossil Valley RV Park** located west of Vernal on US 40. **Steinaker State**

Park, 8 miles north of Vernal on US 191, and **Red Fleet State Park,** another 4 miles beyond that, have lots of lakeside camping. Wilderness camping possibilities are endless in the Ashley National Forest, 20 miles north of Vernal.

LODGING

The closest town offering a choice of accommodations is Vernal, Utah, about 15 miles west of the park. Here you will find about a dozen hotels and motels, including a **Weston Plaza Hotel,** a **Best Western,** a **Days Inn,** and an **Econo Lodge.** Craig, about 55 miles east of the park, has just a handful of hotels and motels to choose from, but there are lots of choices in Steamboat Springs, another 42 miles past Craig.

FOOD

Many of the hotels in Vernal have café-style restaurants serving American food. Chain restaurants such as the **Golden Corral Family Steakhouse** (1046 W. US 40), and the **Crack'd Pot** (1089 E. US 40) have good, basic fare such as steaks, sandwiches, and salads. **Last Chance Steakhouse** (3340 N. Vernal) has a slightly better dining

IT'S INTERESTING TO KNOW . . .

The Dinosaur Quarry at Dinosaur National Monument is one of the richest fossil beds ever discovered. Over 350 tons of fossilized bones have been removed from the quarry; many of the dinosaur bone collections around the country, including complete skeletons, were found here. More than 2,000 bones are exposed in place on the quarry face inside the visitors center, and there are undoubtedly countless thousands of others still entombed in rock layers below.

atmosphere. For Mexican try **Casa Rios** (2015 W. US 40) or **La Cabana** (56 W. Main St.). For Chinese food try **Mei Palace** (3340 N. Vernal).

LAUNDRY

West End Laundromat & Cleaners, 933 W. US 40, Vernal; (435) 789-1990

BIKE SHOP/BIKE RENTAL

Altitude Cycle , 510 E. Main St., Vernal; (435) 781-2595

Basin Saw & Cycle, 450 N. Vernal Ave., Vernal; (435) 781-1226

FOR FURTHER INFORMATION

Dinosaur National Monument— Superintendent, 4545 E. US 40, Dinosaur, CO 81610-9724; (970) 374-3000 or (435) 789-2115; http://www.nps.gov/dino/

Vernal Welcome Center, 235 E. Main St., Vernal, UT 84078; (435) 789-4002

Dinosaurland Travel Board, 25 E. Main St., Vernal, UT 84078; (800) 477-5558

Ashley National Forest—Vernal Ranger District, 355 N. Vernal Ave., Vernal, UT 84078; (435) 789-1181

DON'T MISS

About 10 miles northeast of Vernal, which is about 15 miles west of the park, are the Dry Fork petroglyph panels, considered some of the best left by people of the Fremont culture that once thrived in this area. What make these panels so notable are the number and size of humanoid figures. Most are adorned with elaborate headdresses, necklaces, earrings, and breastplates, all characteristic of Fremont-style petroglyphs. This particular set of panels is believed to be between 1,200 and 1,600 years old.

16

Nestled among the rolling hills, meadows, and ponderosa pine forests of the high country west of Colorado Springs lies Florissant Fossil Beds National Monument. Inside this small, out-of-the-way park awaits a fascinating glimpse into a world frozen in time. During the Cenozoic era, about 33 million years ago in a period called the Oligocene, the region was densely forested swampland surrounded by smoking volcanoes. Lush ferns as well as giant sequoia, cedar, white birch, and oak trees cloaked the slopes surrounding a shallow lake, created when a lava flow from a nearby volcano dammed a valley. The lake, about 12 miles long and 2 miles wide and shaped like a crescent, provided an incredibly rich habitat that attracted thousands of different insects, birds, and mammals to its shores. An impressive variety of fish, mollusks, and aquatic insects also inhabited the waters of the lake.

Suddenly, a massive series of volcanic explosions rained layer upon layer of hot ash on the lake and surrounding area. Butterflies, bees, spiders, and beetles were stopped in their tracks, entombed by a powder-fine ash that coated every hair and antenna, preventing decomposition. Leaves, flowers, and even entire plants and trees were encased in the same process. Unstable layers of ash on the slopes above washed down in mudflows that filled the lake, trapping fish and other aquatic creatures. Thousands of years of eruptions followed, burying deeper and deeper the life that once swam and buzzed around the lake. As groundwater seeped down through the layers of sediments over time, silica was deposited in the cells of the plants and animals, preserving them perfectly.

Some 5 million years later another geologic upheaval, the uplifting of the southern end of the Rocky Mountains, brought the lake's deposits and all its fossil riches back to the surface. Since the discovery of the fossil bed by a U.S. Geological Survey geologist in 1874 over 1,100 species of insects have been identified, and several tons of rock containing fossils have been removed to collections all over the world. Many of the fossils have been taken into private collections. The largest collection, with some 25,000 specimens, exists at the Museum of Comparative Zoology at Harvard University. The several hundred on display at the monument are a good sample of what has been found here. The trails through the park take you to parts of the old lake bed and to the enormous stumps of trees that were fossilized where they stood.

Cycling in the Park

Because this park was designed to protect the lake-bed fossils it is relatively small—only about 6,000 acres—and does not feature scenic drives or trails open to bicycles. The surrounding terrain, however, is very scenic and mountainous and is home to several state parks, reservoirs, large tracts of national forest, and interesting historical tours and towns ideally suited to exploring on two wheels. Pikes Peak, at 14,110 feet, is a formidable barrier between the wild, rolling mountains and high meadows to the west and the sprawling tentacles of Colorado Springs to the east. The monument, ancient lake, and nearby town all earned the name *Florissant*—French for "blooming"—for the incredible variety and beauty of the wildflowers here. Tall, stately ponderosa pines dominate the surrounding area but give way to stands of mixed evergreens and aspens as you move up into the drainages and foothills of Pikes Peak.

The town of Cripple Creek, about 20 miles south of the monument, was the scene of one of this country's richest gold strikes, producing more than $340 million in gold and silver between 1891 and 1916. The road south to Cripple Creek from the monument is an excellent vehicle-supported or all-day adventure through some incredibly scenic terrain. Many of the historic buildings remain in Cripple Creek and nearby Victor, making for an interesting tour of a town that only 100 years ago

CYCLING OPTIONS

There are four rides in this chapter, one a serious road ride, and the other three for mountain bikes. The easy-to-moderate 9.5-mile Twin Rock Loop, which uses both paved and dirt roads, is the only route that traverses the small acreage inside the park. It is a scenic ride cyclists of all abilities will enjoy. Elk Meadow to Cheesman Ranch is just one possible route for fat-tire fans on the many singletrack trails inside Mueller State Park and Wildlife Area. The trail described here is 7.5 miles long and moderate to difficult for intermediate- and advanced-level riders. The ride up to Horsethief Park, on the western slope of Pikes Peak inside the Pike National Forest, is another moderate-to-difficult singletrack that traverses mountainous terrain at high elevations. For road bikers there's the 18-mile ride (36 miles total) from the monument up the scenic Gold Belt Tour Road to the historic mining town of Cripple Creek. A vehicle-supported day trip for riders of varying abilities and fitness levels, this route allows everyone to take some time to enjoy the sights and local history.

was thronged with fortune seekers and the unsavory opportunists who catered to them. Cripple Creek has once again become a place where people are prepared to try their luck: The residents have recently voted to allow gambling on a limited basis.

81. TWIN ROCK LOOP (See map on page 386)

For mountain bikes. This is an easy-to-moderate 9.5-mile loop that traverses some of the really pretty, rolling terrain inside and just outside the monument's boundaries. Plan on stopping and seeing the old Hornbek Homestead along the way, taking at least half an hour to tour the house and outbuildings.

Starting point: Visitors center.

Length: 9.5-mile loop. Allow at least 2 hours to complete this loop.

Riding surface: Pavement, gravel road.

Difficulty: Easy to moderate. No technical riding skills are needed, though a good level of physical fitness is recommended to negotiate some of these hills. Some experience sharing the road with vehicle traffic is recommended as well.

Scenery/highlights: The Hornbek Homestead's well-preserved buildings are a testament to the tenacity and strength of the women settlers, who were often left on their own, to make a new life for themselves on the western frontier. Adeline Hornbek, originally from Massachusetts, came west and settled near Denver with an ailing husband. They did well ranching, but Adeline was soon widowed. She married again, only to have her second husband vanish. Determined to start anew, Adeline brought her four children to the area, and seeing the good pasturage, running water, and proximity to transportation routes, had a sturdy house built for them in the Florissant Valley in 1878. This was no one-room shanty, but a two-story, four-bedroom house with a dozen paned-glass windows, Oriental carpets on the floor, and Victorian-style furniture. It was the first house built in the valley and is on the National Register of Historic Places. Adeline ran a successful ranching operation for many years with her children, and eventually married again. She lived in her house until her death in 1905. The house is open during the summer months and most afternoons. Talks are given hourly during the summer months between 10 A.M. and 4 P.M., and during the off-season when a ranger is available.

Best time to ride: Spring through fall. Afternoon thunderstorms are quite common up here, so if rain is in the forecast, riding earlier in the day is best. These storms can be violent, with lots of lightning and hail.

Special considerations: The elevations here are quite high—between 8,300 and 8,900 feet—so start out slow, pace yourself, and be sure to drink plenty of water before, during, and after your ride.

County Road 1 and the Lower Twin Rock Road are very narrow and have little or no shoulder. There are also several short steep hills and corners with blind spots. Stay to the right and ride in single file. Traffic tends to travel at high speed, so stay alert. Pull over to the right and stop before crossing the road. Water and rest rooms are available at the visitors center but no where else along this route.

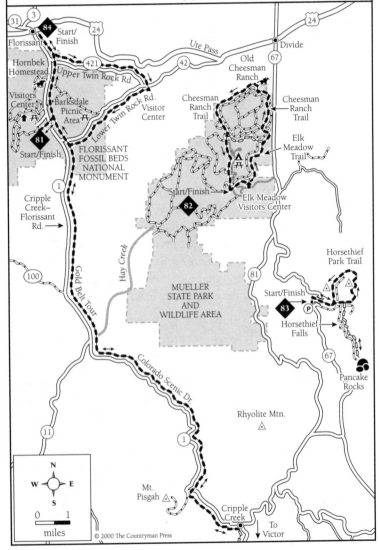

Ride 81 • Twin Rock Loop
Ride 82 • Elk Meadow to Cheesman Ranch
Ride 83 • Horsethief Park
Ride 84 • Florissant to Cripple Creek

31
3
84 Start/Finish
Florissant
24
Ute Pass
Divide
24
67
Hornbek
Homestead
421
42
Old
Cheesman
Ranch
Upper Twin Rock Rd.
Visitors
Center
Barksdale
Picnic
Area
Lower Twin Rock Rd.
Visitor
Center
Cheesman
Ranch
Trail
Cheesman
Ranch
Trail
81 Start/Finish
FLORISSANT
FOSSIL BEDS
NATIONAL
MONUMENT
Elk
Meadow
Trail
1
Start/Finish
82
Elk Meadow
Visitors Center
Cripple
Creek–
Florissant
Rd.
Hay Creek
Horsethief
Park Trail
100
Gold Belt Tour
MUELLER
STATE PARK
AND
WILDLIFE AREA
81
Start/Finish
83 P
Horsethief
Falls
67
Colorado Scenic Dr.
Pancake
Rocks
11
1
Rhyolite Mtn.
N
W E
S
0 1
miles
Mt.
Pisgah
Cripple
Creek
To
Victor

© 2000 The Countryman Press

From the visitors center parking lot ride out onto CR 1 (Florissant–Cripple Creek Road) and ride north for 1 mile to the Hornbek Homestead. Stop here, have a look around, and when you are ready saddle up, ride another 0.7 mile to the gravel CR 421 (Upper Twin Rock Road), and turn right. Pedal east on this road as it rolls along past numerous summer homes, climbing for 3.3 miles to the paved Lower Twin Rock Road. You will have gained over 600 feet in elevation from the start of your ride and reached a high point in this loop of 8,960 feet. Turn right again onto Lower Twin Rock Road (CR 42) descending for 3.2 miles to the intersection with CR 1. You may want to pull into the Barksdale Picnic Area and take a stroll down the Shootin' Star Trail about 1.5 miles from the start of your descent. Otherwise, when you get back to CR 1, go right and ride for 1.3 miles back to the visitors center.

82. ELK MEADOW TO CHEESMAN RANCH (See map on page 386)

For mountain bikes. On this ride within the Mueller State Park and Wildlife Area, you ride through stands of mixed conifers and open meadows, encountering several interesting historical sites along the way. This recreation area is also managed for its wildlife and you may see wild turkeys, deer, elk, or even black bears, which are numerous here. Some sections of trail are steep and loose; use caution. Stop, dismount, and walk your bike around places in the trail you are unsure of. There are over 85 miles of trails in this park, close to half of them designated bike trails, creating almost endless opportunities for designing your own routes.

Starting point: Elk Meadow trailhead, about 0.5 mile past the Mueller State Park Visitors Center. To get to Mueller State Park from Florissant Fossil Beds National Monument go right on CR 1 for just under a mile, then turn left on CR 42 and go east 7 miles to the town of Divide. When you reach Divide go south on CO 67 for approximately 4 miles to the entrance to Mueller State Park. Drive up past the visitors center to the Elk Meadow trailhead.

Length: 7.5-mile loop. Allow at least 2 hours to complete this ride.

Riding surface: Singletrack, pavement.

Difficulty: Moderate to difficult. Good levels of technical riding ability and physical fitness are necessary for negotiating some of these hills and rough spots along the trail, especially at these elevations.

Scenery/highlights: Thick, fragrant forests of mixed conifers and views across open meadows are delightful. Where the Elk Meadow Trail and the Cheesman Ranch Trail intersect is known as Murphys Cut; the old rail line came through here on its way to Cripple Creek. Historic buildings of the Cheesman Ranch can be seen at the north end of this route. Homesteaded in 1900, this was one of the most successful cattle ranch operations in the area.

Best time to ride: Anytime spring through fall, provided the ground is dry and free of snow. Ride morning or evening to see wildlife and avoid the hottest temperatures of the day.

Special considerations: The many biking trails in Mueller State Park allow for groups of varying abilities to go exploring for a day, or several days. Stop in at the visitors center and pick up a map to get an idea of the many opportunities for creating your own routes here. The park has camping, showers, and laundry.

There is a minimal day-use fee to ride in the park. Drinking water and bathrooms are available inside the park at the visitors center or in the campgrounds.

As you begin riding on the Elk Meadow Trail (Trail 18), you head downhill. In 0.5 mile the trail zigzags, then swings around and heads north through open meadows and forests. There are several steep hills here with sections that are loose and dangerous; use caution. Approximately 2.5 miles from the start the Elk Meadow Trail ends where it meets the Cheesman Ranch Trail. This is called Murphys Cut, where the Midland railroad grade came through on its way to Cripple Creek. Continue heading north on the Cheesman Ranch Trail (Trail 17) as it traverses several open meadows. You pass the Greer Ranch, Rule Creek Pond, and the highway in the first mile of this trail before it begins to swing westward. At the northernmost end of the loop you pass the short spur road out to the old Cheesman Ranch (mile 4.5). Just before the ranch turnoff the Buffalo Rock

Trail comes in from your left and then, past the ranch, leaves again from the left. The trail gets more difficult, with steep, loose sections and rocks. Two miles past the last trail junction you come to the Grouse Mountain trailhead in the campground. From the trailhead follow the paved road 1.5 miles through the park campgrounds back to the Elk Meadow trailhead.

Option: You may wish continue on the Cheesman Ranch Trail past the Grouse Mountain trailhead back to the intersection of the Elk Meadow Trail, then ride the Elk Meadow Trail in the opposite direction back to the trailhead and your car. This creates a cherry-stem trail configuration (an out-and-back ride on the same section of trail with a loop at the end) as opposed to a full-circle loop. This option is a total distance of 10 miles.

---

83. HORSETHIEF PARK (See map on page 386)

For mountain bikes. Although this short ride encircles the beautiful wildflower-filled meadow known as Horsethief Park, it is not really what you would call a "ride in the park." Advanced and intermediate riders looking for a challenge will relish the steep climbs, fast-paced singletrack, and lung-expanding elevations along this route. You gain approximately 900 feet in the first 2 miles. A worthwhile spur up to Pancake Rocks adds approximately 3 more miles and another 500 feet of elevation.

Starting point: Horsethief trailhead inside the Pike National Forest. This trailhead is located 9 miles south of the town of Divide on CO 67, on the south side of the old railway tunnel.

Length: 5.5-mile loop; approximately 8 miles if you add the spur up to Pancake Rocks. Allow 1½ to 2 hours to complete this loop—another 1 to 2 hours to ride up to Pancake Rocks and take a look around.

Riding surface: Singletrack.

Difficulty: Moderate to difficult. The loop route involves some steep climbing and intermediate technical skills. The spur up to Pancake Rocks involves even more steep climbing and a lot of technical riding ability. The elevations along this route are very high, so a good-to-excellent level of physical fitness is recommended.

Scenery/highlights: The alpine meadows of Horsethief Park are beauti-

FLORA

Florissant Fossil Beds National Monument is within the montane life zone. Although ponderosa pines dominate around the visitors center, the park also includes Douglas fir, Colorado blue spruce, and limber pine. One of the oldest ponderosa pines in Colorado exists within the park boundaries; ranger-led hikes to see the giant can be arranged by calling ahead. Cinquefoil, or potentilla, which blooms yellow in spring, is one of the only shrubs found here. Grasses such as Nebraska sedge, Arizona fescue, mountain muley, and June grass thrive in these conditions and are what traditionally made for such good ranching in this area.

May and June are the peak times for viewing wildflowers. You are likely to see the delicate pasqueflower, the blue flax for which the park is famous, Indian paintbrush, purple larkspur, monkshood, and harebells. In shadier spots you will find the large white-and-blue blossoms of columbine, the Colorado state flower. The tiny sky-blue clusters of flowers with yellow eyes called forget-me-nots are also here, as are lupine and the low-growing stonecrop. One-day classes in wildflower identification, drawing, and watercolor painting centered on the variety of blooms found at the monument are offered through the park service every June. Call well in advance if you are interested.

ful and likely to host deer or elk near dusk. Beavers also make their home up here in the headwaters of Fourmile Creek, which carries rain and snowmelt out of the Pikes Peak area and becomes a major artery of the Arkansas River. Sentinel Point looms directly to the east at 12,530 feet, and immediately behind it is Pikes Peak (14,110 feet). The views of the back side of Pikes Peak from up here are superb, as are vistas south toward Cripple Creek, and north into the top of the Beaver Creek drainage and Devils Playground.

Best time to ride: Anytime spring through fall, provided the ground is dry and free of snow. Heat is not likely to be a big factor at these elevations, even during the summer months, but the sun is extra strong in the middle of the day, so morning or afternoon is best for riding.

Special considerations: The high elevations, dry air, and rigorous climbing required on this route mean that your body will work extra hard. Keep all your systems functioning smoothly by drinking lots of water.

Be aware of area weather forecasts and do not head up this way if afternoon thunderstorms are likely. You will be very exposed along parts of this trail and on the ridge out to Pancake Rocks. If you see dark thunderclouds rumbling, beat a hasty retreat to lower elevations.

No drinking water or bathrooms are available along this route. The nearest facilities are at the Mueller State Park Visitors Center just a few miles north of the start of this ride, or in the town of Divide 9 miles north. Make sure to bring lots of water.

From the Horsethief trailhead parking lot you begin climbing almost immediately. You first head north and then swing around and begin heading east, crossing over the top of the railway tunnel. The trail follows the upper Fourmile Creek drainage as it climbs steeply. Approximately 0.8 mile from the start you encounter the Horsethief Park Trail coming in from your left. Continue up along the creek another 0.25 mile to where the trail out to Pancake Rocks enters on your right. If you are planning to do this spur now, go right; if not, continue on as the trail becomes flatter and the meadows of Horsethief Park come into view.

Another 0.7 mile from the first intersection you come to a junction where the trail for Horsethief Falls continues straight ahead and the path to Horsethief Park crosses the creek and heads north. The hike up to the falls is a 0.5-mile round-trip if you want to get off your bike and stretch your legs. If not, go left at this junction and climb another 200 feet to reach the high point in this ride. You then drop down and climb back up to almost that same elevation (10,699 feet) following the trail as it swings west and then south 1.5 miles later. From the northernmost point of this loop the trail descends and then rolls along for another 1.5 miles back to the main trail coming up the drainage. Cross over the creek and go right, taking the trail just under a mile back down to the trailhead parking lot.

Note: If you saved the spur out to Pancake Rocks for after your loop, you need to go left and ride 0.25 mile to pick up the trail when you encounter the main trail coming up the drainage. Once on this spur trail you begin climbing immediately, straight up at first and then via several switchbacks. These switchbacks begin 0.5 mile from where you left the main trail and continue for another 0.5 mile before bringing you up to a saddle. From here you roll along at approximately 11,000 feet for just under a mile to the end, at Pancake Rocks. After you have had some time to gaze at the view, turn around and head back the way you came. When you hit the main trail you can either go right and continue on to ride the loop route, or go left down the creek drainage to the trailhead.

84. FLORISSANT TO CRIPPLE CREEK (See map on page 386)

For road bikes. This is a classic trip up the Gold Belt Tour Road to the old gold-mining town of Cripple Creek. Gaining some 1,200 feet over rolling terrain, this route traverses some of this region's most scenic backcountry. Although the road is narrow and almost shoulderless, it receives light traffic and makes a great trip for the avid cyclist who favors either thin or fat tires. It is also a fine vehicle-supported ride for a group with varying abilities, who may want to take some time to wander around the historic mining districts of Cripple Creek and Victor.

Starting point: The town of Florissant at the junction of CR 1 and US 24, a little over 2 miles north of the monument.

Length: 18 miles one-way, 36 miles out-and-back. It's a half- to full-day adventure depending on how much time you spend in Cripple Creek.

Riding surface: Chip-and-sealed pavement.

Difficulty: Moderate to difficult. The elevations along this route are high, ranging between 8,100 and 9,600 feet. Even well-seasoned road riders from lower elevations may find this route challenging because of the thin air. Most of the 1,500-foot elevation gain comes in the 11 miles before you reach Cripple Creek.

If you are doing this route as a vehicle-supported ride, the length and amount of climbing can be tailored to suit the needs of each individual cyclist.

Scenery/highlights: After riding through the open country south of the monument you climb into the tightly compact peaks and ridges of pink granite, overlaid in areas by remnants of old volcanoes. The rich mineralization responsible for the gold and silver deposits around Cripple Creek and Victor occurred in the top of an ancient volcano, or caldera. A

FAUNA

Mule deer are probably the most commonly seen of the larger mammals that pass through the park, but black bear, cougar, and Rocky Mountain elk are sometimes seen here as well. Unique to this area is Abert's squirrel, which is black, has tufted ears, and nests in the park's ponderosas. Richardson's ground squirrel is another park resident not commonly found in other parts of the West. This critter looks like a prairie dog but is smaller, and lives in colonies in the park's meadows. Golden eagles are among the park's avian residents. One particular pair comes every year to nest inside the monument's boundaries and, when they are not hunting or attending to their young, can be seen roosting in a dead tree directly across from the visitors center. Numerous hawk species can be seen in the park, redtails being the easiest to identify. Mountain bluebirds are quite common in the park.

mishmash of broken volcanic and nonvolcanic rock filled this caldera, indicating that tremendous forces must have shattered, then recemented, the rock inside. The volcano most likely collapsed several times, and each time the area was filled back in with sediment and new volcanic rock. Between collapses mineral-rich fluids seeped into the cracks of the broken material inside the caldera, hardening into ore-bearing veins.

The heyday of the mining era here lasted from roughly 1891 to 1920, but gold was still being extracted until 1950, by which time almost 20 million ounces of gold had been produced by the mines of Cripple Creek. Almost twice as much gold was produced here than at the famous Mother Lode in California or Nevada's Comstock Lode. The population of the town mushroomed from a few dozen ranchers to over 50,000 during the first 10 years of the boom, many of them fortune seekers who wound up working long hours in dangerous jobs for little pay. Most of that pay was quickly squandered in more than 70 saloons and numerous "pleasure palaces" and "cribs" where women of ill repute plied their trade. Better mining techniques, new technology, and increase in the price of gold have recently rejuvenated mining in several of the old mines nearby. In the early 1990s the town of Cripple Creek decided to capitalize on its colorful history and, along with Central City and Blackhawk, voted to legalize gambling.

CO 67 is not a good choice for a return route on this ride, as it is congested with tour buses and vehicles full of fun-seekers making their way to and from Colorado Springs. The Gold Camp Road that winds its way due west to Colorado Springs, and the incredibly scenic Shelf Road that heads south out of Cripple Creek to Canon City, are two dirt roads that get very light traffic and make for excellent mountain biking.

Best time to ride: May through October, when temperatures are warm enough to make the ride enjoyable. Despite the high elevations, mid-summer days can get pretty hot with strong sun; if you are riding in July or August, you may want to get an early start.

Special considerations: This is a long day if you are riding this route without a support vehicle. It's best to get an early start so you can give yourself some time to poke around Cripple Creek and have lunch.

Rest rooms and water are available in the town of Florissant, at the visitors center of the park, and in Cripple Creek but nowhere else along the way. Bring plenty of water; staying hydrated is the key to making this a great day. A few energy snacks don't weigh too much and might come in handy on the way up.

From the town of Florissant ride south on CR 1 (Florissant–Cripple Creek Road). For the first 8 miles this road rolls along between 8,300 and 8,500 feet through open ranch country and stands of ponderosa. You then descend over the next 1.25 miles into a shallow valley, where you come to a junction just before Hay Creek. The Gold Belt Tour Road splits here, the west fork heading toward CO 9 and Parkdale. Bear left and stay on course for Cripple Creek. You will cross Hay Creek immediately after this junction. In another 0.5 mile you cross Fourmile Creek, after which the climbing begins. In the next 3 miles you gain just over 800 feet. At this point Copper Mountain and Rhyolite Mountain to the east come into view. Within the next mile Barnard Creek comes out of Box Canyon, and you descend slightly before making the final climb into Cripple Creek. At mile 16 you make a switchback just below the cone-shaped Mount Pisgah, and then ride another mile before gaining the highest elevation on this ride, 9,600 feet. Beyond Mount Pisgah the road drops into the town of Cripple Creek (9,494 feet). Spend some time cruising the town, but beware the tour bus and gambling traffic on Bennett Avenue. When you've had a look around and some lunch, return the same way you came.

Option: It is approximately 5 more miles to the town of Victor, which is worth a visit. The road there is newly paved with wide shoulders and is in excellent condition. The streets in Victor, however, are dirt.

CAMPING

There is no camping inside the monument but there is lots of camping nearby. **Mueller State Park** about 20 minutes from the monument has over 80 sites, as well as showers and laundry facilities. Call (719) 687-2366 or visit http://www.coloradoparks.org. Fees are $4 for a day-use vehicle pass, $9 for a tent campsite, and $12 for an RV campsite. About 0.5 mile south of the entrance to Mueller Park is the Upper Four-mile Road, which takes you to the **Crags Campground** in the Pikes Peak Ranger District of the Pike National Forest. Directly west of the monument, in the South Park Ranger District of the Pike National Forest, are **Riverside Campground** and **Blue Mountain Campground** near the South Platte River.

Lots of private campgrounds in the area offer RV and tent sites as well as showers. Some have laundry facilities, too. In Divide try the **Alpine Lakes Resort** (4145 CR 5). In Woodland Park you have the choice of **Big Pines Campground** (US 24, east of Woodland Park), **Colorado Campground** (31013 CO 67), or **Diamond Campgrounds** (900 CO 67).

LODGING

There are countless possibilities for accommodations in and around Colorado Springs about 40 minutes away. Of note is the elegant old hotel called **The Broadmoor,** built in 1918 and known for decades as the grandest hotel west of the Mississippi. In Woodland Park there are close to a dozen places to stay, half B&Bs and half motel rooms. There are places to stay up in Cripple Creek. No rooms are available in the tiny town of Florissant.

FOOD

If you are looking for a good cup of coffee in the morning, try **Java Junction** (759 Gold Hill Place) in Woodland Park. For breakfast you might want to try **Grandmother's Kitchen** (212 US 24). There are a couple of Chinese restaurants in Woodland Park, including the **Fortune Dragon** (280 US 24) and **Canton China** (1212 E. US 24). **Pazano's Italian Restaurant** (730 E. US 24) is good, and **Tres Hombres Tex-Mex Cantina** (116 ½ Midland Ave.) is worth a try. The **Gold Hill Grill** (609 West Midland Ave.) and the **Paradise**

Mountain Grill (209 E. Midland Avenue) serve a good basic variety of dishes, and you can always find a steak at the **Circle H Smokehouse** (720 West Browning Ave.). In the town of Florissant you can get basic café-style food at the **Fossil Inn** (2651 US 24).

IT'S INTERESTING TO KNOW . . .

The creek that gave its name to the famous mining district of Cripple Creek was labeled by one of the area's first inhabitants, a rancher named Levi Welty. The story goes that Welty and his three sons were building a cabin one day when a heavy log that they were lifting got away from them. It rolled away, hitting one of the boys, knocking over Welty's shotgun (discharging it), and frightening a calf grazing nearby. The boy's leg was badly injured but not broken, Levi Welty's hand and arm had been hit by the shotgun blast, and the calf broke its leg when it jumped the stream in fright. Supposedly Welty commented that the creek that ran through the scene of the calamity was "some kind of cripple creek!" The name stuck.

LAUNDRY

Woodland Laundry, 620 W. Midland Ave., Woodland Park; (719) 687-1222

BIKE SHOP/BIKE RENTAL

There are close to a dozen bike shops in Colorado Springs, a couple of them really good. The two you'll find in Woodland Park are:

Angletech, 318 N. CO 67; (719) 687-7475

Team Telecycle, 615 S. Baldwin; (719) 687-6165; http://www.teamtelecycle.com

FOR FURTHER INFORMATION

Florissant Fossil Beds National Monument—Superintendent, P.O. Box 185, Florissant, CO 80816-0185; (719) 748-3253; http://www.nps.gov/flfo/

Woodland Park Chamber of

Commerce, junction of US 24 and CO 67, Box W, Woodland Park, CO 80866; (719) 687-9885

Pike National Forest, Pikes Peak Ranger District, 601 S. Weber, Colorado Springs, CO 80903; (719) 636-1602

Pike National Forest, P.O. Box 219, Fairplay, CO 80440; (719) 836-2031

DON'T MISS

At the Chamber of Commerce office in Cripple Creek (107 East Eaton) pick up a map and information on a self-guided tour, which includes historic buildings and mine sites in both Cripple Creek and nearby Victor. You can also get a professionally guided tour through a touring company in Cripple Creek; inquire at the Chamber of Commerce office about groups that offer historical tours in town. The Mollie Kathleen Mine Tour is a walk-through of the old Mollie Mine, in operation from 1892 to 1961. Here guides take you 1,000 feet back into the mines to see real gold ore veins, view the equipment used to extract and move the ore, and hear stories of the men and their lives in the mines. The Cripple Creek District Museum (on Bennett Avenue) has a great collection of tools, equipment, ore samples, and old mining artifacts, as well as a re-created assay office where the precious glittering substance was both quantified and qualified as to content and purity.

17

Stumbling upon sand dunes in a valley between two of Colorado's highest mountain ranges seems strange to say the least, but here they lie, the biggest sand dunes in North America. Tucked away in the corner of the San Luis Valley, an enormous, arid expanse between the San Juan Mountains to the west and the Sangre de Cristo Mountains to the east, the Great Sand Dunes got their start eons ago. For thousands and thousands of years the Rio Grande carried southward sand and sediments washed out of the nearby San Juan Mountains. Uplifting mountain ranges, shifting faults, and other geologic processes eventually caused the Rio Grande to change course. As its deposits of silt and sand became exposed, prevailing winds from the southwest carried them across the valley to pile up at the base of the Sangre de Cristo Mountains. As the winds surged upward over Medano and Mosca Passes they carried grains of sand with them, building the dunes.

Wind continues to shape and reshape these dunes, blowing hardest in the spring and fall. Hemmed in on either side by creeks flowing out of the mountains that rise immediately behind them, the 39-square-mile area of the dunes has changed very little over time. Geologists believe that one of the reasons they are so stable is that below the foot or two of shifting sands, the dunes are moist and quite solid. The delicate patterns left in the sand by blowing grasses, a beetle marching by, or a deer coming to drink from one of the creeks are beautiful but fleeting, erased by

Light plays beautifully among the dunes of Great Sand Dunes National Park, which lie nestled against the snowcapped peaks of the Sangre de Cristo Mountains.

the constantly shifting winds. A walk among the finely sculpted ridges and slopes of the Great Sand Dunes, some reaching 750 feet above the valley floor, is a magical experience not often found in North America.

Cycling in the Park

Because of the enormous distances and size of the natural features of this area, opportunities for riding are few and rather spread out. Riding in and around the Great Sand Dunes is very limited due to the extremely steep, rugged character of the nearby Sangre de Cristo Mountains, the sand of the dunes, and the empty nature of flat, arid San Luis Valley. Riding on any of the long, straight county roads that traverse the valley provides excellent views of surrounding mountain ranges, but the distances are significant and the wind blows frequently.

There are some fun trails for mountain bikers of all abilities just south of the dunes at an area called Zapata Falls. You can ride numerous combinations of singletrack trails through piñon and juniper forests in the shadow of 14,345-foot Blanca Peak, and then hike up the short trail to the falls and a refreshing frolic in a clear mountain stream. West of Alamosa in the Rio Grande National Forest there are numerous trails

★

CYCLING OPTIONS

Three rides are listed in this chapter, one for road bikes and two for mountain bikes. Riding in and around Great Sand Dunes National Monument is somewhat limited because of the topography and enormous distances between points. The Medano Pass Road inside the monument is a four-wheel-drive road that skirts the edge of the dunes as it heads north through the park before turning east and climbing up Medano Creek drainage to the pass. There are sections of sand on this easy-to-moderate ride along the dunes. An option for the fit and adventurous takes you up to the pass. There is a network of singletrack trails at Zapata Falls Recreation Area just perfect for aspiring mountain bikers to cut their teeth on. There are approximately 4 miles of trails that loop around a central picnic area. A short hike can be made to Zapata Falls, where hot and dusty bikers can splash around and cool off. A 26-mile road ride from the monument to San Luis Lakes State Wildlife Area is a good taste of the flat, wide-open character of the San Luis Valley. If you'd rather not share the road with cars, there's a network of trails around the lakes that's great for pedaling with the kids while viewing the many migratory bird species that visit.

and old jeep roads perfectly suited to exploring on a mountain bike. The town of Alamosa has several bike shops staffed with friendly faces ready to give you plenty of information on riding in the area.

85. MEDANO PASS ROAD (See map on page 402)

For mountain bikes. This four-wheel-drive road begins in the park, skirts the boundary between the dunes and the mountains, and then heads up over Medano Pass into the Rio Grande National Forest. This road eventually ends up on the east side of the Sangre de Cristo Mountains, where it picks up CO 69. Because it traverses the edge of the dunes, sections of this road are very sandy and may require you to get off your bike and walk to firmer ground.

N
W—E
S
0   2
miles

Medano Pass

SANGRE
DE CRISTO
WILDERNESS

GREAT SAND DUNES
NATIONAL MONUMENT
AND WILDERNESS

Mt. Zwischen
12,006 ft.

Dunes
Visitors Center
Start/Finish

Pinyon Flats
Start/Finish

85

Mosca Pass

SAN LUIS LAKES
STATE WILDLIFE
AREA
Head Lake

86

Carbonate
Mtn.
12,308 ft.

San Luis
Lake

150

SANGRE DE CRISTO RANGE

California
Peak
13,849 ft.

Zapata
Falls

150

© 2000 The Countryman Press

Starting point: Pinyon Flats Campground inside the monument.

Length: 5 miles one-way, 10 miles out-and-back. 13 miles one-way to Medano Pass, 24 miles out-and-back. Allow 2 to 3 hours to complete this ride—more if you want to play and explore in the dunes along the way.

Riding surface: Four-wheel-drive road; extremely sandy in spots.

Difficulty: Easy to moderate. The 10-miles out-and-back are mostly flat, although riding in sand requires some strength and skill. Elevations are fairly high along this route—around 8,000 feet—which adds some difficulty if you have come from a lower elevation and are unused to the thin, dry air.

Scenery/highlights: There are many tantalizing spots to play in the dunes, enjoy the sculpted shapes of their ridges and slopes, and take in their magical beauty. Bird-watching along the creeks and in the cottonwood bosques, or woodlands, is great. Views into the graceful, rippled dunes on one side, and up into the drainages and to the dramatic peaks and ridges of the Sangre de Cristos on the other, are fantastic.

Best time to ride: Spring through fall. Wind and colder temperatures are common at the extreme ends of those seasons. The best time of day to ride out this way is in the morning. You can discover the many interesting tracks left in the sand by the creatures that move around only in the cool of the evening and early morning; in the middle of the summer, temperatures on the surface of the dunes can soar up to 140 degrees, making them too hot to walk on or explore by midday. This road sees moderate-to-heavy traffic during peak visitation times. Evening is also a great time to be out here; the low light plays beautifully in the dunes, temperatures have cooled, and wildlife is more active.

Special considerations: Riding in sand can be challenging. Stay in a low gear so you don't end up having to push hard on your pedals. Also, guide your handlebars gently, putting as little pressure on them as possible; this keeps your front tire from digging in and stopping your forward progress. Be prepared to dismount quickly.

There is no water available at the picnic sites out here, so bring plenty with you and stay hydrated; temperatures can jump as the sun climbs in the sky. Bathrooms and water are available either at the monument's visitors center or in the Pinyon Flats Campground.

If you are interested in hiking into the dunes or exploring one of the trails along the route, bring a lock to secure your bicycle.

From the Pinyon Flats Campground ride out the road that accesses the campground to where the Medano Pass Primitive Road takes off north. Turn onto this road and follow it northward as it skirts the edge of the dunes. The road crosses over several drainages and winds through desert scrub and piñon-juniper forests mixed with some aspens and cottonwoods. The first mile is an easy graded dirt road. At the end of the maintained road you come to a parking area where two-wheel-drive vehicles are encouraged to turn around. You pass Sand Pit Picnic Area less than 0.5 mile from the parking area. Castle Creek Campground, is another 0.5 mile beyond the parking area, is where Castle Creek flows down and hits the edge of the dunes.

Two miles past Castle Creek Campground you encounter the Little

Medano Creek Trail crossing the road. This recently developed hiking trail takes you to this pretty creek in under a mile. If you are interested in walking out this way, leave your bike off the road: Bikes are not allowed on any of the backcountry trails in the park. At this point the road begins to swing northeast and has picked up the main Medano Creek drainage. In another 0.5 mile from the trail crossing you come to the boundary of the Rio Grande National Forest. Turn around here and head back the way you came, or continue up the road for as long as you like. It is another 8 miles to Medano Pass up the Medano Creek drainage.

---

86. SAN LUIS LAKES (See map on page 402)

For road bikes. This ride is a taste of the nice, flat road riding that abounds in the San Luis Valley on one of the lesser-used roads in the area. This route takes you from the visitors center inside the monument to the San Luis Lakes State Wildlife Area, where you can get a glimpse of the avian residents and wetlands habitat found throughout this valley. This is also a state park with camping, showers, and laundry facilities available. If the road ride doesn't appeal to you, drive out and ride the almost 9 miles of trails around the lakes and wetlands on your mountain bike.

Starting point: Visitors center inside the monument.

Length: 13 miles one-way; 26 miles out-and-back. Allow close to 4 hours.

Riding surface: Pavement.

Difficulty: Moderate; only because of the distance. You will experience just a few hundred feet of elevation change along this route.

Scenery/highlights: Views up to the surrounding peaks from the valley floor are impressive. The bird life at San Luis Lakes is great. Stop at one of the bulletin boards or check in with a park ranger to get a list of resident and migratory species that visit the lakes.

Best time to ride: Spring through fall. It can be hot out here in the middle of the day in summer, and windy in the spring.

Special considerations: Bring along some bug spray; as the mosquitoes

FLORA

Several different life zones are found in the park, including the dunes ecosystem, desert shrub and grassland, piñon-juniper forests, and montane conifer and aspen groves. Riparian life also thrives along the creeks that come out of the mountains and run into the dunes. Springtime in and around the dunes brings the billowy white blossoms of evening primrose, red and orange Indian paintbrush, and the purple flowers of nodding onion. A little yellow daisy called groundsel is common here, as is the western wallflower, another yellow bloomer. Later in the summer you begin to see the prairie sunflower and the piñon aster, a little purple daisy. Indian rice grass, blowout grass, and scurf pea live in the dunes and provide important shelter and food for the mice and insects that live here. Several fruit-bearing shrub species are also a good food source for the birds in the area, including wax currant, golden currant, gooseberry, and the three-leaf sumac, or lemonade bush. Narrow leaf cottonwoods dominate in the riparian zones, but are surrounded by piñon-juniper forests and aspen trees in drier areas.

can be bad if a breeze isn't blowing. Drinking water and rest rooms are available at both the visitors center inside the monument and at San Luis Lakes.

From the visitors center simply head out of the monument on the main road, CO 150, and ride 3 miles to the park boundary. You then ride almost another 3 miles to the junction of CO 150 and Sixmile Lane (Great Sand Dunes Road). Bear right onto Sixmile Lane and ride it due west for the next 7.5 miles to San Luis Lakes State Park and Wildlife Area. Turn in here. Refill your hydration packs or water bottles if you need to, toodle around the campgrounds, and check out the bird life. When you're ready, head back the way you came.

Option: Bringing your mountain bike out here and riding around the lakes and wetlands on almost 9 miles of trails is a good option if you're not comfortable sharing the road with cars or have kids who aren't up to pedaling long distances.

Blanca Peak (elevation 14,345 feet), one of the highest peaks in the Sangre de Cristo range, looms above a rider playing on the singletrack trails near Zapata Falls.

SARAH BENNETT ALLEY

87. ZAPATA FALLS (See map on page 407)

For mountain bikes. These singletrack trails that wind around through piñon and juniper forests on the flank of massive Blanca Peak are an excellent place for the whole family to get out and test their bike-handling skills in the dirt. There are at least 4 miles of looped trails that can be ridden without duplication here. There is also a don't-miss 1-mile hike up to the 50-foot Zapata Falls where you can splash around after having worked up a sweat—but beware, for the water comes right out of the mountain and is icy cold.

Starting point: Zapata Falls Recreation Area parking lot. The road up to Zapata Falls is 5 miles south of the monument entrance. It is approximately 4 miles on a gravel road to get to the parking area.

Length: 4 miles of loop trails. The length of this ride can be adjusted to suit the needs of each individual rider.

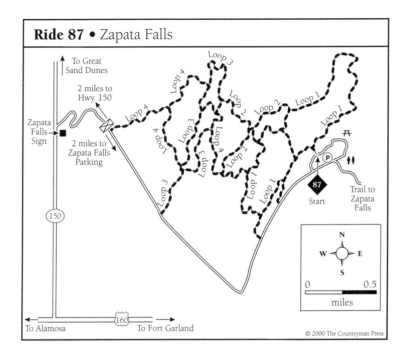

Ride 87 • Zapata Falls

Riding surface: Dirt singletrack.

Difficulty: Easy. The only difficult element of this ride is its overall elevation, which hovers around 9,000 feet. You'll gain and lose only a few hundred feet of elevation among the various loop trails here, but some of the short climbs and a few rocky spots may be challenging for small or beginning mountain bikers.

Scenery/highlights: The views out across the San Luis Valley to the San Juan Mountains to the west are great. You can also see the sand dunes to the north where they tuck in against the mountains. The hike up to Zapata Falls is well worthwhile; plan on spending a little time hanging out by the crystal-clear pools and exploring the falls area. If you are up for a rigorous hike that affords fantastic views for miles around, you can continue up past the falls for approximately 3.5 miles to South Zapata Lake, just below Blanca Peak at an elevation of 12,500 feet.

FAUNA

Many animals in the monument are highly adapted to the conditions found in this arid, high-altitude setting. Kangaroo rats can receive all of their moisture through the plants they eat and never need to drink water. Several species of pocket mice are endemic to the dunes ecosystem, as are the tiger beetle, the circus beetle (which stands on its head when threatened), and the giant sand-treader camel cricket.

The most common birds living around the dunes include the magpie and its cousins the raven and pinyon jay. Common flickers, chickadees, mountain bluebirds, and the orange-and-yellow western tanager are also regulars around the monument. Several species of hummingbirds, including the rufous and broad-tailed, migrate through in the summer. The green-tailed towhee, yellow-rumped warbler, and gray-headed junco are other songbirds found on the monument's bird list. The rodent population of the area keeps golden eagles, peregrine falcons, prairie falcons, and red-tailed hawks well fed, and attracts other animals such as weasels, coyotes, and bobcats. Black bears and cougars are sometimes seen in the park. Rocky Mountain elk sometimes come into the monument in winter, mule deer are year-round residents, and pronghorn antelope like the wide-open spaces around the dunes to the north.

Best time to ride: Late spring through fall. Despite the elevations it can get pretty darn hot out here in the middle of the day, but then again, you have the falls and creek to cool off in.

Special considerations: High elevations, strong sun, and dry air all mean you need to drink plenty of water during a day of playing out here. No water is available along the trail or at the picnic area, so bring your own. Picnic tables and bathrooms are available near the parking area.

After locating the trailhead on the west (downhill) side of the parking lot, simply begin riding in whatever direction you choose. There are four main loops, the westernmost having an outlet onto the main road coming to the falls. Working your way downhill on the trails and then riding up on the dirt road is the easiest option.

CAMPING

There are 88 campsites inside the monument at **Pinyon Flats Campground,** which is managed on a first-come, first-served basis; a fee is charged. There is a six-person, two-vehicle limit at each campsite. Fire grates, picnic tables, flush toilets, and drinking water are all available. Firewood can be purchased in the park. Backcountry camping is permitted at designated sites in the dune wilderness; a camping permit is required. Group campsites are available but in high demand, so make reservations early.

At San Luis State Park and Wildlife Area the **Mosca Campground** is located in low dunes west of San Luis Lake. All sites have hook-ups, sheltered tables, fire grates, and drinking water. A fee is required. The campground also has modern bathrooms, showers, and laundry facilities. Views are great but bugs can be bad in the summer if there isn't a breeze. Call (970) 470-1144 to make reservations.

Wilderness camping is also available in the Rio Grande National Forest.

Three miles south of the visitors center and just outside the park you will find **Great Sand Dunes Oasis and RV Park,** which has showers, a small store, and a nearby restaurant. **Blanca RV Park** has tent sites and hook-ups and is about 30 miles south in Blanca.

IT'S INTERESTING TO KNOW . . .

Geothermal springs in the San Luis Valley have allowed for the success of the Two Mile Creek Wildlife Habitat and Colorado Alligator Farm—that's right, an *alligator* farm! These springs, which stay at a constant 87 degrees, allow the gators to bask and swim happily while grinning for visitors.

LODGING

Alamosa is the nearest town with lodging options. You will find a

Holiday Inn, Comfort Inn, Best Western, and Days Inn as well as a few motels. You may want to try the Cottonwood Inn & Gallery, A Bed & Breakfast Inn in Alamosa. It has private baths and has a great breakfast. An option closer to the park is the Inn at Zapata located 6 miles south of the monument's boundary. It has buffalo grazing in the fields, a golf course, and is open May through October. Other than that you will find the Sand Dunes Motel in Mosca and the Fort Garland Motor Inn in Fort Garland.

FOOD

No food is available inside the monument, but a small general store and a café are located at the monument boundary and open during the summer months only. The Inn at Zapata, located 6 miles south of the monument on CO 150, also has a dining room.

Alamosa offers a few dozen restaurants. For breakfast try Efrem's Place (514 LaVeta) or Bob's Place (423 Main St.), which features family-recipe Mexican dishes. The Sands (801 Main St.) is a good choice for lunch or dinner, and the Old West Café (617 Sixth St.) is touted as the valley's best steakhouse (you can eat outside). For delicious Mexican try Oscar's (710 Main Street); for Asian food Hunan Chinese Restaurant (419 Main St.) is your best bet.

LAUNDRY

B & D's Laundromat, 510 La Veta Ave., Alamosa; (719) 589-6441

Sunshine Laundry, 0217 Market, Alamosa; (719) 589-5254

BIKE SHOP/BIKE RENTAL

Alamosa Schwinn Cycle, 512 Third St., Alamosa; (719) 589-6772

Kristi Mountain Sports, Villa Mall W. US 160, Alamosa; (719) 589-9759

FOR FURTHER INFORMATION

Great Sand Dunes National Monument—Superintendent, 11500 CO 150, Mosca, CO 81146; (719) 378-2312; http://www.nps.gov/grsa/

Alamosa Chamber of Commerce,

Cole Park, Alamosa, CO 81101; (719) 589-3681 or (800) BLU-SKYS

Rio Grande National Forest, 1803 W. US 160, Monte Vista, CO 81144; (719) 852-5941

DON'T MISS

Make an early-morning or evening hike into the dunes; hiking out among the dunes in the moonlight is even better. A morning walk provides the opportunity to discover myriad trails left behind in the night by numerous different creatures. Watching the light play among the sweeping ridgelines and gentle slopes of the dunes at sunset is spectacular. If you sit quietly among the dunes and pay close attention to movement and sounds near their edges and around creeks, you will likely see a deer, a coyote, or even a bobcat in the cool hours before dark.

18

The beautifully constructed stone towers, kivas, and crumbling ruins found at the six sites included in Hovenweep National Monument are fascinating clues to an ancient culture that once thrived among the desolate expanse of Cajon Mesa west of Cortez, and east of Blanding, Utah. This broad sagebrush-covered mesa was first visited some 10,000 years ago by bands of nomadic hunters, who came through seasonally in search of edible plants and small game. By about A.D. 900 these people had developed agricultural skills and began erecting permanent settlements so they could farm the rich soils atop the mesa. By the year 1200 it is thought that they numbered close to 2,500 here. By 1300, however, the mesa was deserted. Depleted soils, disease, hostility from invading tribes, and the effects of drought most likely combined to drive these people off the mesa to find more reliable water and safety elsewhere. Many believe they moved south along the Rio Grande and became the modern-day Pueblo people, although today's Hopi and Zuni tribes also claim ties to the ancient people who lived here.

The ruins protected as Hovenweep National Monument are the most spectacular of those left behind by the Ancestral Puebloans, and were built at the peak of their occupation in the Four Corners region. The structures of Hovenweep, a Ute word meaning "deserted valley," are numerous and varied. Among the most famous are the impressive tower ruins, which are square, D shaped, oval, or circular. Some of them are

SARAH BENNETT ALLEY

The Twin Towers at Hovenweep, Rimrock House, and several other buildings near the visitors center are positioned around the rim of a canyon once fed by a spring.

almost four stories tall. Most are perched on cliff rims, while others are masterfully balanced on freestanding stone pedestals and boulders. Many theories have been offered as to the role these buildings played in the lives of the Ancestral Puebloans. It's possible they served as celestial observatories, defensive structures, storage facilities, civil or religious buildings, homes, or a combination of these. Many of the towers are associated with kivas, sunken round structures known to have religious significance, pointing to a ceremonial use. Whatever their purpose, we know that these people were accomplished farmers, building terraces and catchment basins and growing corns, beans, and squash.

Note: Although the term *Anasazi* is still commonly used to identify the ancient culture that built these beautiful stone cities, the almost two dozen tribes who claim ancestry to these people have collectively rejected this term. *Anasazi* is a Navajo word meaning "enemies of our ancestors," or "ancient foreigners"—a name that casts the Ancestral Puebloans as violent and aggressive invaders, when in fact their history speaks otherwise. The park service is working closely with modern Native Americans to gain better insight into the ruins, symbols, and artifacts found here and have agreed to forward the term *Ancestral Puebloans* in place of *Anasazi.*

Cycling in the Park

The big, empty country that encompasses the ruins of Hovenweep National Monument is paradise for cyclists who delight in wide-open spaces and lonesome roads. There is no pavement for miles around out here, and the road surfaces vary from graded and well maintained to high-clearance, four-wheel-drive jeep roads. While neither of the routes demands more than an intermediate level of riding skill, the combination of distance, elevation, and aridity can make some of these routes challenging. Still, all bikers will enjoy taking the time to pedal out across the mostly rolling terrain of Cajon Mesa to visit and explore these beautiful yet mysterious landmarks in time.

Note: The archaeological resources of this area are extremely precious; please do not disturb or remove any potsherd, stone flake, or other artifact you might find. The place, position, and context of every object is almost as important as the object itself. By removing these pieces of the past, you are taking pieces of a puzzle, preventing a more complete understanding of a people and how they lived. Also, please do not ride off any of the roads in the area or climb in or on top of any of the stone structures, which are fragile and may collapse. Disturbing or removing anything in and around archaeological sites not only detracts from the quality of the next person's experience but is also illegal, punishable by heavy fines. Leave only your footprints around the ruins and your tire tracks on the road, and take away only a wealth of rewarding memories.

88. HORSESHOE, HACKBERRY, AND HOLLY RUINS LOOP (See map on page 416)

For mountain bikes. This route out to Horseshoe, Hackberry, and Holly Ruins looping through the canyons and mesa tops between Bridge Canyon and Hovenweep Canyon along the Utah-Colorado border is a fast-paced cycle through blond sandstone canyons and mesas with significant archaeological sites to visit along the way. To make this a shorter 12-mile route you can simply ride from the visitors center to the ruins and back again instead of looping through the canyons.

Starting point: Visitors center at Square Tower Ruin.

Length: 20-mile cherry-stemmed loop. 13 miles out-and-back to the ruins from the visitors center if you choose not to ride the loop. Set aside at least 4 hours to complete this ride and spend time exploring around the ruins.

Riding surface: Dirt roads; some graded and maintained, some less so.

Difficulty: Easy to moderate. The distance might make this a slightly more difficult ride for some, in which case you can simply ride out to the ruins and back.

Scenery/highlights: Sleeping Ute Mountain to the south, the Abajo Mountains in Utah to the northwest, the San Juan Mountains to the north, and the La Plata Mountains to the northeast make for a magnificent panorama. Cajon Mesa and the surrounding mesas and canyons that lie between these mountain ranges are part of a greater expanse known as the Great Sage Plain that extends across southwestern Colorado and southeastern Utah.

You first visit the Hackberry Unit, where Hackberry and Horseshoe Ruins lie. Horseshoe Ruins was a small village of 50 to 60 people. The main group of ruins consists of a semicircular structure composed of one large room and three smaller rooms. This D-shaped structure follows the same pattern as the Sun Temple at Mesa Verde National Park, suggesting that the people of Hovenweep may have been contempo-

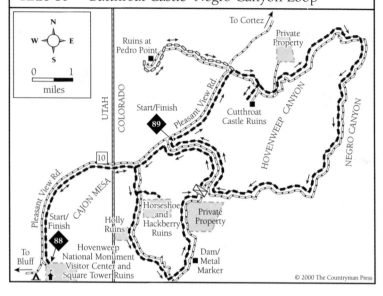

Ride 88 • Horseshoe, Hackberry, and Holly Ruins Loop
Ride 89 • Cutthroat Castle–Negro Canyon Loop

To Cortez
Private Property
Ruins at Pedro Point
N
W E
S
0   1
miles
UTAH
COLORADO
Pleasant View Rd.
Start/Finish
89
Cutthroat Castle Ruins
HOVENWEEP CANYON
NEGRO CANYON
Pleasant View Rd.
10
CAJON MESA
Start/Finish
Holly Ruins
Horseshoe and Hackberry Ruins
Private Property
88
Pleasant View Rd.
To Bluff
Hovenweep National Monument Visitor Center and Square Tower Ruins
Dam/ Metal Marker
© 2000 The Countryman Press

raries, or perhaps predecessors, of those at Mesa Verde. To the west an isolated tower seems to stand guard over the canyons to the south, although archaeologists believe its purpose was probably ceremonial. A short trail leads to a retaining dam, well-preserved handprints on a stone wall, and a small kiva.

The Hackberry site was a larger village, probably housing some 300 to 350 people. It consists of a cluster of room blocks around a spring at the head of a canyon similar to many of the other ruins of Hovenweep. What is unique to this site is its amount of vegetation, due to a productive spring. The large hackberry trees in the canyon help shade the spring, and it is thought that they may have been brought here by the ancients for this purpose. Here it is evident that the people terraced the slopes inside the canyon for planting small plots. With the constant flow of water and shelter from the wind, crops could have been raised here later into the fall and earlier in the spring than on the mesa tops.

The Holly group was once home to an estimated 150 inhabitants.

There are five significant buildings in this group, including Tilted Tower, Holly Tower, Curved Wall House, Great House, and Isolated Boulder House. Many agree that the most spectacular is Holly Tower, a two-story structure gracefully perched on a tall, narrow boulder that was accessed only by hand- and toeholds carved into the rock. Holly Tower is thought to represent one of the finest examples of Montezuma Valley architecture. Also found at Holly is one of the best examples of how the Ancestral Puebloans determined the solstice and equinox by tracking the sun's position. Beneath a nearby ledge are three designs: a complete spiral, a partial spiral, and a complete three-ring concentric circle. Daggers of light of light fall in particular places on these three designs as the sun rises, marking the summer solstice and fall and spring equinoxes. Knowing when to plant crops was something these farming people paid close attention to, as evidenced by astronomical markers such as these found at nearly all the sites. In other places they exist in the form of holes in the eastern walls of certain structures.

Best time to ride: Almost anytime of year, provided the ground is not wet. During the winter you might find a few days that are warm enough and dry enough. Spring and fall are the best, as the temperatures are not too hot. If you are out here in the summer, an early-morning or evening ride is best. The light plays dramatically among the ruins in the morning and evening as well. Be aware that the piñon gnats bite and can drive you crazy in the summer.

Special considerations: There is no water out here, so bring plenty of your own. You may also want to bring some lunch or good energy snacks along to give yourself plenty of time to explore the ruins.

Bring along bug repellent and hope for a little breeze.

Before you head out, spend a little time at the visitors center and visiting Square Tower Ruin, one of the monument's most spectacular sites. The most concentrated remains of buildings at Hovenweep are found along both sides of a Y-shaped canyon just behind the visitors center; this is where Square Tower Ruin stands. Nearly 36 kivas and numerous stone houses were scattered among this canyon, indicating that as many as 500 people once lived here.

From the visitors center ride out onto the Pleasant View Road (CR

10), the road you drove in on, and head north and east for 3.5 miles to the Utah-Colorado border. Just 0.5 mile beyond the border you come to a sign that reads HOVENWEEP, 4 miles from the start; this is the road to Horseshoe, Hackberry, and Holly Ruins. Ride 0.6 mile to the parking area, leave your bike, and follow the footpath to the ruins. When you're ready to move on, go back to the main road and ride another 0.8 mile south to a spur on the right for Holly Ruins. Ride 0.2 mile to the parking area and again, dismount and leave your bike to explore the ruins via a footpath. At this point you have ridden 6.4 miles since setting out. Return 1.8 miles to the main road and return 4 miles to the visitors center if you are not interested in continuing on and riding the loop portion of this route.

If you want to ride the loop head back out on the main road and head south, descending into Bridge Canyon. About 0.3 mile from the Holly Ruins turnoff you come to a fork; bear left on the less-traveled road and follow it approximately 2 miles as it descends into the canyon, crosses the canyon floor, and then heads up the other side. This section is somewhat steep and rocky and may require less-experienced riders to dismount and walk their bikes. Once you are on top of the mesa take the first left-hand turn, which is faint at first. You now pedal northward past two dry ponds, one marked ECLIPSE RETENTION DAM, and parallel the edge of Hovenweep Canyon. Wonderful views into the grassy bottom of Hovenweep Canyon and beyond can be had from here. Approximately 2.3 miles from your last turn you come to a gate. Go through the gate, leave it as you found it, and continue for another 0.3 mile to an intersection. Bear left at the intersection, continuing in a northerly direction. (The road to the right descends steeply into Hovenweep Canyon.) Continue on this road for just over 2 more miles past a corral to the Pleasant View Road. Turn left and ride the 5 miles back to the visitors center at Square Tower Ruin.

---

89. CUTTHROAT CASTLE–NEGRO CANYON LOOP
(See map on page 416)

For mountain bikes. This loop traverses some of the wild, empty country northeast of Hovenweep's visitors center at Square Tower Ruin, and takes you out to Cutthroat Castle Ruins, also protected as part of the monument. This loop route takes you into both Hovenweep and Negro

Square Tower, perched on a boulder and rising almost two stories, was probably not a defensive structure but served some ceremonial purpose instead.

Canyons, where the industrious Ancestral Puebloans once spent their days tending crops. Small grain caches hidden in the cliffs, petroglyphs, and other clues to the past lie hidden in these canyons. This adventure takes most of a day if you plan to explore the ruins and pause along the way to search the canyon walls. There is an optional side trip to Pedro Point ruins too. Enjoy your time out here but please, do not remove or disturb artifacts, climb in or on ruin structures, or ride off the established roadway.

Starting point: The intersection of the Pleasant Valley Road (CR 10) and a road that takes off on your right 1 mile past the turnoff for Horseshoe, Hackberry, and Holly Ruins. Drive a short distance to a corral and park here. The intersection is 5 miles northeast of the monument's visitors center at Square Tower Ruins.

Length: 15.5-mile loop; 21.5 miles if you ride the spur out to Pedro Point. Allow at least 4 hours to do this ride and enjoy the ruins.

Riding surface: Graded dirt, four-wheel-drive jeep roads.

Difficulty: Moderate. There are a few steep, rocky sections and stretches of sandy road to negotiate, requiring an intermediate level of technical riding skills. Good levels of physical fitness and stamina are also recommended, but with the many stops along the way there is plenty of opportunity for taking a break and getting some rest. Elevations range between 5,300 and 6,100 feet.

Scenery/highlights: The ruins of Cutthroat Castle, accessed by a short trail, was the site of a village of substantial size, inhabited by close to 200 individuals. It was built on an S-shaped section of stream that was dammed to create a small reservoir between the two sections of the village. Cutthroat is different from the other ruins at Hovenweep in that it was built down on a streambed rather than clustered high on rock ledges around the head of a canyon with a spring. Another interesting feature of the ruins at Cutthroat is that their towers have no visible entrances. Access to these towers may have been below ground, or from the top by ladders. Cutthroat rests at the highest elevation of all the ruins at Hovenweep, thus receiving more moisture, seeing cooler temperatures, and having deeper and perhaps more fertile soil.

FLORA

On the mesa tops around the Hovenweep ruins the dominant vegetation is piñon-juniper forests and desert scrubland. Types of shrubs you might find are bullberry, cliffrose, and rabbitbrush, which blooms a brilliant yellow in fall. Blooming in the spring are Indian paintbrush, cushion phlox, penstemon, and prickly pear cactus. When the fierce rays of the sun have abated, the large, white blossoms of both evening primrose and sacred datura open in the evening to invite pollinators such as moths and bats, and then closing or fading with the next day's sun. Big sagebrush and yucca are also common here. Lower down in the canyon bottoms the vegetation gets even more sparse, with widely spaced piñons and junipers and a few clump grasses and dryland brushes. Around the springs, however, hackberry is quite lush.

Best time to ride: Spring and fall, provided the ground is dry. There are a few days during the winter that are warm and dry enough to enjoy out here. During the summer it is exceedingly hot and dry in this desert. Plan for an early start or an evening ride. A small creature called a piñon gnat can just about drive you nuts in the summer.

Special considerations: Water and rest rooms are available at the visitors center and nowhere else along this route. Although this is empty country and other travelers on these back roads are seldom seen, you may want to bring a lock to secure your bike if you plan to leave it for any length of time. This is high, arid country, and the sun can be brutally strong. Be sure to bring plenty of water, more than you think you'll need, and some high-energy snacks to get you through the day. Covering up is the best way to protect yourself from the exhausting effects of being in the sun all day; a good slathering of sunscreen is the next best thing. It's also a good idea to have some cold water and drinks in your cooler for when you get back to your car.

From where you parked your car at the road junction by the corral, pedal northeast on the Pleasant View Road (CR 10, the road you drove out on).

Only the towers remain of Hovenweep Castle, which show signs of use as domestic quarters for the inhabitants of the Square Tower Canyon community.

Ride in a northeasterly direction on this graded dirt road for approximately 2.3 miles, over two cattle guards. Just beyond the second cattle guard the road forks next to a sign that reads CARBON DIOXIDE PIPELINE; the lightly traveled road out to Cutthroat Ruins is on the right; Pedro Point is to the left. Turn onto this rocky four-wheel-drive road and pedal mostly level terrain for approximately 1.5 miles to a sign marking the hiking trail to Cutthroat Ruins. Leave your bike by the road and walk down to the ruins. When you're done exploring the ruins hike back out, hop on the saddle, and continue pedaling along this dirt road, bearing left as it descends into Hovenweep Canyon.

The road becomes rougher as you descend into the canyon, and once you reach the canyon floor you encounter sections of sand. These sand stretches are energy traps; the key to escaping them is to work as little as possible. If shifting into a low gear can't get you through, dismount and trudge through to more solid ground.

Continue pedaling across the valley floor, crisscrossing several sand washes, for approximately 2 miles before climbing out of Hovenweep Canyon. As you emerge you pass through a fence; then, just before a metal containment tank, you begin to see bicycle markers where a road branches off to your right. Go right onto this road, now just under 7.8 miles from the start of this ride, and head into Negro Canyon. You traverse Negro Canyon for the next 4 miles, crossing back and forth through several washes and going through several gates as the road takes you south and then west. Approximately 11.8 miles from the start of this ride you begin the climb out of Negro Canyon. You then travel another 3.5 miles over rolling terrain, passing through several gates, soon reaching the corral where you left your car.

Option: Near the start of the ride at 2.3 miles, before you turn right and head out to the Cutthroat Castle Ruins, you might want to take the 3-mile spur that goes left (west) out to the ruins at Pedro Point. This is a lightly used doubletrack road that traces the rim of Cross Canyon, taking you out to this small group of ruins. Riding out and back to these ruins adds 6 miles to your total distance.

CAMPING

Hovenweep Campground has 30 sites and is open year-round. Drinking water and flush toilets are available. There are no hook-ups. A fee is required and camp-sites are managed on a first-come, first-served basis.

Morefield Campground inside Mesa Verde National Park has 477 sites on 92 acres. The camground is open mid-April through mid-October and has showers, laundry, a grocery store, and a gift shop. A fee is required and campsites are managed on a first-come, first-served basis.

There are several private campgrounds in Cortez, including the **A & A Mesa Verde RV Park Resort** (34979 US 160), the **Cortez KOA Kampground** (27432 E. US 160), the **Days Inn & Lazy G Campground** east of Cortez, and the **Mesa Oasis Campground** (5608 US 160).

There are many possibilities for camping in the San Juan National Forest. There is also wilderness camping on BLM lands surrounding the monument.

In Bluff, Utah, you can find a campsite at the **Kokopelli Inn Motel** (no showers) or a tent site at the **Sand Island Recreation Area** 3 miles south of town.

LODGING

In Cortez most of the big chains are represented, including **Holiday Inn Express, Super 8, Best Western, Comfort Inn,** and **Days Inn.** The **Bel Rau Lodge** is one of the more reasonable rooms in town, and the **Anasazi Motor Inn** is among the nicer lodges where you can expect to pay more.

In Bluff, Utah, the **Kokopelli Inn Motel** has reasonable rooms, and **Recapture Lodge** has rooms with knowledgeable owners who can arrange tours and outings in the area.

FOOD

There are at least two dozen non-fast-food restaurants in Cortez to choose from. For getting started in the morning you might try the classic **Ute Coffee Shop** (17 S. Broadway) or **Pippo's Coffee Bar**

(100 W. Main St.). The **San Juan Coffee Company** (508 E. Main St.) also seems to be popular. **Once Upon a Sandwich** (1 W. Main St.) is a good place to stop for lunch. If it's pasta you're after, then **Nero's** (303 W. Main St.) is the place. **Francisca's** (125 E. Main St.) is a favorite for Mexican food among locals, and you can always get basic American fare at **Stromsted's** (1020 S. Broadway). The **Anasazi Motor Inn** has a dining room that serves breakfast, lunch, and dinner, but if beef is on your mind you had better head to the **Purple Sage Rib Company** (2811 Mancos Rd.).

The slightly trendy **Main Street Brewery** (21 E. Main St.) has excellent pizzas, as well as pasta and steaks, and the brewed-on-site beers aren't too bad either.

LAUNDRY

Cortez Laundromat, 1013 E. Main St., Cortez; (970) 565-7959

Plaza Laundry Inc., 2210 E. Main St., Cortez; (970) 565-8467

BIKE SHOP/BIKE RENTAL

Kokopelli Bike & Board, 30 W. Main St.; (970) 565-4408

IT'S INTERESTING TO KNOW . . .

The people who came into the Four Corners area to farm as early as A.D. 550 most likely came from settlements along the Rio Grande near present-day Albuquerque. Using farming techniques imported from Mexico and Central America, their villages expanded rapidly, and eventually they began to suffer from overcrowding. Splinter groups began moving northward into the canyon and mesa country of the Colorado Plateau. With their knowledge of farming these people thrived again in the Four Corners region from roughly A.D. 800 to 1300. The enormous stone structures they left behind were thought to be trade and cultural centers, and artifacts found in them suggest that they traded with tribes as far away as the West Coast of North America and southern Mexico. The many different tribes of Pueblo Indians living throughout New Mexico, and the Hopi and Zuni also living in New Mexico and Arizona, most likely descended from the Ancestral Puebloans of the Four Corners area.

DON'T MISS

The Cortez CU Center, home of the University of Colorado Museum, is a great place to learn more about the ancient cultures of the Southwest. Artifacts from around the Four Corners area are housed here, including pottery, basketry, and tools. Exhibits explaining the construction of Ancestral Puebloan stone cities and displays of more modern Navajo pottery and weaving are also on display, and handmade Native American crafts are for sale at a small gift store. Excellent traveling exhibits come to the museum every summer. Colorful Native American dances and storytelling take place at the museum on summer evenings. These events are not scheduled regularly, so call ahead to get specifics. The museum is located in Cortez half a block north of Main Street (US 160) at 25 N. Market. The phone number is (970) 565-1151.

FOR FURTHER INFORMATION

Hovenweep National Monument, Superintendent, McElmo Route, Cortez, CO 81321; (970) 749-0510 (cellular service at the monument); Art-Hutchinson@NPS.GOV; http://www.nps.gov/hove/

Cortez Visitors Center and **Colorado Welcome Center,** 928 E. Main St., Cortez, CO 81321; (970) 565-4048

Cortez Area Chamber of Commerce, 928 E. Main St., Box 968, Cortez, CO 81321; (970) 565-3414 or (800) 346-6526

San Juan National Forest—Dolores District, 100 N. Sixth, Dolores, CO 81323; (970) 533-7716

San Juan National Forest—Mancos District, 41595 E. US 160, Mancos, CO 81328; (970) 533-7716

19

Mesa Verde, or "green table" in Spanish, is an 80-square-mile plateau that rises more than 1,600 feet above the surrounding desert. The northern rim of the mesa is well defined, dropping away in almost vertical cliffs. The western and eastern rims of the plateau terminate at the edge of steep canyons. Because this expansive mesa top is tilted to the south, eons of rainwater and springs have carved deep canyons that finger their way up into the highest reaches of the plateau.

As early as A.D. 550 groups of Indians were living on the plateau, mostly in these canyons. It is believed they came to this area from overcrowded farming villages along the Rio Grande near present-day Albuquerque. For the next 700 years these people, formerly called Anasazi but now referred to as Ancestral Puebloans, farmed the top of the plateau, hunted wild game, collected plants, and eventually erected the enormous and enchanting stone villages found tucked into alcoves in the canyon cliffs. At their peak there may have been as many as 5,000 individuals living in the canyon villages of Mesa Verde. Artifacts reveal that as their settlements grew, their skills at basketry, potting, tool making, and architecture advanced rapidly. The many kivas, or ceremonial rooms, found among the ruins also suggest that they were a deeply religious people. These things taken together point to one of the most highly developed cultures ever to have flourished in North America.

Then sometime near the year 1300 the people living at Mesa Verde,

Late afternoon sun illuminates Oak Tree House in Fewkes Canyon at Mesa Verde National Park.

and at the many settlements sprinkled throughout the Four Corners area, left their homes. Evidence indicates that the decades leading up to their departure were years of repeated crop failures brought on by a severe drought. But it is likely that other factors were at work, too. Overuse of the area's resources, including timber, game, and soils, likely played a role. These things may have helped precipitate social, political, and even religious upheaval, perhaps compounded by pressure from other tribes moving into the area. The Ancestral Puebloans most likely retreated southward, from where they had come, to find safety and a more reliable water supply among their distant cousins. Today some 24 different tribes, including the Hopi, Zuni, and 18 different Pueblo tribes, claim relation to the people who lived at Mesa Verde.

These ancients were called the Anasazi by the Navajo, meaning "enemies of our ancestors," or "ancient foreigners," a term that is still widely used to describe the people who flourished in the Four Corners region between A.D. 700 and 1300. Recently, however, many of the Native Americans who trace their ancestry to the people who lived here reject it, claiming that the name casts them as violent and aggressive invaders

CYCLING OPTIONS

There are five rides listed for Mesa Verde National Park, two for road bikes and three for mountain. The ride out along the park's main road—which traverses almost the entire length of the mesa, providing access to overlooks along the way—is 28 miles long if all the spurs are ridden; it is the only ride listed inside the park boundaries. The 10-mile (total) mountain-bike ride out to Cannonball Mesa takes you through scenic redrock country and to the ruins of an Ancestral Puebloan village. It is well suited for beginning and intermediate riders. Riding the railroad grade to Cherry Creek is another fat-tire adventure that is longer (16 miles total) but is also appropriate for beginning and intermediate riders. The pedal up to Windy Gap is a 22-mile loop on dirt and jeep roads that reaches elevations of 10,500 feet. Intermediate riders in good-to-excellent physical condition will love the scenery and views along this route. Serious road riders will enjoy the moderately difficult 43-mile loop that begins in Cortez and takes you north to Dolores, east to Mancos, and then west back to your starting point.

when in fact their history speaks otherwise. Today park staff use the term *Ancestral Puebloans,* a phrase that simply means "ancient stone house dwellers."

Cycling in the Park

There are 20 miles of paved roads and loops that roll through piñon-juniper forests and along canyon rims taking you to ruin overlooks at Mesa Verde, but as in all national parks, the roads are exceedingly narrow and sometimes buckled from cycles of freezing and thawing. Traffic is heavy on the roads during peak visitor season, making riding in Mesa Verde a challenge for all but those with the steeliest nerves. Gliding along the top of Chapin Mesa, the main arm of the plateau, taking in the view, and pulling over to peer over into the canyons to see the enchanting ruins hidden there, is a biking experience you won't soon forget.

Make sure you take precautions to make your ride as safe as possible, including riding when you can avoid traffic, staying to the right-hand side of the road, riding in single file, and wearing white or light-colored clothing that can be easily seen by motorists. A properly fitting helmet and a good pair of glasses are essential anytime you're on a bike. The scenic roads between Cortez, Dolores, and Mancos also get very busy during July and August when tourist traffic in the area is at its peak.

There are plenty of options for off-road riding and beating the crowds in the vicinity of Mesa Verde—enough to fill several days if not weeks. Riding out along Cannonball Mesa east of Cortez is a fabulous tour of the colorful redrock country the Four Corners region is known for, and has the added bonus of remote ruins to explore. The Windy Gap ride in the La Plata Mountains just northeast of Mesa Verde provides a good introduction to surrounding alpine environments, and the old railroad grade is a route with historical significance the whole family will enjoy.

---

90. CHAPIN MESA–MESA VERDE NATIONAL PARK
(See map on page 431)

For road and mountain bikes. The route described here takes riders south along Chapin Mesa and around the three different loops where overlooks into the surrounding canyons reveal the famous stone cities of Mesa Verde. Elevations are the highest at the visitors center at just over 8,000 feet, dropping 1,000 feet to the Chapin Museum, and just a few hundred feet more to the end of loops beyond. An option that begins at the Chapin Museum near park headquarters eliminates much of the climbing that must otherwise be done on the return trip.

Starting point: Far View Visitors Center, 15 miles from the park entrance.

Length: 28-mile loop 13-mile loop; from the Chapin Museum. Allow 5 to 6 hours to ride the entire route and spend time at the overlooks.

Riding surface: Pavement.

Difficulty: Moderate to difficult. The combination of narrow, busy roads, distance, and elevation change makes this ride more difficult. The option of starting from Chapin Museum and riding the loops is easy.

Scenery/highlights: There are at least 15 overlooks and points of interest along this route, and none should be missed. Cliff Palace, Balcony

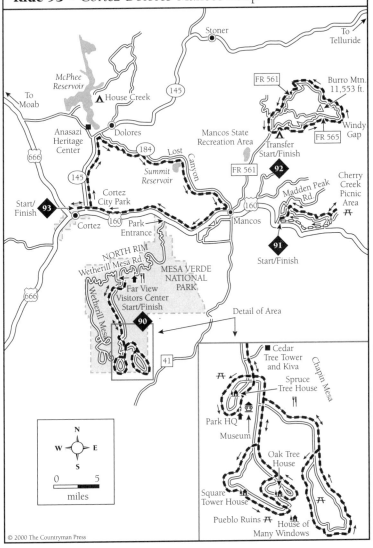

Ride 90 • Chapin Mesa–Mesa Verde National Park
Ride 91 • Railroad Grade to Cherry Creek
Ride 92 • Windy Gap
Ride 93 • Cortez-Dolores-Mancos Loop

Stoner

To Telluride

McPhee Reservoir

House Creek

To Moab

FR 561

Burro Mtn. 11,553 ft.

Windy Gap

FR 565

Anasazi Heritage Center

Dolores

Mancos State Recreation Area

184

Lost Canyon

FR 561

Transfer Start/Finish

92

Cherry Creek Picnic Area

145

Summit Reservoir

Madden Peak Rd.

Start/Finish

93

Cortez City Park

160

Park Entrance

Mancos

91

Start/Finish

NORTH RIM

Wetherill Mesa Rd.

MESA VERDE NATIONAL PARK

Wetherill Mesa

Far View Visitors Center Start/Finish

90

Detail of Area

41

Cedar Tree Tower and Kiva

Chapin Mesa

Spruce Tree House

Park HQ

Museum

Oak Tree House

Square Tower House

Pueblo Ruins

House of Many Windows

N
W E
S

0   5
miles

© 2000 The Countryman Press

House, and Spruce Tree House are some of the most famous and can be visited on foot during scheduled tours. Long House is also open to the public. Check in at the visitors center if you are interested in taking one of the ranger-guided hikes. Square Tower House, New Fire House, Oak Tree House, House of Many Windows, and Sun Temple are closed to the public but can easily be seen from the rim above. It is also worthwhile to stop in and have a look at the early and late pithouses, the structures that preceded the elegant stone buildings found in the canyons. Many artifacts removed from the cliff dwellings over the years are on display at the Chapin Museum, along with other interesting exhibits about life at Mesa Verde. The views from atop this mesa are spectacular, and the craggy old piñon and juniper forests that thrive here are beautiful.

Best time to ride: Spring and fall. The park receives a quarter of a million visitors every year, and most of them come during the months of July and August. Riding in the early-morning and evening hours provides the bonus of catching a glimpse of the park's wildlife when it is most active. Lighting on the ruins at these times of day is also worth seeing.

Special considerations: This can be a long day. Make sure you bring plenty of water and snacks, and eat and drink often to avoid becoming energy depleted before you have to make the trek back up to Far View. Basic food items and water are available at Spruce Tree Terrace Cafeteria, but you'll find little else along the way. Rest rooms are available at the museum and at the visitors center.

Be especially careful around pullouts. Drivers are likely to be looking out into the canyons, not at you.

After you've spent some time at the Far View Visitors Center, head out onto the main Chapin Mesa Road and go south. In approximately 1.5 miles you come to Far View ruins, one of the only stone house ruins on the mesa top. Nearby is Mummy Lake, a catchment basin built by the Ancestral Puebloans to retain water for their crops. When you're ready, head back out to the main road and continue pedaling south. This is an easy downhill coast. In another 4.5 miles you come to the short spur out to Cedar Tree Tower and Kiva. Here you can actually see prehistoric farming terraces. About 0.5 mile beyond (6.5 miles from the start), you come to the 1.3 mile loop that accesses Chapin Museum, Spruce Tree

House, and Spruce Tree Terrace Cafeteria. Another 0.5 mile beyond is the junction of the two mesa-top loops, each about 6 miles in length. The loop to the east takes you to Cliff Palace, Balcony House, and a spectacular overlook that can be reached by a short trail. The western loop takes you to Square Tower Ruins, several pithouse exhibits, Pueblo ruins, and some more stunning overlooks. Ride one loop and then the other, or save one for another day. When you have ridden all the loops and all the spurs, get ready for the climb back to Far View Visitors Center. From the junction of the loops it is 7 miles back to the center.

Option: For a shorter ride with less elevation change, drive out and park at the Chapin Museum and begin your ride from there. Riding both loops from here will give you a total distance of just over 13 miles.

---

91. RAILROAD GRADE TO CHERRY CREEK (See map on page 431)

For mountain bikes. This is an easy route along an old narrow-gauge railroad bed that traverses the rolling terrain of the southern slope of the La Plata Mountains. Beginning and intermediate riders will enjoy the mellow grades of this ride, its fantastic scenery, and the pretty spot at Cherry Creek Picnic Area at the end.

Starting point: The top of Mancos Hill on the Madden Peak Road. Mancos is approximately 7 miles east of the turnoff for Mesa Verde National Park and 15 miles east of Cortez. When you get 5.6 miles past Mancos turn north (left if you are coming from the park or Cortez) onto Madden Peak Road, also Forest Road 316. Drive 1 mile and park at the intersection with FR 568.

Length: 7.2 miles each way, 14.4 miles out-and-back. Allow at least 3 hours to complete this ride.

Riding surface: Dirt railroad bed; friendly grades.

Difficulty: Easy to moderate. There is little technical skill required to negotiate this route, but a moderate level of physical fitness is recommended. Exerting yourself at these elevations in this dry air can be taxing if you are not used to it. Just under 500 feet of elevation is gained on your way out. Elevations run between 7,500 and almost 8,000 feet.

FLORA

There are two dominant vegetation types within the park: piñon-juniper forests and scrub oak. Mesa Verde is where mountain and desert biomes meet. In the higher reaches of the plateau, stands of aspen and mixed conifer can be found. The springs and wetter spots in the canyons are where an entirely different mix of shrubs and trees exist. Here you are likely to find chokecherry and serviceberry. Cliffrose and fendler bush bloom throughout the park in spring, while rabbit-brush blooms bright yellow in the fall. Spring bloomers include Indian paintbrush, scarlet gilia, penstemon, lupine, and bluebells in spots where they can keep their roots damp. In the late spring yuccas send up tall stalks covered with creamy flowers; this plant was used extensively by the Ancestral Puebloans for shoes, mats, needles, thread, and soap. The pods of the yucca were also roasted and eaten. Low-growing claret cup cactus bloom a brilliant red in spring, while prickly pear blooms come in shades of yellow to peach.

Scenery/highlights: One of the best things about this ride is the good grade and nice riding surface. The view of Mesa Verde from this perspective is impressive. The remnants of the old railroad trestle that spanned Starvation Creek drainage can be seen below the road. To get trains across the creek before there was a trestle, the drainage was filled with dirt and rock; a culvert allowed the water through. A flood eventually washed out the fill material, and the tracks were left hanging over the canyon. The story goes that the next train to come along saw what had happened and was able to stop, but not before the front half of the engine was caught cantilevered on unsupported tracks over the canyon below.

Best time to ride: Anytime spring through fall when the ground is dry and free of snow. These roads see light traffic, so anytime during the day is fine.

Special considerations: Bring plenty of your own water and snacks; neither is available along the way. You may want to bring lunch to enjoy at Cherry Creek Picnic Area. Vault toilets are available here.

Begin pedaling east on FR 568, the old railroad grade. You climb gently here as the road hugs a contour around the southern end of the La Plata Mountains. Approximately 4 miles from the start you come to Starvation Creek ford. This creek crossing should be easy unless it is high water due to spring or storm runoff. Use caution if the creek is swollen. Look below you to find the old railroad trestle as you cross Starvation Creek drainage. At 5.7 miles you come to an intersection with FR 320. Continue straight ahead, crossing this road and staying on the railroad bed. The road following the grade continues for another mile, and then turns to a trail that reaches an aspen grove and some beaver ponds in 0.5 mile. This is Cherry Creek Picnic Area; take a break, eat your lunch, and when you get ready to go, simply head back the way you came.

Option: On the return, if you are interested, a slightly longer loop route takes you back to the start on US 160. If you are coming from the picnic area go left onto FR 320 and follow it as it descends over several steep pitches, heads past a gravel pit, and meets US 160 in just under a mile. Turn right when you reach the pavement and ride 5.6 miles west to the Madden Peak Road, and another mile to your car.

---

9 2 . W I N D Y G A P (See map on page 431)

For mountain bikes. This ride is a nontechnical loop through some of the higher country found in the La Plata Mountains northeast of Mesa Verde. Intermediate-level riders in good physical condition will enjoy this route, which varies between 8,800 and 10,800 feet in elevation. Escaping to these cooler elevations in deep conifer forests is a treat on a hot summer day. Views to the southwest of the Mesa Verde Plateau and surrounding country are spectacular.

Starting point: Transfer Campground in the San Juan National Forest. From the town of Mancos, travel north on CO 184 approximately 0.25 mile to County Road 42 (FR 561). Turn right and drive for 10 miles to Transfer Campground. Park near the entrance, not at a campsite.

Length: 22-mile loop. Allow 5 hours to complete this loop.

Riding surface: Dirt forest service roads; some maintained, some not.

Difficulty: Intermediate. This ride does not require much technical bike-

The author mugs for a shot in front of Far View Ruins in Mesa Verde National Park.

handling skills, but some riding experience and a solid level of physical fitness are recommended for this longish route at high altitudes.

Scenery/highlights: The alpine environment found up here is a nice change from the hot, dry desert below. Temperatures will be anywhere from 10 to 20 degrees cooler than on the valley floors. Expect to see wildflowers such as columbine, bluebells, and lupine blooming well into the middle of the summer. Views into surrounding country are fabulous.

Best time to ride: Anytime spring through fall, provided the ground is dry and free of snow (most likely early to mid-May through October). These roads see light-to-moderate traffic at peak season, so anytime of day is fine. In summer and early fall be aware of local weather forecasts; if afternoon thunderstorms are predicted, get an early start. You don't want to get caught out in one of those storms. Also, avoid riding when deer and elk hunts are going on.

Special considerations: Water and vault toilets are available at Transfer Campground, but bring plenty of water with you, as this is a long ride.

Some of the best views along this ride are right at the start. Take a good look around, then pick up FR 565 where it leaves just past the entrance to the campground through a beautiful stand of aspens. Begin riding in a northeasterly direction. Follow FR 565 as it skirts the drainage of the West Fork of the Mancos River, gaining 2,000 feet over the next 8 miles. In the last few miles before Windy Gap, FR 565 joins FR 350. At the junction of these roads your elevation is approximately 10,500 feet; you'll gain a few hundred more feet before reaching Windy Gap between Burro Mountain (11,553 feet) and a collection of peaks that stretch away to the south, including Sharkstooth Peak (farthest north, directly above Windy Gap), Centennial Peak, Hesperus Mountain, and Gibbs Peak (12,286 feet).

Leaving Windy Gap, pick up the northwest-heading FR 561. This road wraps around and begins to descend following the Bear Creek drainage, and then turns south and west as it crosses over the Lost Creek and Fish Creek drainages. Just before you cross over the Lost Creek drainage, go left onto an improved version of FR 561. At this point you are 15 miles from the start of your ride. Another 3 miles down the road you can see the Jersey Jim fire lookout tower (no longer in use) on your left. At mile 20 you come to the log cabin that serves as the Aspen Guard Station for the forest service. Crews working on various improvement projects spend the summer here. Continue past the guard station and straight through the next intersection back to Transfer Campground and your vehicle.

---

93. CORTEZ-DOLORES-MANCOS LOOP (See map on page 431)

For road bikes. This is a super loop through the towns in the vicinity of Mesa Verde that intermediate and advanced road riders will really enjoy. The elevation change is only about 1,000 feet over the entire route, which traverses some lovely open ranch country through the foothills of the San Juan and La Plata Mountains. You can ride in either direction, but the route is described in a clockwise direction here.

Starting point: Cortez City Park next to the Cortez Visitor and Colorado Welcome Centers on Main Street.

Length: 43-mile loop. Allow 4 hours to complete this loop.

Riding surface: Pavement; good roads with wide shoulders.

Difficulty: Moderate to difficult. The distance and elevation make this a more difficult ride.

Scenery/highlights: Pretty country, great ride, good views. You can't go wrong here if you are a skinny-tire enthusiast. Part of this ride traces the actual route taken by the Spanish Fathers Dominguez and Escalante on their 1776 expedition into the western interior while searching for a route from Santa Fe to the newly established missions of California.

Best time to ride: Spring through fall. These roads are busiest during the peak tourist season in July and August. If it's going to be a hot day, plan on an early start.

Special considerations: Water and rest rooms are available in and around the Cortez City Park. This grassy park has shade and a public swimming pool where you may want to cool off when you're done with your ride.

From Cortez (6,200 feet) head east on Main Street, and near the east end of town turn left onto Dolores Road (CO 145). Ride due north on CO 145 for approximately 10 miles almost to the town of Dolores. You gain most of your elevation in these 10 miles. About a mile before you reach Dolores, CO 184 (Dominguez-Escalante Memorial Highway) heads south and east. Go right onto this highway and pedal through this gorgeous, rolling country for the next 17 miles. The middle 5 miles of this route are referred to as Summit Ridge by local riders, because some of the highest elevations of the ride are reached along here. Once you pass Summit Reservoir you descend and then roll along gently before reaching Mancos. When you get to the town of Mancos (6,993 feet), go right onto US 160 and ride the 16 descending miles back to Cortez.

---

94. CANNONBALL MESA (See map on page 439)

For mountain bikes. This ride gaining just over 500 feet is one that beginning and intermediate riders will have little trouble with. However, riders of all abilities should not pass this one up. Located 22 miles west of Cortez in the gorgeous redrock country of the Colorado Plateau, this

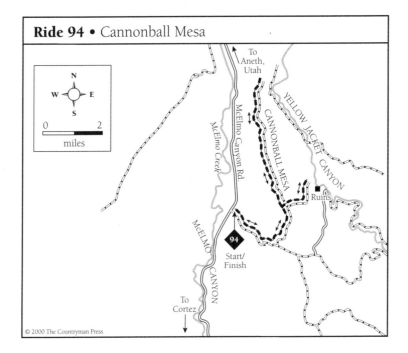

route takes you up onto Cannonball Mesa to enjoy panoramic views of the mountains and mesas that seem to grace every horizon. But that's not the best part. Waiting at the end of this ride are the ruins of an Ancestral Puebloan village overlooking a beautiful canyon and creek.

Starting point: The beginning of an unmarked road just over 22 miles west of Cortez. To get there drive 2 miles south of Cortez on US 666/US 160, making a right-hand turn when you reach the M&M Café onto McElmo Canyon Road. Drive west for 20.4 miles to an unmarked county road on your right with a cattle guard and a sign reading KEEP VEHICLE ON THE ROAD. Park off the road here.

Length: 10 miles (total) out and back, with a spur to the ruins. Allow at least 3 hours to do this ride and check out the ruins.

Riding surface: Jeep roads.

Difficulty: Easy to moderate.

FAUNA

A fabulous variety of birds inhabit the mesa seasonally and year-round. The most noticeable include ravens, gray jays, pinyon jays, turkey vultures, and red-tailed hawks. Golden as well as bald eagles visit the mesa, as do peregrine and prairie falcons. An impressive list of songbirds can be seen on the mesa and in the canyons around water sources each spring, including the mountain bluebird, solitary vireo, Virginia's warbler, yellow-rumped warbler, and both the green-tailed and rufous-sided towhee. Wild turkeys, which were domesticated by the ancient people who lived on the mesa, can still be found here.

Squirrels, chipmunks, marmots, skunks, cottontails, and jackrabbits all live here, as do coyotes. Mule deer, elk, black bear, mountain lion, and bobcat have all been seen on the mesa but are rare. Wild horses also live on the mesa. The distinctively marked collared lizard and short-horned lizard, as well as little brown skinks, are some of the park's most visible wildlife.

Scenery/highlights: Interesting rock formations, incredible views, beautiful country, and 800-year-old Puebloan ruins. The Cannonball Mesa Ruin overlooking the canyon and creek below is a large, late-Pueblo-period structure built at a canyonhead in a style typical of those found in the Yellowjacket Canyon area.

Best time to ride: Early spring to late fall. The elevations here are between 5,100 and 5,600 feet, lower than on Mesa Verde or in the foothills and mountains surrounding Cortez, so the area is warmer and drier. If you are out here in the summer ride early in the day, before temperatures begin to soar skyward. It is not uncommon for temperatures to flirt with the century mark in this country during the summer.

Special considerations: Bring plenty of water, as none is available out here.

Please do not climb on any of the ruins, which are fragile and may collapse. Also, please leave any potsherds, stone flakes, or other artifacts you might find; they are the only clues we have to these ancient people.

The ruins of Cliff Palace, with 220 rooms and 23 kivas, are the largest at Mesa Verde and were first "discovered" by rancher B. K. Wetherill in 1888.

Go left at this fork, following a jeep road as it makes a series of short steep climbs onto Cannonball Mesa over the next 0.5 mile. For the next 2 miles the route is easier, rolling over sections of slickrock and red dirt through piñon and juniper forests where you can enjoy stunning views of surrounding desert and mountains. Approximately 4 miles from the start a road forks off to the right. Follow this rough, four-wheel-drive road approximately 0.5 mile as it descends, eventually leveling out and crossing over more slickrock before ending at the ruins.

After taking some time to explore, return to the main jeep road and go right. Ride due west for another 1.5 miles across the top of Cannonball Mesa. The road begins to descend and ends at a fence 0.5 mile later. Gorgeous views of the fertile McElmo Canyon can be had from here, and to Battle Rock and into Yellowjacket Canyon as well. The road you are on was formerly known as the Wood Road, the original wagon road that accessed Bluff, Utah. When you are ready to turn around simply ride back on the main road.

CAMPING

Morefield Campground inside Mesa Verde National Park has 477 sites on 92 acres. The campground is open mid-April through mid-October and has showers, laundry, a grocery store, and a gift shop. A per-night fee is required and campsites are managed on a first-come, first-served basis.

There are several private campgrounds in Cortez, including the **A & A Mesa Verde RV Park Resort** (34979 US 160), the **Cortez KOA Kampground** (27432 East US 160), the **Days Inn & Lazy G Campground** east of Cortez, and the **Mesa Oasis Campground** (5608 US 160).

There are many possibilities for camping in the San Juan

IT'S INTERESTING TO KNOW . . .

In December 1888 rancher B. K. Wetherill, his son Al, and his brother-in-law Charlie Mason rode up out of Mancos Canyon, where the Ute Indians were letting them graze their cattle, and onto Mesa Verde to look for some missing cows. As they neared the rim of the canyon they looked up and were astonished to see a fabulous stone city tucked into the cliff wall. They immediately dubbed the ruins Cliff Palace and with a great deal of excitement continued to search the rims of the mesa, finding Spruce Tree House later the same day. In the following years Wetherill became obsessed with the ruins and scoured the mesa for abandoned stone dwellings, removing untold thousands of artifacts, which he then sold to museums and private collectors. In 1891 a Swede named Gustaf Nordenskiold excavated several ruins on the mesa top with the help of Wetherill and his sons. His collection of artifacts now resides in the National Museum of Helsinki, Finland. Nordenskiold was the first person to publish a scientific study of his findings, "Cliff Dwellers of the Mesa Verde," printed in 1893. Mesa Verde was declared a national park by Theodore Roosevelt in 1906 in an effort to protect the archaeological resources here.

National Forest. There is also wilderness camping on BLM lands surrounding the monument.

LODGING

In Cortez, most of the big chains are represented, including **Holiday Inn Express, Super 8, Best Western, Comfort Inn,** and **Days Inn.** The **Bel Rau Lodge** is one of the more reasonable rooms in town, and the **Anasazi Motor Inn** is among the nicer lodges where you can expect to pay more.

In Bluff, Utah, the **Kokopelli Inn Motel** has reasonable rooms, and **Recapture Lodge** has rooms with knowledgeable owners who can arrange tours and outings in the area.

FOOD

There are at least two dozen non-fast-food restaurants in Cortez offering a variety of menus. For getting started in the morning you might try the classic **Ute Coffee Shop** (17 S. Broadway) or **Pippo's Coffee Bar** (100 W. Main St.). The **San Juan Coffee Company** (508 E. Main St.) seems to be a favorite with locals. **Once Upon a Sandwich** (1 W. Main St.) is a good place to stop for lunch. If it's pasta you're after then

Nero's (303 W. Main) is the place. **Francisca's** (125 E. Main St.) is a favorite for Mexican food. You can always get basic American fare at **Stromsted's** (1020 S. Broadway). The **Anasazi Motor Inn** has a dining room that serves breakfast, lunch, and dinner, but if beef is on your mind you had better head to the **Purple Sage Rib Company** (2811 Mancos Rd.). The slightly trendy **Main Street Brewery** (21 E. Main St.) has excellent pizzas, as well as pasta and steaks. The brewed-on-site beers aren't too bad, either.

LAUNDRY

Cortez Laundromat, 1013 E. Main St., Cortez; (970) 565-7959

Plaza Laundry Inc., 2210 E. Main St., Cortez; (970) 565-8467

BIKE SHOP/BIKE RENTAL

Kokopelli Bike & Board, 30 W. Main St.; (970) 565-4408

FOR FURTHER INFORMATION

Mesa Verde National Park— Superintendent, Mesa Verde National Park, CO 81330; (970) 529-4465; http://www.nps.gov /meve/

DON'T MISS

Visit one of the ruins on a ranger-guided tour. The up-close inspection of the fine stonework and the smells and sensations of standing in the rooms and passageways add immeasurably to an appreciation of the ancient people who lived here and their way of life.

At the Crow Canyon Archaeological Center, a variety of programs, lasting anywhere from a day to a week, give participants hands-on experience working on digs with trained archaeologists. This research center is devoted to the archaeology of the Southwest and has sophisticated computer links with universities and other researchers, as well as a library and several laboratories all devoted to revealing the secrets of the ancient peoples that once lived in this region. The center is located northwest of Cortez and can be reached by calling (970) 565-8975 or (800) 422-8975.

Cortez Visitors Center and **Colorado Welcome Center,** 928 E. Main St., Cortez, CO 81321; (970) 565-4048

Cortez Area Chamber of Commerce, 928 E. Main St., Box 968, Cortez, CO 81321; (970) 565-3414 or (800) 346-6526

San Juan National Forest— Dolores District, 100 N. Sixth, Dolores, CO 81323; (970) 533-7716

San Juan National Forest— Mancos District, 41595 E. US 160, Mancos, CO 81328; (970) 533-7716

20

ROCKY MOUNTAIN NATIONAL PARK

The jumble of ragged peaks and emerald valleys that comprise Rocky Mountain National Park are stunning examples of the many wonders and incredible beauty found in high-alpine environments. Rocky Mountain National Park was established in 1906 and is one of the oldest and highest parks in the country. Over a third of the park is above tree line, where delicate alpine tundra, evolved to withstand constant wind and weather, dominates the landscape. In fact, this harsh environment supports many of the same plants found above the Arctic Circle. The remainder of the park is cloaked in dense stands of evergreens and quaking aspens interspersed with broad meadows, or parks. Within the boundaries of the park there are 75 peaks above 12,000 feet; the tallest, Longs Peak, rises to a breathtaking 14,255 feet above sea level.

Nestled in among these peaks are glaciers, the remnants of enormous ice flows that shaped this landscape, as well as numerous glittering blue lakes laced together by clear, sparkling streams. Exquisite views into surrounding mountain ranges—with names like the Never Summer mountains, the Mummy Range, and Indian Peaks—abound from the park's main road. The Continental Divide traces the highest peaks and ridges of these ranges, and runs north to south through the park. This invisible boundary is the delineation between waters flowing east toward the Gulf of Mexico, and those flowing west toward the Pacific.

In summer the high peaks and lush meadows of the park are home to

Riding the Trail Ridge Road near the Continental Divide.

an impressive variety of creatures, both large and small. It is not uncommon to see herds of Rocky Mountain elk grazing or resting among the wildflowers of these high mountain meadows, or bighorn sheep traversing the higher ridgelines. Marmots scurry about their business during their brief respite from winter, and occasionally issue short, sharp whistles to alert others to danger whenever an unknowing tourist ventures too close. Coyote, cougar, black bear, deer, mountain goat, and beaver are some of the other magnificent wild creatures that call this park home.

Cycling in the Park

Escaping into the cool mountain air of the high Rockies to do some summer pedaling is an opportunity that many cyclists in the West anticipate all year long. Crystalline blue skies, dazzling fields of colorful blooms, and the scent of pine trees wafting on refreshing breezes make Rocky Mountain National Park and surrounding areas an ideal place get out on your bike. The crisp, clear days of fall, brilliant stands of yellow quakies, and fewer crowds make this time of year preferable for many.

Rocky Mountain National Park receives over 3 million visitors a year; July and August see the heaviest traffic, and riding in the park then can be daunting due to the sheer number of cars on the road. Although speeding vehicles aren't usually a problem, the narrow, winding roads and multitudes of bulky campers can be nerve-racking. Riding in the evening or early-morning hours is a good way to avoid the tourist traffic, and is when the park is graced with some spectacular lighting.

Despite the occasional congestion, a ride up to Fall River Pass, out to Bear Lake, or through the Kawuneeche Valley is sure to be memorable. Just being on a bike and able to move along at your own speed, take in constant 360-degree views, and not have to deal with the hassle of parking your vehicle at every overlook makes the park experience that much more enjoyable. It's a good idea to bring a lock so you can hike along the way without worrying about the security of your bike at the trailhead.

Many of the routes and trails just outside the park offer peace, solitude, and something much closer to a wilderness experience. Traversing the hills and valleys around the town of Estes Park just outside the east entrance of the park allows for spectacular views west into the park's highest peaks. The Grand Lake area on the west side of the park is always less busy and offers some of the best mountain biking anywhere in Colorado. Both Estes Park and Grand Lake cater to outdoor-loving tourists and have good resources for cyclists.

A word of caution here: This is high, mountainous country! Even the comparatively mellower trails and road rides gain and lose elevation. Although none of the rides in and around Rocky Mountain National Park is out of reach for intermediate riders, there are not a lot of easy options, and even the most experienced riders should have a good level of physical fitness to tackle riding at these altitudes. No matter how technically accomplished or fit you are, chances are you've come to Rocky Mountain National Park from a much lower elevation. To make the most of your time here you'll need to start out slow, go for shorter, easier rides and hikes for a day or so, and allow your body to adjust to the thin, dry air and intense sun. Nausea, dizziness, fatigue, and dehydration can result from overexertion at high altitudes before you've had a chance to acclimate. At these elevations your body needs more water than you're probably used to drinking, so bring lots, keep hydrated, and don't forget plenty of tasty, high-energy snacks to enjoy when you break to take in the view.

Weather is another feature of high-alpine environments that must be factored into your cycling adventures. Conditions can change rapidly at

CYCLING OPTIONS

There are nine rides listed in this chapter; four are road rides and the other five are mountain-bike rides. Six rides are accessed from the east side of the park outside the town of Estes Park, and three on the west, or Grand Lake, side of the park. The Old Fall River Road is a dirt road that gains over 3,000 feet of elevation taking you to the Alpine Visitors Center atop Fall River Pass. The Bear Lake Road is a gorgeous 20-mile road tour of some of the park's most famous scenery, while House Rock is an 11-mile mountain-bike ride outside the park boundaries. The easy-to-moderate ride out to the meadows of Big Elk Park is a 15-mile mountain-bike ride good for novice and intermediate cyclists. More serious road riders who are comfortable riding with traffic will appreciate the 32-mile loop between Estes Park and the small towns of Glen Haven and Drake. The Peak to Peak Highway is a classic Colorado road-riding tour that is best suited for superfit and experienced cyclists. The Kawuneeche Road is an excellent option for beginning and intermediate road riders on the west side of the park; if you have the legs and stamina you can continue all the way to the Alpine Visitors Center on Fall River Pass on this road. Just outside the park's west boundary the North Supply–South Supply Jeep Road (8.5 miles) gives beginning and intermediate riders a great excuse to go for a pedal in the woods, while the longer and more technical Wolverine Loop Trail (18.5 miles) will delight more advanced riders.

these elevations. Clouds often build as the day warms, and a day that started out clear blue can turn dark and threatening by afternoon, only to clear again by sunset. The temperature can plummet by 20 to 30 degrees during summer thunderstorms. Carrying a lightweight shell, and perhaps even a polypropylene long-sleeved top, on an all-day excursion is a good idea. Many mountain storms pack a strong electrical punch, so make sure to be well off high, exposed ridgelines and away from open areas if storms are nearby. Remember that there is a lot less atmosphere between you and the sun up here, making the sun's rays doubly intense. Be sure to use sunscreen before you head out, or cover up.

For mountain bikes. This loop route follows the old road to Fall River Pass. Originally built in 1920, this is a narrow, winding dirt road that has recently been opened to two-way bicycle traffic in the spring, before it is opened to cars. From July 4 to sometime in late September or early October both cars and bikes may travel it uphill only. The route gains over 3,000 feet of elevation and makes a loop through the heart of the park.

Starting point: Endovalley Picnic Area. Parking is limited during the busy season and certain times of day. You can begin this ride from Estes Park which will add 7 miles each way to your total distance.

Length: 30 miles. Add 14 to that distance if you ride from Estes Park.

Riding surface: Dirt road and pavement; switchbacks with sections of loose gravel and washboard.

Difficulty: Moderate to difficult. Although not much technical riding skill is required for this ride, the elevation gain and sustained climb require a good to excellent level of physical fitness.

Scenery/highlights: The views from Fall River Pass, and the effort you've made to get there, are breathtaking! Stretching away in all directions is a seemingly endless sea of snowcapped mountains. One of the prettiest vistas is looking across Forest Canyon to the Continental Divide. Mount Ida (12,880 feet) and Stones Peak (12,922 feet) immediately to the south help form the basin and alpine lakes that give birth to the Big Thompson River, a favorite of Colorado trout anglers. The creeks that flow off the far side of that ridge form the headwaters of the mighty Colorado, which winds for hundreds of miles through the Southwest, crosses the border into Mexico, disappears into desert sands before it reaches the Gulf of California.

You encounter the Chapin Creek Trail, which goes up to a pass and other trails that access nearby peaks. You may want to stretch your legs here, or check out one of the other hiking options possible from the Trail Ridge Road (US 34). A stroll out the Alpine Ridge Trail once you reach the top provides plenty of views and a good feeling for the alpine tundra environment that thrives here.

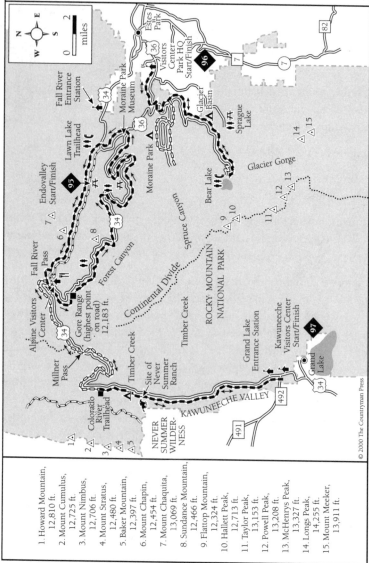

Ride 95 • Old Fall River Road
Ride 96 • Bear Lake Road
Ride 97 • Kawuneeche Valley Road

N E S W
miles
0 2

Estes Park
82
7
7

Moraine Park Museum
Visitors Center
Park HQ Start/Finish
96

Fall River Entrance Station
34
36

Lawn Lake Trailhead
36

Endovalley Start/Finish
95

Fall River Pass

Alpine Visitors Center
34

Gore Range (highest point on road) 12,183 ft.

Millner Pass

Colorado River Trailhead

Timber Creek

Site of Never Summer Ranch

1
2
3
4
5

NEVER SUMMER WILDER-NESS

KAWUNEECHE VALLEY

491
492
34

Grand Lake Entrance Station

Kawuneeche Visitors Center Start/Finish
97

Grand Lake

ROCKY MOUNTAIN NATIONAL PARK

Continental Divide

Timber Creek

Spruce Canyon

Forest Canyon

Moraine Park

Glacier Basin

Sprague Lake

Bear Lake

Glacier Gorge

14
15
13
12
10
11
9
8
7
6

© 2000 The Countryman Press

1. Howard Mountain, 12,810 ft.
2. Mount Cumulus, 12,725 ft.
3. Mount Nimbus, 12,706 ft.
4. Mount Stratus, 12,480 ft.
5. Baker Mountain, 12,397 ft.
6. Mount Chapin, 12,454 ft.
7. Mount Chaquita, 13,069 ft.
8. Sundance Mountain, 12,466 ft.
9. Flattop Mountain, 12,324 ft.
10. Hallett Peak, 12,713 ft.
11. Taylor Peak, 13,153 ft.
12. Powell Peak, 13,208 ft.
13. McHenrys Peak, 13,327 ft.
14. Longs Peak, 14,255 ft.
15. Mount Meeker, 13,911 ft.

A view from the South Supply Jeep Trail just outside the western boundary of Rocky Mountain National Park.

Best time to ride: Spring and fall. The Old Fall River Road is open to only uphill vehicle traffic from July 4 to late September or early October. Recently it has been opened to two-way bicycle traffic in the spring, before it is opened to cars. In July and August, morning and evening hours are good times to pedal when there is not quite so much traffic.

Special considerations: Pit toilets are available at the Endovalley Picnic Area but there is no water. Both water and rest rooms are available in town or at the Aspen Campground, on the right just after the Fall River Entrance Station. There is a snack bar at the Alpine Visitors Center and you can refill your water bottles and hydration packs there.

The ride up the Old Fall River Road to the Alpine Visitors Center requires an elevation gain of almost 3,600 feet. This is a substantial amount of climbing at high altitudes and anyone who is not in reasonably good physical condition should think twice about attempting this ride. This may be a ride to save until your body has had time to acclimate to the high altitudes. Be especially wary when pulling out of overlook pullouts: Drivers are anxious to get out of their cars and are probably looking at the scenery or wildlife, not at you. Speed limits along the park road vary between 10 and 25 miles per hour, so you will be traveling at least as fast as cars and campers—if not faster. Don't be overly concerned about staying way far to the right through the slower sections; cars won't be able to pass you anyway, so don't offer them the temptation to pass on these more dangerous sections of the road. Where the road straightens out and cars can pass you safely is the time to move over.

From the picnic area go back out the short driveway and turn left, through the gate, onto the dirt Old Fall River Road. You start climbing at a grade that requires gearing from low in a middle chain ring to high in your smallest chain ring, depending on your strength. Several sets of switchbacks may require you to shift down and move to the outside of the turn, as the insides of these curves are often loose and badly wash-boarded. Climbing at a steady pace for the first 7 miles you are sur-rounded by deep, fragrant evergreen forests with the sound of the Fall River burbling up from below you. At approximately 7 miles you climb a set of long, steep switchbacks that take you up and out of the Fall River drainage toward a ridge you eventually gain and traverse to get to the Alpine Visitors Center. These last few miles of the Old Fall River Road along the ridge make one of the best stretches to view wildlife. Elk often graze in the meadows here, and you will undoubtedly hear the chirp and whistle of pikas and marmots as they scurry about.

Once you have reached the Alpine Visitors Center at 9.5 miles, take a break, have something to eat, and look at the maps and other interest-ing displays. The rangers are friendly and always full of good informa-tion, but expect stern warnings about riding your bike down the Trail Ridge Road. Take heed: These warnings are well founded. When you get ready to go, make sure the straps of your helmet fit snugly, and that your front wheel is correctly positioned and firmly clamped into your front fork. You go left onto the Trail Ridge Road as you leave the visitors center and climb gradually for just over a mile to the high point in the ride, and the highest point on the Trail Ridge Road. From here, it's all downhill.

At Deer Ridge Junction (the junction of US 34 and 36), go left toward Horseshoe Park, Sheep Lakes, and the Endovalley Picnic Area where you left your car. It is approximately 3 more miles over gently rolling terrain to the picnic area from this junction.

---

96. BEAR LAKE ROAD (See map on page 450)

For road bikes. The Bear Lake Road, ridden from park headquarters, is a tour of some of the park's most picturesque scenery, the kind that inspired the famous 19th-century painter Albert Bierstadt, for whom a lake and trail in the park are named. Like the other roads in the park, it is narrow, winding, and subject to heavy traffic. Total elevation gain is 1,200 feet over rolling terrain.

Starting point: Visitors center on US 36, also the park's headquarters.

Length: Approximately 10 miles one-way, 20 miles out-and-back. Allow 2 to 3 hours, with additional time to visit the Moraine Park Museum, wander around Bear Lake, or take one of the other numerous short hikes along the way. Spurs to Moraine Park and Glacier Basin add approximately 3 miles to your round-trip total.

Riding surface: Pavement; road is narrow and can be rough in spots.

Difficulty: Moderate to difficult. The rolling terrain and overall elevation gain make this an intermediate-to-advanced road ride. Inexperienced riders in good physical condition can give this route a try, although they may be intimidated by the vehicle traffic. The total elevation gain is 1,200 feet over rolling terrain. There may be more actual elevation loss and gain due to the many short climbs and descents along the way. Some of these climbs are somewhat steep.

Scenery/highlights: The Bear Lake Road, ridden from park headquarters, tours of some of the park's most famous scenery. Albert Bierstadt, the 19th-century German-born painter, traveled and painted extensively in this country, and his dreamy, romanticized images of American wilderness enticed Europeans to come westward.

Stop in at the Moraine Park Museum, a beautiful building that offers displays and information on the geologic processes that formed the valleys and peaks of the park. Or if you'd rather stay on your bike, turn right and take the spur up to the Fern Lake trailhead in Moraine Park, a beautiful, broad grassy valley formed by an ancient glacier. The view up this meadow to the peaks beyond is superb.

Short spurs up to the Glacier Basin Campground and Sprague Lake provide stunning views, but the prettiest vistas await at the end of the road at Bear Lake. From here you gaze upward over glistening blue mountain lakes to Hallett Peak (12,713 feet) and Flattop Mountain (12,324 feet) and the icy mantles that cling eternally to their craggy peaks. Andrews Glacier, Tyndall Glacier, and many other smaller glaciers are ancient remnants of a vast ice sheet that helped carve these ridges and valleys. These peaks form part of the Continental Divide.

Best time to ride: Spring and fall. This is the second most popular sight-seeing route in the park and is most crowded from mid-July through mid-September. This road is at a lower elevation than the Trail Ridge or Fall River Road and will be clear of snow sooner. Also, because it is a shorter ride, it is appropriate for an early-morning or late-evening outing, when traffic is sparse and the lighting and wildlife viewing are at their best.

Special considerations: Bring along plenty of your own snacks and water, especially if you plan to spend some time hiking. Water and restrooms are available at the Moraine Park Museum and at the Bear Lake trailhead area. Remember, the sun is strong up here, so wear your sunscreen or cover up! Like the other roads in the park, the Bear Lake Road is narrow and winding and subject to heavy traffic. Speed limits in the park vary between 10 and 25 miles per hour, so cars will not be traveling that much faster than you are, especially when you are heading downhill. Do not worry about staying far to the right in the slow sections; this will only tempt cars to pass you in the most dangerous areas. Take as much of the road as you need to negotiate the curves safely, and then move over in the straightaways to allow traffic to pass.

There are so many great short hikes to take off the Bear Lake Road that you should bring a lock.

From the parking lot at park headquarters go left onto US 36. The road is mostly flat but climbs slightly to the Beaver Meadows Entrance Station. Another 0.25 mile from the entrance station you bear left onto the Bear Lake Road. From this point the road rolls up and down, some-

FLORA

Rocky Mountain National Park has five life zones: aquatic environments and the riparian corridors that surround the mountain meadows and shrublands; montane forests; subalpine forests; and alpine tundra.

Riparian ecosystems provide animals with food, water, and cover, and are a haven for migrating birds. Along the banks of streams and ponds at elevations below 9,000, mountain willow, chokecherry, and gooseberry dominate, while planeleaf willow, alder, river birch, and dwarf birch thrive up to 10,000 feet. Wildflowers include chiming bells, cow parsnip, and elephantella.

Montane forests applies to several types of forests existing between elevations of 8,000 and 10,000 feet, including ponderosa parklands, Douglas fir forests, lodgepole pine forests, and aspen groves. In ponderosa parklands you'll find juniper and mountain sagebrush; in the grassy understory grow sego lily, golden asters, and Wyoming paintbrush. Douglas fir are found on north-facing slopes, and have a sparse understory. Lodgepole pines like to grow in dense stands also, but are closer to ponderosa pines in appearance. In their sparse understory you may find buffaloberry, sticky laurel, or the enchanting blue clematis, fairy-slipper, and pink fireweed. Aspens are easily identified by their broad, round leaves, light bark, and fiery yellow leaves in autumn. Shrubs that might be found growing among aspens include chokecherry, gooseberry, serviceberry, and wild rose, along with Colorado columbine, silvery lupine, white geranium, and yarrow.

Subalpine forests, often referred to as spruce-fir forests, form dense stands of unbroken timber between 9,500 feet and tree line. Good examples of this type of forest dominated by Engelmann spruce and subalpine fir exist along the upper Fall River Road and the Trail Ridge Road. Engelmann spruce are tall, cone-shaped evergreens with short needles. Among stands of these trees at slightly lower elevations you might find Colorado currant, myrtle blueberry, and wild raspberries, or wildflowers such as red columbine, Jacob's-ladder, and curled lousewort. Limber pines—gnarled, twisted, multitrunked pines that remain short and broad even at lower elevations—are most often found on windsweapt ridges. Their understory is usually limited to mountain candytuft, spotted saxifrage, and stonecrop.

Above tree line you will find alpine tundra, a magical world of miniature plant communities comprising meadows and turfs, wet meadows, fellfields (barren rocky places exposed to the wind), shrub communities, and snowbank communities. Tufted grasses and alpine sage dominate turfs, while such beauties as marsh marigold, rose crown, elephantella, and star gentian reign in wet meadows. Fellfields are home to cushion plants, moss campion, alpine nailwort, and alpine phlox. Shrub communities appear in areas that remain sheltered for a time by snowbanks, allowing some plants to grow taller out of the wind. They are usually dominated by willows but chiming bells and paintbrush might also be found. Snowbank communities are restricted to the shortest possible growing season due to the persistence of snow. In these areas a tiny cloverlike plant called sibbaldia thrives, as does the gray lichen (*Lepraria* spp.), which covers the soil.

times dramatically, as it traverses several drainages. About a mile past the turnoff for the Moraine Park Museum (mile 3), the road loops around the bottom of Moraine Park and then begins climbing, steeply at times, along the flank of the glacial moraine for which this area is named. A moraine is a long, low ridge of rocks and boulders pushed aside by a glacier as it makes its way down a valley. Large, tumbled boulders can be seen all along this section.

Almost 5 miles from the start you cross over the Mill Creek drainage at the turnoff for Hollowell Park. This picnic area is a pretty spot halfway along the route and a good place to rest. You climb again from here, and then drop into the Glacier Creek drainage, where the road begins to parallel Glacier Creek. The road continues to climb gradually as it ascends to Glacier Gorge Basin. The last mile of this route is comprised of several long switchbacks that end at the Bear Lake trailhead. When you're finished taking in the sights, remount and head back the way you came.

97. KAWUNEECHE VALLEY ROAD (See map on page 450)

For road bikes. The ride up Kawuneeche Valley to the Colorado River trailhead and nearby picnic area is a straightforward out-back pedal over

A few hardy souls out for a week of sightseeing pose for a shot near Fall River Pass on the Trail Ridge Road.

mostly level terrain for beginning-to-intermediate road riders in good condition. An option allows superfit riders who want a longer ride to continue for another 13.5 miles up to the Alpine Visitors Center at Fall River Pass, elevation 11,796 feet!

Starting point: Kawuneeche Visitors Center at the Grand Lake Entrance Station, just outside the town of Grand Lake.

Length: Approximately 10 miles, 20 miles out-and-back. An option to the Alpine Visitors Center gives you a one-way distance of 23.5 miles, 47 miles round-trip.

Riding surface: Pavement; rough in spots, narrow, no shoulders.

Difficulty: Moderate to difficult. The gain in elevation on your way out is a mere 500 feet over 10 miles. Your starting elevation, however, is approximately 8,500 feet, which will make this ride more difficult for some.

Scenery/highlights: The peaceful, open valley that cradles the beginnings of the Colorado River was gouged out of the earth by one of the largest glaciers in the area. Here, you can leap across the barely whispering Colorado in a single stride, while 1,000 miles downriver it crashes and roars through the Grand Canyon.

Forests of lodgepole pines grow thickly along the sides of the valley, an indication that fire is an integral part of this ecosystem. *Kawuneeche* is an Arapaho word meaning "valley of the coyote," and if you're lucky you might hear them in the evening yipping and howling in unison. During the fall rut it is not uncommon for elk to move out of the forests and into the perimeters of this valley. An evening spent outside listening to their eerie bugling is nothing short of magical. Moose also make their home in this valley and are seen fairly regularly. Trout fishing the Colorado in this valley and farther down below the Shadow Lake Dam is spectacular and delights anglers from all over the country.

Many visitors to the park are curious about the long scar that traverses the side of the Never Summer Mountains on the far side of the valley. This is what remains of the Grand Ditch, a 14.3-mile canal designed to bring water from the Colorado River watershed to the Cache la Poudre River east of the Continental Divide. It was begun in 1890, took almost five decades to complete, and was built entirely by hand. It is 20 feet wide and 6 feet deep at its biggest point and is one of many diversion systems along the divide designed to bring water from these high peaks to the more arid eastern Rockies.

Best time to ride: Anytime June through September when temperatures and weather permit. Early mornings and evenings are a good time to avoid the midday traffic. It is also the best time to glimpse moose or deer.

Special considerations: If you plan on stopping, bring along some bug repellent; the mosquitoes can be fierce in this valley.

Rest rooms are available at the Coyote Valley and Timber Lake trailheads. Water and a phone are available at Timber Creek Campground.

There are several excellent opportunities for hiking along this route. If you're game, bring your bicycle lock and go for a walk along the Colorado River Trail, or take a stroll among the beautiful old buildings of the Never Summer Ranch.

From the Kawuneeche Visitors Center head out onto US 34, the main road through the park, and go right, riding in a northerly direction. You simply cruise along this mostly level, straight road 10 miles to the Colorado River trailhead and picnic area—or points beyond if you have the lungs, legs, and stamina. After you've taken a stroll up the trail and had time to enjoy your surroundings, head on back the way you came.

Option: If you're fit, continue onward and upward another 13.5 miles to the Alpine Visitors Center at Fall River Pass at an elevation of almost 11,800 feet.

---

98. HOUSE ROCK (See map on page 461)

For mountain bikes. This ride is intermediate to advanced in terms of both skill level and fitness. Several significant climbs and descents put the actual elevation change at close to 1,500 feet. An option for the more adventurous allows you to continue past House Rock to Pierson Park and then back to Estes Park, from which the Fish Creek Road and CO 7 take you back to your car.

Starting point: Meeker Park Picnic Area, just over 7 miles south from Estes Park on the left-hand side of CO 7.

Length: Approximately 11 miles out-and-back. The longer loop option is almost 30 miles round-trip. Allow 2 to 3 hours to House Rock and back, 4 to 5 hours for the loop option.

Riding surface: Dirt roads; graded and well-maintained, very primitive jeep roads.

Difficulty: Moderate to difficult. This is an intermediate-to-advanced mountain-bike ride in terms of the technical skill and fitness required. Although point-to-point this route reflects only a 700-foot elevation gain, there are several significant climbs and descents that put the actual elevation *change* closer to 1,500 feet. Sections of loose rocks and dirt and the primitive nature of the trail surface require an intermediate level of technical riding ability.

Scenery/highlights: House Rock itself is simply a rock outcropping that crowns a small mountain. The best views from this ride are at your back on the way up, but can be fully enjoyed on the way back down. The spectacular array of peaks are, from left to right: Horsetooth Peak, Lookout

Mountain, Dragons Egg Rock, Mount Meeker, Longs Peak, Storm Peak, Battle Mountain, and Estes Cone. The two biggest, Longs Peak and Mount Meeker, have served as beacons for prairie travelers for centuries.

Longs Peak (14,251 feet) is the only "fourteener" in Rocky Mountain National Park, and the northernmost peak of that distinction in Colorado. The sheer east-facing rock face of Longs Peak beckons climbers from all over the world, and is considered one of the best summit climbs in the United States. Longs Peak is named after Major Stephen D. Long, who was put in charge of scientific research for the Yellowstone Expedition of 1819.

The mission of the expedition was not only to explore lands recently acquired through the Louisiana Purchase but also to make peace with Indians and begin to remove British influence in the area. Long is credited with discovering the peak in 1820.

Best time to ride: Late May or early June to fall, when this route is free of snow, but wait until the ground has dried out and hardened. Stay off these dirt roads after heavy rains, as they can get ferociously muddy and become rutted and prone to erosion when scarred by tire tracks. In fall you will be surrounded by a riot of gold quaking aspen.

Special considerations: This is a moderate-use area; you may encounter four-wheel-drive vehicles, ATVs, dirt bikes, or equestrians. In every case bikers need to yield the right-of-way. If you hear a motorcycle or ATV coming, move well off the trail—these can be traveling at high speeds and won't be able to stop in time to avoid you. If you encounter people on horseback do the same, and try not to make any loud noise or sudden gesture that might spook the animals.

Rest rooms are available at the route's starting point, but there is no water along the way.

From Meeker Park Picnic Area ride out to CO 7 and go left, riding south for less than a mile to County Road 82 (Cabin Creek Road). Go left onto CR 82 and ride this well-maintained graded dirt road past numerous summer cabins for about a mile to an intersection, where you make a right turn. Continue on CR 82 for another mile to the intersection with Forest Road 119, signed for Pierson Park, House Rock, and Estes Park. Turn left

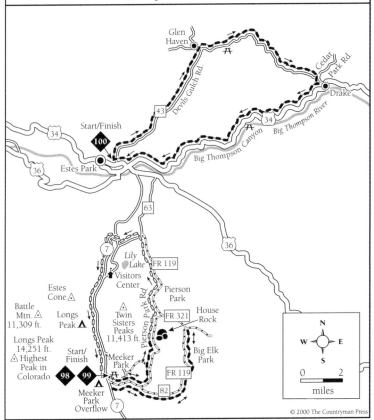

Ride 98 • House Rock
Ride 99 • Big Elk Park–Lake Meadows
Ride 100 • Drake Loop

onto FR 119 and begin climbing up this more primitive four-wheel-drive road. You are now heading north and will continue in this direction.

Another mile into this ride you encounter a fork to the left, and then another. Stay right, continuing up to the base of House Rock at 5.5 miles. Once you have reached House Rock and enjoyed your surroundings, head back down the way you came.

Option: The more adventurous can continue past House Rock another 3 miles to Pierson Park and travel on FR 119 until you reach the Fish Creek Road, where you go left, and go 4 miles to Estes Park. At CO 7 go left again for10 miles to get back to your car. You will encounter several gates along the way; go through them and make sure they are closed behind you.

Note: Although it is hard to get very lost in this area, many dirt roads take off from the main route in all directions. While the mountains to the west and House Rock itself serve as good geographic markers, spending some time with current Roosevelt National Forest and topographic maps will also help orient you.

---

99. BIG ELK PARK–LAKE MEADOWS (See map on page 461)

For mountain bikes. This is an easy-to-moderate cruise into some beautiful ranch country just east of the park. Novice and intermediate riders who are in good shape and acclimated to the area's higher elevations will enjoy this nontechnical trip on well-maintained dirt roads. A total of close to 15 miles is possible, but this route can be adjusted to suit varying ability and fitness levels.

Starting point: Meeker Park Picnic Area, approximately 7 miles south of Estes Park on CO 7.

Length: 5.5 miles one-way to Big Elk Park, 7 miles one-way to Lake Meadows; Close to 15 miles round-trip. Allow 2 to 3 hours to complete this ride.

Riding surface: Graded dirt road; some sections washboarded and rough, others loose and sandy.

Difficulty: Easy. Almost no technical riding ability is required. There are some mellow changes in elevation but most of this ride is nearly flat. If you plan to ride in the area for several days, this might be a good route to start out with. This is an easy ride that the whole family can enjoy. You can adjust the mileage by simply turning around, although you must ride at least 5 miles to reach the open vistas and meadows of Big Elk Park.

Scenery/highlights: The gently rolling terrain and broad, parklike meadows of these valleys are picturesque and call to mind scenes of the Old West. Several established ranching operations still work the land, their quaint old barns and outbuildings a testament to their time here.

Best time to ride: Spring and fall, when car traffic is lighter. This road can get busy during peak tourist season in July, August, and September. It's nice and wide, although the cars can throw quite a bit of dust up in your face.

Special considerations: Private property extends out on either side of this road for a considerable distance. Please stay on the main road, obey all posted signs, and respect the privacy of the ranchers and homeowners who live out here.

From the Meeker Park Picnic Area ride out onto CO 7, go left, and ride south for less than a mile to CR 82 (Cabin Creek Road). For the first mile the route winds around past several side roads and numerous summer cabins. Approximately 1.3 miles from the start you will come to a major intersection; bear right staying on the main route heading east. You will stay on the main road, CR 82, which becomes CR 59 when it crosses over the Larimer County line, for the entire ride. The county line crosses through the valley at Big Elk Park 5.5 miles from the start, but the road continues another 1.5 miles to Lake Pasture, or Lake Meadows as it is listed on some maps. At Lake Pasture the road forks, both forks ending at private gates; turn around and head back the way you came.

---

100. DRAKE LOOP (See map on page 461)

For road bikes. This loop northeast of Estes Park is great for more serious road riders who are comfortable sharing the road with car traffic and riding at higher altitudes. The route traverses some stunning country between Estes Park and the small vacation settlements of Glen Haven and Drake, following the Big Thompson River for a good part of the way.

Starting point: The town of Estes Park.

Length: 32-mile loop. Allow 3 to 4 hours to complete this loop.

Riding surface: Pavement.

Difficulty: Moderate to difficult. Because of changes in elevation, climbing, and vehicle traffic, this is at least an intermediate if not advanced road ride.

Scenery/highlights: The Devils Gulch Road heads up a beautiful draw rimmed by interesting rock formations, before dropping gently into the lower North Fork of the Big Thompson River drainage. From the hamlet of Glen Haven to town of Drake, you ride along the winding North Fork of the Big Thompson, serenaded by its rumbles and gurglings. Riding back up to Estes Park on US 34 you follow the Main Fork of the Big Thompson.

Best time to ride: Anytime June through September when temperatures and weather permit. Early morning is also a good time to get out and enjoy the road before it fills with commuters and sightseers.

Special considerations: The traffic on US 34 coming back into town is not for the weak of heart. The road is narrow, curving, and frequently traveled by large campers and supply trucks going up to Estes Park.

From the intersection of Elk Horn Avenue or US 34/36 and MacGregor Avenue in Estes Park (elevation 7,589 feet), ride north on MacGregor Avenue, which turns into the Devils Gulch Road. You climb to a high elevation of approximately 8,000 feet and then descend into the Piper Meadows–Glen Haven area (6,900 feet). It is 8 miles from Estes Park to Glen Haven. From Glen Haven you descend until reaching the town of Drake (6,130 feet), 12 miles from Glen Haven and 20 from Estes Park. From Drake turn right onto US 34 and begin the arduous climb 12 miles back to Estes Park.

Option: You may want to ride this loop in the opposite direction: Start in Estes Park, pedal down US 34 to Drake, and then pick up CR 43 and take it through Glen Haven and back to your starting point. This gets the busier section out of the way sooner, which may be best if you are doing an early-morning ride. It also means a shorter, faster downhill and a longer, more gradual uphill.

---

101. PEAK TO PEAK HIGHWAY (See map on page 465)

For road bikes. This road ride from Estes Park southward along the Peak to Peak Highway is a classic Colorado skinny-tire route. It can be adjust-

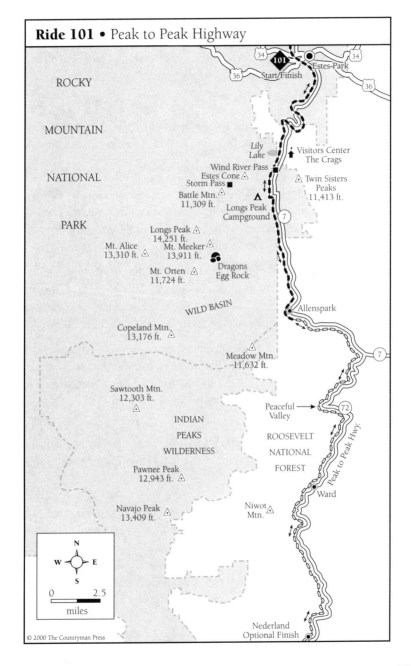

ROCKY

MOUNTAIN

NATIONAL

PARK

Lily
Lake

Visitors Center
The Crags

Wind River Pass
Estes Cone
Storm Pass
Battle Mtn.
11,309 ft.
Longs Peak
Campground

Twin Sisters
Peaks
11,413 ft.

34
101
Start/Finish
36
Estes Park
34
36
36

7

Longs Peak
14,251 ft.
Mt. Alice
13,310 ft.
Mt. Meeker
13,911 ft.
Mt. Orten
11,724 ft.
Dragons
Egg Rock

WILD BASIN

Allenspark

Copeland Mtn.
13,176 ft.

Meadow Mtn.
11,632 ft.

7

Sawtooth Mtn.
12,303 ft.

INDIAN

PEAKS

WILDERNESS

Peaceful
Valley

72

ROOSEVELT

NATIONAL

FOREST

Pawnee Peak
12,943 ft.

Ward

Navajo Peak
13,409 ft.

Niwot
Mtn.

N
W   E
S

0   2.5
miles

Nederland
Optional Finish

Peak to Peak Hwy.

© 2000 The Countryman Press

ed to give you a total distance of from 36 to 78 miles. Parts of this route can be ridden one-way with a shuttle or support vehicle. Sweeping views to majestic peaks that form the Continental Divide, and gorgeous alpine scenery, make this a memorable cycling adventure.

Starting point: The town of Estes Park.

Length: 36 miles out-and-back to Allenspark; 62 miles out-and-back to the town of Ward; 78 miles out-and-back to the town of Nederland.

Riding surface: Pavement; wide shoulders most of the way.

Difficulty: Difficult. This is a strenuous, up-and-down, monster ride for all but very fit and experienced road riders. As this highway rolls across the mountainous terrain just east of the Continental Divide, it gains and loses significant amounts of elevation.

Scenery/highlights: The incredible views up to the peaks of the divide, the dense evergreen and aspen forests, and the deep blue Colorado sky may make you entirely forget how hard you're working and how thin the air is. The vistas between Estes Park and Ward are some of the best.

Best time to ride: Spring to fall. Riding as soon as you can withstand the temperatures in the spring will ensure you have most of the road to yourself. Of course the warmer months are best for road riding, but in the fall, stands of aspen turn to brilliant shades of gold.

Special considerations: Water, rest rooms, and food can be found in Estes Park, Allenspark, Ward, and Nederland. This can be a long day out so be sure to bring plenty of water, some high-energy snacks, and some extra clothing.

From the Elk Horn Avenue (US 34/36) in downtown Estes Park head east on US 34/36 for a few blocks, bearing right onto US 36 where the routes divide. Ride east on US 36 for 0.5 mile to where the routes divide again. Bear right again, this time onto CO 7. Pedal south, gaining 1,700 feet in the first 6 miles to the high point in the ride at Wind River Pass (9,300 feet). Continue riding south on CO 7 for 9 miles until you reach the turnoff for Allenspark. It is 2 miles from CO 7 to Allenspark (at approximately 8,000 feet). Return the way you came, or keep going.

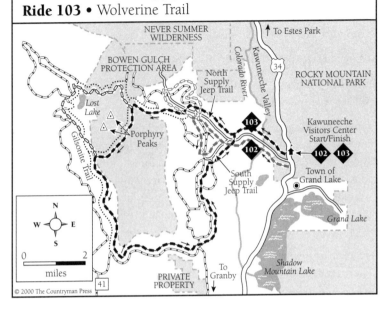

Ride 102 • North Supply–South Supply Jeep Trail
Ride 103 • Wolverine Trail

Continuing on CO 7, just 4 miles past the turnoff to Allenspark pick up CO 72. Keep heading south on CO 72 11 miles to the town of Ward. At Ward your elevation will again climb to over 9,000 feet. If Nederland is your destination, simply keep heading south on CO72 for another 8 miles. You drop again to just over 8,000 feet at the town of Nederland.

102. NORTH SUPPLY–SOUTH SUPPLY JEEP TRAIL
(See map on page 467)

For mountain bikes. This cherry-stem ride is a beautiful trip through an alpine wonderland of fragrant evergreens and wildflowers. It's a great beginning-to-intermediate ride for mountain bikers with a good level of physical fitness. Option for strong riders with good-to-excellent technical riding skills add 2- 4 miles to the total distance.

Starting point: Kawuneeche Visitors Center, just outside the town of Grand Lake.

Length: Approximately 8.5 miles round-trip. Many options for exploring in this area add from 2 to 4 miles to your total distance.

Riding surface: Four-wheel-drive jeep roads, graded dirt roads.

Difficulty: Moderate. Beginning-to-intermediate riding skills and fitness level are recommended for this ride.

Scenery/highlights: This is simply a nice ride in the woods. Big mature stands of spruce and fir, mixed in with some lodgepole at the lower elevations and a few aspen, provide a beautiful forest canopy. In some of the moister drainages you will find delicate ferns and the large nodding heads of white, and sometimes blue, columbine—the Colorado state flower. For the hardy who are able to make it to the top of the North Supply Jeep Road, a fantastic view of the Continental Divide awaits you.

Best time to ride: Spring through fall; when this route is free of snow and dry. It gets good and muddy up here after a hard rain, and mountain-bike tires tend to increase erosion of saturated soils, so stay away if it's wet.

Special considerations: This is a multiple use area so you can expect to see plenty of other bicycles, dirt bikes, ATVs, and jeeps. If you hear a motorized vehicle coming, stop and get well off the trail. They can come around corners pretty quick, and you don't want to be in their way. This graded dirt road is passable to passenger vehicles. Stay to the right when a car approaches.

The biting flies and mosquitoes can be pretty bad up here in the warmest part of the summer. It's a good idea to douse your entire body with bug spray before you go. That includes any parts covered with Lycra; some of the bigger blackflies can bite right through your bike shorts!

The nearest water and facilities are located at the starting point at the Kawuneeche Visitors Center, or in the town of Grand Lake.

From the Kawuneeche Visitors Center parking lot ride out onto US 34 and go right; in only a few hundred feet turn left onto CR 491. If you come to the entrance station, you have gone too far. Follow this dirt road approximately 1 mile until you come to CR 492 and a gate. Go around the gate if it is closed, and continue on the North Supply Jeep Road (FR 120.4). Approximately 1.3 miles past the gate the South Supply Jeep Road comes in from your left. This is where you come out on your return. Continue climbing another 1.4 miles to where your route intersects with the graded Kawuneeche Road (FR 120). Go left and ride the Kawuneeche Road for 1.6 miles until you come to the South Supply Jeep Road, well marked on the left (downhill) side of the road. Go left onto this jeep road and ride it for 1 mile to where it joins the North Supply Jeep Road. From here reverse the route you came out on to get back to the Kawuneeche Visitors Center and your car.

Option: If you've got the legs and the lungs, you can continue onward and upward when you reach the Kawuneeche Road at 3.5 miles from the start. Cross over the road and continue up, up, up on the North Supply Jeep Road. Not only is this a steep and unrelenting climb, but the road is cluttered with fist- to head-sized rocks that require a good amount of technical skill to negotiate. In approximately 2 miles you encounter the Kawuneeche Road (FR 120) again. Go right onto this maintained dirt road and ride back down to the start of the South Supply Jeep Road to return (11.5 miles total), or continue on another mile to where the road ends on a ridge and views to the Continental Divide abound (13.5 miles total).

---

103. WOLVERINE TRAIL (See map on page 467)

For mountain bikes. This 19-mile loop trail is well suited for mountain bikers with an intermediate level of physical fitness and technical riding skills. This route makes a circuit of several peaks just outside the park's western boundary and provides gorgeous alpine scenery, stunning views, and a five-star day of fat-tire fun you won't soon forget.

Starting point: Kawuneeche Visitors Center, just outside the town of Grand Lake. This trail is also accessed by the North Supply trailhead.

Length: Just over 19 miles.

Riding surface: Graded dirt roads, jeep roads; singletrack.

Difficulty: Moderate to difficult. Although intermediate technical skills are sufficient for negotiating this route, its extremely high elevations and length require an excellent level of physical fitness.

Scenery/highlights: As you climb the North Supply Jeep Road you cruise through stands of aspens and lodgepole pines, which give way to large, mature spruce and fir trees. Amid their shadowy understory you might find columbine and ferns growing. As you reach the Wolverine Trail you emerge from montane and subalpine forests into the alpine tundra life zone highlighted inside the park. The Wolverine Trail is almost all above tree line, and the views are superb. The trail is easy to discern in the earth's fragile tundra blanket. Please do not ride off the trail as this will kill the tundra and allow erosion to do its dirty work.

When you first join the Wolverine Trail you may want to go right, to where it ends at the boundary of the Never Summer Wilderness Area. You can stash your bike here and make the short hike down to Bowen Lake, but remember, it is illegal to ride your bike into wilderness areas.

Best time to ride: July through September, when this route is free of snow and dry. It gets good and muddy up here after a hard rain, and mountain-bike tires tend to increase erosion of saturated soils, so stay away if it's wet.

It is best to ride this trail in the early part of the day so you are off portions of the route that are above tree line by afternoon, when the thunderstorms roll in. Check with a park ranger or get a local forecast before you go to avoid risk of cold, exposure, and lightning.

Special considerations: This ride traverses some incredibly beautiful, but very high, alpine country. The highest point on this ride is 11,360 feet, meaning the air is thin and dry and the sun strong. Also, be aware that weather and temperature can change quickly at these elevations. It is a long day, so come with plenty of water and sunblock, high-energy snacks, a shell to keep out wind and rain, and maybe even a lightweight long-sleeved polypro top.

This is a multiple use area so you can expect to see plenty of other bicycles, dirt bikes, ATVs, and four-wheel-drive vehicles. If you hear a

FAUNA

Animal communities, like plant communities, correlate to the five different life zones within the park. In the riparian zones moose, beaver, muskrat, raccoon, and river otter make their home, but visitors such as deer, cougar, and black bear are not uncommon. You'll see water-loving birds such as the American dipper, green-winged teal, spotted sandpiper as well as the Wilson's warbler and song sparrow.

Elk are the dominant species of the meadows and shrublands zone, but must share their niche with mule deer, coyotes, porcupines, pocket gophers, squirrels, and badgers. Avian hunters such as kestrels and nighthawks also favor the more open shrublands, as does the brilliant mountain bluebird. Hooded Steller's jays, northern flickers, chickadees, nuthatches, and the western tanager prefer ponderosa and lodgepole forests, while several varieties of woodpeckers, swallows, and even a warbling vireo can be found among the park's aspen groves.

Porcupines love spruce-fir forests, as do long-tailed weasels and snowshoe hares. Blue grouse, golden-crowned kinglets, and the hermit thrush also spend time in these subalpine forests each year.

In the very highest reaches of the park in summer it's common to see elk lounging about the meadows with pocket gophers, pikas, marmots and ermine. Bighorn sheep are among the park's most magnificent creatures. White-tailed ptarmigans are masters of camouflage and are common in the highest reaches of the park, as are the white-crowned sparrow and horned lark.

Please be aware that some of the park's larger wild creatures can pose a danger to humans if provoked. Elk and moose can charge if they feel threatened, especially if they are caring for young. Mountain lions and bears can be unpredictable and should never be approached. Black bears can be cinnamon, brown, or black in color and are particularly dangerous if they are with cubs. If you are camping in or near the park, either store food in the trunk of your car or hang it between two trees in a sack well away from your tent. Mountain lion numbers have been increasing in the park in recent years, and attacks have been known to occur. If you are hiking or walking in the park, keep pets and small children nearby. Most importantly, never approach and never attempt to feed any of the park's wild animals.

motorized vehicle coming, stop and get well off the trail. They can come around corners pretty quick, and you don't want to be in their way. Cars and four-wheel-drive vehicles tend to travel at high rates of speed on the graded roads.

The biting flies and mosquitoes can be pretty bad up here in the warmest part of the summer. It's a good idea to douse your entire body with bug spray before you go; that includes any parts covered with Lycra.

The nearest water and facilities are located at the starting point at the Kawuneeche Visitors Center or in the town of Grand Lake. *Note:* This ride was written up by Christine "the French Wrench" Gill at Rocky Mountain Sports in Grand Lake. Christine owns and runs the shop and enjoys keeping her fleet of rental bikes and every other bike in town in top working order with the skills she acquired at the Barnett Bicycle Institute. Christine also has sea kayaks for rent if you're interested in paddling around on Grand Lake while you're in the area. Stop in and see her for any kind of gear or advice you might need.

From the visitors center parking lot ride out onto US 34 and go right; in a few hundred feet turn left onto CR 491. If you come to the entrance station, you have gone too far. Follow this dirt road for approximately 1 mile until you come to CR 492 and a gate. Go around the gate if it is closed, and continue on the North Supply Jeep Road (FR 120.4) for approximately 2.7 miles to where it comes out onto the Kawuneeche Road (FR 120). Cross over this graded dirt road and pick up the North Supply Loop Trail, which heads left from this intersection. You climb on this trail for just under 2 miles to where it intersects the Wolverine Trail 5.7 miles from the start. (This and most of the other trails in this area are well marked, so watch for signs.) When you intersect the Wolverine Trail go left and head out across the wide-open, tundra-covered ridges with spectacular views. It is along this stretch that you reach the high point of the ride.

Roll along against the sky for approximately 2 miles before reaching the intersection with the Gilsonite Trail 7.7 miles from the start. Go left onto the Gilsonite Trail and have a ball, as this rollicking singletrack heads downhill for approximately 2.5 miles until it intersects the graded Stillwater Pass Road (FR 123). Turn left and continue downhill for another 3 miles to the Idleglen trailhead. At this trailhead go left onto the Kawuneeche Road (FR 120) and begin the moderate climb up to the South Supply Jeep Road, which leaves from the right-hand side of the road in approximately 3 miles. Go right and head downhill for about 3 more miles, out to the paved highway, and ride the few hundred feet back to your car.

Option: If you are interested in seeing more of the high country and would like to do a shorter loop, you can go right where the Wolverine Trail intersects the Gilsonite Trail and follow the signs for Lost Lake. You can connect back to the North Supply Jeep Road by a trail heading east from the lake, but it is quite steep. You may want to go back the way you came after cooling your heels by the lake. Creating a loop to Lost Lake and back to the North Supply Jeep Road gives you an approximate total distance of 18 miles.

CAMPING

There are five campgrounds and one group camping area in the park with a total of 557 sites. All require a fee. The limit for staying at any of the park's campgrounds is 7 days; Longs Peak campground (tents only) has a 3-day limit. The limits extend to 14 nights at the year-round campgrounds. None of the park's campgrounds have showers or hook-ups. Wood gathering is prohibited but bundled wood is for sale and fires are allowed in fire grates only. Reservations for summer camping in Moraine Park and Glacier Basin are taken beginning March 15. Call (800) 365-CAMP (2267). A permit is required for back-country camping in the park.

EAST SIDE OF THE PARK:

Aspen Glen Campground: Open from mid-May to late September. No reservations but a per night fee is required.

Glacier Basin: Open from early June to Labor Day. Reservations and a per night fee are required.

Glacier Basin Group Sites: Open from early June to Labor Day. Reservations and a fee are required. Tents only.

Longs Peak Campground: Open year-round. No reservations. Tents only.

Moraine Park Campground: Open year-round. Reservations required from Memorial Day to Labor Day. A camping fee is required.

WEST SIDE OF THE PARK:

Timber Creek Campground: Open year-round. No reservations. A camping fee is required.

OUTSIDE THE PARK:

There are several managed campgrounds with facilities in the Arapaho National Forest surrounding the park; many require reservations and a fee. The options for wilderness camping in the national forest are unlimited.

There are at least a dozen private campgrounds outside the park, the majority of them around Estes Park. Several have shower and/or laundry amenities available.

There are some 85 hotels, motels, lodges, and B&Bs in the Estes Park area, and they fill up fast at peak season.

One of the most notable is the **Stanley Hotel.** You can't miss the big, white, castlelike structure on the hillside towering over the valley. First opened in 1909, it is your best bet for upscale lodging. Live music and ballroom dancing on Friday night are standard for the summer season. For reserva-

IT'S INTERESTING TO KNOW . . .

In 1976 the natural ecosystems of the park were collectively deemed to be representative of the Rocky Mountain Biogeographic Province and recognized as an International Biosphere Reserve through the United Nations' Man and the Biosphere Program. This program is devoted to the conservation of nature, the preservation of genetic material, and scientific research in the service of humanity. Rocky Mountain National Park provides a standard against which the effects of human activities and their impacts on the environment can be measured.

tions, call (970) 586-3371 or (800) ROCKIES.

Other lodges are the log-and-stone **Taharaa Mountain Lodge** (970-577-0098) just outside of town; the **Deer Crest** (970-586-2358), offering rooms and cottages right on the Fall River just a mile west of town; and the **Aspen Lodge** (970-586-8133), about 8 miles south of town on CO 7, with both lodge rooms and cabins in a ranch-style atmosphere. **Timberline Motel and Cottages** (970-586-4697) is a blast from the past with nifty fifties decor.

On the Grand Lake side there are at least two dozen possibilities for lodging. Rooms on this side of the park are slightly less expensive than in Estes Park. The **Grand Lake Lodge** (970-627-3967) is one of the best choices; built in 1921, this stately old lodge overlooks the lake from its perch on a hillside, where it provides some stunning views. The **Spirit Lake Lodge** (970-627-3344), located in town, has one- and two-bedroom units, some with kitchenettes.

The **Gala Marina Hotel** (970-627-3220) is right on the water and has fantastic views, patios, and kitchenettes.

The only food available within the park is at the **Alpine Visitors Center** atop Fall River Pass. This center is open from Memorial Day through late September.

Estes Park is packed with restaurants and cafés. If you are looking for that first cup of black gold in the morning, try the **Coffee Clown** (222 E. Elkhorn Ave.) or **Estes Park Coffee Company** (366 E. Elkhorn Ave.). For breakfast the **Topnotch Café and Bakery** (in the Stanley Village Shopping Center) is a good, healthy choice, or you can try the **Mountaineer Restaurant** (540 S. St. Vrain Ave.). **Molly B Restaurant** (200 Moraine Ave. in Gaslight Square) serves three good meals a day, as does **Ed's Cantina and Grill** (362 E. Elkhorn Ave.). **La Casa** (222 E. Elkhorn Avenue) is quite good and has outdoor seating. If Asian food is what you're after, try **Chinatown Super Seafood** (160 S. St. Vrain Ave.). **Mama Rose's** (338 E. Elkhorn Ave.) is a local favorite for Italian food, and the **Dunraven Inn** (2470 County Hwy. Spur 66) also serves good Italian in a nice atmosphere. The **Estes Park Brewery** (470 Prospect) is always a good choice for

a brew, sandwich, or salad, but if you want something more substantial try **Orlando's Steak House** (132 E. Elkhorn Ave.).

For a town the size of Grand Lake, there are a lot of restaurants. For a good cup of coffee try the **Rocky Mountain Coffee Co. & Deli** (913 Grand Ave.); you can get a sandwich for later while you're there. **The Chuckhole Café** (1119 Grand Ave.) is a good choice for breakfast, and you may want to try **E. G.'s Garden Grill** (1000 Grand Ave.) for lunch. A good choice for Mexican food is the **Mountain Inn** (612 Grand

Ave.), always a favorite with locals, but if you're looking for something more upscale try the **Rapids Restaurant and Lodge** (209 Rapids Lane), which serves prime rib, continental fare, and Italian dishes. **Big Ray's Chop House** (10188 US 34) is always a good choice for meat lovers.

In Allenspark, there's the **Hummingbird Café** or the **Meadow Mountain Café**. Try **Alice's Restaurant** or the **Millsite Inn** in Ward. Nederland now has almost a dozen restaurants, including **Annie's Café and Bakery, the Sundance Café,** and **Wolf Tongue Brewery.**

LAUNDRY

ESTES PARK:

Brown's Chinese Laundry & Dry, 183 W. Riverside Dr.; (970) 586-6122

Dad's Maytag Laundry, 457 E. Wonder View Ave.; (970) 586-9847

Dad's Maytag Laundry & Showers, 650 W. Wonder View Ave.; (970) 586-2025

Happy Camper Laundry & Showers, 857 Moraine Ave.; (970) 586-5073

National Park Village Laundry, 900 Moraine Ave.; (970) 586-2702

Rocky Mountain Laundry, 970

Comanche St.; (970) 586-2822

Options for doing laundry on the Grand Lake side of the park are slim. If you are going through Granby (approximately 17 miles from Grand Lake) try:

Granby Eastside Laundromat, 601 E. Jasper Court; (970) 887-3889

BIKE SHOP/BIKE RENTAL

Colorado Bicycling Adventures, 184 E. Elkhorn Ave.; (970) 586-4241

Rocky Mountain Sports, 830 Grand Ave.; (970) 627-8124

FOR FURTHER INFORMATION

Rocky Mountain National Park—Superintendent, Estes Park, CO 80517; (970) 586-1206 (visitors center at park headquarters), (970) 586-1333 (recorded message), (970) 586-1242 (backcountry information), (970) 586-4927 (Alpine Visitors Center), (970) 627-3471 (west side); http://www.nps.gov/romo

Roosevelt National Forest, Estes—Poudre Ranger District, Redfeather Ranger District, 1311 S. College Ave., Fort Collins, CO 80524; (970) 498-2775

Arapaho National Forest, Sulphur Ranger District, 62429 US 40, P.O. Box 10, Granby, CO 80446; (970) 887-4100

Estes Park Chamber of Commerce Visitor Information Center, 500 Big Thompson Rd., P.O. Box 3050, Estes Park, CO 80517; (970) 586-4431 or (800) 443-7837

Grand Lake Chamber of Commerce and Tourist Information Center, US 34, P.O. Box 57, Grand Lake, CO 80447-0057; (970) 627-3402 or (800) 531-1019

G

M